John Locke's Christianity

John Locke's religious interests and concerns permeate his philosophical production and are best expressed in his later writings on religion, which represent the culmination of his studies. In this volume, Diego Lucci offers a thorough analysis and reassessment of Locke's unique, heterodox, internally coherent version of Protestant Christianity, which emerges from *The Reasonableness of Christianity* and other public as well as private texts. In order to clarify Locke's views on morality, salvation, and the afterlife, Lucci critically examines Locke's theistic ethics, biblical hermeneutics, reflection on natural and revealed law, mortalism, theory of personal identity, Christology, and tolerationism. While emphasizing the originality of Locke's Scripture-based religion, this book calls attention to his influences and explores the reception of his unorthodox theological ideas. Moreover, the book highlights the impact of Locke's natural and biblical theology on other areas of his thought, thus enabling a better understanding of the unity of his work.

DIEGO LUCCI is Professor of Philosophy and History at the American University in Bulgaria. Among his publications are the monograph *Scripture and Deism* (2008) and the coedited volume *Atheism and Deism Revalued* (with Wayne Hudson and Jeffrey R. Wigelsworth, 2014).

John Locke's Christianity

Diego Lucci

American University in Bulgaria

CAMBRIDGE
UNIVERSITY PRESS

University Printing House, Cambridge CB2 8BS, United Kingdom

One Liberty Plaza, 20th Floor, New York, NY 10006, USA

477 Williamstown Road, Port Melbourne, VIC 3207, Australia

314–321, 3rd Floor, Plot 3, Splendor Forum, Jasola District Centre, New Delhi – 110025, India

79 Anson Road, #06–04/06, Singapore 079906

Cambridge University Press is part of the University of Cambridge.

It furthers the University's mission by disseminating knowledge in the pursuit of education, learning, and research at the highest international levels of excellence.

www.cambridge.org
Information on this title: www.cambridge.org/9781108836913
DOI: 10.1017/9781108873055

First published 2021

A catalogue record for this publication is available from the British Library.

ISBN 978-1-108-83691-3 Hardback

Contents

Acknowledgments

This book would never have been written without the support of several institutions. My six-month senior fellowship at the Maimonides Centre for Advanced Studies (MCAS), University of Hamburg, in 2018 was crucial to the composition of this book. I am thankful to the MCAS and its fellows and staff – particularly to the MCAS Director, Giuseppe Veltri, and to Bill Rebiger, Maria Wazinski, Christine Wagener, Guido Bartolucci, and Talya Fishman – for their attention and assistance. I am grateful to Gladstone's Library, the Institute of Historical Research at the University of London, and the Institute of Research in the Humanities at the University of Bucharest for their fellowships and hospitality. I gladly recognize my debt to my home institution, the American University in Bulgaria (AUBG), for its continued support and to the faculty, administrators, staff, and students of AUBG for their help and encouragement. Special thanks go to David Evans, Lucia Miree, Steve Sullivan, Robert White, and Emilia Zankina. My deep gratitude goes to the Panitza Library at AUBG and the other libraries where I did research in recent years. I am grateful to all the scholars who have invited me to present my research at their home institutions – particularly to Dana Jalobeanu, Mihnea Dobre, Adam Sutcliffe, Michael Berkowitz, Marco Forlivesi, Paola Rumore, and Cyril Selzner for inviting me to lecture on Locke.

I am indebted to Ruth Boeker, Victor Nuovo, Raffaele Russo, Stephen Snobelen, and two anonymous reviewers for their comments on various parts of this book. I am thankful to Locke experts Peter Anstey, Douglas Casson, Patrick Connolly, Sorana Corneanu, Giuliana Di Biase, Mark Goldie, Jessica Gordon-Roth, Benjamin Hill, Paul Lodge, Antonia LoLordo, John Marshall, Luisa Simonutti, Timothy Stanton, Tim Stuart-Buttle, Kathryn Tabb, Jon Thompson, Felix Waldmann, and Shelley Weinberg for their attention to my research. I am grateful to Rob Iliffe, Dmitri Levitin, Paul Lim, and Brent Sirota for their advice concerning early modern Trinitarian debates. I thank the late Justin Champion, James Herrick, Wayne Hudson, Jonathan Israel, Margaret Jacob, James Lancaster, Ian Leask, Gianluca Mori, Michael Prince, Giovanni Tarantino, and Jeffrey Wigelsworth for contributing to my understanding of

English deism and Locke's relation to it. My studies have benefited from my interaction with many other scholars, all of whom I am grateful to, although I cannot mention all of them here. I just wish to expressly thank a few colleagues and friends – Iordan Avramov, Stephen Benin, Paolo Luca Bernardini, Matteo Bonifacio, Maurizio Cambi, Pierangelo Castagneto, Tomaso Cavallo, Ivo Cerman, Stephen Clucas, Stephen Gaukroger, Doug Geivett, Benjamin Goldberg, Ariel Hessayon, Michael Hunter, Khafiz Kerimov, Fabrizio Lomonaco, Robert Maryks, Rolando Minuti, Riccardo Pozzo, Ronald Schechter, Daniel Schwartz, and James Ungureanu – for significantly contributing to my understanding of seventeenth- and eighteenth-century thought. Special thanks go to my teachers in Naples, particularly to Giuseppe Lissa, Emilia D'Antuono, Paolo Amodio, and Giuseppe Antonio Di Marco.

I am immensely grateful to Hilary Gaskin, Hal Churchman, and Lisa Carter of Cambridge University Press, to my project managers Megalai Soupramaniane and Mathew Rohit, and to my copyeditor Trent Hancock for their invaluable assistance.

My utmost gratitude goes to my mother, Assunta; my father, Gennaro; my sister Roberta; and my sister's partner Valentino for their support, understanding, and love. I am grateful to Maya, Moni, Sylvia, Simona, Veni, and Nikol for their constant care, help, and encouragement. I thank all my friends and relatives who have helped and inspired me in the course of my life. This book is dedicated to my wife Branimira and my son Dario, whose unrelenting support, infinite patience, and unwavering love have enabled me to work on this project with the tranquility and attentiveness needed to complete it.

Introduction

John Locke (1632–1704) is best known for his "way of ideas" and political theory. His empiricist epistemology, which he expounded in *An Essay concerning Human Understanding* (1690), played a crucial role in the development of modern theories of knowledge and significantly influenced the philosophy of the Enlightenment. Moreover, his concept of state authority, which he tasked with the procurement, preservation, and advancement of civil interests, and his views on religious toleration, which entailed the separation of the state from religious societies, had a momentous impact on the liberal political tradition. Along with Isaac Newton, Locke was widely considered the major herald of the Enlightenment in eighteenth-century Europe and America, to such an extent that, starting at least in the 1730s, there was a sort of "international cult" of Newton and Locke.[1] Today, more than three centuries after his death, Locke occupies a solid position in the canon of early modern philosophy, and the study of his political ideas is widely considered essential to comprehending modern political thought. The significance and influence of Locke's way of ideas and political theory are undeniable, but have often been exaggerated, to the extent that labels like "founder of modern empiricism" and "father of political liberalism" are traditionally attached to this author. Locke's foundational role in the history of modern empiricism is indeed debatable, given the early developments of this philosophical tradition in England before Locke and given, also, the skeptical implications of Locke's way of ideas, as Victor Nuovo has aptly noted:

From a historical philosophical perspective, Bacon, Hobbes, Boyle, and Newton are the real founders of British empiricism, and they remained robust natural philosophers, notwithstanding their piety, whereas the customary trinity of Locke, Berkeley,

---

[1] B. W. Young, *Religion and Enlightenment in Eighteenth-Century England: Theological Debate from Locke to Burke* (Oxford: Clarendon Press, 1998), pp. 83–119; Jonathan I. Israel, *Radical Enlightenment: Philosophy and the Making of Modernity 1650–1750* (Oxford: Oxford University Press, 2001), pp. 515–527.

1

and Hume, inspired by Locke's skepticism, leads into a metaphysical dead end, a cul-de-sac.[2]

Concerning the liberal tradition, Locke's political ideas definitely played an important role in the early stages of modern liberalism. However, I deem it incorrect to describe his mature political theory, which he expounded in *A Letter concerning Toleration* (1689) and *Two Treatises of Government* (1689, but dated 1690), as the starting point of this political tradition. In fact, various political dynamics, debates, and writings are at the origin of modern liberalism, the seeds of which, in England, may be found in the discussions on popular sovereignty during the Civil War and Interregnum – particularly in the emergence of what Quentin Skinner has defined "the neo-Roman theory of free states"[3] – although only in the nineteenth century did terms like "liberalism" and "liberal" become of common use to define this political tradition. At any rate, and despite the exaggerations surrounding Locke's intellectual legacy, his achievements as a philosopher and a political thinker have significantly contributed to western culture. Nevertheless, his religious views are comparatively less well known, although they are no less important than his philosophical and political theories, and although his theological ideas conditioned his philosophical and political thought in various respects. Locke was indeed a "religious Enlightener" who endorsed reasonable belief as the coordination of natural reason and scriptural revelation. Thus, whereas I am far from endorsing Locke's or anyone else's religious worldview, I consider a thorough elucidation and reassessment of Locke's religion crucial to a better understanding of this author's work, context, and legacy.

Locke worked intensively on refining his philosophical and political theories during his exile in the Netherlands in the 1680s. He left England in 1683, under suspicion of involvement in the Rye House Plot to murder King Charles II and his brother James, although it is uncertain whether he was actually involved in this plot. In the Netherlands, he befriended such famous scholars as Jean Le Clerc and Philipp van Limborch and the English Quaker merchant and intellectual Benjamin Furly. Following his return to England in the entourage of Princess Mary in February 1689, during the Glorious Revolution, and the publication of his major political and philosophical works in 1689–1690, Locke settled at Oates Manor in Essex in 1691. Oates Manor was the home of Sir Francis Masham and his wife Damaris Cudworth, Lady Masham – a daughter of the Cambridge Platonist Ralph Cudworth and a "proto-feminist" philosopher. Locke brought his library of over 2,000 volumes to Oates, where

[2] Victor Nuovo, *John Locke: The Philosopher As Christian Virtuoso* (Oxford: Oxford University Press, 2017), p. 249.

[3] Quentin Skinner, *Liberty before Liberalism* (Cambridge: Cambridge University Press, 1998).

he devoted his later years mainly to theological writing, besides revising *An Essay concerning Human Understanding* multiple times. In the mid-1690s, he wrote and published anonymously his major book of theology, *The Reasonableness of Christianity, As Delivered in the Scriptures* (1695). He was subsequently involved in heated disputes about his religious views, particularly with the Calvinistic divine John Edwards (a son of the Puritan clergyman and heresiographer Thomas Edwards) and the Bishop of Worcester, Edward Stillingfleet, concerning mainly the anti-Trinitarian potential of his religious and philosophical ideas. In his last decade or so, Locke also wrote many theological manuscripts, most of which are now held at the Bodleian Library at Oxford, and he worked on the unfinished *A Paraphrase and Notes on the Epistles of St Paul*, which appeared posthumously in several volumes between 1705 and 1707.

Although Locke wrote his most important works on religion toward the end of his life, his interest in religious themes permeated his thought since at least the late 1650s and early 1660s. His belief in divine revelation, in a divine creator and legislator, and in an afterlife with reward and punishment informs his philosophical, political, and moral views in all his major works. In fact, Locke's philosophical masterpiece, *An Essay concerning Human Understanding*, is not a secular book. The *Essay* tends toward theological investigation since it affirms God's existence as a creator and lawgiver,[4] the crucial role of biblical revelation as "enlarging" natural reason,[5] and the need to believe in things "above reason" revealed in Scripture.[6] As John Yolton has explained in *The Two Intellectual Worlds of John Locke* (2004), the *Essay* also presents numerous references to "angels," "spirits," and "other intelligent beings" and provides a profoundly religious account of what it means to be human: "Since the human soul turns out to be one of those spirits among the ranks of spirits, we can locate man, human finite Beings, on the chain of being."[7] Locke's way of ideas supports belief in the existence of spiritual beings in that the *Essay* describes revelation as "natural *Reason* enlarged by a new set of Discoveries

---

[4] John Locke, *An Essay concerning Human Understanding*, ed. Peter H. Nidditch (Oxford: Clarendon Press, 1975), I.iv.9, p. 89, II.xxiii.12, pp. 302–303, and IV.x.1–6, pp. 619–621. In the present study, I refer to this edition when not indicated otherwise.

[5] Ibid., IV.xix.4, p. 698.   [6] Ibid., IV.xvii.23, p. 687, IV.xviii.6–10, pp. 693–696.

[7] John W. Yolton, *The Two Intellectual Worlds of John Locke: Man, Person, and Spirits in the "Essay"* (Ithaca: Cornell University Press, 2004), pp. 7–8. In the present study, I abstain from exploring Locke's considerations on the existence of angels, spirits, and other intelligent beings for two reasons. First, Yolton's book provides a thorough analysis of this subject in particular. Second, the present essay focuses on Locke's account of Christianity in the *Reasonableness* and other religious writings, on the moral and soteriological implications of his version of Christianity, and on philosophical, moral, and political issues that, although covered by Locke in other writings, are relevant to his views on morality and salvation.

communicated by God immediately"[8] and admits conjecture as a method to "reach" what sense experience cannot discover. What Locke called "the probable Conjectures of Reason" played an essential part in both his investigation of the natural world and his consideration of scriptural revelation.[9] Thus, Locke's struggle to comprehend religious truth and find the way to salvation in his later theological writings is in continuity with his philosophical inquiry in the *Essay*. Moreover, Locke wrote the *Essay* not only to explore the foundations of human knowledge in matters of natural philosophy, but also to shed light on morality, which he defined as "*the proper Science, and Business of Mankind in general.*"[10] His political writings, too, are informed by a strong attention to morality, which he conceived of in markedly religious terms. For instance, in *A Letter concerning Toleration*, he maintained that the "Business of True Religion" is morality (and, consequently, he denied toleration to atheists and Roman Catholics mainly for moral reasons).[11] Similarly, in the *Second Treatise of Civil Government*, he described human beings as God's workmanship, servants, and property, "sent into the World by his order, and about his business" – namely, to respect the divine moral law of which they are bearers.[12] Briefly, Locke's reflection on morality runs throughout his work and, being grounded in theism and combined with a religious, specifically Christian conception of life, unites his thought.

Several scholars have highlighted the religious dimension of Locke's thought since John Dunn's seminal study *The Political Thought of John Locke* (1969) called attention to "the intimate dependence of an extremely high proportion of Locke's arguments for their very intelligibility, let alone plausibility, on a series of theological commitments."[13] When making this point, Dunn was referring especially to Locke's political theory. Several years later, John Colman's book *John Locke's Moral Theory* (1983) discussed the relation of Locke's religious ideas to his moral philosophy, which Colman described as a "consistent theological ethic" grounded in Locke's consideration of God's Creation and of humanity's position in the Creation.[14] Dunn's and Colman's

---

[8] Locke, *Essay*, IV.xix.4, p. 698.
[9] Ibid., IV.xviii.8, p. 694. See Yolton, *Two Intellectual Worlds*, pp. 47–54.
[10] Locke, *Essay*, IV.xii.11, p. 646.
[11] John Locke, "A Letter concerning Toleration," in John Locke, *A Letter concerning Toleration and Other Writings*, ed. Mark Goldie (Indianapolis: Liberty Fund, 2010), pp. 1–62 (8, 49–53).
[12] John Locke, *Two Treatises of Government*, rev. ed., ed. Peter Laslett (Cambridge: Cambridge University Press, 1988), p. 271.
[13] John Dunn, *The Political Thought of John Locke: An Historical Account of the Argument of the "Two Treatises of Government"* (Cambridge: Cambridge University Press, 1969), p. xi. See, also, Richard Ashcraft, "Faith and Knowledge in Locke's Philosophy," in John W. Yolton (ed.), *John Locke: Problems and Perspectives* (Cambridge: Cambridge University Press, 1969), pp. 194–223.
[14] John Colman, *John Locke's Moral Philosophy* (Edinburgh: Edinburgh University Press, 1983), p. 9.

conclusions regarding Locke's political and moral ideas can be applied to other parts of his thought. In the past four decades or so, several studies have stressed the significance of Locke's religious interests, concerns, and views to virtually all areas of his philosophical production. In this regard, Nicholas Wolterstorff has correctly noted that "a striking feature of Locke's thought is that religious considerations enter into all parts of his thought."[15] Moreover, in a recent, excellent monograph, *John Locke: The Philosopher As Christian Virtuoso* (2017), Victor Nuovo has highlighted the religious character of Locke's work, particularly of his logic, physics, ethics, and theology:

Locke's philosophical work is clarified and explained when it is considered as the production of a Christian virtuoso, which is to say, of a seventeenth-century English experimental natural philosopher, an empiricist and naturalist, who also professed Christianity of a sort that was infused with moral seriousness and with Platonic otherworldliness overlaid with Christian supernaturalism.[16]

I concur with Nuovo's characterization of Locke as a "Christian virtuoso," because Locke always viewed natural reason and biblical revelation as mutually sustaining and complementary. Locke's theological concerns, interests, and ideas indeed pervade his philosophical, political, and moral thought. Consequently, Locke's oeuvre in its different areas is the production of a *Christian* philosopher. But Locke's religious views are significant for yet another reason, as his theological reflections resulted in a unique version of Christianity. Although Locke expounded his religious views unsystematically, given also his dislike of systems of doctrine and his hostility to claims of religious orthodoxy, an original and internally coherent form of Protestant Christianity emerges from his public as well as private writings. In the present study, I aim to provide a thorough, comprehensive, systematic reconstruction of Locke's Christianity, which I consider in its complexity and originality. To this purpose, I concentrate on *The Reasonableness of Christianity* and other writings on religion that Locke composed in his later years. I also take into account Locke's reflections on subjects relevant to his moral and soteriological investigations in his philosophical and political works. While acknowledging that Locke's writings in different areas represent different projects, I disagree with Peter Laslett's, John Dunn's, and others' claim that Locke's work is affected by a sort of incoherence, which these interpreters have described as resulting largely from the theological commitments that conditioned his

---

[15] Nicholas Wolterstorff, "Locke's Philosophy of Religion," in Vere Chappell (ed.), *The Cambridge Companion to Locke* (Cambridge: Cambridge University Press, 1994), pp. 172–198 (174).
[16] Nuovo, *John Locke*, p. 1.

philosophical, moral, and political inquiries.[17] I rather agree with John Marshall, Victor Nuovo, and others whose studies have pointed to the internal coherence of Locke's thought considered in its entirety.[18] Therefore, the present book argues that Locke's different projects cohere and that the religious dimension pervading virtually all the parts of his thought is one of the main factors determining this coherence.

Besides examining several works by Locke, the present study considers the intellectual context of his religious thought and his involvement with various theological currents. Locke's religious ideas are Protestant in nature in that, as Locke himself often declared, he adhered to the Protestant doctrine of *sola Scriptura*, according to which the Christian Scriptures are the only infallible rule of faith and practice. Nonetheless, Locke's religion presents several points in common with heterodox Christian currents such as Socinianism (founded by the Italian anti-Trinitarian and anti-Calvinist author Faustus Socinus in the late sixteenth and early seventeenth century) and Arminianism (named after the Dutch anti-Calvinist thinker Jacobus Arminius, professor of theology at Leiden from 1603 to his death in 1609). Various similarities between Locke's theological ideas and Socinian and Arminian views have led Arthur Wainwright to conclude that "on the theological map of his day [Locke] was somewhere between Socinianism and Arminianism."[19] Both Socinians and Arminians focused, like Locke, on the interplay of biblical revelation and natural reason. An emphasis on Scripture and reason as complementary led Socinians, Arminians, and Locke to reject ecclesiastical tradition and deny, or at least disregard, doctrines that they considered unscriptural or irrational. This approach was inspired by Protestant standard objections, advanced by Lutherans and Calvinists as well, to ecclesiastical tradition, which is the Catholic rule of faith. However, Socinians, Arminians, and Locke rejected as unscriptural or irrational even some of the basic tenets of mainstream Protestantism, especially regarding soteriological issues. Based on their reading of Scripture, they all argued that the essence of Christianity lies in a few simple principles that can be deduced unambiguously from the biblical text. Therefore, Socinianism, Arminianism, and Locke's religion, along with other Protestant irenic currents and authors – from Jacob Acontius and Richard Hooker in the Elizabethan Era to the Arminian-influenced English latitudinarians of

---

[17] Peter Laslett, "Introduction" to Locke, *Two Treatises*, pp. 3–126; Dunn, *Political Thought*. Laslett's edition of *Two Treatises*, with his introduction, first appeared in 1960.

[18] John Marshall, *John Locke: Resistance, Religion and Responsibility* (Cambridge: Cambridge University Press, 1994); Nuovo, *John Locke*.

[19] Arthur W. Wainwright, "Introduction" to John Locke, *A Paraphrase and Notes on the Epistles of St Paul to the Galatians, 1 and 2 Corinthians, Romans, Ephesians*, ed. Arthur W. Wainwright, 2 vols. (Oxford: Clarendon Press, 1987), vol. 1, pp. 1–88 (58).

the seventeenth century – were expressions of the "way of fundamentals."[20] One of the main common features of the currents and authors representing the way of fundamentals was their opposition to Calvinist predestinarianism, with the consequent adoption of a moralist soteriology. Highlighting, albeit to different extents, the role of the human will and reason in accepting God's assisting grace, they regarded both graciously enabled faith and moral works as contributing to salvation. Locke too, like Socinians and Arminians, rejected predestination and upheld a moralist soteriology. His theological writings present several other similarities with Socinianism and Arminianism. For instance, he shared the Socinians' rejection of original sin, their emphasis on Christ's resurrection and exaltation, and their mortalist views, which were in line with *thnetopsychism*, namely the doctrine that the soul dies with the body and will need a divine miracle to be resurrected on Judgment Day. Concerning Locke's relation to Arminianism, his concept of grace as *assisting* grace was consonant with the basic principles of Arminian soteriology. Furthermore, his views on the atonement were inconsistent with the satisfaction theory and echoed, instead, the governmental theory formulated by Hugo Grotius (who was an Arminian in theological matters) and later adopted by Limborch and other Arminians.

---

[20] Several historians have questioned the accuracy and usefulness of the category "latitudinarianism." See, for instance, John Spurr, "'Latitudinarianism' and the Restoration Church," *The Historical Journal*, 31:1 (1988): pp. 61–82; Dmitri Levitin, *Ancient Wisdom in the Age of the New Science: Histories of Philosophy in England, c. 1640–1700* (Cambridge: Cambridge University Press, 2015), pp. 13–21, 143, 542–545. Spurr, Levitin, and others have concentrated on some substantial differences, in doctrinal and ecclesiological matters, between various authors commonly termed "latitudinarians." Moreover, they have called attention to the absence of a "latitudinarian party" in post-Restoration England. Nonetheless, I deem it appropriate to use the category "latitudinarianism," which is rooted in the labeling, and self-labeling, of several Arminian-influenced Church of England divines as "latitude-men" or "latitudinarians." I find this category useful to denote beliefs and attitudes shared by a group of clergymen including, among others, Edward Stillingfleet, John Tillotson, Edward Fowler, and Gilbert Burnet. The "latitude-men" upheld a moralist soteriology emphasizing human reason, free will, and morality. *Contra* Calvinist predestinarianism, they maintained that human beings are able to accept or resist God's *assisting* grace and that good works contribute to salvation. Moreover, the latitudinarians aimed to relax the terms of conformity in such a manner as to "comprehend" Protestant Dissenters – or, at least, the least radical Dissenters – within the Church of England. Finally, the latitudinarians were keen to cooperate with the political authorities and to grant the latter a significant role in ecclesiastical policy-making, particularly after the Glorious Revolution, while the High Church party advocated a larger autonomy for the Church. See Martin I. J. Griffin Jr., *Latitudinarianism in the Seventeenth-Century Church of England* (Leiden: Brill, 1992); William M. Spellman, *The Latitudinarians and the Church of England, 1660–1700* (Athens: University of Georgia Press, 1993). On latitudinarianism and Locke, see John Marshall, "John Locke and Latitudinarianism," in Richard W. F. Kroll, Richard Ashcraft, Perez Zagorin (eds.), *Philosophy, Science, and Religion in England 1640–1700* (Cambridge: Cambridge University Press, 1992), pp. 253–282; G. A. J. Rogers, "Locke and the Latitude-Men: Ignorance As a Ground of Toleration," in Kroll, Ashcraft, Zagorin (eds.), *Philosophy, Science, and Religion*, pp. 230–252.

Briefly, Locke was well acquainted with the main tenets of Socinianism, Arminianism, and still other theological currents and authors – especially English currents and authors belonging to the Protestant tradition of the way of fundamentals. He took into account these theological currents in his reflections on religious issues, particularly in his manuscripts, and he found their views compatible with his own conclusions concerning several theological subjects. But, when reflecting on theological matters, Locke always took the Bible as his point of reference, for he regarded Scripture as the ultimate source of religious truth. Accordingly, he was always careful to make sure that his conclusions were in line with, and indeed grounded in, the biblical text.[21] Locke's conviction that natural reason and scriptural revelation were complementary and mutually sustaining informed his theological investigations, his biblical hermeneutics, and his consideration of specific theological traditions. Thus, he did not hesitate to disagree with the Socinians when he judged some of their doctrines to be at odds with scriptural revelation and natural reason. In fact, Locke did not share Socinus's outright denial of the atonement. Furthermore, he conceived of the Law of Nature as created by God, reaffirmed and contained in the revealed Law of Faith, and hence eternally valid in its entirety. Conversely, according to Socinus and his followers, God's Revealed Word contradicted and invalidated some parts of the Law of Nature and, thus, replaced it. Finally, Locke's Christology was not Socinian proper, because in the *Paraphrase* he hinted at Christ's pre-existence. Though, he never talked of the Son as a divine person, and his Christology was not Arian proper, given also his Socinian-like emphasis on Christ's resurrection and exaltation. He developed an original Christology, presenting both Socinian and Arian elements but irreducible to Socinianism or Arianism. Likewise, Locke's mortalism, his explicit and unambiguous denial of original sin, and his public silence on the Trinity place his religious thought outside of the Arminian theological tradition. Therefore, whereas Wainwright's positioning of Locke's religion "somewhere between Socinianism and Arminianism" on the "theological map of his day" makes sense, Locke was neither a Socinian nor an Arminian. Locke's religion cannot be assimilated to any theological current in particular, for it is a unique, original, Scripture-based form of Protestant Christianity, which the present study attempts to clarify in its various aspects and implications.

---

[21] As a conforming, practicing member of the Church of England, Locke accepted the biblical canon of this church. He owned and annotated several Bibles, including, among others, a 1648 English Bible printed by William Bentley: LL 309, BOD Locke 16.25, Bentley Bible, interleaved. He also used a polyglot New Testament: LL 2864, BOD Locke 9.103–9.107, *Le Nouveau Testament* (Mons, 1673), interleaved and bound in 5 vols.

Chapter 1, "The Context and Background of Locke's Biblical Theology," explains the reasons that led Locke to publish his religious ideas in the mid-1690s. This chapter focuses on Locke's opposition to antinomianism and deism and on his search for scientific or theoretical foundations for morality. While Locke refused antinomianism as denying the efficacy of good works to salvation, he opposed the deistic notion of the religion of nature as sufficient to salvation, and he rejected the deistic view of Jesus as merely the restorer of the Law of Nature. He judged both moral conduct and faith in Jesus *as the Messiah* to be crucial to eternal salvation, as he explained in *The Reasonableness of Christianity*. A markedly religious conception of life and morality, however, pervaded Locke's moral inquiry much before the composition of the *Reasonableness*. In the *Second Treatise of Civil Government* and *An Essay concerning Human Understanding*, he described obedience to the God-given moral law as a duty toward the divine creator and legislator.[22] He regarded the divine moral law as discoverable by natural reason (at least in principle) or through divine revelation. Locke believed that natural reason could not comprehend all divine revelations. However, he argued that assent to anything, including the status of a revelation as divine, ought to be based on rational assessment. Therefore, he abhorred enthusiasts' claims to divine revelation unsubstantiated by rational assessment and inspired, instead, by irrational drives and their unwillingness to employ their rational capabilities. While comparing natural reason to a "dim candle," he affirmed its aptness to serve purposes that "may be of use to us."[23] Nevertheless, the *Essay* contains no rational demonstration of moral principles. Locke acknowledged the limitations of human knowledge in matters of morality and religion, although he thought that ethics and theology had different epistemological statuses, since he regarded morality as demonstrable (at least in principle) while he considered most theological knowledge as falling within the scope of probability – with the significant exception of our knowledge of God's existence, which to Locke is demonstrative and implies an understanding that we have duties toward our creator. His painstaking search for the foundations of morality eventually led him to resolutely turn to biblical theology in the *Reasonableness*. In this treatise on the question of justification – namely, on what it is that "justifies" human beings who have sinned and, hence, enables their salvation – Locke continued his moral inquiry; but, instead of investigating the epistemological foundations of ethics, he aimed to promote the practice of morality and the development of moral character through a Scripture-based theological ethics, as the following chapters explain.

---

[22] Locke, *Two Treatises*, p. 271; Locke, *Essay*, IV.iii.18, p. 549, IV.xviii.5, pp. 692–693.

[23] Ibid., IV.xix.8, p. 700, I.i.5, pp. 45–46.

In Chapter 2, "Engaging with Scripture and Heterodoxy," I examine Locke's approach to Scripture and his involvement with Socinianism and Arminianism. After outlining the tenets of these theological currents and clarifying Locke's familiarity with Socinian and Arminian texts, ideas, and intellectuals, this chapter analyzes Locke's use of Socinus's proof of Scriptural authority. Since Locke claimed, in the *Reasonableness* and its two vindications (written against Edwards's charge of Socinianism), that his account of the Christian religion was based on Scripture alone, he needed to prove the divine authority of Scripture. To this purpose, he followed Socinus in highlighting the excellence of Christ's moral precepts, in pointing out the consistency of Old Testament Messianic prophecies with their fulfillment in the New Testament, and in describing Jesus' miracles as confirming his Messianic mission. According to Locke, biblical miracles, although being only secondary evidence of Christ's and other divine messengers' mission, have a divine origin and can easily be distinguished from fake or demonic wonders, in that biblical miracles either glorify God or reveal matters of great concern to humanity (e.g., matters relevant to deliverance and redemption). Locke's proof of scriptural authority enabled him to develop a historical method of biblical interpretation, according to which he considered the biblical texts in relation to both their respective contexts and the biblical discourse as a whole. Locke emphasized the internal consistency of Scripture but made a distinction between two levels of authority. He thought that the revelations made by Christ during his earthly life, and recorded by the Gospels, were more important than the Apostles' elucidations of Christ's message in their epistles. Drawing particularly on the four canonical Gospels and the Acts of the Apostles, he concentrated on what he took to be the fundamentals of Christianity – that is, faith in Jesus the Messiah, repentance for sin, and obedience to the divine moral law. Thus, while following the way of fundamentals, he developed an original doctrine of the fundamentals.

Chapter 3, "A Scripture-Based Moralist Soteriology," examines Locke's views on the natural and revealed law. Locke saw the Law of Nature as divinely given and, hence, as universally and eternally valid in its entirety. This notion of the Law of Nature, which locates him in the natural law tradition, permeates his political thought. Locke's natural law theory, relying on a view of God as a creator and legislator, is grounded in both natural and biblical theology, given the role that both rational and Scripture-based arguments play in his justification of natural rights and duties in the *Second Treatise of Civil Government*. Locke even saw scriptural revelation as sufficient to establish natural rights and duties, since he regarded Scripture as infallible. In the *Reasonableness*, he maintained that natural reason alone had never grasped the content of the Law of Nature in its entirety. Therefore, the Law of Moses, revealed in the Old Testament, made the divine moral law (i.e., the Law of Works, identical to the Law of Nature) easily accessible. However, the Law of Moses was too rigorous, in that it demanded perfect obedience, and lacked effective incentives to act morally. Locke believed that, conversely, the Christian Law of Faith could promote morality and enable the pursuit of salvation. According to Locke, Jesus Christ, besides restating the Law of Nature completely and plainly, provided an incentive to behave morally in the form of an afterlife with reward and punishment. Moreover, Christ assured humanity of God's forgiveness of the repentant faithful. Comparing the views of Socinians, Arminians, and Locke on the justifying faith, this chapter stresses the specificity of Locke's position on the eternal and universal validity of the Law of Nature. Finally, the chapter elucidates Locke's rejection of original sin and his dislike of the satisfaction theory of atonement, to which he preferred the Arminians' governmental theory of atonement. In this regard, Locke's adherence to *sola Scriptura*, his concept of the mind as a *tabula rasa*, and his stress on free will and individual responsibility contributed to his refusal of original sin and satisfaction.

Chapter 4, "The Soul and the Last Judgment," concentrates on Locke's views on the afterlife and Judgment Day. This chapter argues that Locke's consciousness-based theory of personal identity, which he formulated in the second edition of *An Essay concerning Human Understanding*, published in 1694, perfectly fits with his Scripture-based views on the resurrection of the dead, divine judgment, and otherworldly rewards and sanctions. Locke was a mortalist, specifically a *thnetopsychist*, in that he thought that the human soul is not *naturally immortal*, dies with the body, and will be resurrected only by divine miracle on Judgment Day. Moreover, he believed in the resurrection of the dead, but not of their "frail, mortal bodies," which will be changed into incorruptible, spiritual bodies at resurrection. Given Locke's views on death and resurrection and his agnosticism on the ontological constitution of thinking substances or souls, *Essay* II.xxvii rejects substance-based theories of identity and describes consciousness alone as making personal identity. Locke's theory of personal identity has significant implications concerning moral accountability when it comes not only to human justice, but also to the Last Judgment. In this regard, Udo Thiel and Galen Strawson have questioned the compatibility of Locke's consciousness-based theory of personal identity with his soteriology, particularly with his notion of repentance as necessary to salvation.[24] *Pace* Thiel and Strawson, I argue that, to Locke, it is neither only one's sins and their consciousness thereof, nor merely one's repentance for

---

[24] Udo Thiel, *The Early Modern Subject: Self-Consciousness and Personal Identity from Descartes to Hume* (Oxford: Oxford University Press, 2011), p. 143; Galen Strawson, *Locke on Personal Identity: Consciousness and Concernment*, 2nd rev. ed. (Princeton: Princeton University Press, 2014), pp. 139–149.

their sins that will be considered on Judgment Day. In the *Reasonableness*, Locke recognized the imperfection and weakness of human nature. Thus, he attached importance not only to repentance, but also to the commitment to obey the divine law and to faith in Jesus the Messiah, which entails hope in God's mercy. Accordingly, he maintained that God could forgive and save the repentant faithful who, in their life, endeavor to respect the divine moral law, despite their sins and their consciousness thereof.

Chapter 5, "The Trinity and Christ," deals with a particularly controversial issue. Locke composed most of his theological writings in the 1690s, in the middle of a heated Trinitarian controversy. However, Locke always kept an obstinate public silence on the Trinity, even when Edwards and Stillingfleet pressured him to clarify his view of the Godhead, which was actually non-Trinitarian. And when referring to Locke's view as "non-Trinitarian" I mean that, although Locke never committed himself to an unequivocally anti-Trinitarian stance, belief in the Trinity played no role in his Christianity. Whereas he emphasized faith in Jesus as the Messiah, he never described the Son as a divine person. The *Reasonableness*, the *Paraphrase*, other public writings, and various theological manuscripts, although not offering a systematic account of Locke's position on Christ's nature, present several details of his Messianic Christology. Furthermore, Locke concentrated on Trinitarian issues in several manuscripts, such as *Adversaria Theologica* and *Lemmata Ethica*. A comparative analysis of the passages concerning Christ and the Godhead in Locke's theological writings leads to the conclusion that he held a Christology comprising both Socinian and Arian elements, and that his public silence on the Trinity was due to irenic and prudential reasons. Locke indeed deemed it inappropriate and even immoral to provoke or foster pointless and divisive disputes about non-fundamentals. Moreover, he considered it unwise to challenge the ecclesiastical and political authorities in a time when it was still dangerous to question the Trinitarian dogma.

The irenic attitude emerging from Locke's later writings on religion and its implications are explored in Chapter 6, "Religious Toleration and Christian Irenicism." This chapter argues that Locke's soteriological views in his later theological writings implicitly extend toleration to all those accepting the Christian Law of Faith – be they denominationally committed or not. This approach differs from the mere separation between the state and religious societies in *A Letter concerning Toleration*, which I consider inspired by Locke's political skepticism. In fact, Locke was skeptical about human beings' ability to adequately comprehend and effectively communicate religious truth. But he did not question religious truth itself, which he identified with the salvific message of the Gospel. Nevertheless, Locke never advocated intolerance of antinomians (and, by extension, of Christians rejecting a moralist soteriology) or of non-Christian believers (i.e., deists, Jews, Muslims, and "pagans"), despite their rejection of the Law of Faith, while in the *Letter* and other writings he denied toleration to atheists and Roman Catholics. I argue that Locke's exclusion of antinomians and non-Christian believers from salvation does not imply their exclusion from toleration. To Locke, non-Christian believers acknowledge a divine creator and legislator and are hence able to appreciate and follow at least the essentials of the Law of Nature, which is the only proper rule to govern human conduct and civil institutions in order to preserve natural and civil rights. Moreover, Locke regarded antinomians (and, by implication, other Christians rejecting a moralist soteriology) as only *potentially* intolerable and, hence, actually tolerable as long as they did not engage in immoral and illegal conduct. Conversely, Locke considered atheists to be *intrinsically* immoral, given their denial of a divine creator and legislator and, hence, their failure to acknowledge a divinely given moral law, and he censured Roman Catholics for maintaining some immoral principles which, in his opinion, *actually* informed their conduct.

This book takes into account the contemporary reactions to Locke's religious views. Although *The Reasonableness of Christianity* received some positive responses, the debate on Locke's theological ideas led to some unpleasant consequences – particularly when, in 1697, the Grand Jury of Middlesex reported the *Reasonableness*, along with John Toland's *Christianity Not Mysterious*, to the civil authorities because both books were said to contribute to Arianism, Socinianism, atheism, and deism. These and other charges – including charges of creedal minimalism, skepticism, and even Spinozism and Hobbism – emerged frequently during the debate on Locke's theology. While referring to several critics' objections against specific aspects of Locke's religion, I particularly concentrate on his disputes with John Edwards and Edward Stillingfleet. The Calvinistic divine Edwards openly labeled the author of the *Reasonableness* an anti-Trinitarian, a Socinian, and a creedal minimalist. Furthermore, the latitudinarian Bishop Stillingfleet argued that Locke's way of ideas, with its stress on "clear and distinct ideas," its agnosticism on substance, and its non-substantialist notion of "person," had provided the anti-Trinitarians with new weapons to question the Trinitarian dogma, which was based on a traditional, scholastic understanding of "substance" and "person." During his disputes with Edwards and Stillingfleet, Locke reaffirmed and further elucidated his theological ideas. Therefore, an analysis of his critics' points and his responses facilitates a deeper understanding of the heterodoxy, originality, and significance of his Christianity.

Although having received comparatively less scholarly attention than his way of ideas and his political theory, Locke's religion, in which his thought culminated in his later years, is one of the most thought-provoking elements of his intellectual legacy. Despite the growing number of essays on different parts of Locke's thought, including his religious thought, there is still a need for a thorough analysis of Locke's version of Christianity. This book provides such an analysis of Locke's Christianity, which the following chapters reconstruct and reconsider in its specificity while placing it in the context of his wider work and of the theological debates of his time. This monograph aims to demonstrate that Locke's religion is a unique and internally coherent form of Protestant Christianity, some aspects of which I reassess considering both textual evidence and the intellectual context of Locke's theological writing. Briefly, this study attempts to fill an existing gap in the literature on Locke, in that it provides a systematic analysis and a novel interpretation of Locke's Christianity.

1   The Context and Background of Locke's Biblical Theology

The Reasonableness of Christianity, As Delivered in the Scriptures is Locke's major book of theology. In this treatise on justification, he offered an account of his religious views, or, at least, of his religious views that he did not consider controversial, although the *Reasonableness* still attracted criticism from several quarters, as I explain below in the present study, particularly in Chapters 4 and 5. Before the publication of the *Reasonableness* in 1695, Locke mostly preferred to keep his theological ideas to himself. What led him to publish his religious views? In other words, which events contributed to change him from a simple inquirer, who took notes on theological issues in his private papers, to a writer of theology? The answer to this question is to be found in the intellectual and cultural context in which Locke wrote the *Reasonableness*, as well as in his lifelong struggle with the fundamental questions of ethics. It was both Locke's interest in some of the theological controversies of the day – particularly the antinomian and deist controversies – and his effort to establish morality on solid grounds that led him to write and publish this elucidation of the Christian religion. He was alarmed by the antinomians' denial of the efficacy of good works to salvation. However, he rejected the deists' belief in the sufficiency of natural religion, which, according to Locke, led them to reduce divine revelation to a mere reaffirmation of principles already grasped by unassisted reason. Locke deemed both moral conduct and faith in Jesus the Messiah, and hence in his salvific message, as necessary to salvation. A markedly religious conception of life had conditioned his moral inquiry since at least the composition of the manuscript *Essays on the Law of Nature* in 1664 and influenced his reflections on moral issues in the *Second Treatise of Civil Government* and *An Essay concerning Human Understanding*. In these works, he emphasized the necessity to believe in and obey a divine creator and legislator, and he described the moral law as divinely given and, consequently, discoverable by God-given natural reason (at least in principle) or through divine revelation. Nevertheless, he never offered a thorough demonstration of moral principles based on his "way of ideas." His attempt to ground morality in scientific or theoretical foundations proved fruitless and eventually led him to rely mainly on God's

Revealed Word in his moral inquiry. Although he always believed in the rational demonstrability of morality in itself, he considered Scripture infallible and, hence, sufficient to establish a coherent and cogent ethics, as he actually did when attempting to promote moral practice and the development of moral character in the *Reasonableness*.

Rejecting Antinomianism and Deism

The 1690s were a time of theological controversies. The Trinitarian controversy was only the fieriest of the disputes that heated the English theological arena of the day.[1] That controversy was ignited by Catholic attacks on Protestant Biblicism in the period around the Declaration of Indulgence of James II of 1687. Catholic polemicists challenged their Protestant counterparts to prove that the anti-Trinitarians were wrong in considering the Trinity as unscriptural and, thus, to demonstrate that the Trinitarian dogma could be inferred from clear and intelligible passages in Scripture. If unable to do so, Protestants should then either agree with the anti-Trinitarians' denial of the Trinity, or concur with Catholics that the only way to defend the Trinitarian doctrine was through the Catholic rule of faith, namely ecclesiastical tradition, thus abandoning *sola Scriptura* – that is, the Protestant theory that Scripture alone contains all information needed for salvation.[2] Although English Catholics' attacks on Protestant scripturalism became more vehement in the years of James II's reign, the conflict between Catholics and Protestants over the role of Scripture and ecclesiastical tradition in defining Christian doctrine had started much earlier. This conflict was especially harsh in England throughout the post-Restoration period, starting at least with the publication, in 1665, of a tract by the Catholic priest John Gother, *A Papist Misrepresented and Represented*, which listed many commonly held errors concerning Catholic doctrine and practice and elicited numerous responses from Protestant thinkers, including the famous Church of England divine Edward Stillingfleet.[3] Besides countering attacks by Catholic polemicists, Anglican theologians sought to overcome the scandal of doctrinal divisions among Protestants.[4] Two main ways were proposed to solve the problem of the division among Protestants in

---

[1] For an account of the Trinitarian controversy, see Chapter 5.

[2] [Abraham Woodhead?], *The Protestants Plea for a Socinian* (London, 1686); Anonymous, *A Dialogue between a New Catholic Convert and a Protestant* (London, 1686).

[3] John Gother, *A Papist Misrepresented and Represented* (London, 1665); Edward Stillingfleet, *The Doctrines and Practices of the Church of Rome Truly Represented* (London, 1687).

[4] Although the term "Anglican" came into general usage only in the latter half of the nineteenth century, in this book I use it to denote the specificity of seventeenth- and eighteenth-century Church of England divines' theological reasoning, as distinguished from Roman Catholic, Continental Protestant, and English Nonconformist theological traditions.

England. The first way was endorsed, above all, by latitudinarian clergymen who advocated broad comprehension within the Church of England. In this case, the Church of England needed to admit doctrinal differences among its members, on condition that the faithful adhered to a set of general principles upon which all Christians could easily agree. These principles concerned God's existence, the divine authority of Scripture, Jesus' Messiahship, the moral precepts delivered in the Bible, and reward and punishment in the afterlife. The other solution, which was proposed mainly by Church of England divines with Calvinistic leanings, was the enforcement of strict doctrinal uniformity. Locke chose neither broad comprehension nor the enforcement of uniformity. In *A Letter concerning Toleration* and other writings on this subject, he advocated toleration of different churches, as he argued for the separation between the civil commonwealth and religious societies. To Locke, the civil magistrate has a duty to preserve the citizens' civil interests, whereas religious organizations merely promote the salvation of their members' souls. Therefore, the "Care of the Soul" is not part of the magistrate's purview, and religious organizations cannot interfere in political affairs.[5]

The controversies of the day certainly had an impact on Locke's reflections on Christianity. The Trinitarian controversy and the dispute between Catholics and Protestants over the rule of faith contributed to the further fragmentation of Christendom and to the exacerbation of the divergences between Christians belonging to different churches. Conversely, Locke's intention in the *Reasonableness* was to enable Christians to practice morality and pursue eternal salvation in an effective way – and in a way that would enable them to coexist peacefully. In his attempt to define the fundamentals of Christianity, he described Christ's teachings as the core of the Christian religion, while he deliberately left aside the controversial issues surrounding the Trinitarian dogma. When explaining the motivations behind his decision to write *The Reasonableness of Christianity*, Locke abstained from mentioning the Trinitarian controversy and the ongoing conflicts between Catholics and Protestants over the rule of faith, although, as a Protestant, he always maintained adherence to *sola Scriptura* and rejected tradition. He was more interested in two other controversies, one of which, the antinomian controversy, was limited to the Dissenters, while the other, the deist controversy, was still in its germinal phase in the mid-1690s.[6]

---

[5] See Chapter 6.

[6] On Locke's aversion to antinomianism and deism, see Diego Lucci, "John Locke on Atheism, Catholicism, Antinomianism, and Deism," *Ethics & Politics*, 20:3 (2018): pp. 201–246. On Locke's relation to deism, see John C. Biddle, "Locke's Critique of Innate Principles and Toland's Deism," *Journal of the History of Ideas*, 37:3 (1976): pp. 411–422; Alan P. F. Sell, *John Locke and the Eighteenth-Century Divines* (Cardiff: University of Wales Press, 1997), pp. 203–212; John C. Higgins-Biddle, "Introduction" to John Locke, *The Reasonableness of*

As Locke wrote in a letter to his admirer, the clergyman Samuel Bold, prefaced to *A Second Vindication of the Reasonableness of Christianity* (1697), a controversy that had "made so much noise and heat amongst some of the Dissenters" had drawn him "into a stricter and more thorough Enquiry into the Question about Justification," prompting him to write the *Reasonableness*.[7] Although Locke never used the terms "antinomian" and "antinomianism" in the *Reasonableness* and its two vindications, the above-quoted passage clearly refers to the antinomian controversy that involved several Nonconformist theologians in the first half of the 1690s. This controversy was triggered by the republication, in the year 1690, of the Civil-War Independent divine Tobias Crisp's *Christ Alone Exalted* (1643) by his son Samuel. Elaborating on the doctrine of free grace, Tobias Crisp argued that the elect were justified solely by God's eternal decree, the effects of which their good works and faith could not alter. The Presbyterian minister Daniel Williams refuted Crisp's views in *Gospel Truth, Stated and Vindicated* (1692), which soon received the endorsement of sixteen other Presbyterian theologians. Samuel Crisp gained the support of several Independent divines, who accused Williams and his fellow Presbyterians of advocating a moralist soteriology. The controversy became so bitter that, in 1694, Williams was removed from the Pinners' Hall lectureship. This event had a strongly symbolic significance, given that the Pinners' Hall lectures had been established in 1672 (the same year of the ill-fated Royal Declaration of Indulgence by Charles II)[8] to bring together notable preachers of both factions in order to defend Protestantism from Catholic and anti-Trinitarian threats. The removal of Williams from the Pinners' Hall lectureship led to an irreparable breach between Independents and Presbyterians. Along with other Presbyterian divines who had left in protest, Williams promptly established the Salters' Hall lectureship. In the end, the "Happy Union" between Presbyterians and Independents, established in 1691, was dissolved in 1695.

Christianity, As Delivered in the Scriptures, ed. John C. Higgins-Biddle (Oxford: Clarendon Press, 1999), pp. xv–cxv (xv–xlii); Diego Lucci, *Scripture and Deism: The Biblical Criticism of the Eighteenth-Century British Deists* (Bern: Lang, 2008), pp. 44–52; James A. T. Lancaster, "From Matters of Faith to Matters of Fact: The Problem of Priestcraft in Early Modern England," *Intellectual History Review*, 28:1 (2018): pp. 145–165.

[7] John Locke, "A Second Vindication of the Reasonableness of Christianity," in John Locke, *Vindications of the Reasonableness of Christianity*, ed. Victor Nuovo (Oxford: Clarendon Press, 2012), pp. 27–233 (34).

[8] With this Declaration, issued on March 15, 1672, Charles II attempted to suspend the laws punishing Protestant Nonconformists and Roman Catholics in his realms for their "recusancy," namely for refusing to attend services in the Church of England. In 1673, the Cavalier Parliament compelled Charles II to withdraw this Declaration and, instead, to implement the first of the Test Acts, requiring anyone entering public service in England to deny the doctrine of transubstantiation and take communion within the Church of England.

As Locke himself declared in his letter to Bold, this controversy between two different Dissenting groups had attracted his attention. Locke abhorred Tobias Crisp's antinomian, radically predestinarian ideas. Whereas he avoided using the term "predestination" in the *Reasonableness* and its vindications, his criticism actually involved much more than Crisp's extreme position. Locke considered predestinarian views overall as unscriptural and unreasonable, because he saw belief in predestination as denying any role to good works in the pursuit of salvation. In Locke's opinion, predestinarianism "shook the Foundations of all Religion."[9] At the start of the *Reasonableness*, he criticized the very concept of predestination – a concept he judged grounded in the doctrine of original sin, which he openly rejected:[10]

Some Men would have all *Adam*'s Posterity doomed to Eternal Infinite Punishment, for the Transgression of *Adam*, whom Millions had never heard of, and no one had authorized to transact for him, or be his Representative.[11]

Locke blamed those who endorsed antinomian and, generally, predestinarian ideas for having also provoked the reaction of others who, overestimating the capabilities of natural reason in moral and religious matters, had fallen into the opposite extreme:

This seemed to others so little consistent with the Justice or Goodness of the Great and Infinite God, that they thought there was no Redemption necessary, and consequently that there was none, rather than admit of it upon a Supposition so derogatory to the Honour and Attributes of that Infinite Being; and so made Jesus Christ nothing but the Restorer and Preacher of pure Natural Religion; thereby doing violence to the whole tenor of the New Testament.[12]

To Locke, the opinion that Jesus was "nothing but the Restorer and Preacher of pure Natural Religion" was typical of deism. Whereas Locke did not use terms like "deism" or "deist" in the *Reasonableness*, he wrote the words "deist" or "deists" once in the first vindication and eight times in the second. He employed the term "deists" to refer to those who considered Jesus as merely a moral philosopher – namely, as a man who had simply reasserted a Law of Nature perfectly known to natural reason, without adding anything to this law. It is not easy to understand whom exactly Locke intended to reproach in the above passage from the *Reasonableness*, which he wrote in 1695, at a time when the deist controversy was still in its formative stage. This controversy raged especially between the publication of John Toland's *Christianity Not Mysterious* in 1696 and the 1740s. This period saw the heyday of English deism, with the publication of the major works of the monist and republican

---

[9] Locke, *Reasonableness*, p. 5.   [10] See Chapter 3.   [11] Locke, *Reasonableness*, p. 5.
[12] Ibid.

Toland, the freethinker and determinist Anthony Collins (who was a friend of Locke during the latter's last years), and Matthew Tindal, Thomas Chubb, Thomas Morgan, and Peter Annet, who described Christ's message as only a "republication" of the universal, necessary, and sufficient religion of nature.[13] While sharing a strong confidence in the powers of natural reason, a view of history as a process of corruption, and a consideration of institutional religion as the product of sociocultural, political, and merely human dynamics, these authors (some of whom were also called "freethinkers" because of their advocacy of freedom of thought) employed different concepts of "reason" and held different world views. In late seventeenth- and eighteenth-century England, the term "deism" actually denoted various forms of heterodoxy, such as pantheistic ideas, deterministic theories, and belief in a transcendent, wise, and benevolent creator who had made natural and moral laws perfectly comprehensible to natural reason and who abstained from interfering in worldly affairs. In this period, several theologians, such as the Newtonian scholar Samuel Clarke, the mystic William Law, and Bishop Joseph Butler, reacted to the spread of different "deistic" ideas by reasserting the primacy of revealed religion in various ways. For instance, Clarke maintained the compatibility of natural and revealed religion, but he argued that Christian revelation was a necessary complement to natural reason.[14] Conversely, fideists like Law and Butler claimed that revelation was essential to salvation in that it was different, unrelated, and superior to natural reason, which they judged inadequate to resolve matters of ultimate concern.[15] However, several years before the publication of Toland's *Christianity Not Mysterious*, other English theologians, such as Richard Baxter and Edward Stillingfleet, had already tried to refute deistic views on the sufficiency of natural religion – views that had indeed emerged in England much before the 1690s.[16]

Starting with the mid-eighteenth-century anti-deistic works of the Church of Ireland clergyman Philip Skelton and the Irish Presbyterian minister John Leland,[17] traditional histories of English deism trace its origins to *De veritate*

---

[13] On English deism, see Lucci, *Scripture and Deism*; Wayne Hudson, *The English Deists: Studies in Early Enlightenment* (London: Pickering & Chatto, 2009); Wayne Hudson, *Enlightenment and Modernity: The English Deists and Reform* (London: Pickering & Chatto, 2009); Jeffrey R. Wigelsworth, *Deism in Enlightenment England: Theology, Politics, and Newtonian Public Science* (Manchester: Manchester University Press, 2009).

[14] Samuel Clarke, *A Discourse concerning the Unchangeable Obligations of Natural Religion, and the Truth and Certainty of the Christian Revelation* (London, 1706).

[15] William Law, *The Case of Reason* (London, 1731); Joseph Butler, *The Analogy of Religion, Natural and Revealed, to the Constitution and the Course of Nature* (London, 1736).

[16] Richard Baxter, *More Reasons for the Christian Religion, and No Reason against It* (London, 1672); Edward Stillingfleet, *A Letter to a Deist* (London, 1677).

[17] Philip Skelton, *Deism Revealed*, 2 vols., 2nd rev. ed. (London, 1751); John Leland, *A View of the Principal Deistical Writers*, 2 vols. (London, 1757).

(1624) by Lord Edward Herbert of Cherbury. This late-Renaissance intellectual maintained that human beings could grasp the basic notions of natural religion, which are relevant to the existence of a Supreme Being, the necessity to "worship" this Supreme Being through moral conduct, and reward and punishment in the afterlife. Another seventeenth-century English thinker holding deistic ideas was Charles Blount, who published his works between the early 1680s and his premature death by suicide in 1693.[18] Blount, like Herbert of Cherbury, considered the religion of nature to be universal, necessary, and sufficient. However, whereas Herbert conceded that some revelations (e.g., the Decalogue and Christ's teachings) were compatible with natural religion, Blount's attacks on ancient paganism implied that institutional religion in general was not only superfluous, but also absurd, irrational, and inhumane because it hindered the free development of rationality. Blount became notorious in his time not only because of his deistic views, but also because he drew heavily on the works of Herbert, Hobbes, and Spinoza. Several other English deists were indebted to Hobbes and, above all, to Spinoza.[19] For instance, Toland's monism was inspired by Spinoza's monistic philosophy, although Toland's metaphysics was even more radical than Spinoza's system. In *Letters to Serena* (1704), emphasizing the intrinsic activity of matter and the eternity of the universe, Toland indeed blamed Spinoza for distinguishing thought from matter and for denying that motion was inherent to matter.[20] Yet Spinoza's demystifying biblical hermeneutics significantly influenced Toland's and other deists' approach to Scripture and the history of religion, since Toland, Collins, and other deists and freethinkers denied the Bible and other religious texts any privileged status. In interpreting Scripture, they employed historical-critical and philological methods developed in textual criticism since the Age of Renaissance. Consequently, they questioned, more or less implicitly, the divine authority of Scripture.

---

[18] Blount's works were also collected by his friend and biographer Charles Gildon in: Charles Blount, *Miscellaneous Works*, 2 vols. (London, 1695).

[19] Rosalie L. Colie, "Spinoza and the Early English Deists," *Journal of the History of Ideas*, 20:1 (1959): pp. 23–46; Rosalie L. Colie, "Spinoza in England, 1665–1730," *Proceedings of the American Philosophical Society*, 107:3 (1963): pp. 183–219; Stuart Brown, "'Theological Politics' and the Reception of Spinoza in the Early English Enlightenment," *Studia Spinozana*, 9 (1993): pp. 181–200; Luisa Simonutti, "Premières réactions anglaises au *Traité théologique-politique*," in Paolo Cristofolini (ed.), *The Spinozistic Heresy: The Debate on the "Tractatus Theologico-Politicus," 1670–77* (Amsterdam: APA – Holland University Press, 1995), pp. 123–137; Luisa Simonutti, "Spinoza and the English Thinkers: Criticism on Prophecies and Miracles: Blount, Gildon, Earbery," in Wiep van Bunge, Wim Klever (eds.), *Disguised and Overt Spinozism around 1700* (Leiden: Brill, 1996), pp. 191–211; Lucci, *Scripture and Deism*, pp. 38–44.

[20] John Toland, *Letters to Serena* (London, 1704), pp. 131–239; Gianluca Mori, *L'ateismo dei moderni. Filosofia e negazione di Dio da Spinoza a d'Holbach* (Rome: Carocci, 2016), pp. 147–161.

When Locke, in an above-quoted passage from the *Reasonableness*, blamed those who "thought there was no Redemption necessary . . . and so made Jesus Christ nothing but the Restorer and Preacher of pure Natural Religion," he was probably not thinking of Herbert of Cherbury and Blount, let alone Hobbes or Spinoza. Locke had good knowledge of Herbert's philosophy, which he criticized as a form of innatism in *An Essay concerning Human Understanding*.[21] Nevertheless, nothing in Locke's works indicates that he had Herbert in mind when attacking deism in the *Reasonableness* and its vindications. Concerning Blount, Locke received two volumes of his works only a week before the publication of the *Reasonableness*.[22] Therefore, it is unlikely that he was thinking of Blount when he wrote, in the *Reasonableness*, about the deists' views on redemption and Christ. Finally, when responding to Stillingfleet's charge of materialism and Spinozism in 1699, Locke stated that he was "not so well read in Hobbes or Spinosa, as to be able to say what were their opinions."[23] In this case, Locke was disingenuous. He actually had good knowledge of Spinoza's thought, particularly of his biblical hermeneutics, and he probably discussed Spinoza's ideas with Limborch, Le Clerc, and Furly when he was in the Netherlands.[24] He was also familiar with Hobbes's thought. But the fact that he refrained from labeling these two philosophers as "deists" and from associating them with "deism" is an indication that, most probably, he did not consider them to be deists. So, who were Locke's "deists"? Who did Locke intend to blame, in the *Reasonableness*, for denying the need for redemption and reducing Jesus to merely a moral philosopher? I concur with John Higgins-Biddle that when Locke, in the *Reasonableness*, denounced those who believed only in natural religion, he was probably thinking of Uriel Acosta and John Toland.[25]

Uriel Acosta (also called Uriel da Costa) was born in Porto, around 1585, to a family of "New Christians." He fled Portugal and converted openly to Judaism in the mid-1610s when he moved to Hamburg, whereas part of his family settled in Amsterdam. His opposition to Jewish traditions caused a scandal in 1616–1618 and led to his excommunication by the communities of Venice and Hamburg. He decided to move to Amsterdam in 1623. In the same year, he published *Examination of Pharisaic Traditions* – a tract depicting

---

[21] John Locke, *An Essay concerning Human Understanding*, ed. Peter H. Nidditch (Oxford: Clarendon Press, 1975), I.iii.15–27, pp. 77–84.

[22] The bookseller, and Locke's publisher and friend, Awnsham Churchill billed Locke for "Blunts 2 vols" on August 3, 1695. See MS Locke b. 1, f. 185.

[23] John Locke, "Reply to the Right Reverend the Lord Bishop of Worcester's Answer to His Second Letter," in John Locke, *Works*, 9 vols., 12th ed. (London, 1824), vol. 3, pp. 191–499 (477).

[24] Kim Ian Parker, "Spinoza, Locke, and Biblical Interpretation," in Luisa Simonutti (ed.), *Locke and Biblical Hermeneutics: Conscience and Scripture* (Cham: Springer, 2019), pp. 163–188.

[25] Higgins-Biddle, "Introduction," pp. xxvii–xxxvii.

Rabbinic Judaism as corrupted by unscriptural beliefs and ceremonies and devoid of theological and philosophical truth.[26] Acosta believed that the Law of Nature was universal, necessary, and sufficient, while he judged the rituals and rules of institutional religion inconsistent with both reason and Scripture. When the *Examination* was burned publicly in Amsterdam, Acosta relocated to Utrecht. He was readmitted to the Jewish community of Amsterdam in 1633, but was soon excommunicated because he did not stop expressing heterodox ideas. In the winter of 1639–1640, he was readmitted again to the Amsterdam community, but only after suffering a harsh public punishment. In the end, shortly after his final readmission to the Jewish community of Amsterdam, he committed suicide by shooting himself. Before killing himself, he completed an autobiography, *Exemplar Humanae Vitae*, which remained in manuscript form until Limborch published it in 1687.[27] Locke knew this work through his friend Limborch and, in a note that he wrote in the notebook *Lemmata Ethica* in 1695 (the same year he published the *Reasonableness*), he called Acosta "the father and patriarch of the Deists."[28]

If Locke did not receive a good impression from Acosta's views, he found Toland's ideas even less appealing. Locke and Toland first met in August 1693, when the Irish-born and Scottish- and Dutch-educated Toland was almost twenty-three years old and had recently returned to Britain from the Netherlands. Several friends of Locke had recommended Toland to him. Among Toland's endorsers were Limborch, Le Clerc, Furly, the lawyer John Freke, and the natural philosopher and political writer William Molyneux. Toland sent some papers to Locke through Freke in early 1695, when he was working on *Christianity Not Mysterious*. Freke mentioned Toland's papers in two letters to Locke.[29] Unfortunately, these papers are lost, but it is likely that they contained the drafts of some sections of *Christianity Not Mysterious*. If so, the use that Toland made of Locke's way of ideas must have shocked Locke because, in *Christianity Not Mysterious*, Toland declared acceptable only those revelations consistent with our "natural" or "common Notions."[30] This approach made divine revelation secondary in comparison to natural reason. Toland indeed talked of divine revelations as mere "means of information," the contents of which ought to be consistent with the criteria of

---

[26] Uriel da Costa, *Examination of Pharisaic Traditions*, trans. and ed. H. P. Salomon and I. S. D. Sassoon (Leiden: Brill, 1993).

[27] Philipp van Limborch, *De Veritate Religionis Christianae amica collatio cum Erudito Judaeo* (Gouda, 1687), pp. 341–364.

[28] MS Locke d. 10, "Lemmata Ethica, Argumenta et Authores," p. 33.

[29] John Freke to Locke, March 28, 1695, in John Locke, *The Correspondence of John Locke*, ed. E. S. de Beer, 8 vols. (Oxford: Oxford University Press, 1979–1989), vol. 5, no. 1868; John Freke and Edward Clarke to Locke, April 9, 1695, in Locke, *Correspondence*, vol. 5, no. 1874.

[30] John Toland, *Christianity Not Mysterious* (London, 1696), pp. 31, 79, 128.

natural reason.[31] In other words, Toland completely subjected revelation to natural reason and, thus, he rejected the central place that Locke allocated to revelation.[32]

Locke's insistence on the necessity to refer to scriptural revelation, which also includes things exceeding the capabilities of natural reason, denotes his distance from what he considered the core tenets of deism. According to Locke, the deists believed that natural reason actually grasped the Law of Nature in its entirety, maintained that the Law of Nature was sufficient to salvation, and argued that Jesus had merely reaffirmed the Law of Nature. Conversely, Locke thought that natural reason alone had always failed to comprehend the Law of Nature completely and perfectly and, thus, to build a thorough, convincing, flawless system of ethics. He even regarded many ancient philosophers' reliance on natural reason alone as one of the main factors behind the rise of priestcraft before Christ's Coming. Locke believed that some philosophers, in ancient times, had reckoned the existence of "the One only True God," but they could not persuade the bulk of humankind, who were consequently subjugated by the priests' "wrong Notions, and invented Rites."[33] This was mainly due to those philosophers' circumspection and elitism, as Locke explained in the *Reasonableness*:

The Rational and thinking part of Mankind, 'tis true, when they sought after him, they found the One, Supream, Invisible God: But if they acknowledged and worshipped him, it was only in their own minds. They kept this Truth locked up in their own breasts as a Secret, nor ever durst venture it amongst the People; much less amongst the Priests, those wary Guardians of their own Creeds and Profitable Inventions. Hence we see that *Reason*, speaking ever so clearly to the Wise and Virtuous, had never Authority enough to prevail on the Multitude.[34]

As a result, it was not philosophers who ruled, but "Priests every where, to secure their Empire, having excluded *Reason* from having any thing to do in Religion."[35] Locke's criticism of ancient philosophers in the *Reasonableness* contains an indirect attack on deism, as Mark Goldie has correctly noted:

Locke succeeds in turning anti-clericalism against the deists by showing that it was the flimsy hubris of ancient philosophy – of the advocates of reason – that bred clerical monstrosities by way of a reaction against the vanity and vacuity of secular philosophy. For Locke, undue faith in reason was a type of "enthusiasm." Contemporary deist claims for the great capacity of reason, Locke asserts, cannot be sustained in the face of

---

[31] Ibid., pp. 40–41.

[32] On this point, I agree with G. A. J. Rogers, who has also noted that "Locke was not keen to encourage the deist's overconfident expectations about the power of reason alone to serve man's religious objectives." G. A. J. Rogers, "John Locke: Conservative Radical," in Roger D. Lund (ed.), *The Margins of Orthodoxy: Heterodox Writing and Cultural Response, 1660–1750* (Cambridge: Cambridge University Press, 1995), pp. 97–116 (113).

[33] Locke, *Reasonableness*, pp. 143–144.   [34] Ibid., p. 144.   [35] Ibid., p. 143.

history's evidence to the contrary, for the darkness of error and superstition, and its priestly manipulators, had, through time, overwhelmed the dim light of reason and its partisans.[36]

According to Locke, Jesus Christ reconciled religion and morality, thus avoiding the shortcomings of "the lives of pure idolatry and pure reason [which] were both failed projects."[37] Besides restoring the God-given Law of Nature in its entirety, Christ revealed additional truths concerning otherworldly reward and punishment and God's forgiveness of the repentant faithful. Therefore, Christ's message facilitated the practice of morality and made salvation possible despite the weakness of human nature. But, before coming to this conclusion in *The Reasonableness of Christianity*, Locke had considered the issue of the theoretical foundations of morality in various works, from his early manuscripts of the 1660s to *An Essay concerning Human Understanding*.

Searching for the Foundations of Morality

In the manuscripts *Two Tracts on Government* (1660–1662) and *Essays on the Law of Nature*, Locke insisted that the Law of Nature could be known through natural reason or divine revelation. Far from believing that innate ideas could lead to general consent about morality, Locke rejected innatism and argued that natural reason could demonstrate the existence of a divine lawmaker starting from a consideration of the sensitive world and of the self. Thus, natural reason could appreciate the divinely given Law of Nature and make decisions in accordance with its principles.[38] Nevertheless, he struggled to find

---

[36] Mark Goldie, "John Locke, the Early Lockeans, and Priestcraft," *Intellectual History Review*, 28:1 (2018): pp. 125–144 (132).

[37] Ibid. This theme is present not only in the *Reasonableness*, but also in the 1698 manuscript *Sacerdos*, in which Locke described Christ as reuniting "again Religion and Morality as the inseparable parts of the worship of god, which ought never to have been separated." John Locke, "Sacerdos," in John Locke, *Writings on Religion*, ed. Victor Nuovo (Oxford: Oxford University Press, 2002), pp. 17–18 (17). The original of *Sacerdos* is at p. 93 of the manuscript *Adversaria 1661*, presently in a private collection in France. Microfilm copies of this manuscript are at the Houghton Library, Harvard University (MS. Eng. 860.1), and at the Bodleian Library (MS. Film 77).

[38] John Locke, *Two Tracts on Government*, ed. Philip Abrams (Cambridge: Cambridge University Press, 1967); John Locke, *Essays on the Law of Nature*, ed. Wolfgang von Leyden (Oxford: Clarendon Press, 1954). On the *Essays on the Law of Nature* and their role in the development of Locke's views on natural law, see Wolfgang von Leyden, "Introduction" to Locke, *Essays on the Law of Nature*, pp. 1–92; Franziska Quabeck, *John Locke's Concept of Natural Law from the Essays on the Law of Nature to the Second Treatise of Government* (Zurich-Berlin: Lit Verlag, 2013). The first of the *Two Tracts*, written in 1660, is MS Locke e. 7, "Quest: whether the Civill Magistrate may lawfully impose and determine ye use of indifferent things in reference to Religious Worship." The second, composed in 1662, is in MS Locke c. 28, ff. 3–20, "An Magistratus Civilis posit res adiaphoras in divini cultus ritus asciscere, eosque

rational grounds for morality. Locke was indeed doubtful about the human capacity to *actually* construct a sound system of morality through natural reason alone, as his mature works demonstrate. However, he never questioned the existence, rationality, and demonstrability of morality in itself. Even after acknowledging, in the *Reasonableness*, that "humane reason unassisted, failed Men in its great and Proper business of *Morality*,"[39] he did not tone down his comments about the inherent rationality of morality and the (at least theoretical) possibility of a demonstrative knowledge of morality in later editions of *An Essay concerning Human Understanding*. He always believed in the existence of a God-given moral law compatible with, and hence acceptable to, natural reason. He was indeed committed to both biblical and natural theology.

In the *Essays on the Law of Nature* and *An Essay concerning Human Understanding*, Locke argued that natural reason could deduce God's existence from the observation of Creation. In these works, he made use of the argument from design and the anthropological argument to prove God's existence.[40] Concerning the argument from design, it is stated in *Essay* I.iv.9 that "the visible marks of extraordinary Wisdom and Power, appear so plainly in all the Works of the Creation, that a rational Creature, who will but seriously reflect on them, cannot miss the discovery of a *Deity*."[41] As to the anthropological argument, *Essay* IV.x.1–6 presents a line of reasoning consisting of the following steps. Locke observed "that *Man has a clear Perception of his own Being*; he knows certainly, that he exists, and that he is something."[42] Moreover, he argued:

---

populo imponere? Affirmatur" (Whether the civil magistrate may incorporate indifferent things into the ceremonies of divine worship and impose them on the people: Confirmed). Von Leyden's edition of *Essays on the Law of Nature* presents, in the original Latin and in English translation, Locke's eight lectures or "disputations" on the Law of Nature in his capacity as Censor of Moral Philosophy at Christ Church, Oxford, in 1664. All eight essays are in MS Locke f. 31, ff. 9–119, written probably in 1664. The drafts of essays IV to VIII are also in an earlier manuscript of 1663–1664, MS Locke e. 6, ff. 63v–17v. Moreover, a later manuscript copy of all essays, in the hand of Sylvester Brownover and dating back to 1681, is in MS Locke f. 30, ff. 122–173v. Von Leyden's edition also contains, in both the original Latin and an English translation, Locke's 1664 valedictory speech as Censor of Moral Philosophy, taken from MS Locke f. 31, ff. 120–138. An early draft of this speech is in MS Locke e. 6, ff. 3–6. Finally, von Leyden's edition presents some shorthand writings, mainly from Locke's journal of 1676 (MS Locke f. 1).

[39] Locke, *Reasonableness*, p. 150.

[40] Locke, *Essays on the Law of Nature*, pp. 109, 147–159; Locke, *Essay*, I.iv.9, p. 89, II.xxiii.12, pp. 302–303, and IV.x.1–6, pp. 619–621. However, in MS Locke c. 28, ff. 119–120, "Deus Des Cartes's proof of a God from the idea of necessary existence examined," written in 1696, Locke rejected Descartes's proof of God's existence from the idea of necessary existence. This manuscript was first published in: Peter King, *The Life of John Locke* (London: Colburn, 1829), pp. 312–315.

[41] Locke, *Essay*, I.iv.9, p. 89.   [42] Ibid., IV.x.2, p. 619.

Man knows, by an intuitive Certainty, that bare *nothing can no more produce any real Being, than it can be equal to two right Angles* .... If therefore we know there is some real Being, and that Non-entity cannot produce any real Being, it is an evident demonstration, that from Eternity there has been something; Since what was not from Eternity, had a Beginning; and what had a Beginning, must be produced by something else.[43]

From these premises, Locke concluded the following:

From the Consideration of our selves, and what we infallibly find in our own Constitutions, our Reason leads us to the Knowledge of this certain and evident Truth, That *there is an eternal, most powerful, and most knowing Being.*[44]

Locke considered God as not only the creator, but also a wise and benevolent legislator, and he thought that belief in a divine creator and lawgiver was crucial to moral conduct. As he wrote in *Essay* I.iv.8: "Without a Notion of a Law-maker, it is impossible to have a Notion of a Law, and an Obligation to observe it."[45] He expressed the same view in *Essay* IV.iii.18, where he declared morality capable of demonstration and compared it to mathematics:

The *Idea* of a supreme Being, infinite in Power, Goodness, and Wisdom, whose Workmanship we are, and on whom we depend; and the *Idea* of our selves, as understanding, rational Beings, being such as are clear in us, would, I suppose, if duly considered, and pursued, afford such Foundations of our Duty and Rules of Action, as might place *Morality amongst the Sciences capable of Demonstration*: wherein I doubt not, but from self-evident Propositions, by necessary Consequences, as incontestable as those in Mathematicks, the measures of right and wrong might be made out, to any one that will apply himself with the same Indifferency and Attention to the one, as he does to the other of these Sciences.[46]

In this respect, it is worth noting that Locke's combining of the aforesaid arguments for God's existence with a view of human beings as able to decide about their "Duty and Rules of Action" is rooted in the scholastic natural law tradition. This approach also informed seventeenth-century natural law theories and the theological tradition of English latitudinarianism. Locke himself, in fact, was a natural law theorist, and one who emphasized the connection between humanity and the divine creator and lawgiver, as I explain in Chapter 3. Nonetheless, he doubted the human capacity to *actually* demonstrate moral ideas and provide morality with scientific or theoretical foundations, despite his conviction in the intrinsic rationality of the divine moral law and, hence, in the compatibility of this law with (God-given) natural reason. He called attention to the difficulties that natural reason meets when trying to

---

[43] Ibid., IV.x.3, p. 620.   [44] Ibid., IV.x.6, p. 621.   [45] Ibid., I.iv.8, p. 87.
[46] Ibid., IV.iii.18, p. 549.

demonstrate moral ideas – difficulties like their unfitness for sensible representation and their complexity:

> We have no sensible marks that resemble [moral ideas], whereby we can set them down; we have nothing but Words to express them by: which though, when written, they remain the same, yet the *Ideas* they stand for, may change in the same Man; and 'tis very seldom, that they are not different in different Persons . . . . Another thing that makes the greater difficulty in *Ethicks*, is, That *moral Ideas* are commonly more complex than those of the Figures ordinarily considered in Mathematicks.[47]

Locke noted that these difficulties "may in a good measure be *remedied* by Definitions, setting down that Collection of simple *Ideas*, which every Term shall stand for; and then using the Terms steadily and constantly for that precise Collection."[48] Nevertheless, he admitted that the imperfection and weakness of human nature prevent us from demonstrating moral ideas in the same way as we demonstrate mathematical notions:

> Confident I am, that if Men would in the same method, and with the same indifferency, search after moral, as they do mathematical Truths, they would find them to have a stronger Connection one with another, and a more necessary Consequence from our clear and distinct *Ideas*, and to come nearer perfect Demonstration, than is commonly imagined. But much of this is not to be expected, whilst the desire of Esteem, Riches, or Power, makes Men espouse the well endowed Opinions in Fashion, and then seek Arguments, either to make good their Beauty, or varnish over, and cover their Deformity.[49]

Briefly, whereas Locke did not call into question the existence and rationality of morality in itself, and whereas he deemed morality demonstrable (at least in principle), he doubted the human capacity to *actually* demonstrate morality through the operation of natural reason. Locke himself, in the *Essay*, failed to explain the source of moral obligation in accordance with his way of ideas, for he did not clarify the very idea of moral obligation.[50] Nevertheless, providing epistemological foundations for morality, which the *Essay* defines as "*the proper Science, and Business of Mankind in general*,"[51] was originally one of the main objectives of this work. This has led some Locke specialists, such as John Yolton and John Colman, to maintain that providing epistemological foundations for morality, not for natural philosophy, was Locke's *primary* aim

---

[47] Ibid., IV.iii.19, p. 550.   [48] Ibid., IV.iii.20, p. 552.   [49] Ibid.

[50] Ibid., II.xxii.1–12, pp. 288–295; John Dunn, *The Political Thought of John Locke: An Historical Account of the Argument of the "Two Treatises of Government"* (Cambridge: Cambridge University Press, 1969), pp. 187–192; J. B. Schneewind, "Locke's Moral Philosophy," in Vere Chappell (ed.), *The Cambridge Companion to Locke* (Cambridge: Cambridge University Press, 1994), pp. 199–225 (213).

[51] Locke, *Essay*, IV.xii.11, p. 646.

in the *Essay*.[52] In this regard, I acknowledge that Locke's moral reflection, which was informed by a religious conception of life, played an important role in the development of his thought and indeed unites the different parts of his work in a coherent whole. However, I consider Yolton's and Colman's position too extreme, since I believe that Locke's intent to offer epistemological foundations for natural philosophy was as significant as his intention to find solid grounds for morality.[53] Locke's twofold objective is evidenced by what he wrote in the manuscript *Study*, composed in 1677, six years after the first draft of the *Essay*:

That which seems to me to be suited to the end of man, and lie level to his understanding, is the improvement of natural experiments for the convenience of this life, and the way of ordering himself so as to attain happiness in the other – i.e. moral philosophy, which, in my sense, comprehends religion too, or a man's whole duty.[54]

These two purposes are interconnected in Locke. He viewed not only moral conduct, but also the exercise of understanding (which he considered a moral duty, signifying obedience to the divine moral law that human beings are bearers of) as relevant, useful, and rewarding in both this life and the afterlife. According to Locke, one's exercise of their rational capabilities promotes their intellectual growth and enables them to become as free as any intellectual being can be. Moreover, God will reward the effort to find the truth even when one fails to achieve this goal, because God appreciates sincere intellectual endeavor.[55] Considering the importance of morality and the pursuit of knowledge (and the moral aspects of this pursuit) when working on the *Essay* in the

---

[52] John W. Yolton, *John Locke and the Way of Ideas* (Oxford: Clarendon Press, 1956); John Colman, *John Locke's Moral Philosophy* (Edinburgh: Edinburgh University Press, 1983).

[53] On the relevance of Locke's theory of knowledge to natural philosophy, see Peter Anstey, *John Locke and Natural Philosophy* (Oxford: Oxford University Press, 2011); Peter Anstey, "Locke and Natural Philosophy," in Matthew Stuart (ed.), *A Companion to Locke* (Chichester: Wiley-Blackwell, 2016), pp. 64–81.

[54] John Locke, "Study," in King, *Life*, pp. 90–133 (106). The original of this manuscript is part of MS Locke f. 2, pp. 85–89, 84–85, 87–88, 89–93, 106–114, 116–132 (pagination corrected by the Bodleian Library: pp. 87–93, 95–96, 97–101, 114–122, 124–140). On this manuscript, see Richard Yeo, "John Locke's 'Of Study' (1677): Interpreting an Unpublished Essay," *Locke Studies*, 3 (2003): pp. 147–165. As Sorana Corneanu has observed, in the quoted passage Locke refers to the anonymous tract *The Practice of Christian Graces: Or, the Whole Duty of Man* (London, 1658), a popular primer of ethics written, probably, by the Royalist clergyman Richard Allestree and promoted by the Restoration Church of England. See Sorana Corneanu, *Regimens of the Mind: Boyle, Locke, and the Early Modern Cultura Animi Tradition* (Chicago: The University of Chicago Press, 2011), p. 142. The phrase "the whole duty of man" is taken from Eccl. 12:13: "Let us hear the conclusion of the whole matter: Fear God, and keep his commandments: for this is the whole duty of man." When not noted otherwise, the English translations of the biblical verses quoted in the present book are from the King James Version (KJV).

[55] John Marshall, *John Locke: Resistance, Religion and Responsibility* (Cambridge: Cambridge University Press, 1994), p. 170; Richard Yeo, "John Locke and Polite Philosophy," in Conal

1680s, Locke attempted to create a system of ethics consistent with his way of ideas in the manuscript *Of Ethick in General*, written around 1686 and initially intended as the final chapter of the *Essay*.[56] Though, he eventually discarded this project and left this draft chapter incomplete, after writing twelve sections concerning subjects addressed in other parts of the *Essay* and later covered in the *Reasonableness* as well. After the first two, introductory sections, the sections from 3 to 6 of this manuscript examine the historical evolution of philosophical ethics, particularly among ancient, pre-Christian thinkers, and take this evolution as proof of the existence of a Law of Nature. According to Locke, however, ancient philosophers failed to trace moral laws to their true origin, namely, to the will of a divine legislator. For this reason, they also failed to offer incentives to act morally in the form of otherworldly rewards and sanctions. They concentrated exclusively on worldly incentives, such as praise and blame or civil punishment. To Locke, this approach was unconvincing because it entailed moral relativism and, consequently, it failed to provide universal foundations for morality. He thought that a general criterion or rule to define actions as virtuous or vicious could be found across human societies:

The generall rule whereof & the most constant that I can finde is that those actions are esteemed virtuous which are thought absolutely necessary to the preservation of society & those that disturb or dissolve the bonds of community are every where esteemed ill and vitious.[57]

However, Locke observed that this general rule was adequate to identify only the vices most harmful to society. This general rule could not provide guidance for all sorts of behavior, since different societies have different moral codes concerning "actions that are not thought to have such an immoderate influence on society" and that, consequently, "in some Countrys or Societys ... are virtues in others vices & in others indifferent."[58] Therefore, there was a need of an "obligation or Superior law" beyond social conventions and civil law.[59] In sections 6 and 9, Locke argued that the "Ethicks of the schools" had not provided convincing foundations for morality because, following (and partly misunderstanding) Aristotle's example, teachers of ethics had "become only language masters," unable to distinguish clearly between good and evil and, thus, unable to give us convincing reasons to do good and to shun evil. They

---

Condren, Stephen Gaukroger, Ian Hunter (eds.), *The Philosopher in Early Modern Europe: The Nature of a Contested Identity* (Cambridge: Cambridge University Press, 2006), pp. 254–275 (265); Corneanu, *Regimens of the Mind*, pp. 141–146; Jean-Michel Vienne, "Hermeneutics and the Reasonableness of Belief," in Simonutti (ed.), *Locke and Biblical Hermeneutics*, pp. 105–119 (106–110).

[56] John Locke, "Of Ethick in General," in Locke, *Writings on Religion*, pp. 9–14. On this manuscript, MS Locke c. 28, ff. 146–152, see Victor Nuovo, *John Locke: The Philosopher As Christian Virtuoso* (Oxford: Oxford University Press, 2017), pp. 193–197.

[57] Locke, "Ethick," p. 10.   [58] Ibid.   [59] Ibid.

generally accepted customs and values embedded in language, and they lacked sufficient authority to enforce what they taught.[60] Locke, conversely, believed that morality could be founded on grounds more solid than social convention or language – namely, on "natural" grounds. He devoted sections 7 and 8 of *Of Ethick in General* to this issue. He maintained that "an understanding free agent naturally follows that which causes pleasure to it & flies that which causes pain. i.e. naturally seekes happynesse & shuns misery."[61] Adopting a hedonistic approach, Locke argued that, when making morally relevant decisions, human beings take into account the principles of pleasure and pain, but he highlighted a significant difference between *natural* good and evil and *moral* good and evil:

The difference between morall & natural good & evill is only this that we call that natural good & evill which by the natural efficiency of this thing produces pleasure or peine in us & that is morally Good or Evill which by the appointmt of an Intelligent Being that has power draws pleasure or peine after it not by any natural consequence but by the intervention of that power .... For rewards & punishmts are the good and evil whereby Superiors enforce the observance of their laws it being impossible to set any other motive or restraint to the actions of a free understanding agent but the consideration of good or evill, that is pleasure or pain, that will follow from it.[62]

Following these considerations, Locke called attention, in sections 10 to 12 of this draft chapter, to the effectiveness of incentives to act morally in the form of rewards and punishments enforced by "a Superior power."[63] In this regard, he talked of "a lawgiver" with "power & will to reward & punish" in accordance with "the tenor of the law establishd by him" – a law "sufficiently promulgated and made known to all man kinde."[64] Here, Locke was obviously talking of God, as a lawgiver and judge, and of the Law of Nature; but he did not continue his argument. The manuscript abruptly stops at this point. Locke set this draft chapter aside and decided to not include it in the *Essay*. The exact reasons for this decision are unknown. Nevertheless, what Locke wrote in this manuscript is in line with his considerations on morality in the *Essay* and the *Reasonableness* – two works that, as I explain in the next section of this chapter, are in a relation of continuity.

In the *Essay*, Locke's standards for the demonstration of any truth, including moral truths, could not be satisfied by any available demonstration of moral principles. Whereas he believed that moral demonstrations ought to start from self-evident principles, he could find no self-evident moral principles with substantial content able to ground a moral demonstration. He was aware of the

---

[60] Ibid., pp. 10–12.   [61] Ibid., p. 11.   [62] Ibid., p. 12.   [63] Ibid., p. 13.
[64] Ibid., pp. 13–14.

narrow scope of human knowledge of religious and moral matters.[65] His approach to such matters was indeed conditioned by a sort of "mitigated skepticism," since his philosophy was indebted to the revival of academic as well as Pyrrhonian skepticism in the early modern period.[66] Although Locke was definitely not a full-blown Pyrrhonian skeptic, the early modern revival of skeptical considerations informed his epistemology in a twofold sense.[67] First, according to Locke, we do not get behind ideas to things themselves, to their substance. He described substance as an *unknown* support or substratum of ideas that are "conveyed in by the Senses, as they are found in exteriour things, or by reflection on [the mind's] own operations," and that cannot "subsist by themselves";[68] and he maintained that "we have no clear, or distinct *Idea* of that *thing* we suppose a Support."[69] Second, to Locke we cannot hope to attain certainty in most areas of inquiry, in which we can only aspire to rely on probabilities.[70] He restricted the domain of certain knowledge to only three areas. He maintained that we have *intuitive* knowledge of the existence of thinking in us and of the existence and identity of ideas in our minds. Locke's second area of certain knowledge consists of *demonstrative* knowledge of the existence of God and of mathematics. When considering demonstrative knowledge, he also described morality as demonstrable in principle, despite the difficulties that natural reason meets (and despite natural reason's actual failure) in attempting to demonstrate morality. Finally, Locke argued that we have *sensitive* knowledge of the existence of finite things. Everything else falls in the domain of judgment, or opinion based on probability – not certain knowledge. Locke's recognition of the limits of knowledge significantly influenced his consideration of religious and moral matters. He regarded the amount of knowledge currently available in these domains as strictly limited, although, according to Locke, theological knowledge and moral knowledge do not have the same epistemic status. As we have seen above, Locke regarded morality as demonstrable (at least in principle). Concerning theological knowledge, he thought that we have demonstrative knowledge of God's existence (which implies an understanding that we have duties toward our creator), but he believed that most theological knowledge falls within the scope of probability, as I clarify in the next section of this chapter. At any rate, he was

---

[65] Nicholas Wolterstorff, *John Locke and the Ethics of Belief* (Cambridge: Cambridge University Press, 1996), pp. 12–158; Agostino Lupoli, "Boyle's Influence on Locke's 'Study of the Way to Salvation'," in Simonutti (ed.), *Locke and Biblical Hermeneutics*, pp. 21–54 (27–28).

[66] Sam Black, "Toleration and the Skeptical Inquirer in Locke," *Canadian Journal of Philosophy*, 28:4 (1998): pp. 473–504 (475).

[67] G. A. J. Rogers, "John Locke and the Sceptics," in Gianni Paganini (ed.), *The Return of Scepticism: From Hobbes and Descartes to Bayle* (Dordrecht: Kluwer, 2003), pp. 37–53.

[68] Locke, *Essay*, II.xxiii.1, p. 295.   [69] Ibid., II.xxiii.4, p. 297.

[70] Ibid., IV.xv.2, pp. 654–655, IV.xvi.6, pp. 661–662.

skeptical about the prospects for expanding human knowledge of morality and religion through the operation of natural reason alone. This skepticism played a role in his decision to rely ultimately on scriptural revelation in moral matters.

Reason, Revelation, and Morality

Although Locke decisively turned to biblical theology in his moral investigation in *The Reasonableness of Christianity*, his reliance on scriptural revelation was already obvious in *An Essay concerning Human Understanding*. In *Essay* IV.xviii.3 – a section of the chapter "Of Faith and Reason" – Locke distinguished between "traditional revelation," by which he essentially meant divine revelation as recorded in Scripture, and "original revelation":

I say, *Traditional Revelation*, in distinction to *Original Revelation*. By the one, I mean that first Impression, which is made immediately by God, on the Mind of any Man, to which we cannot set any Bounds; and by the other, those Impressions delivered over to others in Words, and the ordinary ways of conveying our Conceptions one to another.[71]

Locke was confident that the authors of the biblical texts had received "original" revelations from God:

The holy Men of old, who had *Revelations* from God, had something else besides that internal Light of assurance in their own Minds, to testify to them, that it was from God. They were not left to their own Perswasions alone, that those Perswasions were from God; But had outward Signs to convince them of the Author of those Revelations.... *Moses* saw the Bush burn without being consumed, and heard a Voice out of it.[72]

This passage is taken from *Essay* IV.xix, "Of Enthusiasm." Locke composed this chapter upon consulting, in 1695, with his friend William Molyneux about possible additions to the *Essay*, and he inserted it in the fourth edition of the *Essay*, published in 1700.[73] There are, however, previous instances of Locke's belief in the divine origin of the revelations received by Moses and other biblical prophets. For instance, the aforementioned criterion to recognize a divine revelation, along with the example of the burning bush, is present in a 1687 set of comments on *Immediate Inspiration*, which Locke wrote to criticize the Quaker Robert Barclay's justification of "inward and immediate revelation."[74] In this set of comments, Locke stated:

---

[71] Ibid., IV.xviii.3, p. 690.   [72] Ibid., IV.xix.15, p. 705.

[73] Locke to William Molyneux, March 8, 1695, in Locke, *Correspondence*, vol. 5, no. 1857; William Molyneux to Locke, March 26, 1695, in Locke, *Correspondence*, vol. 5, no. 1867; Locke to William Molyneux, April 26, 1695, in Locke, *Correspondence*, vol. 5, no. 1887.

[74] Robert Barclay, *The Possibility and Necessity of the Inward and Immediate Revelation of the Spirit of God* (London, 1686).

For as there were need of signes to convince those they were sent to, that the prophets were messengers sent from god, soe there was need also of some signe some way of distinction where by the messenger him self might be convinced that his message was from god. Thus god spoke to Moses not by a bare influence on his minde, but out of a bush all on fire that consumed not.[75]

Locke wrote both the 1687 manuscript on *Immediate Inspiration* and the later chapter "Of Enthusiasm" to question enthusiasts', particularly Quakers', claims to immediate revelation – a topic he had already addressed several times in his correspondence and private writings between the mid-1650s and the early 1680s.[76] Locke did not deny in principle the possibility of original revelation in post-biblical and modern times, as he clarified in *Immediate Inspiration*: "There may be such an inspiration (which noe body can deny that considers an omnipotent agent & author of us & all our facultys which he can alter & enlarge as seems good to him)."[77] He reaffirmed this opinion in the chapter on enthusiasm in the *Essay*:

I am far from denying, that God can, or doth sometimes enlighten Mens Minds in the apprehending of certain Truths, or excite them to Good Actions by the immediate influence and assistance of the Holy Spirit, without any extraordinary Signs accompanying it.[78]

However, he was suspicious of contemporary claims to immediate revelation because, as he stated in the aforesaid manuscript *Study*, "we are here in the state of mediocrity: finite creatures, furnished with powers and faculties very well fitted to some purposes, but very disproportionate to the vast and unlimited extent of things."[79] In this "state of mediocrity" in which modern humans are, it is extremely difficult, if not impossible, to distinguish between true and false inspiration, especially if one relies exclusively on one's "inner light" or

---

[75] John Locke, "Immediate Inspiration," in Locke, *Writings on Religion*, pp. 37–41 (40). The original of this manuscript is MS Locke c. 27, ff. 73–74.

[76] Peter Anstey, "Locke, the Quakers and Enthusiasm," *Intellectual History Review*, 29:2 (2019): pp. 199–217. The most important references to Quakerism and enthusiasm in Locke's private writings, prior to the composition of *Immediate Inspiration*, are in paragraph 42 of Draft A of *An Essay concerning Human Understanding*, composed in 1671, and in several journal notes taken in 1681–1682: John Locke, *Drafts for the Essay concerning Human Understanding and Other Philosophical Writings*, eds. Peter H. Nidditch and G. A. J. Rogers (Oxford: Clarendon Press, 1990), p. 71; John Locke, *An Early Draft of Locke's Essay: Together with Excerpts from His Journals*, eds. Richard I. Aaron and Jocelyn Gibb (Oxford: Clarendon Press, 1936), pp. 114–125. For later references, see John Locke, "Scriptura Sacra," in Locke, *Writings on Religion*, pp. 42–43 (42). The original of this manuscript, composed in 1692, is MS Locke d. 1, p. 177.

[77] Locke, "Immediate Inspiration," p. 40.   [78] Locke, *Essay*, IV.xix.16, p. 705.

[79] Locke, "Study," p. 105.

"internal perception," as most enthusiasts do.[80] By following this "internal light," enthusiasts persuade themselves to be "under the peculiar guidance of Heaven in their Actions and Opinions," regardless of what the senses and evidence commonly show to humankind.[81] But, as Locke observed in *Immediate Inspiration*, this "internal light" does not prove the divine nature of the revelations claimed by enthusiasts, and it provides no ground to persuade others, "this internal perception being a thing impossible to be made knowne to any but he that has & feels it."[82] Moreover, "such inspirations can be of noe use either for direction or counsel since they cannot be distinguished from illusions."[83] Even putting forward the evidence of miracles to support claims to immediate revelation is problematic, because miracles ought to be verified by rational appraisal and in the context of their occurrence.

Enthusiasts' critical mistake, according to Locke, is to hold experience-based reasoning in low regard. This mistake is grounded in the wrong assumption that God has provided humanity with direct cognitive assistance. This assumption led those whom Locke's friend Molyneux characterized as enthusiasts in philosophy (i.e., Platonists, Cartesians, Malebrancheans, etc.) to maintain the existence of divinely inscribed, innate ideas – a position that Locke refuted in Book I of the *Essay*.[84] Furthermore, this assumption led religious enthusiasts to adopt a "wrong Principle so apt to misguide them both in their Belief and Conduct," as Locke stated in *Essay* IV.xix.8.[85] The meaning of this passage can be properly appreciated if one connects it with Locke's censure of "Propositions that are not in themselves certain and evident, but doubtful and false, taken up for principles" in the chapter following "Of Enthusiasm" – namely, *Essay* IV.xx, "Of wrong Assent, or Errour."[86] The wrong principle on which enthusiasts base their opinions and conduct is indeed their inexplicable "internal perception." But reliance on merely an "inner light" entails circular reasoning, as Locke observes in "Of Enthusiasm": "This Light, they are so dazled with, is nothing, but an *ignis fatuus* that leads them

---

[80] Victor Nuovo, "Enthusiasm," in S.-J. Savonius-Wroth, Paul Schuurman, Jonathan Walmsley (eds.), *The Continuum Companion to Locke* (London – New York: Continuum, 2010), pp. 141–143.

[81] Locke, *Essay*, IV.xix.5, p. 699.   [82] Locke, "Immediate Inspiration," p. 39.

[83] Ibid., p. 37.

[84] William Molyneux to Locke, April 18, 1693, in Locke, *Correspondence*, vol. 4, no. 1622; Nicholas Jolley, "Reason's Dim Candle: Locke's Critique of Enthusiasm," in Peter Anstey (ed.), *The Philosophy of John Locke: New Perspectives* (London: Routledge, 2003), pp. 179–191 (183–187); Nicholas Jolley, "Locke on Faith and Reason," in Lex Newman (ed.), *The Cambridge Companion to Locke's "Essay concerning Human Understanding"* (Cambridge: Cambridge University Press, 2007), pp. 436–455 (446–451).

[85] Locke, *Essay*, IV.xix.8, pp. 699–700.   [86] Ibid., IV.xx.7, p. 711.

continually round in this Circle. *It is a Revelation, because they firmly believe it*, and *they believe it, because it is a Revelation.*"[87]

Locke's criticism of the logical fallacies that underlie enthusiastic belief has led Victor Nuovo to conclude, convincingly, that "Locke imagined enthusiasm, in contrast to authentic divine inspiration, to be a kind of madness, a fixation of the mind upon a religious belief motivated wholly by passion and hence not dependent upon reason."[88] That Locke saw enthusiasm as a sort of madness is confirmed by the connections between *Essay* IV.xix "Of Enthusiasm" and *Essay* II.xxxiii "Of the Association of Ideas" – a chapter that Locke added, with "Of Enthusiasm," to the fourth edition of the *Essay* in the year 1700. Examining Locke's drafts for these additions in MS Locke e. 1, Kathryn Tabb has persuasively argued that these two chapters are part of a unified effort and are linked by Locke's attention to madness.[89] Locke's interest in madness, which developed parallel to his reflections on enthusiasm between the 1670s and his last decade, led him to the conclusion that madness is caused by what he called "association of ideas." By this he meant that madness originates in a "wrong Connexion in our Minds of *Ideas* in themselves, loose and independent one of another" – a "wrong Connexion" that has a strong "influence" and a "great force to set us awry in our Actions, as well Moral as Natural, Passions, Reasonings, and Notions themselves."[90] Enthusiasm provides a good example of "association of ideas," because "in effect it takes away both Reason and Revelation, and substitutes in the room of it, the ungrounded Fancies of a Man's own Brain, and assumes them for a Foundation both of Opinion and Conduct."[91] Enthusiasm, to Locke, is a sort of madness in that it is "founded neither on Reason, nor Divine Revelation, but rising from the Conceits of a warmed or over-weening Brain"; and these conceits, "when got above common Sense, and freed from all restraint of Reason, and check of Reflection," are "heightened to Divine Authority, in concurrence with our own Temper and Inclination."[92] Briefly, irrational drives, not reason, lead

---

[87] Ibid., IV.xix.10, p. 702. On the moral and social dangerousness of enthusiasm according to Locke, see Wolterstorff, *John Locke*, pp. 118–122. See, also, Chapter 6 in the present study.

[88] Nuovo, "Enthusiasm," p. 141.

[89] Kathryn Tabb, "Locke on Enthusiasm and the Association of Ideas," *Oxford Studies in Early Modern Philosophy*, 9 (2019): pp. 75–104. These additions are in MS Locke e. 1, pp. 1–30, 32–56. This manuscript also contains, at pp. 52–260, Locke's draft of *Of the Conduct of the Understanding*, which is largely an inventory of the weaknesses and defects that the mind needs to correct (see Corneanu, *Regimens of the Mind*, p. 145). Locke originally conceived *Of the Conduct of the Understanding* as a new final chapter for the fourth edition of the *Essay* (1700). He wrote it between 1695 and 1701 and partially reorganized it in 1704, shortly before his death, as MS Locke c. 28, ff. 121–130 demonstrates. This work was first published by Peter King in John Locke, *Posthumous Works* (London, 1706), pp. 1–137. Before publishing this writing, King further tried to reorganize it (see MS Locke c. 28, ff. 131–138), but the text he eventually published is fairly close to Locke's draft.

[90] Locke, *Essay*, II.xxxiii.9, p. 397.   [91] Ibid., IV.xix.3, p. 698.   [92] Ibid., IV.xix.7, p. 699.

enthusiasts to claim divine inspiration. To Locke, however, assent to anything, including the status of a revelation as divine, ought to be based on rational assessment, as I elucidate below. Locke was aware of the limits of natural reason, which he compared to a "dim Candle" in the chapter "Of Enthusiasm."[93] Nevertheless, in Book I of the *Essay*, Locke's comparison of natural reason with a candle aims at affirming the aptness of reason to serve purposes that "may be of use to us":

We shall not have much Reason to complain of the narrowness of our Minds, if we will but employ them about what may be of use to us; for of that they are very capable: And it will be an unpardonable, as well as Childish Peevishness, if we undervalue the Advantages of our Knowledge, and neglect to improve it to the ends for which it was given us, because there are some Things that are set out of the reach of it. It will be no Excuse to an idle and untoward Servant, who would not attend his Business by Candle-light, to plead that he had not broad Sun-shine. The Candle, that is set up in us, shines bright enough for all our Purposes.[94]

A few lines below, Locke further clarified his position on this issue with the following words:

Our Business here is not to know all things, but those which concern our Conduct. If we can find out those Measures, whereby a rational Creature put in that State, which Man is in, in this World, may, and ought to govern his Opinions and Actions depending thereon, we need not be troubled, that some other things escape our Knowledge.[95]

These two passages from Book I, which were already present in the first edition of the *Essay* in 1690, shed light on Locke's attitude to enthusiasts, who, in his eyes, behaved as "idle servants" due to their unwillingness to employ their rational capabilities. In *Essay* IV.xix.5, Locke indeed depicted enthusiasts as lazy people who preferred to claim immediate revelation instead of engaging in "strict Reasoning":

Immediate *Revelation* being a much easier way for Men to establish their Opinions, and regulate their Conduct, than the tedious and not always successful Labour of strict Reasoning, it is no wonder, that some have been very apt to pretend to Revelation, and to perswade themselves, that they are under the peculiar guidance of Heaven in their Actions and Opinions, especially in those of them, which they cannot account for by the ordinary Methods of Knowledge, and Principles of Reason.[96]

Moreover, the above-quoted passages from Book I of the *Essay* call attention to the limits and, at the same time, the *powers* of natural reason. In these passages, Locke implies that a much brighter light than human reason can be conceived. However, human beings must be satisfied with the "Candle-light"

---

[93] Ibid., IV.xix.8, p. 700.   [94] Ibid., I.i.5, pp. 45–46.   [95] Ibid., I.i.6, p. 46.
[96] Ibid., IV.xix.5, pp. 698–699.

of natural reason, which "shines bright enough" for purposes relevant to human knowledge and conduct. To Locke, the education of the mind, accompanied by a consistent struggle to overcome its weaknesses and defects, is not only useful and convenient to the individual, but also a duty toward the creator, as Sorana Corneanu has pointed out: "Locke's approach to the limits and corruptions of the mind is shaped by a Christian-philosophical conception of man's task of governing and educating the powers of his mind as a God-assigned duty."[97] One of the tasks of natural reason is the recognition of divine revelations, as I have said above and as Locke explained in another passage already present in the first edition of the *Essay*: "It still belongs to *Reason*, to judge of the Truth of [a proposition's] being a revelation, and of the signification of the Words, wherein it is delivered."[98] Several years later, when writing the chapter "Of Enthusiasm," Locke further clarified this point:

Reason must be our last Judge and Guide in every Thing. I do not mean, that we must consult Reason, and examine whether a Proposition revealed from God can be made out by natural Principles, and if it cannot, that then we may reject it; But consult it we must, and by it examine, whether it be a *Revelation* from God or no: And if *Reason* finds it to be revealed from God, *Reason* then declares for it, as much as for any other Truth, and makes it one of her Dictates.[99]

Briefly, although Locke (unlike Toland and other deists) thought that natural reason is not supposed to comprehend all divine revelations completely and perfectly, he believed that it is still natural reason that decides whether a revelation is truly divine on the basis of relevant evidence and testimony. The famous passage of *Essay* IV.xix.4, in which Locke describes reason and revelation as mutually sustaining and complementary, explains not only that divine revelation comes in where unassisted reason cannot reach, but also that only (divinely given) natural reason can ascertain the divine origin of a revelation:

Reason is natural *Revelation*, whereby the eternal Father of Light, and Fountain of all Knowledge communicates to Mankind that portion of Truth, which he has laid within the reach of their natural Faculties: *Revelation* is natural *Reason* enlarged by a new set of Discoveries communicated by God immediately, which *Reason* vouches the Truth of, by the Testimony and Proofs it gives, that they come from God.[100]

Rational assent is crucial to determining whether a revelation is divine on the basis of available evidence. As Locke wrote in *Essay* IV.xvi.14, "our Assent can be rationally no higher than the Evidence of its being a Revelation."[101]

---

[97] Corneanu, *Regimens of the Mind*, p. 145.   [98] Locke, *Essay*, IV.xviii.8, p. 694.
[99] Ibid., IV.xix.14, p. 704.   [100] Ibid., IV.xix.4, p. 698.
[101] Ibid., IV.xvi.14, p. 667. On the role of reason in matters of religious belief, see Wolterstorff, *John Locke*, pp. 118–133.

Locke's views concerning assent to a revelation represent a continuation of the discourses on "historical faith" and "religious belief" developed by Arminian-influenced English theologians such as William Chillingworth and Isaac Barrow.[102] In *The Religion of Protestants* (1638) – a book that Locke knew well – Chillingworth maintained that "our faith is an assent to this conclusion, that *the Doctrine of Christianity is true*," and he argued that Christ's miracles and "the goodnesse of the precepts of Christianity, and the greatnesse of the promises of it" are at the basis of such an assent.[103] Around three decades later, Isaac Barrow, expressing a position similar to that of Chillingworth, stated that "faith itself is not an arbitrary act, nor an effect of blind necessity . . .. It is a result of judgment and choice, grounded upon reason of some kind, after deliberation and debate concerning the matter."[104] As regards Christ's message, Barrow even wrote that Christ's disciples "were not obliged to accept [his] testimony as true, if it were not also accompanied with other convincing reasons."[105] Locke called attention to Christ's miracles and the excellence of his moral precepts, besides highlighting the fulfillment of Old Testament Messianic prophecies in the New Testament, when attempting to prove the authority of Scripture in his later writings on religion, as we will see in Chapter 2. However, already in the first edition of the *Essay*, published in 1690, he maintained that no genuinely divine revelation is contrary to natural reason:

We can never receive for a Truth any thing, that is directly contrary to our clear and distinct Knowledge . . .. And therefore, *no Proposition can be received for Divine Revelation*, or obtain the Assent due to all such, *if it be contradictory to our clear intuitive Knowledge*. Because this would be to subvert the principles, and Foundations of all Knowledge, Evidence, and Assent whatsoever: And there would be left no difference between Truth and Falsehood, no measures of Credible and Incredible in the World, if doubtful Propositions shall take place before self-evident; and what we certainly know, give way to what we may possibly be mistaken in. In Propositions therefore contrary to the clear Perception of the Agreement or Disagreement of any of our *Ideas*, 'twill be in vain to urge them as Matters of *Faith*. They cannot move our Assent under that, or any other Title whatsoever. For *Faith* can never convince us of any Thing, that contradicts our Knowledge. Because though *Faith* be founded on the Testimony of God (who cannot lye) revealing any Proposition to us: yet we cannot have

---

[102] Ethan H. Shagan, *The Birth of Modern Belief: Faith and Judgment from the Middle Ages to the Enlightenment* (Princeton: Princeton University Press, 2018), pp. 223–227.

[103] William Chillingworth, *The Religion of Protestants a Safe Way to Salvation* (Oxford, 1638), p. 36.

[104] Isaac Barrow, "An Exposition on the Creed," in Isaac Barrow, *Theological Works*, ed. Alexander Napier, 9 vols. (Cambridge: Cambridge University Press, 1859), vol. 7, pp. 3–395 (14).

[105] Ibid., p. 23.

an assurance of the Truth of its being a divine Revelation, greater than our own Knowledge.[106]

Consequently, to Locke "nothing that is contrary to, and inconsistent with the clear and self-evident Dictates of Reason, has a Right to be urged, or assented to, as a Matter of Faith, wherein Reason hath nothing to do."[107] Locke supported his point with a reflection on the relationship between the "bountiful Author of our Being" and natural reason. If we were to accept a "Proposition supposed revealed [that] contradicts our Knowledge or Reason," then we would not be able to "tell how to conceive that to come from God, the bountiful Author of our Being."[108] This would eventually "overturn all the Principles and Foundations of Knowledge he has given us; render all our Faculties useless; wholly destroy the most excellent Part of his Workmanship, our Understandings; and put a Man in a Condition, wherein he will have less Light, less Conduct than the Beast that perisheth."[109] Locke's position on this subject further denotes his view of natural reason and divine revelation as mutually sustaining and complementary and supports his rejection of tradition and human authorities in matters of faith, as Locke himself noted:

In all Things therefore, where we have clear Evidence from our *Ideas*, and those Principles of Knowledge, I have above mentioned, *Reason* is the proper Judge; and *Revelation*, though it may in consenting with it, confirm its Dictates, yet cannot in such Cases, invalidate its Decrees: *Nor can we be obliged, where we have the clear and evident Sentence of Reason, to quit it, for the contrary Opinion, under a Pretence that it is Matter of Faith*; which can have no Authority against the plain and clear Dictates of *Reason*.[110]

To Locke, religious opinions contrary to "the plain and clear Dictates of Reason" either result from incorrect interpretations of Scripture or are inferred through speculations that have nothing to do with Scripture. At any rate, such opinions are not grounded in the biblical text. To a Protestant like Locke, a typical example of an opinion contrary to reason is the doctrine of transubstantiation. Following the example of John Tillotson's *Discourse against Transubstantiation* (1684), Locke rejected the dogma of transubstantiation in that this dogma requires defying the evidence of the senses and is, therefore, incompatible with clear and distinct ideas. According to Locke, this dogma requires Christ's body to be in more than one place at the same time, since the Mass can be celebrated in more than one place at the same time; but this is logically untenable:

---

[106] Locke, *Essay*, IV.xviii.5, p. 692.   [107] Ibid., IV.xviii.10, p. 696.
[108] Ibid., IV.xviii.5, p. 692.   [109] Ibid., IV.xviii.5, pp. 692–693.
[110] Ibid., IV.xviii.6, pp. 693–694.

The *Ideas* of one Body, and one Place, do so clearly agree; and the Mind has so evident a Perception of their Agreement, that we can never assent to a Proposition, that affirms the same Body to be in two distant Places at once, however it should pretend to the authority of a divine *Revelation*.[111]

While rejecting transubstantiation as contrary to reason, Locke argued that natural reason is not always able to achieve certain knowledge, because "most of the Propositions we think, reason, discourse, nay act upon, are such, as we cannot have undoubted Knowledge of their Truth."[112] Therefore, in the numerous instances when we are unable to attain *certainty*, we need to rely on *probability*.[113] This is true, particularly, in religious matters:

There being many Things, wherein we have very imperfect Notions, or none at all; and other Things, of whose past, present, or future Existence, by the natural Use of our Faculties, we can have no Knowledge at all; these, as being beyond the Discovery of our natural Faculties, and above *Reason*, are, when revealed, *the proper Matter of Faith*.[114]

Thus, Locke distinguished propositions *above reason* from propositions *according to reason* and propositions *contrary to reason*:

1. *According to Reason* are such Propositions, whose Truth we can discover, by examining and tracing those *Ideas* we have from *Sensation* and *Reflexion*; and by natural deduction, find to be true, or probable. 2. *Above Reason* are such Propositions, whose Truth or Probability we cannot by Reason derive from those Principles. 3. *Contrary to Reason* are such Propositions, as are inconsistent with, or irreconcilable to our clear and distinct *Ideas*.[115]

As regards a proposition – e.g., a biblical passage – that is neither according nor contrary to reason, we can only conclude that its content is probable. Therefore, as Nicholas Wolterstorff has observed, to Locke "faith is not a mode of knowledge. It consists in believing things on the basis of one's belief that they have been revealed by God rather than on the basis of the premises of some demonstration."[116] In the *Essay*, Locke indeed described faith as assent to merely *probable* matters of fact:

Because the Mind, not being certain of the Truth of that it does not evidently know, but only yielding to the Probability that appears in it, is bound to give up its Assent to such

---

[111] Ibid., IV.xviii.5, p. 692.   [112] Ibid., IV.xv.2, p. 655.   [113] Ibid., IV.xvi.6, pp. 661–662.
[114] Ibid., IV.xviii.7, p. 694.   [115] Ibid., IV.xvii.23, p. 687.
[116] Nicholas Wolterstorff, "Locke's Philosophy of Religion," in Chappell (ed.), *Cambridge Companion*, pp. 172–198 (190). Wolterstorff has also noted: "Assent or belief, says Locke, is *taking* some proposition to be true, whereas knowledge is *seeing* it to be true. To know is to be directly acquainted with some fact, to be immediately aware of it, to perceive it; or, to put the point from the other side, knowledge occurs when some fact is presented directly to the mind .... Knowledge is awareness of some fact; belief or assent, by contrast, is taking something to be a fact" (ibid., pp. 176–177). See, also, Wolterstorff, *John Locke*, 122–124.

a Testimony, which, it is satisfied, comes from one, who cannot err, and will not deceive . . .. For where the Principles of Reason have not evidenced a Proposition to be certainly true or false, there clear *Revelation*, as another Principle of Truth, and Ground of Assent, may determine; and so it may be Matter of *Faith*, and be also above *Reason*. Because *Reason*, in that particular Matter, being able to reach no higher than Probability, *Faith* gave the Determination, where *Reason* came short; and *Revelation* discovered on which side the Truth lay.[117]

According to Locke, a divine revelation, once assented to as such, must take priority over the uncertain conjectures of unassisted reason. This is the case with scriptural revelation. To Locke, scriptural revelation also contains things "whose truth our mind, by its natural faculties and notions, cannot judge" – things that we have to accept as "above reason."[118] These things include the notions "that part of the Angels rebelled against God, and thereby lost their first happy state: And that the dead shall rise, and live again."[119] These revelations, according to Locke, transcend the capacities of natural reason, but do not contradict it. Therefore, "these, and the like, being beyond the Discovery of *Reason*, are purely Matters of *Faith*; with which *Reason* has, directly, nothing to do."[120]

In stressing the limits of natural reason and regarding some revelations as being above reason, Locke followed the example of several seventeenth-century "rational supernaturalists," including, among others, the natural philosopher Robert Boyle, who argued that some religious truths transcend the cognitive powers of natural reason.[121] Locke's acceptance of things above reason distinguished him from deists and freethinkers, who subjected any kind of proposition, including supposedly divine revelations, to the judgment of unprejudiced reason. Hostility to the supernatural had already emerged in the works of Herbert of Cherbury and Charles Blount, but it was the deists and freethinkers of the late seventeenth and eighteenth centuries who made this hostility more explicit, although they held different views of "reason." Under the influence of Spinoza's metaphysics and biblical hermeneutics, Toland and Collins rethought and "radicalized" Locke's way of ideas. They argued that "clear and distinct ideas" were necessary to attaining proper knowledge in all matters and, consequently, they rejected the very concept of "things above

---

[117] Locke, *Essay*, IV.xviii.8–9, pp. 694–695.   [118] Ibid., IV.xviii.9, p. 695.
[119] Ibid., IV.xviii.7, p. 694.   [120] Ibid.
[121] Robert Boyle, *Some Considerations about the Reconcileableness of Reason and Religion* (London, 1675); Robert Boyle, *A Discourse of Things above Reason* (London, 1681); Jan W. Wojcik, "The Theological Context of Boyle's Things above Reason," in Michael Hunter (ed.), *Robert Boyle Reconsidered* (Cambridge: Cambridge University Press, 1994), pp. 139–156; Jan W. Wojcik, *Robert Boyle and the Limits of Reason* (Cambridge: Cambridge University Press, 1997), pp. 100–108; Thomas Holden, "Robert Boyle on Things above Reason," *British Journal for the History of Philosophy*, 15:2 (2007): pp. 283–312. On Boyle's influence on Locke in this regard, see Lupoli, "Boyle's Influence."

reason." Conversely, in the central decades of the eighteenth century, Tindal and other deists employed concepts of reason compatible with a notion of natural religion like that formulated by Herbert of Cherbury more than one century earlier. Although their epistemological and hermeneutical methods differed from Toland's and Collins's methodologies of historical, exegetical, and philosophical inquiry, Tindal, Chubb, Morgan, and Annet, too, denied the supernatural. However, the fact that deists and freethinkers had confidence in the powers of natural reason and rejected the supernatural does not mean that they disregarded the limits of human reason. They simply refused to go beyond the boundaries of experience and to accept, as "truths above reason," things that natural reason could not make sense of. According to Toland and Collins, this approach was in line with the basic tenets of Locke's way of ideas – or, at least, with their interpretation and use of the basic tenets of Locke's way of ideas – while acceptance of the supernatural was incompatible with the fundamental principles of this epistemological method. They were clear on this point. In 1696, Toland wrote in *Christianity Not Mysterious* that "there is nothing in the Gospel Contrary to Reason, Nor Above it," and that "an implicit Assent to any thing above Reason ... contradicts the Ends of Religion, the Nature of Man, and the Goodness and Wisdom of God."[122] Over a decade later, Collins stated: "All propositions, consider'd as objects of assent and dissent, are adequately divided into propositions agreeable or contrary to reason; and there remains no third idea under which to rank them."[123] Briefly, Toland and Collins started from Locke's way of ideas, but they reached conclusions that Locke would have never subscribed to.

Locke's stress on the limited scope of natural reason and the imperfection and weakness of human nature was matched by his skepticism about the human capacity to *actually* demonstrate moral ideas and build a perfect system of morality. This skepticism contributed to leading him to highlight, in his mature writings, the importance of rewards and punishments as incentives to promote moral conduct.[124] Locke emphasized, in particular, *otherworldly* rewards and sanctions as powerful incentives to act morally. Locke's stress on otherworldly incentives for moral action has led some interpreters, such as John Colman and Michael Rabieh, to describe his ethics as essentially a "mercenary" ethics (as Rabieh defines it) and hence, I would say, as a form of what Kant called heteronomous ethics.[125] I disagree with this interpretation

---

[122] Toland, *Christianity,* pp. 77, 139.

[123] Anthony Collins, *An Essay concerning the Use of Reason in Propositions* (London, 1707), pp. 24–25.

[124] Schneewind, "Locke's Moral Philosophy," p. 208.

[125] Colman, *John Locke's Moral Philosophy,* pp. 226–236; Michael S. Rabieh, "The Reasonableness of Locke, or the Questionableness of Christianity," *The Journal of Politics,* 53:4 (1991): pp. 933–957.

of Locke's ethics. It is true that Locke valued the effectiveness of otherworldly incentives to promote moral conduct; but he never abandoned his conviction in the existence of a universal, eternal, intrinsically rational, God-given moral law – namely, the Law of Nature – which all human beings *have to obey*. He deemed it necessary to moral conduct to hold belief in a divine creator and legislator – a belief that can be reached through the operation of natural reason, since knowledge of God's existence is demonstrative. Belief in a divine creator and legislator indeed entails that we humans, as God's rational creatures, owe obedience to the divinely given moral law, which we are bearers of. Thus, Locke regarded obedience to the divine moral law as primarily a *duty* to the divine creator and lawgiver, whose workmanship, servants, and property all human beings are, as he maintained in the *Second Treatise*:

For Men being all the Workmanship of one Omnipotent, and infinitely wise Maker; All the Servants of one Sovereign Master, sent into the World by his order, and about his business; they are his Property, whose Workmanship they are, made to last during his, not one another's Pleasure . . .. Every one, as he is *bound to preserve himself,* and not to quit his Station wilfully, so by the like reason, when his own Preservation comes not in competition, ought he, as much as he can, *to preserve the rest of Mankind.*[126]

Locke considered reward and punishment in the afterlife as foreseeable outcomes of one's conduct and, thus, as *mere incentives* to the practice of morality – in other words, as incentives useful to *promote* moral action despite the imperfection and weakness of human nature – but *not* as the main *motivation* to act morally. He also envisioned worldly incentives to moral action, since in the *Essay*, the *Second Treatise*, the *Reasonableness*, and other writings he frequently referred to convenience or utility as resulting from moral conduct. However, I do not consider Locke a utilitarian. My view is that Locke's ethics is a sort of theistic and rationalist deontological ethics. Being both theistic and rationalist, Locke's ethics blurs the distinction between "voluntarism" and "intellectualism" or "rationalism," since in it both the inherently rational moral law and natural reason are God-given. In this regard, I concur with Alex Tuckness that, "since God created us with reason in order to follow God's will, human reason and divine reason are sufficiently similar that natural law will not seem arbitrary to us."[127] This divinely given, intrinsically rational moral law is *universally binding*, even regardless of incentives to

---

[126] John Locke, *Two Treatises of Government*, rev. ed., ed. Peter Laslett (Cambridge: Cambridge University Press, 1988), p. 271. See, also, Locke, *Essay*, IV.iii.18, p. 549, IV.xviii.5, pp. 692–693.

[127] Alex Tuckness, "Locke's Political Philosophy," *Stanford Encyclopedia of Philosophy* (2016), https://plato.stanford.edu/entries/locke-political/. See, also, Alex Tuckness, "The Coherence of a Mind: John Locke and the Law of Nature," *Journal of the History of Philosophy*, 37:1 (1999): pp. 73–90.

observe it. It is true that Locke's ethics presents utilitarian elements, but I consider these elements as a sort of "superstructure" in Locke's ethics. I follow John Simmons in arguing that the "rule utilitarian" aspects of Locke's ethics concern only the advancement of the end of morality – not its foundations.[128] Locke himself, in the *Essays on the Law of Nature*, wrote that "utility is not the basis of the law or the ground of obligation, but the consequence of obedience to it."[129] Furthermore, in *The Reasonableness of Christianity*, he praised the "Conveniences of common life," but he maintained that human beings' "Obligation was throughly known and allowed, and they received as Precepts of a Law; Of the highest Law, the Law of Nature" thanks to "a clear knowledge and acknowledgment of the Law-maker."[130] According to Locke, human beings' ability to demonstrate the existence of a divine creator and lawmaker through the operation of natural reason indeed enables them to acknowledge the *existence* of a divinely given, eternally valid, universally binding moral law – even though natural reason alone has always failed to grasp the *content* of this law in its entirety. This law, nevertheless, is revealed clearly in Scripture and is consistent with, and hence acceptable to, natural reason.

Locke, however, did not believe that natural reason alone could attain certain knowledge of an afterlife with reward and punishment. According to Locke, only scriptural revelation assures us of a life after this life, and this revealed truth transcends the capacities of natural reason. *Essay* IV.xviii.7 indeed mentions the fact "that the dead shall rise, and live again," which is unambiguously revealed in Scripture, as an emblematic example of truth above reason.[131] Concerning reward and punishment in the afterlife, *Essay* II.xxi.60, quoting from Rom. 2:6–9, hints at belief in otherworldly incentives as effective to resist evil urges and act morally:

---

[128] A. John Simmons, *The Lockean Theory of Rights* (Princeton: Princeton University Press, 1992), pp. 57–58. Besides Simmons, others have argued that, to Locke, convenience or utility is not the basis for accepting natural law principles: see Henry Sidgwick, *Outlines of the History of Ethics for English Readers* (London: Macmillan, 1886), pp. 174–175; Martin Seliger, "Locke's Natural Law and the Foundation of Politics," *Journal of the History of Ideas*, 24:3 (1963): pp. 337–354; Morton White, *The Philosophy of the American Revolution* (Oxford: Oxford University Press, 1978), pp. 43–44. Interpretations of Locke's ethics as neither "mercenary" nor fundamentally utilitarian, but rationalist, theistic, and deontological, obviously clash with Leo Strauss's notion of the Lockean Law of Nature as the principle of utility and as essentially based on consent – a notion in line with Strauss's (untenable) view of Locke as fundamentally an atheist and a Hobbesian political thinker. See Leo Strauss, *Natural Rights and History* (Chicago: The University of Chicago Press, 1953), pp. 209–251; Leo Strauss, "Locke's Doctrine of Natural Law," *American Political Science Review*, 52:2 (1958): pp. 490–501.

[129] Locke, *Essays on the Law of Nature*, p. 215.   [130] Locke, *Reasonableness*, p. 154.

[131] Locke, *Essay*, IV.xviii.7, p. 694.

Change but a Man's view of these things [i.e., earthly desires and enjoyments]; let him see, that Virtue and Religion are necessary to his Happiness; let him look into the future State of Bliss or Misery, and see there God the righteous Judge, ready to *render to every Man according to his Deeds; To them who by patient continuance in well-doing, seek for Glory, and Honour, and Immortality, Eternal Life; but unto every Soul that doth Evil, Indignation and Wrath, Tribulation and Anguish.* To him, I say, who hath a prospect of the different State of perfect Happiness or Misery, that attends all Men after this Life, depending on their Behaviour here, the measures of Good and Evil, that govern his choice, are mightily changed. For since nothing of Pleasure and Pain in this Life, can bear any proportion to the endless Happiness, or exquisite Misery of an immortal Soul hereafter, Actions in his Power will have their preference, not according to the transient Pleasure, or Pain that accompanies, or follows them here; but as they serve to secure that perfect durable Happiness hereafter.[132]

Furthermore, *Essay* II.xxviii.8 stresses God's power to reward and punish "in another Life":

The *Divine* Law, whereby I mean, that Law which God has set to the actions of Men, whether promulgated to them by the light of Nature, or the voice of Revelation. That God has given a Rule whereby Men should govern themselves, I think there is no body so brutish as to deny. He has a Right to do it, we are his Creatures: He has Goodness and Wisdom to direct our Actions to that which is best: and he has Power to enforce it by Rewards and Punishments, of infinite weight and duration, in another Life: for no body can take us out of his hands. This is the only true touchstone of *moral Rectitude*; and by comparing them to this Law, it is, that Men judge of the most considerable *Moral Good* or *Evil* of their Actions; that is, whether as *Duties, or Sins*, they are like to procure them happiness, or misery, from the hands of the Almighty.[133]

However, it was when elucidating Scripture in the *Reasonableness* that Locke resolutely emphasized the promise, made by Christ, of otherworldly rewards and sanctions as incentivizing moral conduct. In his major theological treatise, Locke abstained from attempting to ground morality on scientific or theoretical foundations. He had recourse, instead, to a Scripture-based theological ethics in order to promote the practice of morality and the development of moral character. In the *Reasonableness*, Locke openly acknowledged the failure of unassisted reason to comprehend the content of the Law of Nature in its entirety and, thus, to construct a sound system of ethics, given the actual

---

[132] Ibid., II.xxi.60, pp. 273–274. Locke included a heavily revised, extended version of *Essay* II. xxi, "Of Power," in the second edition of 1694. As regards the passage cited here, the part between "God the righteous Judge" and the end of this quote was already in the first edition of 1690, although in paragraph 38 of the same chapter. The 1690 edition reads "God the righteous Judge will render . . ." because these words are preceded by a premise different from that in the 1694 edition – a premise expressing, nevertheless, the same concept, namely, the prospect of otherworldly reward and punishment. See John Locke, *An Essay concerning Human Under-standing* (London, 1690), II.xxi.38, pp. 126–127.

[133] Locke, *Essay*, II.xxviii.8, p. 352. See Nuovo, *John Locke*, pp. 182–213.

difficulty of demonstrating morality. Locke's increasing attention to biblical theology in the 1690s was indeed attributable to his growing conviction that a *scientia moralis*, although possible in theory, was actually far from being achieved.[134] The outcomes of Locke's moral investigation in the *Essay* eventually led him to turn, in continuing his moral inquiry in the *Reasonableness*, to the New Testament. According to Locke, Christ's message discloses the Law of Nature plainly and completely and complements it with other divine, revealed truths about otherworldly rewards and sanctions and God's mercy of the repentant faithful. Thus, Christian revelation facilitates moral conduct and makes salvation possible despite the weakness of human nature. In conclusion, there is continuity between *An Essay concerning Human Understanding* and *The Reasonableness of Christianity*, as Victor Nuovo has accurately noted:

Locke concluded the *Essay* by declaring that in the light of the human situation in the world and the capacities and limitations of human knowledge, morality is the proper business of mankind and that to be efficacious it must be joined to religion. The *Reasonableness* was intended to accomplish this. This turning toward religion, however, does not require the abandonment of natural reason, rather its enlargement through revelation, not by endowing it with transcendent capacities, but by showing the reasonableness of extending belief to matters beyond the capacity of reason and experience to discover.[135]

Locke's position on the matter also emerges from his correspondence with Molyneux. In a letter dated August 27, 1692, Molyneux asked Locke to "think of Obleidging the World, with a *Treatise of Morals*, drawn up according to the Hints you frequently give in your Essay, of their being Demonstrable according to the Mathematical Method."[136] Locke did not accede to this request, which Molyneux reiterated after the publication of the *Reasonableness*.[137] In a letter written in April 1696, Locke eventually wrote to Molyneux that "the Gospel contains so perfect a body of ethics, that reason may be excused from that inquiry, since she may find man's duty clearer and easier in revelation, than in herself."[138] To Locke, natural reason and Scripture are

---

[134] Several scholars agree on this point. See, for instance, Schneewind, "Locke's Moral Philosophy"; Wolterstorff, "Locke's Philosophy of Religion," p. 185; Raffaele Russo, *Ragione e ascolto. L'ermeneutica di John Locke* (Naples: Guida, 2001), pp. 168–174; Nuovo, *John Locke*, pp. 215–218, 248–249; Patrick J. Connolly, "Locke's Theory of Demonstration and Demonstrative Morality," *Philosophy and Phenomenological Research*, 98:2 (2019): pp. 435–451.

[135] Nuovo, *John Locke*, p. 216.

[136] William Molyneux to Locke, August 27, 1692, in Locke, *Correspondence*, vol. 4, no. 1530.

[137] Locke to William Molyneux, September 20, 1692, in Locke, *Correspondence*, vol. 4, no. 1538; William Molyneux to Locke, March 28, 1696, in Locke, *Correspondence*, vol. 5, no. 2050.

[138] Locke to William Molyneux, April 5, 1696, in Locke, *Correspondence*, vol. 5, no. 2059.

complementary and mutually sustaining by their very nature, because they are both God-given. Though, as regards religious and moral matters, Scripture reveals much more than natural reason alone has ever managed to discover. Therefore, Locke, while still believing in the intrinsic rationality and in the (at least theoretical) demonstrability of morality, relied on Scripture as an authoritative, infallible, and sufficient source in matters of ethics and religion.

While being in continuity with the philosophical and moral inquiry developed in *An Essay concerning Human Understanding*, Locke's major writing on religion, *The Reasonableness of Christianity*, is a book of biblical theology revolving around the question of justification. In some of his previous works, including the *Essay*, Locke attempted to provide a scientific or theoretical basis for morality. In the *Reasonableness*, which represents the culmination of Locke's moral investigation, he concentrated, instead, on promoting the practice of morality and the development of moral character on the basis of a coherent, convincing Scripture-based theological ethics. This attempt at a theological ethics is an essential part of Locke's endeavor as a biblical theologian who aimed to reconcile historical-critical learning with faith. To Locke as a theologian, it was not God's nature that counted above all. His focus was rather on "the supposed originating events of Christianity, which in turn are set in a narrative of sacred history, looking toward the fulfillment of the divine purpose in the establishment of the kingdom of God."[1] Locke maintained that his account of the Christian religion in the *Reasonableness* was based on Scripture alone. However, his public as well as private writings on religion, including the *Reasonableness* itself, denote many similarities with the Socinian and Arminian theological traditions, which he knew well. When justifying his reliance on the biblical text, he adopted Socinus's proof of scriptural authority, popularized by the Arminian scholar Hugo Grotius. This proof highlighted the excellence of Christ's moral precepts, called attention to the fulfillment of Old Testament Messianic prophecies in the New Testament, and described Christ's miracles as confirming his Messianic mission. This proof enabled Locke to develop and employ a historical method of biblical interpretation, which, stressing the internal consistency of the Bible, considered the biblical texts in relation to both their respective historical contexts and the biblical discourse as a whole. Attaching special importance to the four canonical Gospels and the Acts of the Apostles, Locke offered an elucidation of the

---

[1] Victor Nuovo, *John Locke: The Philosopher As Christian Virtuoso* (Oxford: Oxford University Press, 2017), p. 250.

Christian religion revolving around what he took to be the fundamentals of Christianity – that is, faith in Jesus the Messiah, repentance for sin, and obedience to the divine moral law. Locke's account of Christianity placed him in the Protestant irenic tradition of the way of fundamentals, to which Socinians and Arminians also belonged, although he formulated an original doctrine of the fundamentals. In fact, he regarded Scripture alone as the ultimate source of religious truth and saw scriptural revelation as complementing natural reason. Therefore, even when considering other theologians' views, he was always careful to make sure that his conclusions were in line with, and actually grounded in, Scripture. However, his involvement with such heterodox currents as Socinianism and Arminianism, which definitely had an impact on his religious thought, deserves serious consideration.

Socinianism and Arminianism

Socinianism, named after the sixteenth-century Italian theologian Faustus Socinus, was an anti-Trinitarian and anti-Calvinist current that developed in the late sixteenth and seventeenth centuries.[2] From the late 1570s to his death in 1604, Socinus resided in Poland, where he lived among the mostly Polish and German members of the Minor Reformed Church, also called "Polish Brethren." These anti-Trinitarians had settled in the village of Rakow, where they established a printing press in the year 1600 and an academy in 1602. During Socinus's later years, he and his immediate disciples formulated the core tenets of this theological tradition in the *Racovian Catechism* (1605), completed and published shortly after Socinus's death.[3] Second-generation Socinians, such as Johann Crell, Jonas Schlichting, Johann Ludwig von Wolzogen, and Samuel Przypkowski, significantly contributed to the development of Socinian thought. Their works, along with Socinus's writings, were collected in the nine-volume *Bibliotheca Fratrum Polonorum* (1665–1692)

---

[2] On Socinian thought and history, see Earl M. Wilbur, *A History of Unitarianism*, 2 vols. (Cambridge, MA: Harvard University Press, 1945–1952); George H. Williams (ed.), *The Polish Brethren: Documentation of the History and Thought of Unitarianism in the Polish-Lithuanian Commonwealth and in the Diaspora 1601–1685*, 2 vols. (Missoula: Scholars Press, 1980).

[3] The *Racovian Catechism* is a summa of Socinian thought originally published in Polish in 1605. Its first Latin translation appeared in Rakow in 1609. Between the seventeenth and the nineteenth century, this book received several editions in different languages. Revised Latin editions appeared in the Netherlands in 1665 (dated "Irenopoli, post 1659"), 1680, and 1684. The 1684 edition was a reissue of the "post 1659" edition. The 1680 Latin *Catechism* presents further revisions and is considered the "final edition" of this work prepared by Socinians, mainly by Socinus's grandson Andrzej Wiszowaty (who died two years before its publication) and great-grandson Benedykt Wiszowaty, who drew on Johann Crell, Jonas Schlichting, Martin Ruar, and other Socinian authors in revising the text. The 1680 edition was later translated into English: *The Racovian Catechism*, trans. and ed. Thomas Rees (London, 1818).

and their theological views were reflected in the final Latin edition of the *Racovian Catechism*, which appeared in Amsterdam in 1680.[4]

According to Socinus and his disciples, the Trinitarian dogma was unscriptural, in that this dogma could not be inferred from clear and intelligible passages in Scripture, but resulted from the Platonic corruption of ancient Christianity. They interpreted in non-Trinitarian terms the biblical passages commonly alleged to support the Trinitarian dogma. These passages include, among others, John 1:1 ("In the beginning was the Word, and the Word was with God, and the Word was God"). The Socinians interpreted the term "beginning" in this verse as simply the beginning of Christ's ministry. Concerning Rom. 9:5 ("Christ came, who is over all, God blessed for ever") and other biblical passages in which Christ is called "God," they claimed that this appellative is to be understood as a synonym for "Lord," and the term "Lord" denotes, simply, Christ's Messiahship, not his divinity. Finally, they denied the authenticity of the *Comma Johanneum* ("Johannine Comma"), namely 1 John 5:7–8 ("For there are three that bear record in heaven, the Father, the Word, and the Holy Ghost: and these three are one. And there are three that bear witness in earth, the Spirit, and the water, and the blood: and these three agree in one"). These two verses, which are absent in the oldest Greek manuscripts of the Bible and the oldest Vulgate manuscripts (i.e., the sixth-century Codex Fuldensis and the early eighth-century Codex Amiatinus), first appeared in some Latin manuscripts of the Scriptures between the fifth and tenth centuries. Following Erasmus's exclusion of the Johannine Comma from the first two editions of his Greek New Testament in 1516 and 1519, a heated dispute erupted. Erasmus declared that the Comma did not appear in any ancient Greek manuscript of the Bible and that, consequently, he would include it in his New Testament only if at least one Greek manuscript containing it was found. When such a manuscript was shown to him, he added the Johannine Comma to the 1522 edition of his work, but he accompanied it with a long note setting out his suspicion that this manuscript had been concocted exactly to refute his position on the Comma. In the early modern period, other scholars, such as Hugo Grotius, Isaac Newton, William Whiston, Samuel Clarke, and Edward Gibbon, challenged the authenticity of this biblical passage, which also attracted Locke's attention, as we will see in Chapter 5.[5] While these Protestant scholars

---

[4] *Bibliotheca Fratrum Polonorum quos Unitarios vocant*, 9 vols. (Irenopoli – Eleutheropoli [Amsterdam], "post annum Domini 1656" [1665–1692]); *Racovian Catechism*.

[5] On the debate on the Johannine Comma in the early modern period, see Stephen D. Snobelen, "'To us there is but one God, the Father': Anti-Trinitarian Textual Criticism in Seventeenth- and Early Eighteenth-Century England," in Ariel Hessayon, Nicholas Keene (eds.), *Scripture and Scholarship in Early Modern England* (Aldershot: Ashgate, 2006), pp. 116–136; Rob Iliffe, "Friendly Criticism: Richard Simon, John Locke, Isaac Newton and the *Johannine Comma*," in Hessayon, Keene (eds.), *Scripture and Scholarship*, pp. 137–157; Grantley McDonald, *Biblical*

rejected the Johannine Comma as inauthentic, the French Catholic priest Richard Simon's studies indirectly questioned its authority, because Simon had recourse to the Catholic rule of faith – ecclesiastical tradition – to uphold the "authenticity" of this passage and defend the Trinitarian doctrine, as Rob Iliffe has explained:

> For Simon, any dispute about the authenticity of the passage was pointless, since the passage could not *by itself* establish a doctrine that was so strongly supported both by tradition and by other passages . . . . Whatever the current manuscript evidence, the present Greek and Latin churches agreed that only "the bare Authority of the Church" obliged Christians to accept the passage as authentic.[6]

The Socinians judged the Trinitarian dogma not only unscriptural, but also illogical, in that it maintained the consubstantiality of the three divine persons. They concurred with the sixth-century philosopher Boethius's definition of person as an "individual substance of a rational nature" and, thus, they argued that three persons could not share one substance.[7] Therefore, they saw Jesus as simply the Messiah – namely, as a man (although not an ordinary man) charged by God the Father with a message of salvation hitherto unknown to humankind. They thought that natural reason could comprehend the Law of Nature, but they considered the Law of Nature insufficient to salvation because it disposed humankind to merely the preservation of earthly goods. Consequently, they judged saving faith to be unattainable by natural reason alone. To the Socinians, saving faith resulted from the free choice to accept the assistance of God's grace, which could be known of thanks to biblical revelation. They argued that Scripture contains all information necessary to salvation, particularly Christ's precepts, which offer a better prospect than worldly benefits – the prospect of eternal salvation. This position, stressing the superiority of God's Revealed Word over the Law of Nature and affirming the primacy of eternal salvation over worldly interests, was at the root of Socinus's and his followers' radical pacifism and advocacy of non-resistance.[8] Moreover, the Socinians endorsed wide religious toleration because they regarded the acceptance of God's assisting grace, and hence the pursuit of salvation, as a matter of free choice.[9] Accordingly, they rejected the Calvinist concept of predestination, which they considered unscriptural and unreasonable. They held, instead, a moralist soteriology that emphasized free will,

---

Criticism in Early Modern Europe: Erasmus, the Johannine Comma and Trinitarian Debate (Cambridge: Cambridge University Press, 2016); Rob Iliffe, *Priest of Nature: The Religious Worlds of Isaac Newton* (Oxford: Oxford University Press, 2017), pp. 354–389.

[6] Ibid., p. 379. On Simon's biblical criticism, I say more in the next section of this chapter.

[7] William S. Babcock, "A Changing of the Christian God," *Interpretation*, 45:2 (1991): pp. 133–146.

[8] See Chapter 3.   [9] See Chapter 6.

stressed individual responsibility and the importance of both faith and good works for salvation, denied original sin, and rejected satisfaction and, generally, the atonement. They argued that Adam's sin had not changed human reason and morality. Therefore, humanity did not need to be reconciled to God through the sacrifice of Christ. Following Adam's sin, humanity became mortal, but this was not a punishment. To the Socinians, Adam's immortality was not natural: he had acquired it as simply part of his condition in Paradise, and he consequently lost it when he had to leave Paradise. Thus, they saw mortality as part of humanity's natural condition outside of Paradise. They regarded not only the human body, but also the soul as not naturally immortal, since they thought that the soul dies with the body and will be resurrected by divine miracle on Judgment Day.[10]

In late sixteenth- and seventeenth-century Europe, the Socinians were not alone in opposing Calvinism. The disciples of the Dutch scholar Jacobus Arminius, professor of theology at Leiden from 1603 to his death in 1609, shared the Socinians' hostility to predestination.[11] Like Socinianism, Arminianism experienced dramatic developments throughout the seventeenth century, thanks to the famous jurist Hugo Grotius and theologians like Simon Episcopius, Etienne de Courcelles, and Philipp van Limborch. Arminian soteriology was outlined in the *Five Articles of Remonstrance* (1610).[12] Following the publication of this document, the Dutch Arminians who stuck to these articles were also known as Remonstrants. The *Five Articles of Remonstrance* maintained that only the Holy Spirit, which one could know through the Sacred Scriptures, could enable one to respond to God's Will and that God's grace informed the beginning, continuance, and accomplishment of any good. Most Arminians believed that God foreknew those who would accept His grace. However, they stressed the possibility for human beings to receive or reject the Holy Spirit's aid and, hence, to embrace or resist God's grace, which they viewed as *assisting* grace. Arminian authors upheld a moralist soteriology, in that they argued that salvation was conditioned by both graciously enabled faith and moral works, and they saw the atonement as qualitatively adequate for all human beings, although they thought that only the Christian faithful could enjoy the forgiveness of sins on Judgment Day.

Concerning the nature of the Godhead, most Arminian theologians openly affirmed belief in the Trinity. Nonetheless, the works of Arminius, Episcopius, Courcelles, and other Arminians denote a heterodox, subordinationist notion

---

[10] See Chapter 4.

[11] On the Arminian theological tradition, see Carl Bangs, *Arminius: A Study in the Dutch Reformation* (Nashville: Abingdon Press, 1971); Roger E. Olson, *Arminian Theology: Myths and Realities* (Downers Grove: Intervarsity Press, 2000).

[12] For an English translation, see Philip Schaff, *The Creeds of Christendom, with a History and Critical Notes*, 3 vols. (New York: Harper, 1877), vol. 1, pp. 516–519.

of the Trinity. They maintained this view in opposition to Calvin's *autothean-ism* – namely, the theory that the Son is God "of himself" ("*autotheos*"), which Calvin had formulated, in the mid-sixteenth century, to refute the anti-Trinitarianism of Giovanni Valentino Gentile and Michael Servetus.[13] *Contra* Calvin, Arminius argued that only the Father has aseity (i.e., the property by which a being exists in, of, and from itself), while the Son and the Holy Spirit do not have this property, because the Son was begotten by the Father, and the Holy Spirit was "spired" by the Father and the Son.[14] Therefore, Arminius and his disciples depicted the Son and the Holy Spirit as subordinate to the Father. Nevertheless, the Arminians did not reduce the Son to a creature distinct from the Father and, hence, did not maintain an Arian view of the Godhead. Arianism is indeed different from Trinitarian subordinationism. Several ancient Christian currents were labeled "Arian" after the third- and fourth-century Alexandrian presbyter Arius, later known as a prominent heresiarch. Although holding different positions on the Son's nature and relation to God the Father, those ancient Christian currents known as Arian considered the Son as a creature and, thus, as neither consubstantial, nor coequal, nor coeternal with the Father. Arian theologians of different stripes were among the many early Christian thinkers who, while disagreeing with each other about various theological issues, saw themselves as keepers of the apostolic doctrine and attempted to unite traditional biblical language with philosophical, especially Neoplatonic, ideas and methods. However, Arian views of the Godhead were declared heretical at the First Council of Nicaea in the year 325, and Arianism was later regarded as one of the major heresies in the early centuries of Christianity. Arian ideas experienced a revival between the sixteenth and eighteenth centuries, especially in England, where, among others, Isaac Newton and his associates William Whiston and Samuel Clarke held essen-tially Arian (although different in several respects and, also, Socinian-influ-enced) views of Christ and the Godhead.[15] The Remonstrants were far from

[13] John Calvin, *Institutio Christianae Religionis* (Geneva, 1559), Book I, Chapter xiii; John Calvin, *Expositio impietatis Valentini Gentilis* (Geneva, 1561); Stephen Hampton, *Anti-Armi-nians: The Anglican Reformed Tradition from Charles II to George I* (Oxford: Oxford Univer-sity Press, 2008), pp. 166–175; Brannon Ellis, *Calvin, Classical Trinitarianism, and the Aseity of the Son* (Oxford: Oxford University Press, 2012), pp. 20–63, 109–127.

[14] Jacobus Arminius, "On the Person of Our Lord Jesus Christ," in Jacobus Arminius, *Works*, trans. and ed. James Nichols and W. R. Bagnall, 3 vols. (Auburn – Buffalo: Derby, Miller, Orton and Mulligan, 1853), vol. 2, pp. 83–84; Jacobus Arminius, *Arminius and His Declaration of Sentiments*, trans. and ed. W. Stephen Gunter (Waco: Baylor University Press, 2012), pp. 144–148; Simon Episcopius, "Institutiones Theologicae," in Simon Episcopius, *Opera theologica*, 2 vols. (Amsterdam, 1650), vol. 1, part 1, pp. 1–425 (332–344); Etienne de Courcelles, "De vocibus Trinitatis," in Etienne de Courcelles, *Opera Theologica* (Amsterdam, 1675), pp. 811–883 (879–883).

[15] On Arianism and its revival in the early modern period, see Maurice Wiles, *Archetypal Heresy: Arianism through the Centuries* (Oxford: Oxford University Press, 2001).

endorsing Arianism, since they upheld a Trinitarian albeit subordinationist (and hence heterodox to most Protestants) theology. Nevertheless, they considered belief in the Trinity as inessential to salvation, and they deplored the divisions and enmity provoked, among Christians, by disputes on the Trinity. They called for toleration and unity among Christians, claiming that the essence of the Christian religion consisted of a few, simple, fundamental principles. To the Arminians, faith in Christ's salvific message and observance of his precepts were crucial to salvation, while non-fundamental beliefs and doctrines, being unnecessary to salvation, ought not to harm peace among Christians. Due to their moralist soteriology, the Remonstrants suffered severe persecution after the Synod of Dort (1618–1619), which condemned their theories and drove many of them into exile until, in the year 1630, they were formally allowed to reside again in all the United Provinces, where they established a theological seminary in Amsterdam in 1634. The Dutch Remonstrants' irenicism led them to welcome and assist a number of Socinian exiles, and even to admit them to worship together, after the suppression of the Socinian academy and press in Rakow in 1638 and the expulsion of anti-Trinitarians from Poland in 1658, under pressure by Catholic clergymen and politicians.

Both before and after the Synod of Dort, Arminianism spread outside the Netherlands and found fertile ground in England, where its moralist soteriology strongly influenced several anti-Calvinist theologians, including the members of the Great Tew Circle and other supporters of Archbishop William Laud in the 1630s and 1640s. During the Civil War and Interregnum, several Royalist clergymen, such as Jeremy Taylor, Henry Hammond, and Gilbert Sheldon, although ejected from their livings, kept Arminianism alive in England. After the Restoration of the Stuart monarchy in 1660, Arminian views had a significant impact on the "latitude men," including such prominent divines as Edward Stillingfleet, Gilbert Burnet, and John Tillotson. Besides upholding a moralist soteriology, several latitudinarians adopted Arminian irenicism in their efforts to relax the terms of conformity in such a manner as to "comprehend" the least radical Dissenters within the Church of England. Nevertheless, these efforts proved fruitless, because latitudinarianism met with hostility not only among Nonconformists who opposed Arminian soteriology and resisted all attempts at "comprehension," but also among Calvinistic, "anti-Arminian" divines of the Church of England, due to the persistence of the Reformed tradition among a number of clergymen after the Restoration.[16]

Besides Arminian doctrines, Socinian views, too, reached England in the first half of the seventeenth century, particularly during the Civil War and

---

[16] Hampton, *Anti-Arminians*, pp. 1–38.

Interregnum.[17] In that period, the adventurer Paul Best wrote the first Socinian book in English, *Mysteries Discovered* (1647), after adopting Socinian ideas during his travels in Continental Europe in the 1620s and 1630s, while the schoolmaster and writer John Biddle developed anti-Trinitarian theories based on his own reading of the Bible, which he then found consistent with Socinian theology.[18] Even before the publication of Best's book, the Continental Socinians' views on salvation, toleration, and non-resistance played a role in the making of the anti-predestinarian, moralist, irenic ideas of English Arminians like William Chillingworth, Lord Falkland, John Hales, and other members of the Great Tew Circle.[19] In the same period, the Trinitarian dogma met with new challenges coming from several radical groups, which did away with theological learning in favor of their personal union with God. Although direct attacks on the Trinity from radical groups were rather infrequent, their blurring of the Creator-creature distinction furthered the appearance of implicitly non-Trinitarian forms of Christianity.[20] The spread of expressly anti-Trinitarian ideas in mid-seventeenth-century England provoked the reaction of various Puritan divines – including, among others, Francis Cheynell and John Owen – and led to the persecution and imprisonment of Best and Biddle.[21] After the Restoration, the English Socinians – mostly disciples of Biddle, who died in 1662 – continued their activities underground, until Socinian ideas reemerged on the theological scene during a heated Trinitarian controversy in the late seventeenth century, leading, in the long run, to the institutionalization of Unitarianism in England in the 1770s.

Although Locke did not know the *Five Articles of Remonstrance*, as he confessed to Limborch in a letter of 1701,[22] he had good knowledge of the

---

[17] Wilbur, *History of Unitarianism*, vol. 2, pp. 185–343; H. John McLachlan, *Socinianism in Seventeenth-Century England* (Oxford: Oxford University Press, 1951); Philip Dixon, *Nice and Hot Disputes: The Doctrine of the Trinity in the Seventeenth Century* (London: T&T Clark, 2003); Sarah Mortimer, *Reason and Religion in the English Revolution: The Challenge of Socinianism* (Cambridge: Cambridge University Press, 2010); Paul C. H. Lim, *Mystery Unveiled: The Crisis of the Trinity in Early Modern England* (Oxford: Oxford University Press, 2012); Christopher J. Walker, *Reason and Religion in Late Seventeenth-Century England: The Politics and Theology of Radical Dissent* (London: I. B. Tauris, 2013).

[18] Paul Best, *Mysteries Discovered* (London, 1647); John Biddle, *Twelve Arguments Drawn out of the Scripture* (London, 1647); John Biddle, *A Confession of Faith Touching the Holy Trinity* (London, 1648); John Biddle, *The Apostolical and True Opinion concerning the Holy Trinity Revived and Reasserted* (London, 1653); John Biddle, *A Twofold Catechism* (London, 1654). As I note in Chapter 5, Locke knew Biddle's writings, some of which he referred to in his manuscript notes on the Trinitarian doctrine.

[19] Mortimer, *Reason and Religion*, pp. 63–118.   [20] Lim, *Mystery Unveiled*, pp. 69–123.

[21] Mortimer, *Reason and Religion*, pp. 147–232; Lim, *Mystery Unveiled*, pp. 172–216.

[22] Locke to Philipp van Limborch, June 1, 1701, in John Locke, *The Correspondence of John Locke*, ed. E. S. de Beer, 8 vols. (Oxford: Oxford University Press, 1979–1989), vol. 7, no. 2935. In this letter, Locke also asked Limborch where he could find and read the *Five Articles of Remonstrance*. Limborch replied in astonishment: "I believed that our five

Arminians' views on salvation and toleration, he owned a number of Arminian works, and he was a good friend of several Arminian scholars. One of Locke's most cherished friends was the leading Remonstrant theologian of his generation – the aforementioned Limborch, who helped him during his exile in the Dutch Republic and remained one of his correspondents upon his return to England. In the Netherlands, Locke also befriended a famous intellectual and theologian who upheld Arminian ideas, Jean Le Clerc.[23] Moreover, he was on friendly terms with several Church of England divines with Arminian leanings, such as John Tillotson, Archbishop of Canterbury from 1691 to his death in 1694, and he had good knowledge of the works of English theologians strongly influenced by Arminianism – above all, Chillingworth's *The Religion of Protestants*. Locke was, also, well acquainted with anti-Trinitarian literature, which he started to read extensively at least in the late 1670s. He had direct knowledge of the Continental Socinians' theories, for he owned most of their major works, including at least three different editions of the *Racovian Catechism*, eight books by Socinus, the nine-volume *Bibliotheca Fratrum Polonorum*, and several writings by Socinian thinkers like Johann Crell, Jonas Schlichting, Valentin Schmaltz, Johannes Völkel, Martin Ruar, Samuel Przypkowski, Johann Ludwig von Wolzogen, and still others. He also owned books by other prominent anti-Trinitarians, such as the bishop of the Unitarian Church of Transylvania George Enyedi and the German Arian Christoph Sand. Furthermore, he had in his library a number of books published during the aforesaid Trinitarian controversy of the late seventeenth century, including the first three collections of Unitarian tracts (the first volume of which contained several writings by Biddle) and various treatises by Stephen Nye, the leading anti-Trinitarian polemicist of late seventeenth-century England. Besides collecting, reading, and quoting anti-Trinitarian works (especially in some of his theological manuscripts), Locke befriended many anti-Trinitarians, such as Isaac Newton, Alexander Beresford, the merchants Thomas Firmin and William Popple (the latter being the English translator of *A Letter concerning Toleration*), and Samuel Crell, a grandson of Johann Crell and a pastor in the Minor Reformed Church of Poland.[24] Briefly, Locke was familiar with Socinianism and Arminianism, and his familiarity with Socinian and Arminian

---

articles ... were known to everybody." Philipp van Limborch to Locke, July 8, 1701, in Locke, *Correspondence*, vol. 7, no. 2953.

[23] On Locke in the Netherlands, see Luisa Simonutti, "Religion, Philosophy, and Science: John Locke and Limborch's Circle in Amsterdam," in James E. Force, David S. Katz (eds.), *Everything Connects: In Conference with Richard H. Popkin. Essays in His Honor* (Leiden: Brill, 1999), pp. 295–324; John Marshall, *John Locke, Toleration and Early Enlightenment Culture* (Cambridge: Cambridge University Press, 2006), pp. 469–499; Roger Woolhouse, *Locke: A Biography* (Cambridge: Cambridge University Press, 2007), pp. 197–265.

[24] In the past, Locke's interest in Socinian texts, his friendship with anti-Trinitarian intellectuals, and the similarities between Socinianism and his religious thought led some scholars –

thought is manifest in his considerations on various theological issues – starting with the question of scriptural authority and the method to interpret Scripture.

Scriptural Authority and Historical Method

As Locke repeatedly stated in the *Reasonableness* and its two vindications, his account of Christianity was based on Scripture – not on ecclesiastical tradition, systems of divinity, or any human authority whatsoever. This approach to religious truth was in line with the Protestant doctrine of *sola Scriptura*, according to which Scripture is the sole infallible rule of faith and practice. However, in the second half of the seventeenth century, before Locke wrote the *Reasonableness*, several scholars had questioned the divine authority of Scripture. The most corrosive criticism to scriptural authority came from the monist philosopher Baruch Spinoza, whose *Tractatus Theologico-Politicus* (1670) portrayed the Bible as a collection of texts relating the history and traditions of the ancient Hebrews and providing, in a clear and straightforward manner, moral principles which anyone could easily comprehend and respect. In the *Tractatus*, Spinoza provided a naturalistic and demystifying account of miracles and prophecy. To Spinoza, belief in miracles originated in the human inability to understand the natural causes of unusual, extraordinary events. Concerning biblical miracles, in Chapter 6 of the *Tractatus*, he maintained that many natural phenomena narrated in the Scriptures were commonly, but mistakenly, believed to be miraculous because of the hyperbolic style employed by the authors of the biblical texts, who used rhetorical figures and expressions incomprehensible to a modern audience.[25] As to prophecy,

---

especially anti-Trinitarian historians – to incorrectly describe him as a Socinian: see Robert Wallace, *Antitrinitarian Biography*, 3 vols. (London: Whitfield, 1850), vol. 3, pp. 399–428; H. John McLachlan, *The Religious Opinions of Milton, Locke, and Newton* (Manchester: Manchester University Press, 1941), pp. 69–114. For more reliable considerations on Locke's ownership of Socinian sources, friendship with anti-Trinitarian intellectuals, and relation to the Socinian theological tradition, see John R. Harrison, Peter Laslett, *The Library of John Locke* (Oxford: Oxford University Press, 1965); Richard Ashcraft, "John Locke's Library: Portrait of an Intellectual," *Transactions of the Cambridge Bibliographical Society*, 5:1 (1969): pp. 47–60; John C. Higgins-Biddle, "Introduction" to John Locke, *The Reasonableness of Christianity, As Delivered in the Scriptures*, ed. John C. Higgins-Biddle (Oxford: Clarendon Press, 1999), pp. xv–cxv (lviii–lx); John Marshall, "Locke, Socinianism, 'Socinianism,' and Unitarianism," in M. A. Stewart (ed.), *English Philosophy in the Age of Locke* (Oxford: Clarendon Press, 2000), pp. 111–182; Stephen D. Snobelen, "Socinianism, Heresy and John Locke's *Reasonableness of Christianity*," *Enlightenment and Dissent*, 20 (2001): pp. 88–125; Luisa Simonutti, "John Locke e il socinianesimo," in Mariangela Priarolo, Maria Emanuela Scribano (eds.), *Fausto Sozzini e la filosofia in Europa* (Siena: Accademia Senese degli Intronati, 2005), pp. 211–249.

[25] Benedict de Spinoza, *Theological-Political Treatise*, trans. Michael Silverthorne and Jonathan I. Israel, ed. Jonathan I. Israel (Cambridge: Cambridge University Press, 2007), pp. 81–96.

the first three chapters of the *Tractatus* depict it as an ingenious way to discipline the ignorant and superstitious multitude through the use of a vivid imagination.[26] Briefly, Spinoza's work implicitly questioned the divine authority of Scripture while expressly describing the Bible as a collection of texts irrelevant to politics, law, and philosophy. Another hard blow to biblical authority came from the aforesaid Catholic priest Richard Simon, although his works were inspired by pious intentions.[27] Simon attempted to defend ecclesiastical tradition, which was the Catholic rule of faith, against the Protestant doctrine of *sola Scriptura*. He noted that no originals remained of texts from biblical and apostolic times. Moreover, modern readers could not have a clear understanding of how the Scriptures had been composed and how the biblical texts had been transmitted over the centuries. The biblical texts present numerous obscurities, corruptions, and interpolations, frequently resulting not from intentional frauds, but from accidental transcription errors, misinterpretations, mistranslations, and even sincere efforts to shed light on unclear passages. Simon called attention to these issues, which made reliance on Scripture alone impracticable, in order to reject the Protestant theory that Scripture is the only infallible rule of faith. Thus, he reaffirmed the crucial role of ecclesiastical tradition in interpreting the Bible and defining the true theological doctrine. However, his erudite and accurate comparative analysis of the Old and New Testaments had an unintended (and undesirable to both Catholics and Protestants) side effect, in that it implicitly questioned the unity and internal consistency of Scripture and, consequently, its divine authority.

Spinoza's and Simon's theories soon reached and spread into England, especially among the heterodox.[28] Therefore, if Locke wanted to use the Bible as the only source of religious truth, he could not simply assume the divine authority of Scripture: he needed to prove it. The proof of scriptural authority he gave was extremely similar to that formulated by Faustus Socinus in *De Sacrae Scripturae auctoritate* (1588).[29] According to Socinus, the divine authority of the Bible is proven by the truth of the Christian religion, which

---

[26] Ibid., pp. 13–56.

[27] Simon's major works were promptly translated into English: see, for instance, Richard Simon, *A Critical History of the Old Testament* (London, 1682); Richard Simon, *A Critical History of the Text of the New Testament* (London, 1689).

[28] On the reception of Simon's theories in England, see Justin Champion, "Père Richard Simon and English Biblical Criticism, 1680–1700," in Force, Katz (eds.), *Everything Connects*, pp. 37–61; Iliffe, "Friendly Criticism"; McDonald, *Biblical Criticism*, pp. 144–156. On Spinoza's impact in England, see Chapter 1.

[29] Socinus's *De Sacrae Scripturae auctoritate* was first published in Seville in 1588 under the pseudonym "Dominicus Lopez" and was translated into French in 1592. Its most famous Latin edition was made in 1611 by the Dutch Remonstrant scholar Conrad Vorstius, whose sympathies for Socinian thought caused him to lose the theology chair at Leiden upon King James's request. An English translation appeared in 1731: Faustus Socinus, *An Argument for the Authority of Holy Scripture*, trans. Edward Combe (London, 1731).

lies in the moral excellence of the biblical precepts. To Socinus, the Bible, particularly the New Testament, delivers an irrefutable moral message, combining universally acceptable moral principles with the promise of immortality and eternal reward. In Socinus's words: "No one who accepts that the Christian religion is true can reasonably doubt the authority of the New Testament; and because the truth of the Old Testament is confirmed by the New, this applies to the whole Bible."[30] This passage denotes the Socinians' belief in biblical prophecies and miracles. In line with the Christian hermeneutical doctrine known as typology, which emphasizes the consistency of Old Testament prophecies with their fulfillment in the New Testament, the Socinians believed that the New Testament confirmed the truth of Old Testament prophecies concerning the Coming of the Messiah. Moreover, they thought that Christ's miracles further proved his Messianic mission. Nonetheless, Christ's miracles were only secondary evidence of the truth of the Christian religion, which the Socinians considered manifest, above all, in Christ's moral precepts and living example. Socinus's strategy to establish the divine authority of the Bible on the moral excellence of Christianity had a significant advantage. Thanks to this strategy, historical and critical objections to the divine authority of Scripture could be dismissed easily, according to the Socinians, because these objections concentrated on matters of fact that were only probable and could not be warranted with certainty, while the moral precepts and the message of salvation delivered in the New Testament were universally acceptable.

Although there is no conclusive evidence that Locke read Socinus's *De Sacrae Scripturae auctoritate*, he knew of this proof, most probably, from Grotius's *Pro veritate religionis Christianae* (1627) and from a manuscript version of Bishop Thomas Barlow's posthumously published *De Studio Theologiae* (1699), which he referred to and copied in part in one of his notebooks, MS Locke e. 17.[31] Moreover, he cited a 1660 edition of Grotius's *Pro veritate religionis Christianae* fifteen times in MS Locke f. 14, a notebook for miscellaneous notes from c.1659 to c.1667. Despite their doctrinal divergences and their hostility to Socinianism concerning various subjects, both the Remonstrant scholar Grotius and the Calvinistic clergyman Barlow approved of Socinus's proof, which could be utilized to support the Protestant doctrine of *sola Scriptura* against Catholic claims on ecclesiastical authority as the rule of faith. Furthermore, William Chillingworth's demonstration of the truth of "*the*

---

[30] Ibid., p. 3.

[31] Hugo Grotius, *Sensus librorum sex, quos pro veritate religionis Christianae* ... (Paris, 1627), pp. 83–84; Thomas Barlow, *De Studio Theologiae* (Oxford, 1699); MS Locke e. 17, pp. 23–71; Victor Nuovo, *Christianity, Antiquity, and Enlightenment: Interpretations of Locke* (Dordrecht: Springer, 2011), pp. 53–73; Nuovo, *John Locke*, pp. 220–225, 233–235.

Doctrine of Christianity" in *The Religion of Protestants* – a book that Locke knew well – is very similar to Socinus's proof, in that it emphasizes Christ's miracles and "the goodnesse of the precepts of Christianity, and the greatnesse of the promises of it."[32]

Like Socinus and Grotius, Locke inferred the divine authority of the Bible from the moral excellence of the principles preached in it – principles that Christ not only taught but also practiced, as Locke frequently pointed out in the *Reasonableness* and other writings on religion. As Locke declared in *A Second Vindication of the Reasonableness of Christianity*, he was struck by the "Discovery of the marvellous and divine Wisdom of our Saviour's Conduct, in all the Circumstances of his promulgating this Doctrine."[33] In Locke's opinion, Christ's "doctrine" combined universally acceptable moral precepts with the promise of eternal bliss. This doctrine persuaded Locke "of the necessity that such a Law-giver should be sent from God for the reforming the Morality of the World."[34] Locke, like Socinus, believed that Christ's miracles were only secondary evidence of his Messiahship, and he thought that the miracle of Christ's resurrection served to authenticate his Messianic mission and to assure the righteous that they will be rewarded with eternal life.[35] To Locke, miracles just confirmed Christ's (and the biblical prophets' and other divine messengers') divine mission, since truly divine miracles either glorified God or revealed matters of great concern to humankind – for instance, matters regarding deliverance and redemption.[36] Locke paid attention to the issue of miracles throughout his mature life, both before and after writing the *Reasonableness*. One of his later writings, *A Discourse of Miracles* (written in 1702 and published in the *Posthumous Works* in 1706) was devoted specific-

---

[32] William Chillingworth, *The Religion of Protestants a Safe Way to Salvation* (Oxford, 1638), p. 36.

[33] John Locke, "A Second Vindication of the Reasonableness of Christianity," in John Locke, *Vindications of the Reasonableness of Christianity*, ed. Victor Nuovo (Oxford: Clarendon Press, 2012), pp. 27–233 (35).

[34] Ibid.

[35] Locke, *Reasonableness*, pp. 23, 37, 47–50, 56–57, 142–143, 146–147, 153; Locke, "Second Vindication," pp. 156–158, 162, 185–186; John Locke, *A Paraphrase and Notes on the Epistles of St Paul to the Galatians, 1 and 2 Corinthians, Romans, Ephesians*, ed. Arthur W. Wainwright, 2 vols. (Oxford: Clarendon Press, 1987), 1 Cor. 2:4–5, vol. 1, p. 172.

[36] On Locke on miracles, see T. Brian Mooney, Anthony Imbrosciano, "The Curious Case of Mr. Locke's Miracles," *International Journal for Philosophy of Religion*, 57:3 (2005): pp. 147–168; J. J. MacIntosh, "Locke and Boyle on Miracles and God's Existence," in Michael Hunter (ed.), *Robert Boyle Reconsidered* (Cambridge: Cambridge University Press, 1994), pp. 193–214; Travis Dumsday, "Locke on Competing Miracles," *Faith and Philosophy*, 25:4 (2008): pp. 416–424; Nuovo, *Christianity*, pp. 43–46; Marcy Lascano, "Locke's Philosophy of Religion," in Matthew Stuart (ed.), *A Companion to Locke* (Chichester: Wiley-Blackwell, 2016), pp. 469–485 (480–485); Nathan Rockwood, "Lockean Essentialism and the Possibility of Miracles," *The Southern Journal of Philosophy*, 56:2 (2018): pp. 293–310.

ally to this subject.[37] In this tract, he defined "a miracle" as "a sensible operation, which being above the comprehension of the spectator, and in his opinion contrary to the established course of nature, is taken by him to be divine."[38] Concerning the origin and purpose of divine miracles, he added:

> To know that any revelation is from God, it is necessary to know that the messenger that delivers it is sent from God, and that cannot be known but by some credentials given him by God himself . . .. Divine revelation receives testimony from no other miracles, but such as are wrought to witness his mission from God who delivers the revelation.[39]

Locke was aware that miracles could be alleged by non-Christians to substantiate their claims to have received divine revelations. In this respect, he called attention to the lack of "any miracles recorded in the Greek or Roman writers, as done to confirm any one's mission and doctrine."[40] As regards other religions, Locke dismissed Zoroastrianism and Hinduism as unworthy of consideration, whereas he noted that "Mahomet having none to produce, pretends to no miracles for the vouching his mission."[41] Locke, unlike Robert Boyle, disregarded the Islamic idea that the Quran is itself a miracle, possibly because he was unaware of this claim, or perhaps he was unimpressed by it.[42] According to Locke, the only revelations attested by miracles are those of Moses and Christ, which are complementary.[43] As a result, there is no problem of competing miracles. Nevertheless, Locke believed in supernatural forces other than God, including demonic forces, who were able to perform miracles. He also took into account the possibility of impostors capable of faking miracles. And a demonic or fake miracle could contradict a divine miracle. In this case, Locke argued, we ought to accept the greater miracle as attesting a truly divine revelation, because God, being omnipotent and benevolent, would not allow a malevolent force or an impostor to prevail and deceive us:

> For since God's power is paramount to all, and no opposition can be made against him with an equal force to his; and since his honour and goodness can never be supposed to suffer his messenger and his truth to be born down by the appearance of a greater power on the side of an impostor, and in favour of a lye; wherever there is an opposition, and two pretending to be sent from heaven clash, the signs, which carry with them the evident marks of a greater power, will always be a certain and unquestionable evidence, that the truth and divine mission are on that side on which they appear.[44]

This happened, for instance, when Moses performed miracles that the Egyptian sorcerers could not duplicate.[45] Locke employed the same criterion when stressing the divine origin of Christ's miracles:

---

[37] Here, I refer to the following edition: John Locke, "A Discourse of Miracles," in John Locke, *Works*, 9 vols., 12th ed. (London, 1824), vol. 8, pp. 256–265.

[38] Ibid., p. 256.   [39] Ibid., p. 257.   [40] Ibid.   [41] Ibid., p. 258.

[42] MacIntosh, "Locke and Boyle," pp. 203–204; Dumsday, "Locke on Competing Miracles," pp. 417, 423.

[43] Locke, "Discourse of Miracles," p. 258.   [44] Ibid., p. 260.   [45] Ibid.

The number, variety, and greatness of the miracles wrought for the confirmation of the doctrine delivered by Jesus Christ, carry with them such strong marks of an extraordinary divine power, that the truth of his mission will stand firm and unquestionable, till any one rising up in opposition to him shall do greater miracles than he and his apostles did. For any thing less will not be of weight to turn the scales in the opinion of any one, whether of an inferiour or more exalted understanding.[46]

Finally, drawing a conclusion concerning Christ's miracles, Locke noted:

Miracles being the basis on which divine mission is always established, and consequently that foundation on which the believers of any divine revelation must ultimately bottom their faith, this use of them would be lost ... if miracles be defined to be none but such divine operations as are in themselves beyond the power of all created beings, or at least operations contrary to the fixed and established laws of nature.[47]

Whereas *A Discourse of Miracles* presents an interesting attempt to make sense of miracles – mainly, but not exclusively, biblical miracles – Locke's main argument for the acceptance of supernatural occurrences is in *An Essay concerning Human Understanding*:

Though the common Experience, and the ordinary Course of Things have justly a mighty Influence on the Minds of Men, to make them give or refuse Credit to any thing proposed to their Belief; yet there is one Case, wherein the strangeness of the Fact lessens not the Assent to a fair Testimony given of it. For where such supernatural Events are suitable to ends aim'd at by him, who has the Power to change the course of Nature, there, under such Circumstances, they may be the fitter to procure Belief, by how much the more they are beyond, or contrary to ordinary Observation. This is the proper Case of *Miracles*, which well attested, do not only find Credit themselves; but give it also to other Truths, which need such Confirmation.[48]

Locke admitted, though, that not all biblical texts have the same importance. He was aware of a dispute on this matter between Richard Simon and Jean Le Clerc. In *Sentimens de quelques theologiens de Hollande* (1685), Le Clerc responded to the comments that Simon had made on several biblical texts in *Histoire critique du Vieux Testament* (first published in Paris in 1678 and then reissued, with various amendments, in Rotterdam in 1685, after being also translated into English in 1682).[49] Simon's thesis was that several books of the Old Testament were collections of other, older sources and that, although these

---

[46] Ibid., pp. 260–261.   [47] Ibid., p. 264.

[48] John Locke, *An Essay concerning Human Understanding*, ed. Peter H. Nidditch (Oxford: Clarendon Press, 1975), IV.xvi.13, p. 667.

[49] Jean Bernier, "Le Problème de la tradition chez Richard Simon et Jean Le Clerc," *Revue des Sciences Religieuses*, 82:2 (2008): pp. 199–223. On Locke's interest in this dispute, see John Marshall, *John Locke: Resistance, Religion and Responsibility* (Cambridge: Cambridge University Press, 1994), pp. 337–346; Champion, "Père Richard Simon," pp. 39, 45–47; Raffaele Russo, *Ragione e ascolto. L'ermeneutica di John Locke* (Naples: Guida, 2001), pp. 143–149; Iliffe, "Friendly Criticism."

writings were originally inspired by God, a number of mistakes, alterations, and interpolations had affected their transmission. Le Clerc conceded that the Scriptures – not only the Old Testament, but also the New Testament – presented some variations and mistakes, which showed that the biblical writers (including, also, the Evangelists and the Apostles) were not always divinely inspired when compiling their texts. According to Le Clerc, this was true, in particular, for the New Testament epistles, which were influenced by their authors' specific views and objectives. However, to Le Clerc, the Scriptures unambiguously expounded the fundamental tenets of the Christian religion, and all the Evangelists agreed upon these tenets. This is why, in Le Clerc's opinion, the essential elements of Christianity were plainly explained and easily intelligible. Le Clerc adopted this strategy because he thought that disregarding Simon's well-grounded remarks, and uncritically asserting the reliability of all biblical texts, would expose the Bible to attacks from "libertines" – namely atheists, deists, and disbelievers. However, one of the side effects of Le Clerc's approach to Scripture was that it diminished the significance of various biblical texts, especially the New Testament epistles.

Locke expressed his concerns about some points made by Le Clerc in a letter he sent to Limborch upon reading *Sentimens* in 1685. He acknowledged the need to make a clear distinction between authoritative and dubious passages in the Bible; but, although he appreciated Le Clerc's intention to salvage the Scriptures from destructive criticism, he believed that Le Clerc had not accomplished this task adequately.[50] Therefore, when writing the *Reasonableness* a decade later, Locke employed a slightly different strategy. Repairing to the divinely inspired Scriptures and rejecting systems of divinity, tradition, and any human authority whatsoever, he distinguished two levels of authority within the Scriptures. He argued that the revelations made by Christ during his earthly life were more important than the Apostles' explanations of Christ's teachings in their epistles to the early Christians. According to Locke, the first Christian communities already believed in Christ's precepts, knew the fundamental notions of Christianity, and, thus, did not need to receive any additional revelations. Locke based his theory on an interpretation of Acts 1:3 – a verse relating that, after his resurrection, Christ appeared to the Apostles for a period of forty days and spoke to them about "things *concerning the Kingdom of God.*"[51] Given the relative silence of biblical narratives about Christ's preaching to the Apostles in the period between his resurrection and his ascension, Locke thought that Christ had not revealed anything new to the Apostles

---

[50] Locke to Philipp van Limborch, September 26/October 6, 1685, in Locke, *Correspondence*, vol. 2, no. 834.
[51] Locke, *Reasonableness*, p. 105. The King James Version reads "things pertaining to the kingdom of God."

during that forty-day period. According to Locke, during that forty-day period, Christ only repeated what he had taught up until his death on the cross. This argument established the primacy of the Gospels over the Apostles' epistles, although Locke himself devoted a significant part of his later years to writing *A Paraphrase and Notes on the Epistles of St Paul*. As Victor Nuovo has correctly noted, Locke indeed considered the Pauline and other New Testament epistles to be "works of counsel and edification addressed to Christian communities, and although they contain fundamental doctrines, it is not their primary purpose to teach them, but to apply them with other pertinent truths to the problems and circumstances of these communities."[52]

Locke's defense of the unity, internal consistency, and authority of Scripture opposed Catholic claims of a secret oral tradition about Christ's supposed revelations following his resurrection. Moreover, his strategy confirmed that, although not all biblical texts are equally important, the Scriptures still contain all that is necessary to salvation. Therefore, ecclesiastical tradition and extra-scriptural speculations are unnecessary to salvation. In this regard, John Higgins-Biddle has aptly observed:

In his opposition to tradition Locke placed the "historical" accounts of Jesus' life and teachings in a position of ultimate authority, superior not only to tradition but also to the interpretations of Christianity in the Epistles .... His presupposition that faith was a matter of assent to propositions was complemented by the assumption that those propositions – the fundamental articles of faith – were clearly stated in the Scripture. To elucidate those propositions Locke adopted a strictly historical, but not always literal, method of interpretation and concentrated his attention on those portions of the New Testament that seemed most historical.[53]

With his historical method of biblical interpretation, Locke distanced himself from the literalism of some Protestant groups and, at the same time, he rejected the subjection of Scripture to systems of divinity and theological doctrines of extra-scriptural origin.[54] Starting at least with his Latin essay of 1661 on

---

[52] Victor Nuovo, "Introduction" to John Locke, *Writings on Religion*, ed. Victor Nuovo (Oxford: Oxford University Press, 2002), pp. xv–lvii (lv). On the *Paraphrase*, see Arthur W. Wainwright, "Introduction" to Locke, *Paraphrase*, vol. 1, pp. 1–88; Maria-Cristina Pitassi, *Le philosophe et l'écriture: John Locke exégète de Saint Paul* (Geneva: Cahiers de la Revue de Théologie et de Philosophie, 1990); Russo, *Ragione e ascolto*, pp. 205–246; Raffaele Russo, "The Thread of Discourse: Primary and Secondary Paraphrase in Locke's Hermeneutics," in Luisa Simonutti (ed.), *Locke and Biblical Hermeneutics: Conscience and Scripture* (Cham: Springer, 2019), pp. 121–141; Maria-Cristina Pitassi, "Locke's Pauline Hermeneutics: A Critical Review," in Simonutti (ed.), *Locke and Biblical Hermeneutics*, pp. 243–256.

[53] Higgins-Biddle, "Introduction," p. xxiii.

[54] On Locke's historical method of biblical interpretation, see Nuovo, *John Locke*, pp. 220–225; Victor Nuovo, "Locke's Hermeneutics of Existence and His Representation of Christianity," in Simonutti (ed.), *Locke and Biblical Hermeneutics*, pp. 77–103; Justin Champion, "'An Intent and Careful Reading': How John Locke Read His Bible," in Simonutti (ed.), *Locke and Biblical*

infallibility – an essay in which he declared that "the most certain interpreter of Scripture is Scripture itself, and it alone is infallible"[55] – he always deplored readings of Scripture influenced by systems of theology, as he explained in *A Second Vindication of the Reasonableness of Christianity*:

If the reading and study of the Scripture were more pressed than it is, and Men were fairly sent to the Bible to find their Religion; and not the Bible put into their hands only to find the Opinions of their peculiar Sect or Party, Christendom would have more Christians, and those that are, would be more knowing, and more in the right, than they now are. That which hinders this, is that select bundle of Doctrines, which it has pleased every Sect to draw out of the Scriptures, or their own inventions, with an Omission ... of all the rest .... Thus Systems, the Inventions of Men, are turn'd into so many opposite Gospels; and nothing is truth in each Sect, but what just suits with them. So that the Scripture serves but like a Nose of Wax, to be turn'd and bent, just as may fit the contrary Orthodoxies of different Societies.[56]

Locke recommended a holistic reading of the biblical texts, rather than reading them "piecemeal," as he maintained in *An Essay for the Understanding of St Paul's Epistles* prefaced to the *Paraphrase*.[57] This holistic approach to Scripture would indeed undermine the credibility of those who "snatch out a few Words, as if they were separate from the rest, to serve a Purpose."[58] Thus, Locke attempted to read the biblical texts in relation to their respective contexts and tried to elucidate their meaning in light of the biblical discourse taken as a whole. He stated in the *Reasonableness*:

We must look into the drift of the Discourse, observe the coherence and connexion of the Parts, and see how it is consistent with it self, and other parts of Scripture; if we will conceive it right. We must not cull out, as best suits our System, here and there a Period or a Verse; as if they were all distinct and independent Aphorisms.[59]

To Locke, the true meaning of Scripture could be comprehended only by making sense of "the coherence and connexion" of its various parts. To this purpose, historical knowledge and familiarity with the biblical languages are of utmost importance:

[Scripture is] to be understood in the plain direct meaning of the words and phrases, such as they may be supposed to have had in the mouths of the Speakers, who used them according to the Language of that Time and Country wherein they lived, without

---

Hermeneutics, pp. 143–160; Kim Ian Parker, "Spinoza, Locke, and Biblical Interpretation," in Simonutti (ed.), *Locke and Biblical Hermeneutics*, pp. 163–188.

[55] John Locke, "Infallibility," in Locke, *Writings on Religion*, pp. 69–72 (72), in English translation. The Latin original of this manuscript is in the British National Archives (PRO 30/24/47/33) and has been published in John C. Biddle, "John Locke's Essay on Infallibility: Introduction, Text, and Translation," *Journal of Church and State*, 19:2 (1977): pp. 301–327.

[56] Locke, "Second Vindication," pp. 125–126.   [57] Locke, *Paraphrase*, vol. 1, pp. 105–107.

[58] Ibid., p. 106.   [59] Locke, *Reasonableness*, p. 165.

such learned, artificial, and forced senses of them, as are sought out, and put upon them in most of the Systems of Divinity, according to the Notions, that each one has been bred up in.[60]

Nonetheless, Locke was aware of the difficulties of interpreting Scripture. These difficulties were mainly due to lack of a clear understanding of the historical circumstances in which the biblical texts were composed, as Locke acknowledged in the prefatory essay to the *Paraphrase*:

I know Expressions now out of use, Opinions of those times, not heard in our days, Allusions to Customs lost to us, and various Circumstances and Particularities of the Parties, which we cannot come at, etc. must needs continue several Passages in the dark now to us at this distance, which shon with full Light to those they were directed to.[61]

While Locke did not share the different objectives of Spinoza's or Simon's biblical hermeneutics, which he considered harmful to scriptural authority, he recognized, as they had done, the problem of the obscurity of Scripture, which led him to doubt the possibility of achieving complete and perfect understanding of its meaning. This is why he distinguished between the *meaning* of Scripture, which is tied to the historical contexts of the biblical texts and necessitates careful investigation, and the *truth* that Scripture delivers, which is transhistorical and clearly discernible.[62] Consequently, in the *Reasonableness*, he concentrated mainly on the fundamentals of Christianity, which he considered plainly revealed in Scripture and, hence, essential to salvation and acceptable to all Christians. And this approach had significant irenic implications.

The Way of Fundamentals

In *The Reasonableness of Christianity*, Locke pursued the way of fundamentals, thus following the example of Socinians, Arminians, and several English scholars, such as the members of the Great Tew Circle and various latitudinarian divines. According to these theologians, the essence of Christianity consists of few simple principles regarding God's existence and assisting grace, the divine authority of Scripture, the existence of an afterlife with

---

[60] Ibid., p. 6.   [61] Locke, *Paraphrase*, vol. 1, p. 112.

[62] On this point, see Parker, "Spinoza, Locke," pp. 176–182. Parker has also highlighted some important methodological similarities between Spinoza's and Locke's biblical hermeneutics: "Even though Spinoza and Locke are worlds apart theologically – Spinoza's naturalism is very much antithetical to Locke's theism – both tend to interpret the Bible in a similar manner. They are equally adamant that there are two wrong directions that biblical hermeneutics could take, either by interpreting the text without using reason, or by making Scripture conform to an a priori philosophical position. Both Spinoza and Locke also agree that the proper way to interpret Scripture is by 'Scripture alone,' and both also agree that historical evidence be brought to bear on the text to avoid misreading it" (ibid., p. 172).

reward and punishment, and the necessity of moral conduct to achieve salvation. Other disparate beliefs and practices may originate from different interpretations of Scripture, which every Christian is allowed to understand according to their intellectual capabilities; but non-fundamental beliefs and practices are secondary in comparison with the fundamental tenets of Christianity. Therefore, divergences about non-fundamental doctrinal, ceremonial, and ecclesiological issues ought not to hinder peace among Christians. Peaceful coexistence among Christians should be attained either through mutual toleration between different churches, as the Socinians proposed, or through "comprehension" into one church (frequently conceived of as a *national* church) admitting differences in secondary doctrines and practices, as most Arminians and latitudinarians argued. Locke himself made a distinction between fundamentals and non-fundamentals, as John Higgins-Biddle has noted:

[Locke] distinguish[ed] consistently between beliefs necessary to make one a Christian and beliefs that a Christian might subsequently hold. He maintained that the former were so simple and readily discernible that all persons could discover and understand them, whatever their intellectual capacities. At the same time, by allowing Christians to pursue subsequent beliefs to the extent of their intellectual capacity and in the direction of their religious preference, he maintained the flexibility necessary for toleration, which was the goal of the way of fundamentals.[63]

Whereas I acknowledge that Locke's doctrine of the fundamentals had important irenic *implications*, I believe that the main *motivation* behind this doctrine was in Locke's preoccupation with morality and salvation. I think that his Christian irenicism was actually a (desired) consequence of the moralist soteriology he expounded in the *Reasonableness*. Like Socinians, Arminians, and other Protestant irenicists, Locke refused the main tenets of Calvinist theology and, instead, he upheld a moralist soteriology. He rejected predestination, he believed in the power of the human will to accept or resist saving grace, and he highlighted the role of good works in the pursuit of salvation. Concerning Locke's rejection of predestination and his emphasis on individual choice and responsibility in the pursuit of salvation, it is unclear whether he agreed with most Arminian thinkers (including the leading Remonstrant theologians) that God foreknew those who would accept God's assisting grace, or he thought that God simply saves those who in fact respond to the call of the Gospel.[64] Neither Locke's public writings nor his private manuscripts are helpful to clarify this issue. While being unable to provide an explanation of Locke's position on this point, I can only speculate that he either dismissed the

---

[63] Higgins-Biddle, "Introduction," p. lxvi.

[64] Marshall, *John Locke: Resistance*, p. 431; Alan P. F. Sell, *John Locke and the Eighteenth-Century Divines* (Cardiff: University of Wales Press, 1997), p. 234.

above distinction as irrelevant, or simply disregarded or ignored the Remonstrants' and other Arminians' clarifications of their views on this matter. At
any rate, Locke's approach to saving belief differs from the views of other
representatives of the way of fundamentals in a significant respect. Several
Arminian authors, including Arminius himself, Limborch, and other Remonstrants, and Socinian writers like Socinus himself and Johann Crell limited the
essence of the Christian religion to a few fundamental principles (i.e., principles concerning God's existence and grace, scriptural authority, morality,
and the afterlife), while they left it to each Christian to infer non-fundamentals
from their own reading of the Bible. Nonetheless, Remonstrants and Socinians
affirmed much more than what they saw as the fundamentals of Christianity
when they formulated and endorsed comprehensive, detailed, complex
systems of doctrine, and consequently they showed what Locke called "Zeal
for their Orthodoxy."[65] Conversely, other Protestant irenicists, especially in
England, avoided any attempt to detail even the fundamental tenets of Christianity. For instance, Chillingworth wrote in *The Religion of Protestants* that
Christians should "syncerely endeavour to finde the true sense of [Scripture],
and live according to it."[66] But he considered it undesirable, and actually
impossible, to create a unique list of fundamentals to be followed by all
Christians. Unlike Chillingworth, Locke embarked on identifying the fundamental articles of Christianity; but, unlike Remonstrants and Socinians, he
refrained from expressly proposing a specific, thorough, complex system of
doctrine. He formulated original and internally coherent religious views, but he
did so in an unsystematic way, and he focused on difficult and controversial
theological issues (e.g., the Trinity and satisfaction) especially in his private
writings. In his public writings on religion, he rather concentrated on issues
that, in his opinion, Scripture addressed in an explicit, plain, unambiguous way
and, thus, on principles that all Christians could accept. Locke did not wish to
endorse a particular, detailed, comprehensive system of doctrine to others
because, in his opinion, saving belief does not result from the acceptance of
some theological system. Since saving belief is rooted in Scripture, the faithful
ought to study Scripture to the best of their abilities in order to live the
Christian life and pursue salvation. As Locke deemed intellectual effort useful
and rewarding not only in this life but also in the "other life," so he thought
that the exercise of understanding in the interpretation of scriptural revelation
would contribute to salvation.[67] He even admitted the possibility of mistakes in

---

[65] Locke, "Second Vindication," p. 126. Locke used this expression – "Zeal for their Orthodoxy" –
in reference to the Socinians in particular.

[66] Chillingworth, *Religion of Protestants*, p. 180.

[67] Jean-Michel Vienne, "Hermeneutics and the Reasonableness of Belief," in Simonutti (ed.),
Locke and Biblical Hermeneutics, pp. 105–119 (110). On God's appreciation of intellectual
effort, see Chapter 1.

interpreting Scripture, since he acknowledged the problem of the obscurity of many biblical texts. In the *Reasonableness* and its vindications, he argued that much was not plain in Scripture and that, consequently, searching for religious truth was more important than (often supposedly) finding and maintaining it. He even claimed that error about non-fundamentals, if held after sincere search, could still lead to salvation.[68] In this regard, he wrote in the *Reasonableness*:

A great many of the Truths revealed in the Gospel, every one does, and must confess, a man may be ignorant of; nay, disbelieve, without danger to his Salvation: As is evident in those, who allowing the Authority, differ in the Interpretation and meaning of several Texts of Scripture, not thought Fundamental.[69]

Concerning the reasons why Locke judged some Christian doctrines – even some doctrines based on interpretations of biblical texts – to be debatable and inessential to salvation, I agree with G. A. J. Rogers, who, on this point, has noted the following:

There are three reasons why doctrines of the Christian religion may be open to debate, discussion, and dispute without in any way threatening the moral or theological integrity of the disputants. First, it may be a genuine intellectual issue as to which way the text should be interpreted, and we should recognize that neither side may have clear demonstration, and therefore, knowledge to settle the matter. Or, secondly, it may be that no right answer to some question has actually been revealed in the text, and the question must remain open. Or, finally, it may be that in addition to the text not revealing any settled conclusion, reason itself may be incapable of reaching an answer. That these difficulties exist should not in itself prevent anyone attempting to seek answers for himself either from the text or from his own intellectual resources, so long as we always remember that where no demonstration can be given we may not demand acceptance of the proposed solution from others.[70]

Though, Locke maintained that "some of the Truths delivered in Holy Writ are very plain: 'Tis impossible, I think, to mistake their Meaning; And those certainly are all necessary to be explicitly believ'd."[71] These "very plain" truths are what Locke identified as the three fundamentals of Christianity – namely, faith in Jesus the Messiah, repentance for sin, and obedience to the divine moral law. Locke declared in the *Reasonableness* that Jesus' Messiahship "is the sole Doctrine pressed and required to be believed in the whole

---

[68] Locke, *Reasonableness*, 168–171; John Locke, "A Vindication of the Reasonableness of Christianity," in Locke, *Vindications*, pp. 3–26 (11–12); Locke, "Second Vindication," pp. 44–45, 75–76, 174–177, 192–194, 230–233; Marshall, "Locke, Socinianism," p. 172.

[69] Locke, *Reasonableness*, p. 168.

[70] G. A. J. Rogers, "John Locke: Conservative Radical," in Roger D. Lund (ed.), *The Margins of Orthodoxy: Heterodox Writing and Cultural Response, 1660–1750* (Cambridge: Cambridge University Press, 1995), pp. 97–116 (109–110).

[71] Locke, "Second Vindication," p. 175.

tenour of our Saviour's and his Apostles Preaching."[72] According to Locke, faith in Jesus' Messiahship is necessary to believe in his teachings, including his moral precepts, which disclose the divine moral law in its entirety and emphasize repentance and obedience to it.[73] To Locke, repentance and obedience go hand in hand, because sincere repentance involves a mental act of sorrow and entails a change of life in accordance with the divinely given moral law:

[Repentance is] not only a sorrow for sins past, but (what is a Natural consequence of such sorrow, if it be real) a turning from them, into a new and contrary Life .... Repentance is an hearty sorrow for our past misdeeds, and a sincere Resolution and Endeavour, to the utmost of our power, to conform all our Actions to the Law of God. So that Repentance does not consist in one single Act of sorrow ... But in *doing works meet for Repentance*, in a sincere Obedience to the Law of Christ, the remainder of our Lives.[74]

Without repentance for all sins and without the consequent, sincere commitment to abide by the divine moral law, it is impossible to achieve a moral renovation and strive to live an exemplary life inspired by faith in Christ. Concerning faith in Christ, it is worth noting that Locke described Jesus as simply the Messiah, namely, as he who had delivered a salvific message hitherto unknown to humankind. He never referred to Jesus Christ as a divine person. This means that, to Locke, belief in the Trinity was not among the fundamentals of Christianity and, consequently, was not necessary to salvation. Locke never clarified his views on the Trinitarian dogma, even when his critics John Edwards and Edward Stillingfleet pressured him to do so in the second half of the 1690s. Locke's Christological reflections in his public and private writings and his consideration of Trinitarian issues in some manuscripts indicate that he had a non-Trinitarian view of the Godhead, as I explain in detail in Chapter 5. However, his emphasis on the necessity of faith in Jesus as the Messiah (and not necessarily as also a person of the Trinity) is

---

[72] Locke, *Reasonableness*, p. 109.

[73] Around half a century before the publication of the *Reasonableness*, an emphasis on repentance and obedience, besides faith in Christ, had appeared in another English work representative of the way of fundamentals, *A Discourse of the Liberty of Prophesying* (1646) by the Laudian and Royalist clergyman Jeremy Taylor. Moreover, repentance is the main subject in Taylor's *Unum Necessarium* (1655). See Jeremy Taylor, "Of the Liberty of Prophesying," in Jeremy Taylor, *Treatises* (London, 1648), pp. 1–267 (5–18); Jeremy Taylor, *Unum necessarium*, 4th ed. (London, 1705), pp. 1–325. In his attack on Locke, which I examine in Chapter 5, John Edwards called attention to the similarities between the *Reasonableness* and Taylor's work.

[74] Locke, *Reasonableness*, pp. 111–112. Incidentally, I believe that, in Locke, the fact that repentance must be accompanied by obedience does not make death-bed repentance pointless. If, to Locke, what counts in repentance is a sincere resolution to obey the divine moral law, and if one, upon repenting, fails to translate this resolution into actions (and to examine God's Revealed Word and live a Christian life) because of their death, then one is not accountable for this failure and it would consequently be unjust to penalize them for this.

compatible with the irenic ideas of various Trinitarian thinkers belonging to the Arminian theological tradition, including, among others, John Tillotson and Philipp van Limborch. Tillotson was one of several seventeenth-century Protestant as well as Catholic scholars who fostered, often inadvertently, the marginalization of the Trinitarian dogma, in that they shifted focus toward Scripture's relation to reason – not to tradition – in their attempts to reject atheism and disbelief. Besides Tillotson, this diversified group of theologians included the Jesuit Leonard Lessius, the Minim friar Marin Mersenne, the Lutheran Abraham Calov, the Reformed Francis Turretin, and still others. Their main objective was to fight against atheism and disbelief and to affirm the truth of the Christian religion in its essential principles, regardless of the specific tenets of different Christian confessions and, thus, regardless of the numerous points of disagreement between different Christian groups. Their stress on elements of the Christian religion other than the Trinitarian doctrine was, however, one of the factors that caused the gradual weakening of the role of the Trinitarian dogma in Christian belief. Thus, the relative neglect of the Trinitarian doctrine by several prominent Christian theologians contributed to the revival of Arian ideas, to the emergence of anti-Trinitarian theories, and to the spread of creedal minimalism among Christian irenicists.[75] Furthermore, even some of those renowned theologians who inadvertently contributed to the marginalization of the Trinitarian doctrine in Christian belief held heterodox views of the Trinity. Tillotson is the most emblematic example in this regard, for he had a subordinationist notion of the Trinity, which denoted his closeness to the theories of Remonstrant scholars such as Episcopius and Courcelles. He followed Episcopius in arguing that self-existence (namely, aseity) "is peculiar to the Father as he is the principle and fountain of the Deity."[76] To Tillotson, although the other two divine persons share with the Father "the most incommunicable properties and perfections of the Deity," self-existence "is not, nor can be said of the Son and Holy Ghost."[77] Tillotson also followed the Remonstrants in their dislike of doctrinal conflicts – especially of conflicts provoked by disagreements about the Trinitarian dogma, as he felt uncomfortable with the divisions caused, within the Church of England, by the Trinitarian controversy of the late seventeenth century. In a letter to the Bishop of Salisbury, Gilbert Burnet, dated October 23, 1694 (one month before Tillotson's death), he deplored the use of the Athanasian Creed by the Church of England: "The account given of Athanasius's creed seems to me nowise

---

[75] William C. Placher, *The Domestication of Transcendence: How Modern Thinking about God Went Wrong* (Louisville: Westminster John Knox Press, 1996), pp. 164–178.

[76] John Tillotson, *Sermons, concerning the Divinity and Incarnation of Our Blessed Saviour* (London, 1693), p. 121.

[77] Ibid.

satisfactory. I wish we were well rid of it."[78] Locke held Tillotson in great esteem and was attached to him, as is shown by a letter he sent to Limborch shortly after the archbishop's death:

As soon as I find leisure I shall examine your *Theologia Christiana* diligently, for I think that I ought now to give my mind for the most part to such studies, and I wish so much the more that I were with you because, now that that great and candid searcher after truth, to say nothing of his other virtues, has been taken from us, I have scarcely anyone whom I can freely consult about theological uncertainties.[79]

In this letter, Locke mentioned Limborch's important book *Theologia Christiana*, which presents several similarities with the *Reasonableness*. Locke had probably read some draft sections of *Theologia Christiana* during its making in the mid-1680s, before Limborch completed and published it in 1686, when Locke was still in the Netherlands. However, after receiving this book in late 1694, he did not rush to examine it "diligently." As Locke wrote in a letter to Limborch in May 1695, shortly after finishing the *Reasonableness* and reading Limborch's book, he had delayed scrutinizing the Dutch theologian's work, as well as other "systems of divinity," until after completing his own treatise of biblical theology.[80] Nevertheless, this letter shows Locke's appreciation of Limborch's work. While Locke criticized the writings of Calvin and Turretin as "discordant ... with the sense and simplicity of the Gospel," he praised Limborch's *Theologia Christiana* as a book that had brought him "very great joy" because, at last, he had found "one theologian ... for whom I am not a heretic."[81] When commending Limborch's work in this letter, Locke referred, in particular, to Book V, Chapter 8 of *Theologia Christiana*, entitled "De Fide in Jesum Christum" ("On Faith in Jesus Christ") – a chapter that testifies to the Arminians' tolerant attitude and their preference for broad doctrinal comprehension. The Arminians were Trinitarians and believed in the atonement, whereas they rejected predestination and granted an important role to human reason and will in the pursuit of salvation.[82] Limborch himself, in *Theologia Christiana*, defended the Trinity against the Socinians and attempted to refute the latter's anti-Trinitarian reading of John 1:1 ("In the beginning was the Word, and the Word was with God, and the Word was God") – a verse he regarded as proof of the scriptural foundations of the Trinitarian doctrine. Nevertheless, the Arminians did not deny the possibility of salvation to

---

[78] John Tillotson to Gilbert Burnet, October 23, 1694, in John Tillotson, *Works*, ed. Thomas Birch, 3 vols. (London, 1752), vol. 1, p. 95.

[79] Locke to Philipp van Limborch, December 11, 1694, in Locke, *Correspondence*, vol. 5, no. 1826.

[80] Locke to Philipp van Limborch, May 10, 1695, in Locke, *Correspondence*, vol. 5, no. 1901.

[81] Ibid.

[82] On Limborch's and other Remonstrants' views on the atonement and salvation, see Chapter 3.

Socinians and other anti-Trinitarian Christians. As I have said in the first section of this chapter, the Dutch Remonstrants even admitted to communion with them several Polish Brethren, who had taken refuge in the Netherlands after their expulsion from Poland in 1658. Limborch's soteriological views were emblematic of the Arminians' irenic, conciliatory attitude to anti-Trinitarian Christians. While stating that belief in Jesus the Messiah was the fundamental article of the Christian religion, and was therefore essential to salvation, Limborch distinguished belief in Jesus' Messiahship from belief in the Trinity, as he explained in *Theologia Christiana*:

True it is, the Person to whom the office of a Saviour is committed by God, ought to be apprehended who is denoted by the Name of Jesus; which Name signifies a certain Man Anointed by God the Father and installed in that office. But whether this person consists of two Natures, one Eternal and Divine, the other Human, both united in one Person, has no reference to the Truth of this Proposition [that Jesus is the Messiah], but ought to be enquired after in other Places of Scripture.[83]

Limborch went even further in *De veritate religionis Christianae* (1687). In this book, he replied to the objections made by the Jewish controversialist Isaac Orobio de Castro against the idea that Jesus was the Messiah. Limborch attempted to demonstrate that Old Testament Messianic prophecies were fulfilled by Christ's Coming as related in the New Testament. However, while still portraying belief in Jesus the Messiah as the fundamental tenet of Christianity, he described belief in Christ's divinity as unnecessary to salvation. Locke must have felt relieved when he saw that Limborch concurred with him that faith in Jesus the Messiah was essential to make one a Christian, regardless of any speculation on the nature of Christ and the Godhead – in other words, regardless of belief (or disbelief) in the Trinity. Both Trinitarian and non-Trinitarian Christians indeed believed that Jesus was the Messiah announced by the Old Testament. Therefore, faith in Jesus as the Messiah could serve as a common ground for moderation, charity, and toleration among Christians.[84]

Locke considered acceptance of the fundamentals of Christianity – that is, faith in Jesus the Messiah, repentance, and obedience – as necessary to *become* a Christian. Locke's stress, in the *Reasonableness*, on these three fundamentals led some of his critics, including, among others, John Edwards, to accuse him of creedal minimalism. The second half of the seventeenth century had seen the publication of several works of creedal minimalism, such as Bishop Herbert Croft's *The Naked Truth* (1675), which reduced the Protestant faith

---

[83] Philipp van Limborch, *Theologia Christiana* (Amsterdam, 1686), pp. 433–434. This English translation is from: Victor Nuovo (ed.), *John Locke and Christianity: Contemporary Responses to "The Reasonableness of Christianity"* (Bristol: Thoemmes, 1997), p. 68.

[84] Concerning the similarities between Locke and Limborch on this issue, see Marshall, *John Locke: Resistance*, pp. 331–346.

to only a few simple principles, and Arthur Bury's *The Naked Gospel* (1690), which adopted a minimalist strategy in order to avoid the constraints of Trinitarian Christianity. These books demonstrate that, in some cases, the pursuit of the way of fundamentals could indeed lead to creedal minimalism. Nevertheless, an emphasis on the fundamentals of Christianity, potentially leading to creedal minimalism, is also present in the work of an author distant from all strands of English "theological liberalism" – namely, Thomas Hobbes, who delineated the fundamentals of Christianity in Chapter 43 of *Leviathan* (1651):

All that is Necessary to Salvation, is contained in two Vertues, Faith in Christ, and Obedience to Laws. The latter of these, if it were perfect, were enough to us. But because wee are all guilty of disobedience to Gods Law, not onely originally in Adam, but also actually by our own transgressions, there is required at our hands now, not onely Obedience for the rest of our time, but also a Remission of sins for the time past; which Remission is the reward of our Faith in Christ. That nothing else is Necessarily required to Salvation, is manifest from this, that the Kingdome of Heaven is shut to none but to Sinners; that is to say, to the disobedient, or transgressors of the Law; nor to them, in case they Repent, and Beleeve all the Articles of Christian Faith, Necessary to Salvation.[85]

In the same chapter of *Leviathan*, Hobbes subscribed to a Messianic Christology, in which Christ is, first and foremost, a "king":

By the name of Christ, is understood the King, which God had before promised by the Prophets of the Old Testament, to send into the world, to reign (over the Jews, and over such of other nations as should beleeve in him) under himself eternally; and to give them that eternall life, which was lost by the sin of Adam.[86]

In Hobbes's account, faith in Christ and obedience, which presupposes repentance, are "All that is Necessary to Salvation." Conversely, Locke believed that accepting and living by the fundamentals of Christianity was *necessary but not sufficient* to salvation. This important aspect of Locke's soteriology was obviously ignored by John Edwards and other critics, such as the London preacher William Payne, the Nonconformist minister and anti-Arminian theologian Stephen Lobb, the Oxford scholar and anti-Socinian writer Jonathan Edwards, and the anti-Calvinistic divine Daniel Whitby, all of whom thought that Locke's characterization of Jesus as the Messiah and his disregard of the satisfaction theory of atonement denoted creedal minimalism.[87] In the first of his four attacks on the *Reasonableness*, which provoked a bitter polemic with

---

[85] Thomas Hobbes, *Leviathan*, ed. C. B. Macpherson (London: Penguin, 1985), pp. 610–611.

[86] Ibid., p. 615.

[87] William Payne, *The Mystery of the Christian Faith and of the Blessed Trinity Vindicated* (London, 1697); Stephen Lobb, *The Growth of Error* (London, 1697); Jonathan Edwards, *A Preservative against Socinianism*, 3rd ed. (Oxford, 1698), pp. 46–47; Daniel Whitby, *A Paraphrase and Commentary on All the Epistles of the New Testament* (London, 1700), pp. 627–629.

Locke, John Edwards blamed this book for having ignored the New Testament epistles in favor of the Gospels alone and for having reduced the Gospel message to a rational creed, which could be summarized in one simple principle: "That nothing is required to be believed by any Christian man but this, that Jesus is the Messiah."[88] However, as Locke explained in the *Reasonableness* and repeated in its two vindications, faith in Jesus the Messiah, which entails repentance for sin and obedience to the divine moral law, is required to *become* a Christian, but is not enough to achieve salvation. To Locke, the faithful have to not only accept the three fundamentals, but also study the Bible conscientiously, because the study of Scripture is a significant element of the Christian life. According to Locke, acceptance of Jesus as the Messiah binds one to not only this article of faith, but to Scripture as a whole. Though, Locke argued that all that is necessary to be believed by Christians is in the four Gospels and the Acts of the Apostles and, when responding to Edwards, he challenged his opponent to prove that the Apostles' epistles contained anything new or essential to salvation.[89] Locke's insistence on the Christian duty to study the Bible without bias and in accordance with one's intellectual abilities – a task that could lead to divergent, and frequently mistaken, interpretations of Scripture – distinguishes his doctrine of the fundamentals from Hobbes's, Croft's, and Bury's minimalist positions. Therefore, I consider it incorrect to label Locke a "minimalist," and I agree with Victor Nuovo that Locke's position is not even a sort of "foundationalism," because to Locke belief in the fundamentals of Christianity is not a *basic* belief, but it is rather a *threshold* belief.[90] Briefly, to Locke, accepting the three fundamentals of Christianity, namely, faith, repentance, and obedience, is enough to *become* a Christian; but, after becoming a Christian, one also has to study Scripture diligently. All these things are required for salvation.

---

[88] John Edwards, *Some Thoughts concerning the Several Causes and Occasions of Atheism* (London, 1695), p. 105.

[89] Locke, "Second Vindication," pp. 87–90, 102–103, 151–152, 167, 198–200.

[90] Victor Nuovo, "Introduction" to Nuovo (ed.), *John Locke and Christianity*, pp. ix–xli (xxiv); Nuovo, *John Locke*, pp. 224–225.

3   A Scripture-Based Moralist Soteriology

Locke's doctrine of the fundamentals of Christianity was inspired mainly by his preoccupation with morality and salvation, whereas his soteriology had significant irenic implications. In *The Reasonableness of Christianity*, Locke described acceptance of the fundamentals of Christianity – that is, faith in Jesus the Messiah, repentance for sin, and obedience to the divine moral law – and the conscientious study of Scripture as necessary for salvation. He regarded the Law of Nature as divinely given and, hence, universally and eternally valid. His notion of the Law of Nature informed his political theory, which relied both on Scripture-based points and on rational arguments employing conceptual and terminological categories typical of natural theology. However, he believed in the superiority of the Law of Faith, delivered by Christ, both over the Law of Nature (knowable, at least in principle, by natural reason alone, consistent with natural reason, and confirmed by Christ) and over the Law of Moses (comprising a ceremonial part and a moral part – the Law of Works – identical to the Law of Nature). According to Locke, Christ not only reaffirmed the Law of Nature as a complete and authoritative system of moral rules, but also assured humanity of otherworldly rewards and sanctions and emphasized God's forgiveness of the repentant faithful who sincerely endeavor to obey the divine moral law. Thus, to Locke, the Law of Faith effectively promotes the practice of morality and the development of moral character and enables human beings to pursue salvation. Maintaining the necessity both of good works and of acceptance of God's assisting grace for salvation, Locke rejected predestination as unscriptural, irrational, and inconsistent with human freedom and responsibility. For the same reason, he denied original sin – a doctrine he considered unscriptural, irrational, and incompatible with individual responsibility – and he excluded the satisfaction theory of atonement from his account of the Christian religion. In an attempt to justify this exclusion, in *A Second Vindication of the Reasonableness of Christianity* he defined satisfaction as a disputed doctrine not grounded in Scripture and he clarified that, in the *Reasonableness*, he had explained only principles plainly expounded in Scripture and hence acceptable to all Christians.[1] However, some of his manuscripts denote his dislike for the satisfaction theory, to which he preferred the Arminians' governmental theory of atonement – a theory compatible with his moralist soteriology.

Natural Theology, Biblical Theology, and Natural Law Theory

Locke believed that disregarding the three fundamentals of Christianity when reading the Bible was likely to lead to either one of two equally extreme, albeit diametrically opposed, outcomes – antinomianism and deism, both of which he rejected as unreasonable, inconsistent with Scripture, and detrimental to salvation.[2] Locke blamed antinomianism, and more generally predestinarianism, for denying the efficacy of good works to salvation. However, he considered deism ineffective to morality and salvation because deists relied on natural reason alone. They thought that natural reason actually knew the Law of Nature completely and perfectly and was thus able to establish a sound system of ethics, without any need of a supernatural revelation. Conversely, although Locke regarded morality in itself as rational and demonstrable, he was skeptical about the human capacity to *actually* demonstrate morality. Moreover, he was skeptical about the prospect of enlarging human knowledge in religious matters through the operation of natural reason alone. This is why he had recourse to Christian revelation. And this is another point of similarity between Locke's religious thought and the Socinian theological tradition. One of the main tenets of Socinianism is indeed that God's Revealed Word is superior to the Law of Nature.[3] This is a significant difference between the Socinians and the Magisterial Reformers, whose position on this subject is detailed in Philip Melanchthon's *Loci Communes* (1521). According to Melanchthon, human beings have an innate knowledge of God and of the divine law in its entirety – a sort of knowledge not dependent on revelation.

---

[1] John Locke, "A Second Vindication of the Reasonableness of Christianity," in John Locke, *Vindications of the Reasonableness of Christianity*, ed. Victor Nuovo (Oxford: Clarendon Press, 2012), pp. 27–233 (227).

[2] See Chapter 1.

[3] For the Socinians' emphasis on the saving power of God's Revealed Word, see Faustus Socinus, "De Jesu Christo Servatore," in *Bibliotheca Fratrum Polonorum quos Unitarios vocant*, 9 vols. (Irenopoli – Eleutheropoli [Amsterdam], "post annum Domini 1656" [1665–1692]), vol. 2, pp. 115–246; Johann Crell, *Ad librum Hugonis Grotii … de satisfactione Christi* (Racoviae, 1623). Socinus wrote *De Jesu Christo Servatore* after a heated discussion with the Huguenot pastor Jacques Couet in Basel in 1576. This treatise was completed in 1578 and first published in 1594 in Poland. Crell defended Socinus's views on salvation in his book of 1623, written to rejoin Grotius's attack on Socinus in *Defensio fidei Catholicae de satisfactione Christi adversus Faustum Socinum* (1617). See Sarah Mortimer, "Human and Divine Justice in the Works of Grotius and the Socinians," in Sarah Mortimer, John Robertson (eds.), *The Intellectual Consequences of Religious Heterodoxy, 1600–1750* (Leiden: Brill, 2012), pp. 75–94 (76–81).

Melanchthon, like other Magisterial Reformers, identified the divine law with a perfect Law of Nature, which Christian revelation had restated and clarified.[4] He argued that Christian revelation, with the promise of grace (which he particularly emphasized), was necessitated because of sin, but he did not make a sharp distinction between natural and revealed morals. He considered the revealed moral law as simply more thorough and clear, but not different in its tenets and aims, than the Law of Nature accessible to unassisted reason. Briefly, Melanchthon and the other Magisterial Reformers thought that faith in God and a correct understanding of the divine law were fundamentally grounded in human nature. Socinus and his followers rejected this view. They thought that natural reason alone could understand the Law of Nature and, hence, natural rights. However, they judged the Law of Nature insufficient to salvation, because it disposed human beings to merely the preservation of earthly goods. They considered saving faith – namely, Christian faith – unattainable by natural reason alone. Therefore, Socinus and his disciples distinguished true and saving religious belief from human nature. This distinction supported their emphasis on the role of free will in the pursuit of salvation. According to the Socinians, before Christian revelation humanity had no assurance of an afterlife with reward and punishment and of God's mercy. Only after Christian revelation could human beings know of the true faith and choose to embrace it and, thus, effectively pursue salvation.[5] To the Socinians, saving faith originated in one's free choice to accept the assistance of God's grace. While they thought that the possibility to freely accept the assistance of God's grace was rooted in natural liberty, they believed that one could know of God's assisting grace only thanks to Christian revelation as recorded in Scripture. They argued that Scripture contains all information necessary to salvation, including Christ's moral precepts, which they considered more coherent, convincing, and rewarding than the Law of Nature. To the Socinians, Christian revelation indeed offered a better prospect than worldly benefits – the prospect of eternal salvation. Prior to Christian revelation, human morality was still imperfect, because it focused on worldly interests alone. Only after Christ's ministry on earth could humanity comply with moral standards facilitating the pursuit of salvation; and these moral standards, in some cases, clashed with the dictates of the Law of Nature. This position was at the origin

---

[4] Philipp Melanchthon, *On Christian Doctrine: Loci Communes 1555*, trans. and ed. Clyde L. Manschrek (Oxford: Oxford University Press, 1965), pp. 51–53, 73–75.

[5] On the Socinians' distinction between human nature and saving religious belief, see Sarah Mortimer, "Human Liberty and Human Nature in the Works of Faustus Socinus and His Readers," *Journal of the History of Ideas*, 70:2 (2009): pp. 191–211; Sarah Mortimer, "Freedom, Virtue and Socinian Heterodoxy," in Quentin Skinner, Martin van Gelderen (eds.), *Freedom and the Construction of Europe*, 2 vols. (Cambridge: Cambridge University Press, 2013), vol. 1, pp. 77–93.

of the Socinians' radical pacifism and advocacy of non-violence and non-resistance. Socinus and his disciples admitted that the Law of Nature disposed human beings to defend their natural rights, namely, their life, property, and freedom, when harmed by others. Nevertheless, they inferred from the New Testament (particularly from Jesus' imperative to turn the other cheek)[6] that doing violence to another human being, even for reasons of self-defense or to preserve one's rights against a despotic power, would hinder the attainment of the supreme good – eternal beatitude.[7] In the seventeenth century, Socinian political writers like Samuel Przypkowski, Johann Crell, and Jonas Schlichting continued to advocate non-violence and non-resistance to the government, although they made some concessions to merely defensive warfare waged by the civil magistrate. They argued that it was the civil magistrate's task and duty to protect the citizens' civil interests, which were grounded in their natural rights. One such right was liberty of religion. Socinus's theory that acceptance of, or resistance to, God's assisting grace was a matter of free individual choice led him and his followers to endorse extensive religious toleration.[8] Nonetheless, according to the Socinians, if the rulers neglected their duty or abused their powers and infringed upon the citizens' rights (including, among others, religious liberty), the subjects could *not* resist nor revolt against the political authorities in order to defend their civil interests – unless they unreasonably renounced the opportunity to achieve eternal salvation, which the Socinians considered immensely more valuable than any worldly good.

Locke shared the Socinians' opinion that Christian revelation was superior to the Law of Nature. However, he disagreed with the Socinian idea that God's Revealed Word contradicted and invalidated some elements of the Law of Nature, such as the rights to self-preservation and self-defense. Here, a discussion of Locke's justification of natural rights is needed, in order to understand his approach to the natural and revealed law and, thus, his divergence from

---

[6] Matt. 5:39: "But I say unto you, That ye resist not evil: but whosoever shall smite thee on thy right cheek, turn to him the other also."

[7] Socinus, "De Jesu"; Samuel Przypkowski, *Dissertatio de pace et concordia ecclesiae* (Eleutheropoli [Amsterdam], 1628); Johann Crell, *Prima ethices elementa* (Racoviae, 1635); Johann Crell, *Vindiciae pro religionis libertate* (Eleutheropoli [Amsterdam], 1637); Jonas Schlichting, *Confessio fidei Christianae* (n.p., 1642). Przypkowski's *Dissertatio* and Crell's *Vindiciae* were translated into English: Johann Crell, *A Learned and Exceeding Well-Compiled Vindication of Liberty of Religion*, trans. N. Y. (London, 1646); Samuel Przypkowski, *Dissertatio de pace, &c. Or, A Discourse Touching the Peace and Concord of the Church* (London, 1653). While the English translation of Crell's *Vindiciae* is commonly attributed to the irenicist Scottish Calvinist minister John Dury, the translation of Przypkowski's *Dissertatio* is attributed by some to Dury and by others to the English anti-Trinitarian John Biddle. I have found no evidence for these attributions. On the Socinians' pacifism and advocacy of non-resistance, see Mortimer, "Human Liberty," pp. 194–195; Sarah Mortimer, *Reason and Religion in the English Revolution: The Challenge of Socinianism* (Cambridge: Cambridge University Press, 2010), pp. 18–20.

[8] See Chapter 6.

Socinianism concerning this subject. In this respect, Locke was not a Socinian. He was a natural law theorist, and his natural law theory is grounded in both natural and biblical theology. Whereas he decisively turned to biblical theology to continue his moral investigation in *The Reasonableness of Christianity*, natural as well as biblical theological points already played a role in his political works, most prominently in *Two Treatises of Government*. Locke indeed described divine revelation as complementing and sustaining natural reason not only in *An Essay concerning Human Understanding* and his later writings on religion, but also in his political writings. In the *Second Treatise of Civil Government*, he provided mixed arguments, based on rational reasoning and scriptural revelation, to justify natural rights, since both natural theology and biblical theology enabled him to emphasize God's dignity as a creator and lawgiver. He even regarded biblical revelation as sufficient to establish natural rights, since he saw Scripture as infallible and, hence, trumping rational doubt.[9] In fact, when summarizing the findings of the *First Treatise* and making a premise to his explanation of equality and natural rights at the start of the *Second Treatise*, he made reference to the Old Testament (which he referred to copiously in *Two Treatises of Government*):

Adam had not either by natural Right of Fatherhood, or by positive Donation from God, any such Authority over his Children, or Dominion over the World as is pretended. ... It is impossible that the Rulers now on Earth, should make any benefit, or derive any the least shadow of Authority from that, which is held to be the Fountain of all Power, Adam's Private Dominion and Paternal Jurisdiction.[10]

It is worth specifying that, here, Locke is talking of *natural equality*, which, as Bruce Hunt has pointed out, "is inclusive of all human beings [and] implies rights to life, liberty, and property."[11] This concept of equality, which affirms universal human dignity, is different from the other concept of equality entrenched in Locke's political theory – namely, *law-abiding equality*, "which includes the potentially very large subset of people who sufficiently recognize and abide by the principles of civility and decency codified in natural law"[12]

---

[9] Several scholars have observed, correctly, that Locke's theism and reliance on Scripture had a significant impact on his political theory. See, for instance, Kirstie M. McClure, *Judging Rights: Lockean Politics and the Limits of Consent* (Ithaca: Cornell University Press, 1996); Richard Ashcraft, "Religion and Lockean Natural Rights," in Irene Bloom, J. Paul Martin, Wayne L. Proudfoot (eds.), *Religious Diversity and Human Rights* (New York: Columbia University Press, 1996), pp. 195–212; Kim Ian Parker, *The Biblical Politics of John Locke* (Waterloo: Wilfried Laurier University Press, 2004), pp. 125–146; Yechiel J. M. Leiter, *John Locke's Political Philosophy and the Hebrew Bible* (Cambridge: Cambridge University Press, 2018).

[10] John Locke, *Two Treatises of Government*, rev. ed., ed. Peter Laslett (Cambridge: Cambridge University Press, 1988), p. 267.

[11] Bruce A. Hunt Jr., "Locke on Equality," *Political Research Quarterly*, 69:3 (2016): pp. 546–556 (546).

[12] Ibid.

and who, therefore, are able and entitled to exercise political rights. Concerning every human being's right to property acquisition, too, Locke referred to Scripture. In Chapter 5 of the *Second Treatise*, "Of Property," he maintained:

Whether we consider natural *Reason*, which tells us, that Men, being once born, have a right to their Preservation, and consequently to Meat and Drink, and such other things, as Nature affords for their Subsistence: Or *Revelation*, which gives us an account of those Grants God made of the World to *Adam*, and to *Noah*, and his Sons, 'tis very clear, that God, as King *David* says, *Psal.* CXV. xvi. *has given the Earth to the Children of Men*, given it to Mankind in common. But this being supposed, it seems to some a very great difficulty, how any one should ever come to have a *Property* in any thing: I will not content my self to answer, That if it be difficult to make out *Property*, upon a supposition, that God gave the World to *Adam* and his Posterity in common; it is impossible that any Man, but one universal Monarch, should have any *Property*, upon a supposition, that God gave the World to *Adam*, and his Heirs in Succession, exclusive of all the rest of his Posterity. But I shall endeavour to shew, how Men might come to have a *property* in several parts of that which God gave to Mankind in common, and that without any express Compact of all the Commoners.[13]

Below in the same chapter, Locke wrote:

And thus, without supposing any private Dominion, and property in *Adam*, over all the World, exclusive of all other Men, which can no way be proved, nor any ones Property be made out from it; but supposing the *World* given as it was to the Children of Men *in common*, we see how *labour* could make Men distinct titles to several parcels of it, for their private uses; wherein there could be no doubt of Right, no room for quarrel.[14]

These Scripture-based arguments from the *Second Treatise* represent a continuation of Locke's attack on Robert Filmer's patriarchalism in the *First Treatise*. Locke disapproved of Filmer's theory that "not only *Adam*, but the succeding *Patriarchs* had, by Right of Father-hood, Royal Authority over their Children [and] were endowed with Kingly Power" – which entails that "Civil Power ... is by Divine Institution."[15] Interpretations of Adam as *monarch* were fundamentally based on Gen. 1:28 – a biblical verse relating God's donation to Adam of "dominion over the fish of the sea, and over the fowl of the air, and over every living thing that moveth upon the earth." Conversely, drawing also on Ps. 115:16, which maintains that "the earth hath [the Lord] given to the children of men" and thus, in Locke's words, "to Mankind in common," Locke argued that the Bible referred to Adam as *representative of humankind*.[16] Therefore, Scripture-based arguments play a significant role in Locke's rejection of divine-right theory.

---

[13] Locke, *Two Treatises*, pp. 285–286.   [14] Ibid., p. 296.

[15] Robert Filmer, *Patriarcha, or the Natural Power of Kings* (London, 1680), p. 12.

[16] Locke, *Two Treatises*, pp. 286, 156–171; Leiter, *John Locke's Political Philosophy*, pp. 171–173, 210–211.

Locke's reliance on Scripture also informs *The Reasonableness of Christianity*, although this book draws mainly on the New Testament, to which the *Two Treatises*, conversely, devote scarce attention. In both the *Reasonableness* and the *Second Treatise*, Locke substantiated his belief in the intrinsic rationality and eternal validity of the Law of Nature, and hence of natural rights, with rational arguments typical of a natural theological approach. These arguments underpin and combine with Scripture-based points, which, even though being sufficient thanks to the infallibility of Scripture, require prior rational assent to the contents of Scripture as divinely revealed. In this respect, Locke followed his conviction, expounded in *An Essay concerning Human Understanding*, that "it still belongs to *Reason*, to judge of the Truth of [a proposition's] being a revelation, and of the signification of the Words, wherein it is delivered."[17] To Locke, natural reason and divine revelation were complementary and mutually sustaining. Natural reason, if utilized properly, could not only grant assent to revealed propositions *above reason*, but also discover truths *according to reason* – namely, truths knowable to natural reason alone and, in some cases, also revealed in Scripture. One of such truths *according to reason* is God's existence. Locke argued in the *Essay* that natural reason could demonstrate God's existence through the argument from design and the anthropological argument.[18] And acknowledging the existence of a divine creator and legislator is logically required to recognize that there is a divine moral law. This law is the Law of Nature, which Locke always judged intrinsically rational and hence consistent with and acceptable to natural reason, despite the latter's repeated failure to grasp on its own the content of this law in its entirety – a failure Locke acknowledged in both the *Essay* and the *Reasonableness*.[19] Briefly, according to Locke, rational thinking enables human beings to conceive of a God-given moral law and, consequently, to accept its content, which is knowable (at least if not only in principle) to natural reason alone, consistent with natural reason, and revealed completely and plainly in Scripture. In the *Second Treatise*, too, Locke insisted on human beings' *rational* recognition of their dependence on a divine creator and lawgiver in his justification of natural rights and of the duty to preserve oneself, as well as "the rest of Mankind." He indeed described the state of nature with the following words at the start of Chapter 2 in the *Second Treatise*:

A *State of perfect Freedom* to order their Actions, and dispose of their Possessions, and Persons as they think fit, within the bounds of the Law of Nature, without asking leave, or depending upon the Will of any other Man. A *State* also *of Equality*, wherein all the

---

[17] John Locke, *An Essay concerning Human Understanding*, ed. Peter H. Nidditch (Oxford: Clarendon Press, 1975), IV.xviii.8, p. 694.
[18] See Chapter 1.   [19] See Chapters 1 and 2.

Power and Jurisdiction is reciprocal, no one having more than another: there being nothing more evident, than that Creatures of the same species and rank promiscuously born to all the same advantages of Nature, and the use of the same faculties, should also be equal one amongst another without Subordination or Subjection, unless the Lord and Master of them all, should by any manifest Declaration of his Will set one above another, and confer on him by an evident and clear appointment an undoubted Right to Dominion and Sovereignty.[20]

Given that Locke opposed divine-right theory, the closing remarks in this passage imply that natural rights are divinely established and all humans have an equal duty to respect others' natural rights. These rights and duties are logically correlative and equally important elements of the divine, rational moral law that governs the state of nature – that is, the Law of Nature.[21] As regards Locke's state of nature, several scholars, including, among others, John Dunn and Richard Ashcraft, have characterized it as a merely fictional, theoretical analysis of interpersonal relations or as an account of the human condition in the absence of a political society.[22] However, this characterization of the state of nature as a mere "fiction" is inconsistent with Locke's parallel between the natural state of humankind and Adam's condition as a *fact* described in Scripture, which Locke utilized as a political document. On this point, I agree with Barry Hindess that "the idea of an original condition of freedom and equality played a central role in Locke's argument," for it served the important purpose "to undermine the view that humans were born into a natural condition of subjection to the rule of others."[23] Furthermore, in the *Second Treatise*, Locke expressly maintained that there are and have been people in the state of nature.[24] Thus, I think that Locke believed in the historicity of the state of nature, which he described through both examples drawn from Scripture and rational explanations employing terms and concepts typical of natural theology. Concerning property acquisition, too, Locke combined his consideration of Adam's condition as a *fact* with a rational clarification, which was grounded in natural theology in that his anthropocentrism was founded on his religious worldview. In Chapter 5 of the *Second Treatise*,

---

[20] Locke, *Two Treatises*, p. 269.

[21] Ibid., p. 271. See A. John Simmons, *The Lockean Theory of Rights* (Princeton: Princeton University Press, 1992), pp. 68–120.

[22] John Dunn, *The Political Thought of John Locke: An Historical Account of the Argument of the "Two Treatises of Government"* (Cambridge: Cambridge University Press, 1969), pp. 97, 101, 113; John Dunn, "The Contemporary Political Significance of John Locke's Conception of Civil Society," *Iyyun: The Jerusalem Philosophical Quarterly*, 45 (1996): pp. 103–124; Richard Ashcraft, "Locke's State of Nature: Historical Fact or Moral Fiction?," *American Political Science Review*, 62:3 (1968): pp. 898–915.

[23] Barry Hindess, "Locke's State of Nature," *History of the Human Sciences*, 20:3 (2007): pp. 1–20 (3–4).

[24] Locke, *Two Treatises*, pp. 276–277.

Locke's reference to the "Grants God made of the World to *Adam*" is indeed followed by these words:

God, who hath given the World to Men in common, hath also given them reason to make use of it to the best advantage of Life, and convenience. The Earth, and all that is therein, is given to Men for the Support and Comfort of their being. And though all the Fruits it naturally produces, and Beasts it feeds, belong to Mankind in common, as they are produced by the spontaneous hand of Nature; and no body has originally a private Dominion, exclusive of the rest of Mankind, in any of them, as they are thus in their natural state: yet being given for the use of Men, there must of necessity be a means *to appropriate* them some way or other before they can be of any use, or at all beneficial to any particular Man. . . .. Though the Earth, and all inferior Creatures be common to all Men, yet every Man has a *Property* in his own *Person*. This no Body has any Right to but himself. The *Labour* of his Body, and the *Work* of his Hands, we may say, are properly his. Whatsoever then he removes out of the State that Nature hath provided, and left it in, he hath mixed his *Labour* with, and joyned to it something that is his own, and thereby makes it his *Property*.[25]

Finally, concerning the duty to preserve oneself and "the rest of Mankind," Locke essentially adopted the "Golden Rule" obligation to "love thy neighbour as thyself," which is present in Christ's teaching – precisely in Mark 12:31 – and, albeit expressed in different terms, in the Old Testament too (e.g., in Deut. 6:5 and Lev. 19:9-18).[26] However, for this biblical commandment to be acceptable to humanity, it requires contents compatible with reason and experience – contents that Locke spelled out in Chapter 2 of the *Second Treatise*:

For Men being all the Workmanship of one Omnipotent, and infinitely wise Maker; All the Servants of one Sovereign Master, sent into the World by his order, and about his business; they are his Property, whose Workmanship they are, made to last during his, not one another's Pleasure. And, being furnished with like Faculties, sharing all in one Community of Nature, there cannot be supposed any such *Subordination* among us that may Authorize us to destroy one another, as if we were made for one another's uses, as the inferior ranks of Creatures are for ours. Every one, as he is *bound to preserve himself*, and not to quit his Station wilfully, so by the like reason, when his own Preservation comes not in competition, ought he, as much as he can, *to preserve the rest of Mankind*, and may not unless it be to do Justice on an Offender, take away, or impair the life, or what tends to the Preservation of the Life, the Liberty, Health, Limb, or Goods of another.[27]

In this passage from the *Second Treatise*, Locke described human beings as God's "Property," while in an above-quoted passage from the same text he

---

[25] Ibid., pp. 286–288.
[26] Ian Harris, *The Mind of John Locke: A Study of Political Theory in Its Intellectual Setting* (Cambridge: Cambridge University Press, 1994), pp. 219–222; Leiter, *John Locke's Political Philosophy*, p. 213.
[27] Locke, *Two Treatises*, p. 271.

claimed that "every Man has a *Property* in his own *Person*." However, these two statements do not contradict each other. In the passage on human beings owning themselves, Locke concentrated on interpersonal dealings with the purpose of stressing freedom from interference by others, as is also proven by the next sentence ("This [i.e., one's person] no Body has any Right to but himself"). Conversely, in the passage on divine ownership, he focused on the relation between God and humanity in order to emphasize all human beings' duty toward God. And this duty goes hand in hand with freedom from interference by others, as is also demonstrated by Locke's statement, in the passage on divine ownership, that "there cannot be supposed any such *Subordination* among us that may Authorize us to destroy one another, as if we were made for one another's uses."

Briefly, Locke's natural law theory, which encompasses both natural rights and duties, is neither grounded merely in rational arguments, nor rooted only in Scripture-based points. He actually employed mixed arguments in justifying natural rights and duties, since he saw natural reason and scriptural revelation as complementary and mutually sustaining. Thus, Locke's natural law theory, which relies on a view of God as the legislator of the moral law, stands on both natural and biblical theology. Yet, he considered Scripture infallible and hence sufficient to establish natural rights and duties. Concerning Locke's drawing on Scripture in his political thought, Yechiel Leiter has argued, in a recent and extremely erudite book, that Locke was a political Hebraist, given his use of Scripture, particularly of the Old Testament, as a political document in *Two Treatises of Government*.[28] In this regard, I would like to point out that Locke's theological writings emphasize Christ's role as restorer of the divinely given moral law, king, and supreme archetype or model for humanity. This provides Locke's political theology with an eschatological, Messianic, and inherently Christian character.[29] Therefore, if we accept the thesis that Locke was a political Hebraist in that he drew heavily on the Old Testament in his major political writing, I deem it more correct to define him as a *Christian* political Hebraist, and as one whose political theory definitely belongs to the natural law tradition.

In order to appreciate the distance between Locke's and the Socinians' views on the natural and revealed law, it is worth noting that Locke's natural theological reflections, albeit developed in combination with Scripture-based points, are in general agreement with the ideas of seventeenth-century natural law theorists such as Hugo Grotius and, above all, Samuel Pufendorf.[30] Grotius considered the Law of Nature as created by God. This is certainly a

---

[28] Leiter, *John Locke's Political Philosophy*.   [29] See Chapters 5 and 6.
[30] Richard Tuck, *Natural Rights Theories: Their Origin and Development* (Cambridge: Cambridge University Press, 1979), pp. 168–173; Jean-Fabien Spitz, "Le concept d'état de nature

point in common between Grotius and Locke. However, in *De jure belli ac pacis* (1625), Grotius declared the Law of Nature to be objectively valid even if we were to suppose "that there is no God, or that he takes no Care of human Affairs."[31] Such a move implied a disentanglement of natural law from theology and was definitely foreign to Locke's thinking. Conversely, Pufendorf reaffirmed the indispensable theological foundation of natural law and combined it with a focus on individual needs in *De jure naturae et gentium* (1672). Accordingly, he saw the state as a moral person whose will is the sum of the citizens' individual wills and aims to their preservation.[32] These concepts are compatible with Locke's views on the Law of Nature, the civil magistrate's tasks, and the foundations of political power. Starting with his *Essays on the Law of Nature* of 1664, Locke also drew on English theologians belonging to the natural law tradition, such as Robert Sanderson, Nathaniel Culverwell, and, above all, Richard Hooker, whose eight-volume book *Of the Laws of Ecclesiastical Politie* (1594–1617) was his main source on scholastic natural law.[33] Locke never abandoned the scholastic belief in the intrinsic rationality and demonstrability (at least in principle) of the moral law, but in his mature political works he stressed the individual level associated to natural rights. His emphasis on individual needs, rights, and duties was in line with the seventeenth-century natural law tradition, particularly with Pufendorf's thought, but diverged significantly from the Socinian understanding of the natural and revealed law, mainly concerning self-preservation and self-defense.

Both the Socinians and Locke regarded Christian revelation as superior to the Law of Nature, given the salvific power of Christ's message. However, Socinus and his followers considered the natural rights to self-preservation and self-defense superseded by the Christian imperative of non-violence. To

---

chez Locke et chez Pufendorf: Remarques sur le rapport entre épistémologie et philosophie morale au XVIIe siècle," *Archives de Philosophie*, 49:3 (1986): pp. 437–452; Michael J. Seidler, "The Politics of Self-Preservation: Toleration and Identity in Pufendorf and Locke," in T. J. Hochstrasser, Peter Schröder (eds.), *Early Modern Natural Law Theories: Contexts and Strategies in the Early Enlightenment* (Dordrecht: Kluwer, 2003), pp. 227–255.

[31] Hugo Grotius, *The Rights of War and Peace*, ed. Richard Tuck, 3 vols. (Indianapolis: Liberty Fund, 2005), vol. 1, p. 89.

[32] Samuel Pufendorf, *Of the Law of Nature and Nations*, trans. Basil Kennett (London, 1729).

[33] Richard Hooker, *Of the Laws of Ecclesiastical Polity*, ed. W. Speed Hill, 2 vols. (Binghamton: Folger Library, 1993). See Wolfgang von Leyden, "Introduction" to John Locke, *Essays on the Law of Nature*, ed. Wolfgang von Leyden (Oxford: Clarendon Press, 1954), pp. 1–92 (43–60); John Colman, *John Locke's Moral Philosophy* (Edinburgh: Edinburgh University Press, 1983), pp. 187–198; Harris, *Mind of John Locke*, pp. 219–223; Alan P. F. Sell, *John Locke and the Eighteenth-Century Divines* (Cardiff: University of Wales Press, 1997), pp. 112–113; Jeremy Waldron, *God, Locke, and Equality: Christian Foundations in Locke's Political Thought* (Cambridge: Cambridge University Press, 2002), pp. 154–156; Leiter, *John Locke's Political Philosophy*, pp. 121–127, 158–159, 189–190, 212–213.

Locke, conversely, the Law of Nature gives us an inalienable right and duty to preserve and make good use of the life that God has given us, of the goods produced or acquired through our work, and of the freedom to make use of our persons and possessions while respecting others' like rights.[34] According to Locke, Christ's precepts had neither nullified nor replaced any element of the Law of Nature. In *The Reasonableness of Christianity*, he argued that Christ had restored the Law of Nature in its entirety, complementing it with newly revealed truths concerning otherworldly rewards and sanctions and God's mercy, as I explain below in this chapter. Therefore, after Christian revelation, we still have a right and a duty (toward God) to preserve our (and others') natural rights, even when this necessitates a violent reaction to those violating such rights. Under the Christian covenant, one still can, and must, repel an aggressor and resist or even revolt against a despotic power. Thus, the *Reasonableness* does not contradict the nineteenth and last chapter of the *Second Treatise*, "Of the Dissolution of Government." This chapter argues that, under the social contract, the people may, as a last resort, instigate a revolution against the government when the latter acts against the citizens' civil interests. This revolution's aim would be to replace a government that abuses its powers, or neglects its duties, with a new government that will serve the citizens' rights sanctioned by the divinely given, eternally valid Law of Nature.[35] Locke indeed thought that the civil magistrate's powers flow not only from the citizens' consent, but also from the Law of Nature, which the rulers must respect when making and enforcing the civil law.[36] The magistrates who ignore the Law of Nature, and thus disregard their subjects' natural and civil rights, should expect legitimate resistance and even revolution from the citizens. This is why the threat of rebellion, acting as a warning to rulers, makes tyranny less likely to occur.[37] In conclusion, according to Locke, even under the Christian covenant the Law of Nature cannot be disregarded or abolished, given its divine origin and nature.

Law of Nature, Law of Moses, Law of Faith

In *The Reasonableness of Christianity*, Locke openly described the Law of Nature as divinely established and, hence, universally and eternally valid.[38] This law, which can be "promulgated . . . by the light of Nature, or the voice of Revelation" (especially traditional, namely, scriptural, revelation) "stands as

---

[34] Locke, *Two Treatises*, pp. 269–272.   [35] Ibid., pp. 406–428.   [36] Ibid., pp. 313–314.

[37] Ibid., pp. 414–416. On the context and development of Locke's arguments for resistance and revolution, see Richard Ashcraft, *Revolutionary Politics and Locke's Two Treatises of Government* (Princeton: Princeton University Press, 1986), pp. 286–405, 521–589.

[38] John Locke, *The Reasonableness of Christianity, As Delivered in the Scriptures*, ed. John C. Higgins-Biddle (Oxford: Clarendon Press, 1999), pp. 13–15.

an Eternal Rule to all Men," since it is "the Will and Law of ... God," as is explained in *An Essay concerning Human Understanding* and the *Second Treatise of Civil Government*.[39] Locke never discarded this concept of the Law of Nature, as is shown by what he wrote on this matter in *A Paraphrase and Notes on the Epistles of St Paul*. In commenting on Paul's Epistle to the Romans, Locke indeed talked of a "natural and eternal rule of rectitude, which is made known to men, by the light of reason" – in other words, "that rule of rectitude which God had given to mankind, in giving them reason."[40] In the *Reasonableness*, Locke also talked of the Law of Nature as a law of convenience promoting utility. Most human beings know some of its elements in the form of prescriptions of civil law or moral principles formulated by philosophers.[41] However, as I have explained in Chapter 1, the *Reasonableness* clarifies that convenience, which is equivalent to utility, is not the basis for accepting natural law principles and, consequently, to act morally.[42] Convenience or utility, to Locke, is rather a *consequence* of obedience to the Law of Nature – *not* the *motivation* behind obedience to this moral law, which he considered divinely given, intrinsically rational, eternally valid, and universally binding. In the *Reasonableness*, he did not abandon his conviction in the inherent rationality and theoretical demonstrability of morality, but he maintained that, before Christ's ministry on earth, unassisted reason had always failed to grasp the Law of Nature in its entirety:

'Tis too hard a task for unassisted Reason, to establish Morality in all its parts upon its true foundation; with a clear and convincing light.... Such trains of reasoning the greatest part of Mankind have neither leisure to weigh; nor, for want of Education and Use, skill to judge of. We see how unsuccessful in this, the attempts of Philosophers were before our Saviour's time. How short their several Systems came of the perfection of a true and compleat *Morality*, is very visible.... Experience shews that the knowledge of Morality, by meer natural light, (how agreeable soever it be to it) makes but slow progress, and little advance in the World. And the reason of it is not hard to be found in Men's Necessities, Passions, Vices, and mistaken Interests; which turn their thoughts another way. And the designing Leaders, as well as following Herd, find it not to their purpose to imploy much of their Meditations this way. Or whatever else was the cause, 'tis plain in fact, that humane reason unassisted, failed Men in its great and Proper business of *Morality*. It never from unquestionable Principles, by clear deductions, made out an entire body of the *Law of Nature*.[43]

According to Locke, ecclesiastical tradition, priestcraft, and power politics were the other factors that had negatively affected the human capacity to

---

[39] Locke, *Essay*, II.xxviii.8, p. 352; Locke, *Two Treatises*, p. 358; Locke, *Essay*, I.iii.6, p. 69.

[40] John Locke, *A Paraphrase and Notes on the Epistles of St Paul to the Galatians, 1 and 2 Corinthians, Romans, Ephesians*, ed. Arthur W. Wainwright, 2 vols. (Oxford: Clarendon Press, 1987), Rom. 2:26, vol. 2, p. 502, Rom. 1:32, vol. 2, p. 496.

[41] Locke, *Reasonableness*, pp. 151–154.   [42] Ibid., p. 154.   [43] Ibid., pp. 148–150.

comprehend and observe the Law of Nature. He lived in a time that witnessed numerous attacks on priestcraft. Deists like Herbert of Cherbury in *De religione gentilium* (1663, posthumous) and Charles Blount in *Great Is Diana of the Ephesians* (1680) argued that natural religion had been corrupted, in ancient times, by priestly frauds, which had led to the making of institutional religions founded on abstruse dogmas and supported by oppressive ecclesiastical institutions.[44] Moreover, a virulent attack on priestcraft is present in the poetic political satire *Absalom and Achitophel* (1681) by John Dryden, whose brother-in-law, Sir Robert Howard, attempted to explain "how religion has been corrupted, almost from the beginning, by priestcraft" in his *History of Religion* (1694). Locke shared these authors' hostility to priestcraft.[45] In some of his manuscripts, he rejected the clerical interpretations of the Bible endorsed by Catholics, whom he called "Romanists."[46] Furthermore, in his assault on Filmer in the first of the *Two Treatises of Government*, he argued for the necessity to interpret Scripture in accordance with principles of reason – not authoritative tradition.[47] In this regard, he wrote in *A Second Vindication of the Reasonableness of Christianity*: "I know no other infallible guide, but the Spirit of God in the Scriptures."[48] Furthermore, when dealing with the imperfection and abuse of words in the *Essay*, he stated that "the Precepts of Natural Religion are plain, and very intelligible to all Mankind";[49] but "the several *Sects* of Philosophy and Religion" had magnified the natural difficulties of the use of language by coining "insignificant" words, "either affecting something singular, and out of the way of common apprehensions, or to support some strange Opinions, or cover some Weakness of their Hypothesis."[50] Moreover, as I have explained in Chapter 1, in the *Reasonableness* Locke blamed ancient philosophers for relying on natural reason alone and for separating morality from religion – an attitude that, in Locke's opinion, had fostered priestcraft.[51] Finally, he argued in the same book that the imperfection and weakness of

---

[44] For an English translation of *De religione gentilium*, see Edward Herbert of Cherbury, *Pagan Religion*, trans. and ed. John A. Butler (Ottawa: Dovehouse, 1996).

[45] On Locke's views on priestcraft, see John Marshall, *John Locke: Resistance, Religion and Responsibility* (Cambridge: Cambridge University Press, 1994), pp. 353–357, 405–410; Mark Goldie, "John Locke, the Early Lockeans, and Priestcraft," *Intellectual History Review*, 28:1 (2018): pp. 125–144; James A. T. Lancaster, "From Matters of Faith to Matters of Fact: The Problem of Priestcraft in Early Modern England," *Intellectual History Review*, 28:1 (2018): pp. 145–165. On the debate on priestcraft in early Enlightenment England, see Justin Champion, *The Pillars of Priestcraft Shaken: The Church of England and Its Enemies 1660–1730* (Cambridge: Cambridge University Press, 1992).

[46] John Marshall, "Locke, Socinianism, 'Socinianism,' and Unitarianism," in M. A. Stewart (ed.), *English Philosophy in the Age of Locke* (Oxford: Clarendon Press, 2000), pp. 111–182 (145).

[47] Locke, *Two Treatises*, pp. 141–263.   [48] Locke, "Second Vindication," p. 176.

[49] Locke, *Essay*, III.ix.23, p. 490.   [50] Ibid., III.x.2, p. 491.

[51] Locke, *Reasonableness*, pp. 143–144.

human nature make human beings prone to be misled by their own mistakes and by priestly frauds as well.[52]

Locke believed that, because of human imperfection, the abuse of words by philosophers as well as priests, and priestcraft in ancient times, God had reaffirmed the Law of Nature through the covenant of works, establishing the Law of Moses. This law consisted of a ceremonial part and a moral part, the latter of which Locke termed "the Law of Works" and considered identical to the Law of Nature.[53] The main advantage of the Law of Works over the Law of Nature was that the former was stated clearly in the Old Testament and, thus, was easily intelligible. Nevertheless, the Law of Moses was excessively demanding, in that it required perfect obedience, and did not offer any incentive to act morally. Moreover, the Law of Moses had gradually become more complex, and less loyal to the original in its intentions and objectives, due to "the corrupt and loosening glosses of the Scribes and Pharisees."[54] This is why a new covenant, the covenant of grace or covenant of faith, was necessary. With this new covenant, God established a new and final law – the Law of Faith – through Jesus Christ, the Messiah, who disclosed the divine law completely. In this respect, it is worth noting that what Locke meant by completeness was different from comprehensiveness, as Victor Nuovo has observed:

> By claiming completeness, however, Locke did not mean that Jesus offered in his teaching a comprehensive code of law to which nothing can be added, but a complete system of principles. In this respect, he also simplified it. ... Jesus is supposed to have perfected the law by increasing its rigor not only with respect to actions but the intentions of the moral agent.[55]

In other words, Jesus put an end to the formalism that, in Locke's opinion, had corrupted the Mosaic Law. According to Locke, Christ revealed the Law of Nature in its entirety. However, the Law of Faith, although overlapping with, and actually encompassing, the Law of Nature, is not coextensive with the Law of Nature, because the Law of Faith has a wider scope than the Law of Nature. In fact, Christ complemented the Law of Nature with important revelations,

---

[52] Ibid., pp. 161–163.

[53] Ibid., pp. 17–22. Locke highlighted the religious, legal, and moral nature of the Law of Moses, also, in a manuscript comment on the Socinian Johannes Völkel's *De vera religione* (1630), which he owned in its Amsterdam 1642 edition: John Locke, "Volkelii Hypothesis lib. De vera religione," in Mario Sina, "Testi teologico-filosofici lockiani dal MS. Locke c.27 della Lovelace Collection," *Rivista di filosofia neo-scolastica*, 64:1 (1972): pp. 54–75, and 64:3 (1972): pp. 400–427 (424–427). The original of this manuscript is MS Locke c. 27, ff. 238–245 (ff. 239v–245 blank). Concerning the differences between the ceremonial and moral parts of the Law of Moses, see Chapter 6.

[54] Locke, *Reasonableness*, p. 123.

[55] Victor Nuovo, *John Locke: The Philosopher As Christian Virtuoso* (Oxford: Oxford University Press, 2017), p. 227.

such as the promise of reward and punishment in the afterlife, thus providing a powerful incentive to act morally.[56] Locke called attention to this incentive in both the *Reasonableness* and the *Paraphrase*, in which he wrote: "We the preachers of the Gospel are but labourers imploid by God, about that which is his work, and from him shall receive reward here-after every one according to his own labour."[57] This incentive was also one of the main tenets of Socinian soteriology, since the Socinians believed that, before Christ's Coming, human-kind had no assurance of an afterlife with reward and punishment.[58] According to Locke, due to the weakness of human nature and to the difficulties faced by natural reason in attempting to demonstrate morality, Jesus complemented the Law of Nature with the promise of otherworldly rewards and sanctions to promote the performance of the moral duty. However, Locke did not claim that accepting the Law of Faith and believing in an afterlife with reward and punishment leads one, necessarily and unfailingly, to act morally. In *An Essay concerning Human Understanding* (which Locke revised multiple times in his later years) and in the *Reasonableness* as well, he admitted that even those who believe in otherworldly sanctions are still liable to commit evil deeds because of human imperfection.[59] While insisting on human rationality, Locke never disregarded the weakness of human nature.[60] Therefore, he shared another important tenet of Socinian soteriology – belief in God's mercy. Socinus and his disciples maintained that Christ, emphasizing God's forgiveness, had offered humanity a concrete hope of salvation, despite the limits of human nature. The Socinians rejected the opinion that God necessarily ought to punish sinners. They argued that God is merciful and omnipotent and, hence, not bound by any law – unlike human judges, who have to apply the laws of the state. To the Socinians, God could therefore waive his right to punishment and forgive the sins of the repentant faithful who, during their life, sincerely endeavor to obey the divine moral law. Thus, the Socinians' consideration of God as a judge recalls the image of an absolute ruler, instead of that of a judge who must apply laws that cannot be neglected.[61] The importance that Locke

---

[56] Locke, *Reasonableness*, pp. 22–25, 110–112. See, also, John Locke, "Voluntas," in John Locke, *Political Essays*, ed. Mark Goldie (Cambridge: Cambridge University Press, 1997), p. 321. The original of this manuscript, written in 1693, is MS Locke c. 28, f. 114.

[57] Locke, *Paraphrase*, 1 Cor. 3:8, vol. 1, p. 183.

[58] David Wootton, "John Locke: Socinian or Natural Law Theorist?," in James E. Crimmins (ed.), *Religion, Secularization and Political Thought: Thomas Hobbes to J. S. Mill* (London: Routledge, 1989), pp. 39–67 (49).

[59] Locke, *Essay*, II.xxi.60–73, pp. 273–287, II.xxviii.12, pp. 356–357; Locke, *Reasonableness*, pp. 19, 120, 130.

[60] William M. Spellman, *John Locke and the Problem of Depravity* (Oxford: Clarendon Press, 1988), p. 57; Sell, *John Locke*, p. 230.

[61] Socinus, "De Jesu," pp. 121–132; Crell, *Ad librum*, pp. 164–167; Mortimer, "Human and Divine Justice."

attached to faith as one of the fundamentals of Christianity was in line with the Socinians' stress on God's forgiveness, since he wrote in the *Reasonableness* that "*by the Law of Faith, Faith is allowed* to supply the defect of full Obedience; and so the Believers are admitted to Life and Immortality as if they were Righteous."[62] To Locke, Christ "did not expect ... a Perfect Obedience void of all slips and falls: He knew our Make, and the weakness of our Constitution too well, and was sent with a Supply for that Defect."[63] This supply was faith:

Christian Believers have the Privilege to be under the *Law of Faith* too; which is that Law whereby God Justifies a man for Believing, though by his Works he be not Just or Righteous, *i.e.* though he came short of Perfect Obedience to the Law of Works. God alone does, or can, Justifie or make Just those who by their Works are not so: Which he doth by counting their Faith for Righteousness, *i.e.* for a compleat performance of the Law.[64]

As Jean-Michel Vienne has noted, Locke's position on God's forgiveness in the *Reasonableness* parallels the views that he expressed in the *Essay* (and that I have examined in Chapter 1) concerning God's appreciation of intellectual effort even when one's intellectual pursuits are flawed or unsuccessful:

In the *Essay*, reason discovers that we have to examine, understand and reason to find truth or probability. However, even if we fail, our endeavours will be counted by God as if we had reasoned rightly: intention is counted for success. In the *Reasonableness*, the Gospels tell us that we have to obey the law of nature ... but if we fail, faith will be counted for works.[65]

The importance that Locke attached to the justifying faith in his religious writings led him to develop a new concept of faith – a concept that he expressed in the *Paraphrase* and that complements his notion of faith expounded in the *Essay*. While in the *Essay* he talked of faith as assent to probable matters of fact,[66] in the *Paraphrase* he wrote that the faithful are those "who relye upon God and his promise of grace and not upon their own performances, they are the children who shall inherit and this is plain in the Sacred Scripture."[67] These words denote a notion of true, saving faith as not merely a sort of assent, but as *fiducia*, as trust in Christ, entailing reliance on and commitment to God's Revealed Word.[68] Yet, this does not mean that, in the *Paraphrase*, Locke discarded the view of faith he had explained in the

---

[62] Locke, *Reasonableness*, p. 19.   [63] Ibid., p. 120.   [64] Ibid., pp. 20–21.

[65] Jean-Michel Vienne, "Hermeneutics and the Reasonableness of Belief," in Luisa Simonutti (ed.), *Locke and Biblical Hermeneutics: Conscience and Scripture* (Cham: Springer, 2019), pp. 105–119 (112).

[66] Locke, *Essay*, IV.xviii.8–9, pp. 694–695.   [67] Locke, *Paraphrase*, Gal. 3:7, vol. 1, p. 136.

[68] Arthur W. Wainwright, "Introduction" to Locke, *Paraphrase*, vol. 1, pp. 1–88 (41–43); Sell, *John Locke*, pp. 87–88.

Essay. His idea that saving faith entails trust in Christ, and hence in scriptural revelation, is actually compatible with his conviction that "it still belongs to *Reason*, to judge of the Truth of [a proposition's] being a revelation, and of the signification of the Words, wherein it is delivered."[69] In fact, when accepting as true, in the *Paraphrase*, Paul's claim to have received direct revelation from God, Locke described Paul as communicating the divine truths bestowed to him through concepts and arguments suitable to rational understanding. Therefore, Paul was no enthusiast.[70] As Locke wrote in the *Essay*, "*Reason* must be our last Judge and Guide in every Thing"[71] – in both our opinions and our actions, which must not be misguided by wrong principles "*that are not in themselves certain and evident.*"[72] Both our opinions and actions, if guided by sound reasoning, contribute to our salvation. Those who, like enthusiasts, Roman Catholics, and antinomians of various stripes, are misguided by wrong, ill-grounded principles in their opinions and actions jeopardize their own salvation. Since Locke believed that both opinions and actions contribute to the achievement of eternal salvation, he disapproved of the principle of *salvation by faith alone*, as Dewey Wallace has observed:

By the law of faith Locke does not intend a new way of serving God but the same moral law, which may, however, under the new covenant be only partially fulfilled, the defect in its fulfillment being compensated for by the faith of the believer.[73]

As Locke himself explained in the *Reasonableness*, saving faith has practical consequences, since it goes hand in hand with repentance and obedience:

[Jesus' followers] were required to believe him to be the *Messiah*; Which Faith is of Grace promised to be reckoned to them for the compleating of their Righteousness, wherein it was defective: But Righteousness, or Obedience to the Law of God, was their great business; Which if they could have attained by their own Performances, there would have been no need of this Gracious Allowance, in Reward of their Faith. . . . But their past Transgressions were pardoned, to those who received *Jesus*, the promised *Messiah*, for their King; And their future slips covered, if renouncing their former Iniquities, they entered into his Kingdom, and continued his Subjects, with a steady Resolution and Endeavour to obey his Laws. This Righteousness therefore, a compleat Obedience and freedom from Sin, are still sincerely to be endeavoured after. And 'tis no where promised, That those who persist in a wilful Disobedience to his Laws, shall be received into the eternal bliss of his Kingdom, how much soever they believe in him.[74]

[69] Locke, *Essay*, IV.xviii.8, p. 694.
[70] Victor Nuovo, "Enthusiasm," in S.-J. Savonius-Wroth, Paul Schuurman, Jonathan Walmsley (eds.), *The Continuum Companion to Locke* (London: Continuum, 2010), pp. 141–143 (141).
[71] Locke, *Essay*, IV.xix.14, p. 704.   [72] Ibid., IV.xx.7, p. 711.
[73] Dewey D. Wallace, "Socinianism, Justification by Faith, and the Sources of John Locke's *The Reasonableness of Christianity*," *Journal of the History of Ideas*, 45:1 (1984): pp. 49–66 (53–54).
[74] Locke, *Reasonableness*, p. 130.

To Locke, the faithful still ought to obey the eternally valid principles of the divinely established Law of Nature, also confirmed by Christ. According to the Law of Faith, the believer's faith compensates for their failure to perfectly comply with the divine moral law – a failure that, due to the weakness and imperfection of human nature, is inevitable, even when one is sincerely committed to obedience. Therefore, the faithful will receive "the Pardon and Forgiveness of Sins and Salvation"[75] thanks to their faith,. but only on condition that, in their life, they repent for their sins and wholeheartedly endeavor to observe the divine moral law. It is in this sense that, in Locke's soteriology, faith "justifies." The justifying faith includes good works. Thus, Locke's concept of justification, which involves a stress on conscious freedom and individual responsibility, significantly differs from the Calvinist theory that Christ's righteousness, imputed by God to the believer, justifies.[76] Locke's position on justification rather resembles that of Richard Baxter, of various Laudian Arminians (e.g., Jeremy Taylor, Henry Hammond, and Herbert Thorndike), and of several latitudinarians and other Arminian-inspired clergymen of the Restoration era, such as Isaac Barrow, George Bull, and Locke's friends Edward Fowler and John Tillotson. Locke indeed shared with these theologians the ideas that faith is assent to propositions, faith itself is imputed as righteousness, the justifying faith includes good works, the new covenant is conditional, and grace is *assisting* grace.[77]

Locke's views on justification distinguish him, on the one hand, from antinomians and predestinarians of different stripes and, on the other, from deists. Locke's position is in line with the Socinian and Arminian idea that human beings are able to accept or resist assisting grace. Locke thought that accepting divine assistance and adhering to the Law of Faith was reasonable, thanks to the "advantages" of Christ's Coming, which he summarized in five points in the *Reasonableness*.[78] According to Locke, human beings could demonstrate God's existence from "the works of nature." But, in ancient times, priestcraft and the stronger powers of the senses prevented the bulk of humankind from acknowledging their creator's existence. For this reason, Christ revealed the existence of "the One Invisible True God," thus putting an end to pagan polytheism, idolatry, and superstition. This is the first advantage of Christ's Coming.[79] The second is that Christ's message obviated the failure of unassisted reason to comprehend the Law of Nature completely, because Christ revealed to humankind "a true and complete Morality," clarifying all the principles and implications of the Law of Nature.[80] The third advantage is that Christ reformed the public worship, depriving it of its ritualistic

[75] Ibid., p. 133.   [76] Wallace, "Socinianism," p. 56.   [77] Ibid., p. 66.
[78] Locke, *Reasonableness*, pp. 139–164.   [79] Ibid., pp. 142–147.   [80] Ibid., pp. 147–159.

elements.[81] The fourth is that Jesus, through his teachings and his resurrection, gave humankind a "clear revelation" and an "unquestionable assurance" of an afterlife with reward and punishment. Thus, Jesus gave humanity an effective incentive to act virtuously – an incentive that no philosopher before him had ever provided.[82] The fifth and last advantage is in Christ's promise of assistance by the Holy Spirit to those willing to accept divine grace.[83] The two final advantages demonstrate, once again, that Locke disagreed with the deists about Christ's message. He thought that Christianity was more reasonable than deism, and by "reasonable" he did not mean that the Christian religion could be discovered by rational inquiry or proven true through rational arguments – which was not the case, according to Locke. He indeed regarded biblical revelation as a necessary complement to natural reason and he believed that some important truths of Christianity were *above reason*.[84] When characterizing Christianity as reasonable, Locke actually meant that even the weakest intellect could accept Christ's message: "And if the poor had the Gospel preached to them, it was, without doubt, such a Gospel, as the poor could understand, plain and intelligible: and so it was . . . in the preachings of Christ and his Apostles."[85] Furthermore, Christ's message is reasonable, convenient, advantageous, and hence easily acceptable, thanks to its saving power.

Original Sin, Satisfaction, and Atonement

Locke described God's mercy as essential to salvation because he acknowledged the human propensity to evil, the origins of which he investigated in several writings. He always rejected the opinion that this propensity was innate or naturally inherited from the previous generations. In a letter he sent to his friend, the politician Edward Clarke, in 1684, more than ten years before writing the *Reasonableness*, he stated that most human beings are good or evil by their education, although a small portion of humanity is equipped with exceptional intellectual skills and can therefore achieve moral excellence.[86] Moreover, he denied original sin on several occasions. In Book II, Chapter 27 of *An Essay concerning Human Understanding* – a chapter that Locke added to the second edition of the *Essay* in 1694, shortly before writing the *Reasonableness* – he maintained:

---

[81] Ibid., pp. 159–160.   [82] Ibid., pp. 160–163.   [83] Ibid., pp. 163–164.
[84] See Chapter 1.   [85] Locke, *Reasonableness*, p. 171.
[86] Locke to Edward Clarke, July 9/19, 1684, in John Locke, *The Correspondence of John Locke*, ed. E. S. de Beer, 8 vols. (Oxford: Oxford University Press, 1979–1989), vol. 2, no. 782. Locke wrote this letter before reading the works of Socinians like Johannes Völkel and Johann Crell, but most probably after reading the writings of other anti-Trinitarians, such as John Biddle and Christoph Sand. See Marshall, "Locke, Socinianism," p. 155.

In the great Day, wherein the Secrets of all Hearts shall be laid open, it may be reasonable to think, no one shall be made to answer for what he knows nothing of; but shall receive his Doom, his Conscience accusing or excusing him.[87]

In this passage, Locke used a formula borrowed from 1 Cor. 14:25 ("And thus are the secrets of his heart made manifest ...") – a Pauline verse which he expressly referred to in another paragraph from the same chapter of the *Essay*: "The Apostle tells us, that at the Great Day, when every one shall receive according to his doings, the secrets of all Hearts shall be laid open."[88] These two passages concerning "the Great Day" are part of Locke's explanation of his consciousness-based theory of personal identity, which I consider in Chapter 4. Here, I would only like to note that Locke's persuasion that, on Judgment Day, "no one shall be made to answer for what he knows nothing of" and "every one shall receive according to his doings" is logically inconsistent with the idea that human beings are to be held accountable for another person's deeds and, hence, for Adam's sin. This persuasion is in line with Locke's explicit rejection of original sin in *The Reasonableness of Christianity*, in which he criticized those who "would have all *Adam*'s Posterity doomed to Eternal Infinite Punishment for the Transgression of *Adam*, whom Millions had never heard of, and no one had authorized to transact for him, or be his Representative."[89] Locke focused especially on Adam's sin and its impact on human nature in two short manuscripts written before the *Reasonableness* and entitled, respectively, *Peccatum originale* (1692) and *Homo ante et post lapsum* (1693).[90] In these two manuscripts, Locke advanced some arguments he later repeated and further developed in his major book of theology. In *Peccatum originale*, he objected to the theory that Adam's sin was imputed to his posterity – a theory he judged illogical and incompatible with God's goodness and justice. Nevertheless, Adam's sin still had an effect on human life, as Locke observed in *Homo ante et post lapsum*:

By this sin Adam & Eve came to know good & Evil. i e the difference between good & evill for without sin man should not have known evil. upon their offence they were affraid of god, this gave them frightfull Ideas and apprehensions of him & that lessened

---

[87] Locke, *Essay*, II.xxvii.22, p. 344.

[88] Ibid., II.xxvii.26, p. 347. In this passage, Locke also drew on, and expressly referred to, 2 Cor. 5:10: "For we must all appear before the judgment seat of Christ; that every one may receive the things done in his body, according to that he hath done, whether it be good or bad."

[89] Locke, *Reasonableness*, p. 5.

[90] John Locke, "Peccatum originale," in John Locke, *Writings on Religion*, ed. Victor Nuovo (Oxford: Oxford University Press, 2002), pp. 229–230; John Locke, "Homo ante et post lapsum," in Locke, *Writings on Religion*, p. 231. The original of *Peccatum originale* is at pp. 294–295 of the manuscript *Adversaria 1661* (see Chapter 1 for more details of this manuscript). *Homo ante et post lapsum* is MS Locke c. 28, f. 113v. On Locke's views on original sin, see Spellman, *John Locke*; Aderemi Artis, "Locke on Original Sin," *Locke Studies*, 12 (2012): pp. 201–219.

their love which turnd their minds to the creature this root of all evill in them made impressions & soe infected their children, & when private possessions & labour which now the curse on the earth had made necessary, by degrees made a distinction of conditions, it gave roome for coviteousnesse pride & ambition, which by fashen and example spread the corruption which has soe prevailed over man kind.[91]

In this passage, Locke maintained that, following Adam's and Eve's sin, their children were "infected." But he clarified that it was fashion and example to "spread the corruption," and he spoke of this "corruption" as coming from a world of covetousness, pride, and ambition. In other words, to Locke this "infection" of humankind was caused by environmental factors. He did not believe that humanity suffered from an *inherited* guilt or propensity to evil due to the Fall. As John Marshall has accurately noted, it is indeed unlikely that the philosopher who described the human mind at birth as a *tabula rasa* "meant to be supporting an infection of 'impressions' to be taken in an inherited as opposed to an environmental, or contagious sense, the latter being also the more usual way of talking of both infection and impression."[92]

While denying that humankind as a whole had been "punished" for Adam's sin, Locke argued that Adam's disobedience had still brought about consequences for him and his posterity as well. In *Homo ante et post lapsum*, he inferred from Gen. 2:17 ("... in the day that thou eatest thereof thou shalt surely die") that, following his disobedience, Adam became liable to suffer "a natural death."[93] Does this mean that Adam was created immortal? On this specific point, Locke's position is ambiguous. *Homo ante et post lapsum* and the introductory sections of the *Reasonableness* argue that Adam was not created immortal but, in Paradise, he was provided with the means to attain immortality, since God gave him a probationary law, which he then transgressed. However, in the *Reasonableness* it is also written:

Adam being the Son of God ... had this part also of the *Likeness* and *Image* of his Father, *viz.* That he was Immortal. But *Adam* transgressing the Command given him by his Heavenly Father, incurred the Penalty, forfeited that state of Immortality, and became Mortal. After this, *Adam* begot Children: But they were *in his own likeness, after his own image*; Mortal, like their Father.[94]

Locke restated that Adam had been created immortal, but had lost the state of immortality following his sin, in a manuscript dated 1702, *Christianae Religionis Synopsis*, in which he also repeated that Adam, having become mortal, "begat children in his own likeness i e Mortal."[95] Although Locke did not clarify this ambiguity about Adam's original status, his views on the mortality

[91] Locke, "Homo ante et post lapsum," p. 231.   [92] Marshall, "Locke, Socinianism," p. 162.
[93] Locke, "Homo ante et post lapsum," p. 231; Locke, *Reasonableness*, p. 5.   [94] Ibid., p. 113.
[95] John Locke, "Christianae Religionis Synopsis," in Locke, *Writings on Religion*, pp. 242–244 (242). The original of this manuscript is MS Locke c. 27, ff. 213–216 (ff. 215–216 blank).

of human beings are still compatible with his opinion that Adam's posterity was not punished for his sin. Locke viewed human mortality as naturally resulting from the mortal condition of the progenitor of humanity "out of Paradise."[96] In other words, he saw death as inherent to human nature "out of Paradise." Consequently, he did not consider human mortality as a punishment, given that humanity "has no right to" immortality, as he explained in the *Reasonableness*: "The state of Immortality in Paradise is not due to the Posterity of *Adam* more than to any other Creature."[97] Locke's idea that every individual person is to be held accountable exclusively for their own sins (and not for others' sins) contradicts a view about original sin that focuses on what humans *are* – not on what humans *do*. According to this view of original sin, human beings are fundamentally fallen following Adam's sin, and their fallen condition will certainly be relevant to God's judgment of them. But this view is inconsistent with Locke's denial of a naturally inherited propensity to evil following Adam's sin. Moreover, this view of original sin is incompatible with Locke's opinion that human mortality is not a punishment. Finally, this view clashes with Locke's notion of the human mind as a *tabula rasa*.

Despite Locke's ambiguity concerning the creation of Adam as originally mortal or immortal, his notion of Adam's condition in Paradise and then out of it is in line with the Socinian theory that Adam's immortality, far from being natural, was simply part of his condition in Paradise, which he lost when he had to leave it. The Socinians did not see human mortality as a punishment for Adam's sin, but merely as part of human nature. Thus, they denied the doctrine of original sin, as they argued that Adam's sin had not changed human nature, reason, and morality. Besides echoing Socinian arguments, Locke's view that humanity was mortal after the Fall, and yet Adam's sin had not affected human reason and morality, is indebted to still other influences, particularly to Arminian authors. For instance, a position similar to that of Locke on this subject can be found in *Unum necessarium* (1655) by the Laudian clergyman Jeremy Taylor, who upheld a moralist soteriology.[98] Moreover, Locke's friend and leading Remonstrant theologian Philipp van Limborch argued, in *Theologia Christiana*, that the term "original sin" did not have a scriptural origin, and he maintained that Adam's sin was not the cause of human sinfulness. Nevertheless, Limborch believed that human beings are *born* with a propensity to evil; and this position contrasts with Locke's opinion that the human propensity to evil was not innate or naturally inherited, but was caused by upbringing and other environmental influences.[99]

---

[96] Locke, *Reasonableness*, pp. 6, 9, 11, 115.   [97] Ibid., p. 10.

[98] Jeremy Taylor, *Unum necessarium*, 4th ed.(London, 1705), pp. 43–49.

[99] Philipp van Limborch, *Theologia Christiana* (Amsterdam, 1686), pp. 182–200. On the similarities and differences between Locke, Taylor, and Limborch on this subject, see Spellman, *John Locke*, pp. 97–101, 130–134.

According to Locke, whereas human beings "out of Paradise" are mortal, God offered immortality again to humankind through Jesus, whom Locke, in the *Reasonableness*, described as a "second Adam."[100] The definition of Jesus as a "second" or "last" Adam dates back to Paul's Christology in Rom. 5:12–21 and in 1 Cor. 15:20–23 and 15:45–49, and was frequently used by seventeenth-century English theologians, such as the aforementioned Jeremy Taylor, the Puritan preacher Robert Harris, and the Royalist clergyman Thomas Bradley.[101] Adopting this characterization of Jesus, Locke clarified that Jesus, like Adam, had no natural father, for he did not descend from Adam and was, instead, an "immediate" Son of God.[102] Locke's position on this subject is partly in line with Socinian Christology. The Socinians, too, believed that Christ was an "immediate" Son of God, in that God the Father was *literally* Jesus' father, but they considered Jesus as created mortal and then made immortal by divine miracle upon his death. Conversely, in Locke's *Reasonableness*, the fact that Jesus was an "immediate" Son of God, miraculously born of a virgin, means that he was a bearer of the image of God. This means that Jesus was created immortal and, hence, did not have to suffer death.[103] Nevertheless, Jesus chose to die in order to fulfill his Messianic office, because, without his death, his resurrection would not be possible. As Locke stated in the *Reasonableness*, "the great Evidence that Jesus was the *Son of God*, was his Resurrection. Then the Image of his Father appeared in him, when he visibly entered into the state of Immortality."[104] Christ was rewarded for his suffering with his kingdom in heaven – a kingdom in which the righteous will be admitted to immortal life on Judgment Day.[105]

---

[100] Locke, *Reasonableness*, p. 12.

[101] Jeremy Taylor, "Of the Liberty of Prophesying," in Jeremy Taylor, *Treatises* (London, 1648), pp. 1–267 (224); Robert Harris, *A Brief Discourse of Man's Estate in the First and Second Adam* (London, 1654); Thomas Bradley, *Nosce te ipsum, in a Comparison between the First, and the Second Adam* (York, 1668); Thomas Bradley, *The Second Adam* (York, 1668).

[102] Locke, *Reasonableness*, p. 113. Victor Nuovo has connected Locke's use of the Pauline doctrine of the two Adams with his disregard of Eve in the *Reasonableness* (whereas, as we have seen above, Eve is mentioned in *Homo ante et post lapsum*): "In this schema, there is no place for Eve, for the primal or archetypal man requires no consort, nor, for that matter, does the Messiah whom Locke equates with the second Adam. They are pure, although not genderless, archetypes." Victor Nuovo, "Locke's Hermeneutics of Existence and His Representation of Christianity," in Simonutti (ed.), *Locke and Biblical Hermeneutics*, pp. 77–103 (93).

[103] Locke, *Reasonableness*, pp. 113–115.

[104] Ibid., p. 115. See, also, Locke, "Second Vindication," p. 161, where Locke talks of Jesus' "Resurrection from the dead" as "the great and demonstrative Proof of his being the *Messiah*." As I explain in Chapter 5, Locke's position on Jesus' sonship in the *Paraphrase* denotes a subtle shift from the *Reasonableness*. In the *Paraphrase*, he attached scarce importance to Christ's virgin birth, while he put a strong emphasis on Christ's resurrection as distinguishing him as the Son of God.

[105] On Locke's views on Judgment Day, see Chapter 4. On his Christology, see Chapter 5.

Locke's account of Christ's death and resurrection denotes that he did not approve of the satisfaction theory of atonement, according to which Christ suffered death on the cross as a substitute for human sin, satisfying God due to his infinite merit. This theory is based on the idea of substitutionary atonement, namely, the idea that Jesus died "for us," which was, and is still, upheld by the Roman Catholic Church and by the large majority of Protestants. The satisfaction theory of atonement was first formulated by Anselm of Canterbury, then refined by Thomas Aquinas, and later accepted by the Magisterial Reformers. Though, Calvin adapted this theory to his views on predestination, as he limited Christ's atonement in its effect only to those whom God has elected to save, and he talked of Christ as being "punished" for human sin – a view that developed into the doctrine of penal substitution. Concerning Locke's position on satisfaction, the *Reasonableness* was silent on this subject at a time when a major Nonconformist controversy about justification – the antinomian controversy – was taking place. As Locke himself admitted, this controversy prompted him to write and publish the *Reasonableness* in 1695.[106] However, he wrote in this book that "we know little of this visible, and nothing at all of the state of that Intellectual World ... and therefore know not what Transactions there were between God and our Saviour, in reference to his Kingdom."[107] Two years later, in the *Second Vindication*, Locke justified his silence on the satisfaction theory in the *Reasonableness* by maintaining that "satisfaction" was "a term not used by the Holy Ghost in the Scripture, and very variously explained by those that do use it."[108] According to Locke, the satisfaction was one of the many "disputed doctrines of Christianity," but he had chosen to take into account, in his elucidation of Christianity *as delivered in the Scriptures*, "such Particulars only as were agreed on by all Christians, and were capable of no Dispute."[109] Yet, Locke concentrated on satisfaction in some of his private manuscripts, particularly in *Adversaria Theologica*. This notebook, which Locke wrote for the most part in 1694–1695 and slightly revised and augmented over the next five years or so, presents a sort of theological map of the intellectual world in which Locke lived, for it contains a comprehensive checklist of the major theological subjects discussed by European scholars in the seventeenth century.[110] The entries in this notebook can be classified in two categories – namely, extracts from Locke's readings

---

[106] Locke, "Second Vindication," p. 34. See Chapter 1.
[107] Locke, *Reasonableness*, pp. 141–142.   [108] Locke, "Second Vindication," p. 227.
[109] Ibid.
[110] John Locke, "Adversaria Theologica 94," in Locke, *Writings on Religion*, pp. 19–33. The original of this manuscript is MS Locke c. 43, pp. 1–46. On this manuscript, see Victor Nuovo, "Introduction" to Locke, *Writings on Religion*, pp. xv–lvii (xxix–xxxiii); Victor Nuovo, *Christianity, Antiquity, and Enlightenment: Interpretations of Locke* (Dordrecht: Springer, 2011), pp. 22–31.

and his own thoughts about topics that fall mostly within two groups, some concerning God and others concerning humanity. The group of topics regarding God includes, among other subjects, the Trinity, Christ's nature, and the Holy Spirit, while the group concerning humanity contains entries on topics such as the immateriality or materiality of the soul, the human condition after the Fall, the differences between the Law of Works and the Law of Faith, satisfaction, divine election, and redemption. Some of these topics (e.g., the Law of Works and the Law of Faith) cover themes that Locke also examined in the *Reasonableness*. Moreover, Locke partly drew on this manuscript (e.g., on the entries about the soul) when writing the *Paraphrase*.[111] Nevertheless, Locke consistently abstained from publicly clarifying his views on some controversial topics covered in this notebook, such as the Trinity, Christ's nature, and the satisfaction doctrine. When noting points that supported divergent views on a certain subject, Locke signaled his endorsement of a specific argument by signing with his initials next to this argument. In some cases, as with the question of the immateriality or materiality of the soul, he endorsed opposing arguments, thus manifesting an ambiguous or undecided position on the matter. However, Locke judged the question of the ontological constitution of the thinking substance, or soul, to be irrelevant to salvation.[112] In other cases, as in the entries on the Trinity and Christ's nature, there is a significant imbalance in the number of arguments that Locke listed, and this imbalance is in favor of non-Trinitarian interpretations, since Locke mainly drew on anti-Trinitarian sources.[113] As regards the entries on satisfaction in *Adversaria Theologica*, Locke recorded no argument and left the page blank under the heading "Satisfactio Christi Aff." ("the satisfaction of Christ affirmed").[114] Probably, he did not judge any argument supporting the satisfaction doctrine to be worthy of consideration. Conversely, in the entry "Satisfactio Christi Neg." ("the satisfaction of Christ denied"), he cited the English Unitarian Stephen Nye's *Considerations on the Explications of the Doctrine of the Trinity* (1693) when relating the views on satisfaction held by Socinians like Martin Ruar, Jonas Schlichting, and the editors of the final Latin edition of the *Racovian Catechism*, Andrzej and Benedykt Wiszowaty.[115] Under the influence of Remonstrant theology, especially of Simon Episcopius's soteriology, these anti-Trinitarian theologians deviated from Socinus's and several of his followers' outright denial of the atonement. This is how Locke summarized their views on the matter:

---

[111] See Chapter 4.   [112] See ibid.   [113] See Chapter 5.
[114] Locke, "Adversaria Theologica," p. 32.
[115] Ibid. On the *Racovian Catechism* and its final Latin edition, published in Amsterdam in 1680, see Chapter 2.

What we deny is this: That this Sacrifice was by way of true & proper satisfaction, or full & coequate payment to the justice of God. We say, this sacrifice (as all other Sacrifices) was only an oblation or application to the mercy of god: A sacrifice it was which it pleased god to accept for us though he might have refused it. And for this reason tis said all along in the Holy Scripture that god forgives to us our sins; & not that he received a Satisfaction, or an equivalent for them.[116]

A few lines below in this manuscript, Locke wrote an entry entitled "Redemptio & Ransom." In this entry, he outlined a position compatible with the Socinians' refusal of the notion of a "coequal payment" – a notion central to the satisfaction theory of atonement:

By Christs sufferings & death we are redeemed not from punishment but from Sin primarily & from punishment because free from sin. . ... Christ by his death redeems us from sin in that his death is a demonstration of the truth of his doctrine & the great argument to bring them into an obedience to the Gospel whereby they leave sin & soe scape punishment To restore the law of nature or natural religion almost blotted out by corruption god yields his son to death which is therefor cald a Ransome. . . . The first & principal end of Christs death is by being a proof of the Gospel to be a motive to holynesse, & for all such as it thus works on god accepts it as a Sacrifice & forgives their sins. . . . Tis gods acceptance not its merit makes it expiatory.[117]

In this passage, Locke restated his view of Christ's death on the cross as necessary to confirm the truth of his doctrine. Moreover, he introduced the idea that Christ's death was a ransom paid to God for our sins – a point he also made in another manuscript, *Redemtion, Death*, written probably in 1697.[118] Locke's position on this matter is in line with the governmental theory of atonement, first formulated by Hugo Grotius in opposition to Socinus's rejection of the atonement.[119] Later, besides being accepted by most Remonstrants (including, among others, Limborch, who further developed and clarified it), this theory influenced the aforesaid Socinian thinkers who deviated from Socinus's denial of the atonement. According to the governmental theory of atonement, God offered Christ's death as a public display of how seriously he takes sin, in order to uphold his moral government of Creation.[120] Limborch's version of this theory was particularly refined, as John Mark Hicks has pointed out:

According to Limborch's theory of the atonement, Christ paid a real, but not a full, price to the justice of God. The price was his physical death which demonstrated that God

---

[116] Locke, "Adversaria Theologica," p. 32.   [117] Ibid., p. 33.
[118] John Locke, "Redemtion, Death," in Locke, *Reasonableness*, pp. 205–208. The original of this manuscript is in MS Locke c. 27, ff. 112–113.
[119] Grotius, *Defensio fidei*, pp. 56–157.
[120] Roger E. Olson, *Arminian Theology: Myths and Realities* (Downers Grove: Intervarsity Press, 2000), p. 229.

hated evil and loved justice. The price had no relation to the eternal penalty of sin except that it opens the way of reconciliation by the suspension of the Father's wrath. Since this wrath was publicly displayed through Jesus, the Father is appeased and the way is now open for reconciliation with man. The Father has opened the way of salvation by the establishment, through his Son, of a new covenant in which the forgiveness of sins is proffered upon the condition of faith and repentance.[121]

According to Limborch, who was a Trinitarian, God the Father accepted Christ's sacrifice because of his dignity, since Christ was both divine and human. Nevertheless, Limborch explained that, even if Christ were considered as only the Messiah and, hence, as a man (as he was actually considered by Socinians and other anti-Trinitarian Christians), he was still dignified beyond other human beings. Therefore, Limborch judged Christ's deity important, but not essential to accept this view of the atonement.[122] This is one more reason why Locke could approve of this notion of the atonement. Locke's manuscript notes on this subject indeed indicate that he agreed with the Remonstrants' governmental theory, and particularly with Limborch's sophisticated account of it. Limborch's position was actually consonant with the Arminian soterio-logical tradition, which influenced Locke's views on justification. Yet, Locke's silence on the satisfaction in the *Reasonableness*, along with his omission of the Trinitarian dogma from the fundamentals of Christianity, led some critics to accuse him of Socinianism. In fact, Locke's views on the atonement aligned not only with the Remonstrants' governmental theory, but also with the views on this matter expressed by several Socinians, such as the aforementioned Ruar, Schlichting, and editors of the final version of the *Racovian Catechism*. Nonetheless, Locke disagreed with the Socinians – including *these* Socinians – on several points. Socinus and all his followers believed that both Adam and Jesus had been created mortal, since the Socinians considered mortality as inherent to human nature. They thought that only a divine miracle had made possible Christ's resurrection, exaltation, and immortality. Moreover, most Socinians argued that Jesus was commissioned as Messiah only before his ministry. Unlike the Socinians, Locke maintained in the *Reasonableness* that Jesus was created immortal and was the Messiah since birth. However, in both the *Reasonableness* and the *Paraphrase*, Locke, like the Socinians, described Christ's resurrection – and not Christ's suffering and death on the cross – as what really counted in the economy of salvation. This was a central element of the Socinian theological tradition, since the Socinians shifted the focus of Christianity from the crucifixion to the resurrection of Christ, which they

---

[121] John Mark Hicks, "The Theology of Grace in the Thought of Jacobus Arminius and Philip van Limborch," PhD dissertation, Westminster Theological Seminary, 1985, p. 206. See Limborch, *Theologia Christiana*, pp. 224–241, 264–273.

[122] Marshall, "Locke, Socinianism," pp. 168–169.

saw as definitive proof of eternal reward.[123] At any rate, Locke's views on original sin, satisfaction, and the atonement cannot be ascribed to any theological tradition in particular. In this as in other cases, Locke indeed attempted to formulate ideas ultimately grounded in Scripture, although his familiarity with various theological currents, particularly Socinianism and Arminianism, had an impact on his reading of Scripture. The influence that other theologians and currents exercised on Locke's approach to hermeneutical, theological, and soteriological questions is indeed demonstrated not only by the remarkable similarities between his religious thought and the Socinian and Arminian theological traditions, but also by his frequent references to other authors, texts, and currents, mainly in his private writings.

---

[123] On this similarity between Socinianism and Locke's religion, see Wootton, "John Locke," p. 45. Locke also expressed this position on Christ's death and resurrection in a note on Hebrews inserted in his polyglot New Testament: LL 2864, BOD Locke 9.103–9.107, *Le Nouveau Testament* (Mons, 1673), interleaved and bound in 5 vols., p. 249. This manuscript note has been published as: John Locke, "On the Priesthood of Christ: Analysis of Hebrews," in Locke, *Writings on Religion*, pp. 238–241. On this manuscript, see Nuovo, "Introduction," pp. lv–lvi; Nuovo, *Christianity*, pp. 84–86. On Locke's emphasis on Christ's resurrection, I say more in Chapter 5.

4   The Soul and the Last Judgment

Locke thought that God, far from predestining only the "elect" to Heaven, leaves salvation open to all human beings, on condition that they adhere to the Law of Faith. He believed in eternal life, as is demonstrated by his emphasis on an afterlife with reward and punishment. But he did not believe in the natural immortality of the soul, since his writings on this subject indicate belief that the soul dies with the body. He conceived of the soul and the body as distinct but interdependent.[1] Accordingly, he thought that bodily death entails the death of the soul. He maintained that the resurrection of the dead will take place by divine miracle on Judgment Day, when the saved will be admitted to eternal beatitude while the wicked will experience a second, final death. Moreover, he was agnostic about the ontological constitution of the soul. His account of substance as an unknown substratum of ideas in *An Essay concerning Human Understanding* entails that we have no clear and distinct idea of a thinking substance or soul and that, therefore, we do not know whether the soul is immaterial or material. Furthermore, he questioned the resurrection of the body, as he maintained that the corruptible, frail, mortal bodies of the saved will be changed into incorruptible, spiritual bodies at resurrection, when every saved soul will need an incorruptible body to sustain it for eternity. Locke's position on the soul and the resurrection of the dead implies that personal identity is neither in the soul, nor in the body, nor in a union of soul and body. In *Essay* II.xxvii – a chapter he added, in 1694, to the second edition of the *Essay* – he argued that consciousness alone makes personal identity.[2] Between physical death and resurrection there is a gap in existence, and the same self exists diachronically, in this life and beyond it, only "by the same consciousness." Locke's approach to these matters further denotes the heterodox nature of his religious thought and necessitates some clarifications, especially

---

[1]   Liam P. Dempsey, "'A Compound Wholly Mortal': Locke and Newton on the Metaphysics of (Personal) Immortality," *British Journal for the History of Philosophy*, 19:2 (2011): pp. 241–264 (242).

[2]   John Locke, *An Essay concerning Human Understanding*, ed. Peter H. Nidditch (Oxford: Clarendon Press, 1975), II.xxvii.9, p. 335.

concerning his views on moral accountability and eternal salvation. In this regard, Udo Thiel and Galen Strawson have questioned the compatibility of Locke's consciousness-based theory of personal identity with his soteriology, particularly with his notion of repentance.[3] *Pace* Thiel and Strawson, I argue that, in *The Reasonableness of Christianity*, Locke described repentance as *necessary but not sufficient* to salvation, since he thought that repentance, obedience, *and* faith, along with the diligent study of Scripture contribute, all together, to the achievement of eternal life.[4] Locke indeed believed that God, being aware of human weakness and imperfection, will forgive the sinful acts and thoughts of the repentant faithful who sincerely endeavor to obey the divine moral law. Therefore, to Locke the Last Judgment is not merely a matter of one's consciousness of their sins. And repentance, far from being sufficient to salvation, plays only a partial role in the pursuit of eternal life.

Death and Resurrection

When reflecting on the afterlife and the Last Judgment, Locke expressed mortalist views. Mortalism is the theory that the human soul is not naturally immortal or, at least, is not comprehending during the time between bodily death and resurrection. This position has been aptly defined as an emphatically *Christian* heresy.[5] Mortalist ideas diverge from the views on eschatological judgment maintained by the major Christian theological traditions, which generally agree that the soul is naturally immortal. For instance, Roman Catholics believe that, immediately upon physical death, the soul undergoes particular judgment and, depending upon its state, it goes to Heaven, Purgatory, or Hell. All souls in Purgatory will reach Heaven, while souls in Hell will be there eternally. The Last Judgment will take place at the time of Christ's Second Coming and the universal resurrection of the dead, when each person's relationship with God will be laid bare, their faith and works will be considered, and everyone will be judged in perfect justice in Christ's presence. At the Last Judgment, eternal bliss or torment will be perfected, because all those present will also be capable of physical pleasure or pain, upon the reuniting of their souls with their bodies at resurrection. Eastern Orthodox Christians, too, believe in

---

[3] Udo Thiel, *The Early Modern Subject: Self-Consciousness and Personal Identity from Descartes to Hume* (Oxford: Oxford University Press, 2011), p. 143; Galen Strawson, *Locke on Personal Identity: Consciousness and Concernment*, 2nd rev. ed. (Princeton: Princeton University Press, 2014), pp. 139–149.

[4] Concerning my disagreement with Thiel and Strawson on this subject, see, also, Diego Lucci, "Reconciling Locke's Consciousness-Based Theory of Personal Identity and His Soteriology," *Locke Studies*, 20 (2020), https://ojs.lib.uwo.ca/index.php/locke/article/view/7321.

[5] Bryan W. Ball, *The Soul Sleepers: Christian Mortalism from Wycliffe to Priestley* (Cambridge: James Clarke, 2008), pp. 10–11.

two judgments, although they do not have an understanding of "Purgatory." They believe that, upon physical death, the soul journeys to the abode of the dead, also called "Hades," where it remains in a condition of waiting. They think that the "particular judgment" is God's decision of where the soul is to spend the time until Judgment Day, given that Hades consists of different layers in which some souls foresee the glory to come and others foretaste their eternal suffering. As to Protestant theological traditions, Calvin argued that the souls of the departed are conscious, and are either in bliss or in torment, while awaiting the Last Judgment. Mortalist ideas, however, were not always deemed heretical and, in fact, were not uncommon among Christians in the early centuries of Christianity. In Late Antiquity, various early Christian writers, particularly in the East, held mortalist views, which were later denied by several prominent Christian theologians in the Middle Ages – from John of Damascus in the eighth century to Pope Benedict XII in the fourteenth century. Mortalist ideas reemerged and spread, in different varieties, soon after the Reformation.

Mortalist theories can be classified into three categories.[6] The mortalist view closest to natural immortality does not entail the view that the soul dies, but rather maintains that the soul sleeps until its awakening on Judgment Day. This sort of mortalism, known as *psychopannychism*, was upheld by Luther but was opposed by Reformers such as Calvin and Bullinger. Another version of mortalism is *thnetopsychism*, namely, the doctrine that the soul dies with the body and will be raised again by divine miracle on Judgment Day. Among others, the Socinians and other anti-Trinitarians, such as Michael Servetus, Simon Budny, John Biddle, and John Milton, approved of *thnetopsychism*. The third kind of mortalism is *annihilationism*, which considers the soul absolutely and permanently mortal. Some versions of *thnetopsychism* also present *annihilationist* and *conditionalist* elements, in that they describe the soul as naturally mortal while affirming belief in *conditional immortality* – namely, belief that the saved will eventually be granted immortality as a divine gift, whereas the unsaved cease to exist *permanently* either at physical death or on Judgment Day.

By the late sixteenth century, mortalism was a minor but influential heresy in Protestant Europe. Both *psychopannychist* and *thnetopsychist* views were actually compatible with some points of Protestant doctrine, such as the rejection of Purgatory and the conviction that the soul's destiny in the afterlife depends exclusively on God – not on some ecclesiastical or other human authorities or intercessions.[7] In England, the Forty-Two Articles of the Church

---

[6] Norman T. Burns, *Christian Mortalism from Tyndale to Milton* (Cambridge, MA: Harvard University Press, 1972), p. 2; Richard Sugg, *The Smoke of the Soul: Medicine, Physiology and Religion in Early Modern England* (Basingstoke: Palgrave Macmillan, 2013), p. 207.

[7] Burns, *Christian Mortalism*, pp. 9, 51; Ball, *Soul Sleepers*, pp. 28, 44–49; Sugg, *Smoke of the Soul*, p. 211.

of England (1553) condemned both soul-sleep and soul-death. Anglicans in the early modern period almost always held to natural immortality, believing that there is an intermediate state between physical death and the resurrection of the dead. In this intermediate state, the soul is conscious and exists in happiness or misery until Judgment Day, when it will be reunited to the body and receive its final reward. However, the Thirty-Nine Articles of 1563, which were revised several times and finalized in 1571, contained no explicit censure of mortalist ideas, perhaps in recognition that mortalism was less "heretical" than Calvin and Bullinger insisted.[8] During the Civil War and Interregnum, mortalist views appealed to heterodox intellectuals such as the physician Thomas Browne, the Leveller pamphleteer Richard Overton, Thomas Hobbes, and the aforesaid Biddle and Milton, as well as sectarians from marginal groups like the Ranters and the Familists. The spread of mortalist ideas in mid-seventeenth-century England was promoted by both the development of the natural sciences, especially medicine and anatomy, and Puritan Biblicism. English mortalists whose views were essentially *thnetopsychist*, such as Overton, Hobbes, and Milton, referred to both natural philosophical observations and biblical passages (e.g., Gen. 2:7 and Eccl. 3:19)[9] when criticizing belief in the natural immortality of the soul, which they described as a sort of pagan-influenced, unscriptural, illogical sophistry.[10] Conversely, Ranters and Familists based their peculiar mortalism on their mystical pantheism, which entailed the idea that the soul, when returning to God, will be devoid of its individuality and absorbed into God's essence.[11]

Locke's father was acquainted with mortalism, since he read Overton's *Mans Mortalitie* (1644).[12] However, Locke's mortalist ideas are identical to some Socinian authors' views on the matter, although not to Socinus's position. Socinus rejected the idea that the human soul was naturally immortal. Though, he did not believe in the resurrection of the wicked to punishment. He thought that only the righteous will be raised to eternal salvation and that the punishment of the wicked is annihilation at physical death. A slightly different version of *thnetopsychism* presenting also, like Socinus's version, *annihilationist* and *conditionalist* elements eventually prevailed among Socinians in the seventeenth century. Socinian writers like Johann Crell, Jonas Schlichting,

---

[8] Ball, *Soul Sleepers*, pp. 59–61.

[9] Gen. 2:7: "And the Lord God formed man of the dust of the ground, and breathed into his nostrils the breath of life; and man became a living soul." Mortalists argued that, in this verse, by "a living soul" is meant, simply, "a living being." Eccl. 3:19: "For that which befalleth the sons of men befalleth beasts; even one thing befalleth them: as the one dieth, so dieth the other; yea, they have all one breath; so that a man hath no preeminence above a beast: for all is vanity."

[10] Sugg, *Smoke of the Soul*, pp. 215–222.

[11] Burns, *Christian Mortalism*, pp. 74–87; Sugg, *Smoke of the Soul*, p. 223.

[12] Roger Woolhouse, *Locke: A Biography* (Cambridge: Cambridge University Press, 2007), p. 7.

and the editors of the final Latin version of the *Racovian Catechism* believed, unlike Socinus, in a general resurrection of both the righteous and the wicked, followed by the enjoyment of eternal beatitude by the righteous and the final annihilation of the wicked after unspeakable albeit brief sufferings.[13] Locke shared these Socinians' mortalist views. He believed that, upon Christ's Second Coming, a general resurrection of the dead will take place by divine miracle and will be followed by the Last Judgment. Whereas the righteous will be admitted to eternal bliss in Heaven, the wicked will be resurrected for only a short time, to suffer a brief but terrible torment and die a second, and final, death.[14]

The most comprehensive account of Locke's views on the matter is in a manuscript, *Resurrectio et quae sequuntur*, which he wrote, most probably, in 1699, at the time when he was working on *A Paraphrase and Notes on the Epistles of St Paul*.[15] The views that Locke expressed in this manuscript are indeed the same he formulated when elucidating Paul's epistles on this subject in the *Paraphrase*, particularly 1 Cor. 15.[16] *Resurrectio et quae sequuntur* too is mainly, albeit not exclusively, based on Paul's stance on the resurrection of the dead in 1 Cor. 15. In this manuscript, Locke maintained that "all men by the benefit of Christ shall be restored to life."[17] He clarified that the Second

[13] George H. Williams (ed.), *The Polish Brethren: Documentation of the History and Thought of Unitarianism in the Polish-Lithuanian Commonwealth and in the Diaspora 1601–1685*, 2 vols. (Missoula: Scholars Press, 1980), vol. 1, pp. 106–107, 202–204, 237, 326, vol. 2, pp. 407, 416, 686.

[14] On Locke's mortalism and its relation to his theory of personal identity and to early modern mortalist theories, see Arthur W. Wainwright, "Introduction" to John Locke, *A Paraphrase and Notes on the Epistles of St Paul to the Galatians, 1 and 2 Corinthians, Romans, Ephesians*, ed. Arthur W. Wainwright, 2 vols. (Oxford: Clarendon Press, 1987), vol. 1, pp. 1–88 (51–56); Philip C. Almond, *Heaven and Hell in Enlightenment England* (Cambridge: Cambridge University Press, 1994), pp. 129–130, 140–143; John Marshall, *John Locke: Resistance, Religion and Responsibility* (Cambridge: Cambridge University Press, 1994), pp. 399–401; John Marshall, "Locke, Socinianism, 'Socinianism,' and Unitarianism," in M. A. Stewart (ed.), *English Philosophy in the Age of Locke* (Oxford: Clarendon Press, 2000), pp. 111–182 (159–161); John C. Higgins-Biddle, "Introduction" to John Locke, *The Reasonableness of Christianity, As Delivered in the Scriptures*, ed. John C. Higgins-Biddle (Oxford: Clarendon Press, 1999), pp. xv–cxv (cxxi–cxxii); Stephen D. Snobelen, "Socinianism, Heresy and John Locke's *Reasonableness of Christianity*," *Enlightenment and Dissent*, 20 (2001): pp. 88–125 (114–120); Ball, *Soul Sleepers*, pp. 120–126; Chiara Giuntini, *Presenti a se stessi. La centralità della coscienza in Locke* (Florence: Le Lettere, 2015), pp. 239–285; Nicholas Jolley, *Locke's Touchy Subjects: Materialism and Immortality* (Oxford: Oxford University Press, 2015), pp. 99–115; Jon William Thompson, "Personal and Bodily Identity: The Metaphysics of Resurrection in 17th Century Philosophy," PhD dissertation, King's College London, 2019, pp. 137–179.

[15] John Locke, "Resurrectio et quae sequuntur," in John Locke, *Writings on Religion*, ed. Victor Nuovo (Oxford: Oxford University Press, 2002), pp. 232–237. A transcription of this manuscript is also in Locke, *Paraphrase*, vol. 2, pp. 679–684. The original of this manuscript is MS Locke c. 27, ff. 162–173, "Resurrectio et quae sequuntur."

[16] Locke, *Paraphrase*, 1 Cor. 15, vol. 1, pp. 246–256.   [17] Locke, "Resurrectio," p. 232.

Coming of Christ will be followed by the resurrection of "Those that are his" and, subsequently, by "the resurrection of the wicked," which will take place "before our Saviour delivers up the Kingdom to his father, for then is the end."[18] He argued that the wicked "shall not live forever" because "the wages of sin is death," as is stated in Rom. 6:23, while "the reward of the righteous is everlasting life."[19] Upon the resurrection of the dead, there will be "life to the just, to beleivers, to the obedient; & death to the wicked & unbeleivers."[20] Locke expressly denied that, when Scripture threatens death as "the ultimate punishment & last estate to which the wicked must all come," by "death" is meant "eternal life in torment."[21] He referred to several biblical verses in support of his point. He maintained that, when Gal. 6:8 states that "he that soweth to his flesh shall of the flesh reap corruption; but he that soweth to the spirit shall of the spirit reap life everlasting," the terms "corruption & life everlasting are opposed," and by corruption is meant "the dissolution & final destruction of a thing whereby it ceases to be."[22] Moreover, when considering "the everlasting fire threatened by our saviour to the wicked" in Matt. 18:8 and Matt. 25:41–46, he argued that "everlasting in a true scripture sense may be said of that which endures as long as the subject it affects endures" and, consequently, "the wicked shall die & be extinguished at last."[23]

Although Locke wrote his most thorough account of his mortalist ideas in the late 1690s, various passages concerning 1 Cor. 15 and other relevant biblical texts in *The Reasonableness of Christianity* and in several theological manuscripts (most of which are drafts of different sections of the *Reasonableness*) demonstrate that he already held mortalist views by the mid-1690s.[24] Concerning human mortality, the *Reasonableness* indeed states:

By *Death* here I can understand nothing but a ceasing to be, the losing of all actions of Life and Sense. Such a Death came on *Adam*, and all his Posterity by his first Disobedience in Paradise, under which *Death* they should have lain for ever, had it not been for the Redemption by Jesus Christ.[25]

---

[18] Ibid., pp. 232–234.   [19] Ibid., p. 233.   [20] Ibid., p. 234.   [21] Ibid.
[22] Ibid., pp. 235–236.   [23] Ibid., p. 236.
[24] Locke, *Reasonableness*, pp. 7–16, 104, 117; John Locke, "On the Immortality of the Soul," in John Locke, *An Early Draft of Locke's Essay: Together with Excerpts from His Journals*, ed. Richard I. Aaron and Jocelyn Gibb (Oxford: Clarendon Press, 1936), pp. 121–123 (original: MS Locke f. 6, "Locke's journal, 1682," February 20, 1682, pp. 25–33, "On the Immortality of the Soul," first published by Peter King in 1830); John Locke, "MS Locke c. 27, f. 101, Christianitie," in Locke, *Reasonableness*, pp. 198–200 (written around 1695); John Locke, "MS Locke c. 27, f. 103, Adam ante lapsum immortalis," in Locke, *Reasonableness*, p. 201 (written around 1695); John Locke, "MS Locke c. 27, ff. 104–111," in Locke, *Reasonableness*, pp. 201–205 (containing a list of biblical verses compiled, probably, around 1695); John Locke, "Spirit, Soul, and Body," in Locke, *Paraphrase*, vol. 2, pp. 675–678 (original: MS Locke c. 27, ff. 131–137, "Spirit, Soul, and Body," composed in 1697 or later); Wainwright, "Introduction," pp. 52–53.
[25] Locke, *Reasonableness*, pp. 8–9.

In the *Reasonableness*, Locke described resurrection and eternal life as made possible, following redemption by Christ, only by a divine miracle. As regards otherworldly sanctions, he maintained that "Immortality and Bliss belong to the Righteous," who will be "re-instated in an Happy Immortality," while the wicked will suffer a "second Death."[26] In this respect, too, the *Reasonableness* anticipated the thesis of *Resurrectio et quae sequuntur*, since it argued that, in Scripture, by "death" is meant literal termination – not "endless torment in Hell-fire" and "Eternal Life in Misery."[27] Drawing on 2 Thess. 1:9 ("Who shall be punished with everlasting destruction from the presence of the Lord, and from the glory of his power"), he indeed wrote:

The state the unrighteous are at last destined to is a final cessation of life, *i.e.* of all sense perception and activity. ... The punishment of those that know not God and obey not the gospel shall be *everlasting destruction*.[28]

Locke never stated expressly that the human soul is mortal. But his theory that a divine miracle will be needed for the resurrection of the dead, and for the subsequent admission of the saved to eternal life, while the unsaved will suffer complete annihilation on Judgment Day implicitly denies the *natural immortality* of the soul. Locke's view of the soul as not *naturally immortal* implies that there is no temporal continuity between a soul's existence in this world and its existence in the afterlife upon resurrection – whether to enjoy eternal bliss, or to suffer horrible torments and then be destroyed again and forever. Furthermore, Locke's agnostic approach to substance in *An Essay concerning Human Understanding* entails that we do not know whether the soul, or thinking substance, is immaterial or material. In *Essay* II.xxiii.1, substance is described as an *unknown* support, or "substratum," of ideas that are "conveyed in by the Senses, as they are found in exteriour things, or by reflection on [the mind's] own operations" and that cannot "subsist by themselves."[29] In this respect, *Essay* II.xxiii.4 states that "we have no clear, or distinct *Idea* of that *thing* we suppose a Support."[30] In regard to our own thinking, we are aware of our thoughts and we have an idea of our thinking; but we have no clear and distinct idea of the underlying entity in which our thinking takes place and of its ontological constitution – whether it is immaterial or material.[31] In other words, we have no clear and distinct idea of a thinking substance, or soul. Locke's ambiguity, or rather agnosticism, about the immateriality or materiality of the soul emerges not only from the *Essay*, but also from two manuscripts he composed at different times. In a journal entry dated February 20, 1682, he

---

[26] Ibid., pp. 13, 104, 117.   [27] Ibid., p. 7.   [28] Ibid., p. 15.
[29] Locke, *Essay*, II.xxiii.1, p. 295.   [30] Ibid., II.xxiii.4, p. 297.
[31] Ibid., IV.iii.6, pp. 539–543. See Ruth Boeker, "Locke on Personal Identity: A Response to the Problems of His Predecessors," *Journal of the History of Philosophy*, 55 (2017): pp. 407–434 (412).

questioned the compatibility between two attributes commonly ascribed to the soul, namely, its (natural) immortality and its immateriality, since immortality would make sense only in the presence of sensibility.[32] Over one decade later, in the entries on this subject in the manuscript *Adversaria Theologica*, he endorsed opposing arguments with his initials, thus manifesting an ambiguous or undecided position.[33] For instance, he endorsed the following argument in favor of the view that the soul is immaterial: "We cannot conceive one material atom to think nor any Systeme of Atoms or particles to think."[34] But he also endorsed the following argument, which is compatible with the hypothesis of the materiality of the soul:

We can conceive noe movable substance without extension, for what is not extended is nowhere. i e is not. From this & the opposite view we must conclude there is something in the nature of Spirits or thinking beings which we cannot conceive.[35]

However, when Edward Stillingfleet, commenting on Locke's agnostic approach to substance in the late 1690s, accused him of being a materialist at heart like Spinoza,[36] Locke rejected this inference, although he still kept an agnostic position on the subject:

It requires some skill for any one to represent me, as your lordship does here, as one ignorant or doubtful whether matter may not think; to that degree, "that I am not certain, or I do not believe that there is a principle above matter and motion in the world, and consequently all revelation may be nothing but the effects of an exalted fancy, or the heats of a disordered imagination, as Spinosa affirmed."[37]

Concerning the body in which the soul will be resurrected, Locke wrote in *Essay* II.xxvii.15: "We may be able without any difficulty to conceive, the same Person at the Resurrection, though in a Body not exactly in make or parts the same which he had here."[38] In the *Reasonableness*, referring to 1 Cor. 15:54, he stated that our "frail Mortal Bodies" will be changed into "Spiritual Immortal Bodies at the Resurrection," and he talked of the

---

[32] Locke, "Immortality."

[33] John Locke, "Adversaria Theologica 94," in Locke, *Writings on Religion*, pp. 19–33 (28–30). For more details of this manuscript, written for the most part in 1694–1695, see Chapter 3.

[34] Locke, "Adversaria Theologica," p. 28.   [35] Ibid., p. 30.

[36] Edward Stillingfleet, *An Answer to Mr. Locke's Second Letter* (London, 1698), pp. 29–30. On the Locke-Stillingfleet controversy of 1697–1699, I say more below in this chapter and Chapter 5.

[37] John Locke, "Reply to the Right Reverend the Lord Bishop of Worcester's Answer to His Second Letter," in John Locke, *Works*, 9 vols., 12th ed. (London, 1824), vol. 3, pp. 191–499 (294). The charge of Spinozism was also leveled at Locke, after his death, by the Irish clergyman William Carroll in *A Dissertation upon the Tenth Chapter of the Fourth Book of Mr Locke's Essay Concerning Humane Understanding* (London, 1706).

[38] Locke, *Essay*, II.xxvii.15, p. 340.

"Resurrection of the dead," not of their bodies.[39] He repeated the notion that "the saints shall then have spiritual & immortal bodys" in *Resurrectio et quae sequuntur*.[40] In this manuscript, he clarified, drawing on several passages from 1 Cor. 15:

We shall all be changed in the twinkleing of an eye ... Because this corruptible thing must put on incorruption & this mortal thing put on immortality. how? by putting off flesh & bloud by an instantaneous change because ... Flesh & bloud cannot inherit the kingdom of god. ... Men alive are flesh & bloud, the dead in the graves are but the remains of corrupted flesh & bloud. But flesh & bloud can not inherit the kingdom of god, neither can corruption inherit incorruption i e immortality.[41]

Here, Locke's use of the term "change" needs some explanation. Considering his mention of the "putting off" of flesh and blood and his explicit denial that "the resurrection of the same body ... is an article of the Christian faith,"[42] I believe that he did not mean that God will revive and modify the deceased body. I think that he meant that God will provide a new, "spiritual" body for the saved at the resurrection. As to the bodies of the wicked, he abstained from drawing any conclusion, given the lack of scriptural references to this subject:

Nor doe I remember any mention of the change of the bodys where the resurrection of the wicked can be supposed to be comprehended. ... But of the change of their bodys of their being made spiritual or of their putting on incorruption or immortality I doe not remember any thing said. They shall be raised is said over & over, But how they are raised or with what bodys they shall come the Scripture as far as I have observed is perfectly silent.[43]

Finally, whereas Locke had referred to the resurrection of "bodies" in the first three editions of *An Essay concerning Human Understanding*, he repeatedly spoke of the "resurrection of the dead" – not of their bodies – in the fourth edition of the *Essay*, published in 1700, and in the *Paraphrase*, particularly when paraphrasing and commenting on 1 Cor. 15:42–50.[44] Locke's paraphrase and notes on 1 Cor. 15:42 actually present the same points made in *Resurrectio*

---

[39] Locke, *Reasonableness*, pp. 115–116. 1 Cor. 15:54 reads: "So when this corruptible shall have put on incorruption, and this mortal shall have put on immortality, then shall be brought to pass the saying that is written, Death is swallowed up in victory."

[40] Locke, "Resurrectio," p. 232.

[41] Ibid., p. 233. While attaching great importance to Christ's resurrection as evidence of his Messiahship (see Chapters 2 and 5), and while maintaining that "corruptible" flesh and blood cannot inherit the Kingdom of God, Locke did not consider the fact that Christ's body at resurrection still bore the wounds of crucifixion. Moreover, none of his opponents ever confronted him on this subject.

[42] Locke, "Reply to the ... Answer to His Second Letter," p. 303. As we will see in the next section of this chapter, Locke made this point during his dispute with Stillingfleet.

[43] Locke, "Resurrectio," p. 237.

[44] Locke, *Essay*, IV.iii.29, pp. 559–560, IV.xvii.23, p. 687, IV.xviii.7, p. 694; Locke, *Paraphrase*, 1 Cor. 15:42–50, vol. 1, pp. 253–255.

et quae sequuntur about "flesh and blood," and "corruption," which cannot inherit immortality.[45] In the *Paraphrase*, Locke also reasserted his agnostic position on the bodies of the wicked at resurrection, given Paul's silence on this subject, and he reaffirmed the view that the saved "shall have from Christ the second Adam spiritual body," which will enable them to "subsist perpetually" in a "state of immutable incorruptibility."[46]

Besides denoting various points in common with the Socinian theological tradition, Locke's views on the afterlife present some striking similarities to Hobbes's position on this subject. In an attempt to reconcile the biblical references to eternal punishment with biblical passages implying that death is the fate of the reprobate, Hobbes argued in *Leviathan* that the sufferings of the wicked might be of limited duration, even though the fire in which they will burn might be everlasting.[47] Moreover, he questioned the natural immortality of the soul and maintained that the resurrection of the soul depends "on Grace, not on Nature."[48] Despite the similarities between Locke's and Hobbes's views on this matter, it is difficult to ascertain whether Locke drew on Hobbes in this regard, because Locke was very careful to never associate himself with Hobbism. Locke was accused of Hobbism by some contemporaries, such as the clergyman (and later Bishop of Gloucester, Salisbury, and Winchester) Richard Willis, the Oxford theologian Richard West, and the Calvinistic divine John Edwards.[49] Even Locke's friend Isaac Newton took him for a Hobbist, given Locke's position on the immateriality or materiality of the soul, before apologizing to him in written form in 1693.[50] Nevertheless, the charge of Hobbism against Locke, during the long debate on his religious views, revolved mainly around the similarities between his emphasis on faith in Jesus the Messiah and Hobbes's considerations on Jesus as the Messiah.[51] Some of Locke's critics actually saw his (implicit) rejection of the natural immortality of the soul as inspired mainly by Socinian influences.

---

[45] Ibid., 1 Cor. 15:42, vol. 1, p. 253.

[46] Ibid., 1 Cor. 15:44, vol. 1, p. 254, and 1 Cor. 15:50, vol. 1, p. 255. On Locke's views on the body at resurrection, see Luisa Simonutti, "Locke's Biblical Hermeneutics on Bodily Resurrection," in Luisa Simonutti (ed.), *Locke and Biblical Hermeneutics: Conscience and Scripture* (Cham: Springer, 2019), pp. 55–74.

[47] Thomas Hobbes, *Leviathan*, ed. C. B. Macpherson (London: Penguin, 1985), pp. 478–496; Wainwright, "Introduction," p. 53; Luc Foisneau, "Personal Identity and Human Mortality: Hobbes, Locke, Leibniz," in Sarah Hutton, Paul Schuurman (eds.), *Studies on Locke: Sources, Contemporaries, and Legacy* (Dordrecht: Springer, 2008), pp. 88–105; Jolley, *Locke's Touchy Subjects*, pp. 116–131.

[48] Hobbes, *Leviathan*, pp. 644–649.

[49] Richard Willis, *The Occasional Paper*, 10 vols. (London, 1697–1698), vol. 1, pp. 20–27; Richard West, *Animadversions on a Late Book Entituled The Reasonableness of Christianity* (Oxford, 1698), pp. 64–65; John Edwards, *A Brief Vindication of the Fundamental Articles of the Christian Faith* (London, 1697), sig. A3r; Higgins-Biddle, "Introduction," pp. lxxiv–cxv.

[50] Liam P. Dempsey, "John Locke, 'Hobbist': Of Sleeping Souls and Thinking Matter," *Canadian Journal of Philosphy*, 47:4 (2017): pp. 454–476.

[51] See Chapter 2.

Locke's agnostic stance on the immateriality or materiality of the soul in the *Essay* and the mortalism emerging from his public writings raised criticism from various intellectuals, such as the Cambridge scholar Richard Bentley, the Malebranchean philosopher John Norris, and the aforesaid Richard West.[52] Locke's views on the soul were also criticized in three anonymous sets of remarks published between 1697 and 1699 and commonly attributed to the theologian and cosmogonist Thomas Burnet.[53] However, a recent article has persuasively argued that the author of these three sets of remarks was not Burnet, but the aforementioned clergyman Richard Willis, given the evidence coming from several contemporary sources and the stylistic affinities between these three pamphlets and Willis's other works.[54] Regardless of who was the author of these anonymous pamphlets, Locke was very annoyed by his criticism. He was particularly disturbed by this author's claim that his agnosticism about the immateriality or materiality of the soul implies that we cannot have any assurance of divine sanctions in the afterlife and, consequently, we have no incentive to act morally. This position was obviously inconsistent with Locke's soteriological and moral views. Thus, replying to this and other objections raised by this author, Locke judged these criticisms untenable and based on gross misinterpretations of his views on morality and the soul.[55] Another, and more acute, critique of Locke's mortalism came from the renowned German philosopher Gottfried Wilhelm Leibniz in *Nouveaux essais sur l'entendement humain* (*New Essays on Human Understanding*).[56] In these essays, Leibniz connected Locke's mortalism, which he judged influenced by Socinianism, with the fact that Locke did not dismiss the possibility that the soul might be material. Moreover, Leibniz maintained that Locke's considerations on the mortality of the soul were in line with his way of ideas, especially

---

[52] Richard Bentley, *Observations upon a Sermon Intituled, A Confutation of Atheism from the Faculties of the Soul* (London, 1692); John Norris, *An Account of Reason and Faith, in Relation to the Mysteries of Christianity* (London, 1697); West, *Animadversions*.

[53] Thomas Burnet, *Remarks on John Locke, with Locke's Replies*, ed. George Watson (Doncaster: Brynmill, 1989).

[54] J. C. Walmsley, Hugh Craig, John Burrows, "The Authorship of the *Remarks upon An Essay concerning Human Understanding*," *Eighteenth-Century Thought*, 6 (2016): pp. 205–243.

[55] Another defense of Locke from the objections raised in these three pamphlets came, in 1702, from the novelist, playwright, and philosopher Catharine Trotter Cockburn in "A Defence of Mr. Lock's Essay of Human Understanding," now in Catharine Trotter Cockburn, *Philosophical Writings*, ed. Patricia Sheridan (Peterborough: Broadview Press, 2006), pp. 35–85. See Jessica Gordon-Roth, "Catharine Trotter Cockburn's Defence of Locke," *The Monist*, 98:1 (2015): pp. 64–76; Emilio Maria De Tommaso, "'Some Reflections upon the True Grounds of Morality': Catharine Trotter in Defence of John Locke," *Philosophy Study*, 7:6 (2017): pp. 326–339.

[56] For an English translation, see Gottfried Wilhelm Leibniz, *New Essays on Human Understanding*, trans. and ed. Peter Remnant and Jonathan Bennett (Cambridge: Cambridge University Press, 1982). On this work, see Nicholas Jolley, *Leibniz and Locke: A Study of the New Essays concerning Human Understanding* (Oxford: Oxford University Press, 1984).

with his denial of innate ideas and his theory that the soul does not think continuously.[57] However, Locke could not respond to Leibniz's criticism because the latter completed *Nouveaux essais* in 1704 and, following Locke's death in late October of that year, he preferred to withhold the publication of these essays, which were first published, posthumously, in 1765.

At any rate, although Locke's mortalist ideas were identical to the views held by some Socinians on this matter, he always made sure that his religious views – including his views on the resurrection of the dead and the Last Judgment – were consistent with, and indeed grounded in, scriptural revelation. But, although grounded in Scripture, Locke's mortalism, along with his agnosticism on substance, had heterodox implications concerning personal identity. Locke's theory that the human soul perishes with the body and will need a divine miracle to be resurrected on Judgment Day, his idea that our "frail Mortal Bodies" will be changed into "Spiritual Immortal Bodies at the Resurrection," and his view that we do not have a clear and distinct idea of a thinking substance or soul and its ontological constitution make it difficult, or even impossible, to argue that personal identity is in the soul, or in the body, or in a union of body and soul. Locke was aware of this problem and its moral implications. According to Locke, personal identity indeed entails moral accountability, which is not only taken into account in matters relevant to human justice, but will also be considered on the Last Judgment. Given his emphasis on individual responsibility in matters relevant to salvation, he needed to provide an account of personal identity consistent with his mortalism and his way of ideas.

Personal Identity and Moral Accountability

Locke decided to expound his theory of personal identity when, in a letter dated March 2, 1693, his friend William Molyneux encouraged him to clarify his position on the *principium individuationis* (principle of individuation).[58] The *principium individuationis*, as Udo Thiel has put it, defines "what it is that makes an individual the individual it is and distinguishes it from all other individuals of the same kind."[59] Locke concentrated on this issue in the second edition of *An Essay concerning Human Understanding*, published in 1694, precisely in Book II, Chapter xxvii, "Of Identity and Diversity." In this chapter, Locke paid great attention to the principle of individuation of persons

---

[57] Leibniz, *New Essays*, pp. 110–116.

[58] William Molyneux to Locke, March 2, 1693, in John Locke, *The Correspondence of John Locke*, ed. E. S. de Beer, 8 vols. (Oxford: Oxford University Press, 1979–1989), vol. 4, no. 1609.

[59] Udo Thiel, "The Trinity and Human Personal Identity," in Stewart (ed.), *English Philosophy*, pp. 217–243 (217–218).

and to personal identity, delineating a theory that significantly diverges from the traditional Christian understanding of these concepts.

Christian thought since the sixth century has largely shared Boethius's definition of "person" as an "individual substance of a rational nature." In the early modern era, even the Socinians and other anti-Trinitarians accepted this definition of person. They argued that the Trinitarian dogma, which maintains the consubstantiality of the three divine persons, is not only unscriptural but also illogical, because a person is an individual substance and, therefore, three persons cannot share one substance. The Socinians' and other anti-Trinitarians' use of the Boethian theory of personhood entails a substantialist view of the *divine* persons consistent with a notion of *human* person based on Boethius's definition. However, in the traditional Christian account of personhood, adopted with different purposes by both Trinitarian and anti-Trinitarian theologians in the early modern period, the concept of *human* person assumes the union of soul and body, both described in substantialist terms. According to this notion of individuation, human individuality is constituted by the particular union of soul and body, which is a particular subsistence, or manner of subsistence, of human nature. Bishop Stillingfleet's points on this subject, during his dispute with Locke about the anti-Trinitarian potential of the latter's way of ideas, exemplify this position. Claiming that Locke's way of ideas, with its agnostic account of substance, was incompatible with the traditional, substantialist notion of person underlying the Trinitarian dogma, Stillingfleet reaffirmed that a "person" is a "compleat intelligent Substance, with a peculiar manner of Subsistence."[60] He added that "we take *Person* with Relation to *Soul* and *Body* united together. And so the *Identity* of *Person* must take in both, not only here, but at the Resurrection."[61] Stillingfleet's claim that Locke had departed from the traditional, substantialist understanding of person was not ill grounded. In fact, when Locke embarked on offering a solution to the problem of individuation and formulating a theory of personal identity in the 1694 edition of the *Essay*, he provided a non-substantialist account of personal identity and developed, instead, a consciousness-based theory of personal identity.[62]

---

[60] Edward Stillingfleet, *A Discourse in Vindication of the Doctrine of the Trinity* (London, 1697), p. 261.

[61] Stillingfleet, *Answer to Mr. Locke's Second Letter*, p. 175. See, also, ibid., pp. 33–44.

[62] Several aspects of Locke's theory of personal identity are still issues for debate, due to Locke's conciseness or, in some cases, ambiguity. There is no consensus among Locke experts concerning matters such as the ontological status of Lockean persons (which have been variously interpreted as modes or substances), the metaphysical constitution of the unifying component of consciousness, the role of appropriation in making personal identity, and whether the nature of thinking substances is simply *unknown* or *unknowable* to us. Here, a discussion of these controversial issues (which I abstain from providing) would be irrelevant to my analysis of the connections between Locke's mortalism, his theory of personal identity, and his soteriology. For an accurate account of the debate on these issues, see Jessica Gordon-Roth, "Locke

Essay II.xxvii makes a distinction between the *principium individuationis* as an ontological notion and identity as an epistemic notion. To Locke, the *principium individuationis* is "Existence it self, which determines a Being of any sort to a particular time and place incommunicable to two Beings of the same kind."[63] Identity, in Locke, is a more complex concept, which Udo Thiel has accurately explained as follows:

Our concepts determine what is required for the identity of objects over time. . . . According to Locke, then, what constitutes the identity of a being through time is the continued fulfilment of those requirements which are specified by that abstract idea under which we consider the being: there can be no satisfactory treatment of identity through time independently of our abstract ideas of those things whose identity is in question.[64]

This means that, as Locke himself admitted, different people could determine different requirements for the identity of objects over time. *Essay* II.xxvii.29 considers the case of the identity of "man":

For supposing a rational Spirit be the *Idea* of a *Man*, 'tis easie to know, what is the *same Man*, *viz*. the *same Spirit*, whether separate or in a Body will be the *same Man*. Supposing a rational Spirit vitally united to a Body of a certain conformation of Parts to make a *Man*, whilst that rational Spirit, with that vital conformation of Parts, though continued in a fleeting successive Body, remains, it will be the *same Man*. But if to any one the *Idea* of a *Man* be, but the vital union of Parts in a certain shape; as long as that vital union and shape remains, in a concrete no otherwise the same, but by a continued succession of fleeting Particles, it will be the same *Man*. For whatever be the composition whereof the complex *Idea* is made, whenever Existence makes it one particular thing under any denomination, the same Existence continued, preserves it the same individual under the same denomination.[65]

This said, although different people might have different notions of "man," Locke was persuaded that his own notion of man was the most appropriate and best-conforming to the idea of man "in most Peoples Sense."[66] His view of the identity of man is closely connected to his description of the identity of living creatures, which he distinguished from atoms and masses of atoms:

Let us suppose an Atom, *i.e.* a continued body under one immutable Superficies, existing in a determined time and place: 'tis evident, that, considered in any instant of its Existence, it is, in that instant, the same with it self. For being, at that instant, what it

on Personal Identity," *Stanford Encyclopedia of Philosophy* (2019), https://plato.stanford.edu/entries/locke-personal-identity/.

[63] Locke, *Essay*, II.xxvii.3, p. 330.

[64] Thiel, *Early Modern Subject*, p. 106. See, also, K. Joanna S. Forstrom, *John Locke and Personal Identity: Immortality and Bodily Resurrection in 17th-Century Philosophy* (London: Continuum, 2010), pp. 18–24.

[65] Locke, *Essay*, II.xxvii.29, p. 348.

[66] Ibid., II.xxvii.8, p. 335; Thiel, *Early Modern Subject*, p. 106.

is, and nothing else, it is the same, and so must continue, as long as its Existence is continued: for so long it will be the same, and no other. In like manner, if two or more Atoms be joined together into the same Mass, every one of those Atoms will be the same, by the foregoing Rule: And whilst they exist united together, the Mass, consisting of the same Atoms, must be the same Mass, or the same Body, let the parts be never so differently jumbled: But if one of these Atoms be taken away, or one new one added, it is no longer the same Mass, or the same Body. In the state of living Creatures, their Identity depends not on a Mass of the same Particles; but on something else.[67]

According to Locke, the identity of living creatures depends on the continued organization of a common life – namely, on the continued organization of all their parts in a way fit to convey life to the whole creature. Likewise, the *principium individuationis* of a living creature is the existence of an organized, common life.[68] This is also true for man, because human beings are living creatures. In *Essay* II.xxvii.6, Locke wrote that "the Identity of the same *Man* consists … in nothing but a participation of the same continued Life, by constantly fleeting Particles of Matter, in succession vitally united to the same organized Body."[69] He further clarified that "'tis not the *Idea* of a thinking or rational Being alone, that makes the *Idea* of a *Man* in most Peoples Sense; but of a Body so and so shaped joined to it."[70] Locke made a distinction between the identity of a "man" and that of a "person," as he located personal identity in "consciousness, which is inseparable from thinking."[71] He substantiated this point with the following explanation:

For since consciousness always accompanies thinking, and 'tis that, that makes every one to be, what he calls *self*; and thereby distinguishes himself from all other thinking things, in this alone consists *personal Identity*, *i.e.* the sameness of a rational Being: And as far as this consciousness can be extended backwards to any past Action or Thought, so far reaches the Identity of that *Person*; it is the same *self* now it was then; and 'tis by the same *self* with this present one that now reflects on it, that that Action was done.[72]

To Locke, consciousness makes personal identity as an epistemic notion and also determines the *principium individuationis* of a person as an ontological notion. The *principium individuationis* of a person indeed defines what it is that makes an individual person the individual person this person is and that, consequently, distinguishes this individual person from all other individual persons. Here, a clarification of what "consciousness" means in Locke's philosophy is in order. Locke maintained that "Consciousness is the perception

---

[67] Locke, *Essay*, II.xxvii.3, p. 330.   [68] Ibid., II.xxvii.3–5, pp. 330–331.

[69] Ibid., II.xxvii.6, pp. 331–332. On Locke's concept of "man," see John W. Yolton, *The Two Intellectual Worlds of John Locke: Man, Person, and Spirits in the "Essay"* (Ithaca: Cornell University Press, 2004), pp. 9–37.

[70] Locke, *Essay*, II.xxvii.8, p. 335.   [71] Ibid., II.xxvii.9, p. 335.   [72] Ibid.

of what passes in a Man's own mind."[73] In this regard, I find Shelley Weinberg's clarification of Locke's concept of consciousness very helpful:

[Consciousness] is a non-evaluative self-referential form of awareness internal to all perceptions of ideas. It is the perception that *I am perceiving* an idea, or the perception of *myself as perceiving* an idea. . ... Perceptions of ideas, for Locke, are complex mental states in which we are conscious of more than just the idea perceived. In any perception of an idea, there is, at the very least, an act of perception, an idea perceived, and consciousness (that *I am perceiving*).[74]

According to Locke, the fact of being conscious denotes an *immediate awareness*, which is a crucial part of all acts of thinking. Consciousness is, indeed, "inseparable from thinking." Therefore, consciousness is different from "reflection," which Locke described as "the *Perception of the Operations of our own Minds* within us."[75] Reflection is relevant to contemplation, not to immediate awareness, because reflection takes place when the mind considers its own operations and objectifies them – or, in other words, when the mind produces *ideas* of its own operations. Therefore, reflection is not an essential element of thinking. Consciousness is also to be distinguished from intuition, which, in Locke's way of ideas, is immediate knowledge of self-evident truths. Intuition has a more limited scope than consciousness, because intuition, unlike consciousness, is not necessarily always present in thinking. Finally, consciousness cannot be identified with memory, because consciousness is an integral part of all acts of thinking at any time, while memory consists of one's recollection of their experiences from the past. Thus, memory is only a part of consciousness – precisely that part of consciousness that, as Locke wrote in an above-quoted passage from *Essay* II.xxvii.9, "as far as [it] can be extended backwards to any past Action or Thought, so far reaches the Identity of that *Person*; it is the same *self* now it was then; and 'tis by the same *self* with this present one that now reflects on it, that that Action was done."[76] Briefly, consciousness is more fundamental than reflection, has a broader scope than intuition, and is also broader than memory.[77]

Nevertheless, in the *Essay*, the term "consciousness" seems to denote two different senses, which Weinberg has accurately explained: "Locke seems to see consciousness as (1) *a mental state inseparable from an act of perception by means of which we are aware of ourselves as perceiving*, and (2) *the ongoing self we are aware of in these conscious states*."[78] While the first sense of consciousness signifies a momentary psychological state based on a momentary subjective experience, the second sense denotes the objective fact

---

[73] Ibid., II.i.19, p. 115.

[74] Shelley Weinberg, *Consciousness in Locke* (Oxford: Oxford University Press, 2016), p. xi.

[75] Locke, *Essay*, II.i.4, p. 105.   [76] Ibid., II.xxvii.9, p. 335.

[77] Thiel, *Early Modern Subject*, pp. 109–120.   [78] Weinberg, *Consciousness*, p. 153.

of the diachronic existence of a self – "by the same consciousness."[79] Here, nevertheless, a problem arises, given that consciousness presents gaps, whereas life has no gaps. Locke considered this issue in *Essay* II.xxvii.20:

Suppose I wholly lose the memory of some parts of my Life, beyond a possibility of retrieving them, so that perhaps I shall never be conscious of them again; yet am I not the same Person, that did those Actions, had those Thoughts, that I was once conscious of, though I have now forgot them? To which I answer, that we must here take notice what the Word *I* is applied to, which in this case is the Man only. And the same Man being presumed to be the same Person, *I* is easily here supposed to stand also for the same Person.[80]

However, despite the undeniable gaps in consciousness, in this section of the *Essay* Locke still argued that consciousness alone makes personal identity:

But if it be possible for the same Man to have distinct incommunicable consciousness at different times, it is past doubt the same Man would at different times make different Persons; which, we see, is the Sense of Mankind in the solemnest Declaration of their Opinions, Humane Laws not punishing the *Mad Man* for the *Sober Man*'s Actions, nor the *Sober Man* for what the *Mad Man* did, thereby making them two Persons; which is somewhat explained by our way of speaking in *English*, when we say such an one *is not himself*, or is *besides himself*; in which Phrases it is insinuated, as if those who now, or, at least, first used them, thought that *self* was changed, the *self* same Person was no longer in that Man.[81]

Locke also emphasized that it is consciousness alone that makes an individual person the individual person that this person is, despite the temporal interruptions in consciousness, in *Essay* II.xxvii.10, where he argued that the question whether the same substance exists continuously is irrelevant to the question of personhood:

This consciousness, being interrupted always by forgetfulness, there being no moment of our Lives wherein we have the whole train of all our past Actions before our Eyes in one view: But even the best Memories losing the sight of one part whilst they are viewing another; and we sometimes, and that the greatest part of our Lives, not reflecting on our past selves, being intent on our present Thoughts, and in sound sleep, having no Thoughts at all, or at least none with that consciousness, which remarks our waking Thoughts. I say, in all these cases, our consciousness being interrupted, and we losing the sight of our past *selves*, doubts are raised whether we are the same thinking thing; *i.e.* the same substance or no. Which however reasonable, or unreasonable, concerns not *personal Identity* at all. The Question being what makes the same *Person*, and not whether it be the same Identical Substance, which always thinks in the same *Person*, which in this case matters not at all. Different Substances, by the same consciousness (where they do partake in it) being united into one Person; as well as

[79] The phrase "by the same consciousness" appears in Locke, *Essay*, II.xxvii.10, p. 336, II.xxvii.21, p. 343, II.xxvii.25, p. 345.
[80] Ibid., II.xxvii.20, p. 342.   [81] Ibid., II.xxvii.20, pp. 342–343.

different Bodies, by the same Life are united into one Animal, whose *Identity* is preserved, in that change of Substances, by the unity of one continued Life. For it being the same consciousness that makes a Man be himself to himself, *personal Identity* depends on that only, whether it be annexed only to one individual Substance, or can be continued in a succession of several Substances. For as far as any intelligent Being can repeat the *Idea* of any past Action with the same consciousness it had of it at first, and with the same consciousness it has of any present Action; so far it is the same *personal self*. For it is by the consciousness it has of its present Thoughts and Actions, that it is *self* to it *self* now, and so will be the same *self* as far as the same consciousness can extend to Actions past or to come.[82]

Locke repeated the concepts expressed in the conclusion of this passage in other sections of *Essay* II.xxvii. For instance, in *Essay* II.xxvii.16, he maintained that "consciousness ... unites Existences, and Actions, very remote in time, into the same Person, as well as it does the Existence and Actions of the immediately preceding moment."[83] In the next section, he further argued that consciousness is that "which makes the same *Person*, and constitutes this inseparable *self*," and he declared that "That with which the *consciousness* of this present thinking thing can join it self, makes the same *Person*, and is one *self* with it, and with nothing else."[84]

The fact that consciousness makes personal identity has important practical, moral implications, because to Locke "in this *personal Identity* is founded all the Right and Justice of Reward and Punishment."[85] The moral aspects of Locke's theory of personal identity are manifest in his considerations on the continuity of personal identity, and hence of moral accountability, "by the same consciousness" during a person's life:

This every intelligent Being, sensible of Happiness or Misery, must grant, that there is something that is *himself*, that he is concerned for, and would have happy; that this *self* has existed in a continued Duration more than one instant, and therefore 'tis possible may exist, as it has done, Months and Years to come, without any certain bounds to be set to its duration; and may be the same *self*, by the same consciousness, continued on for the future. And thus, by this consciousness, he finds himself to be the *same self* which did such or such an Action some Years since, by which he comes to be happy or miserable now. In all which account of *self*, the same numerical Substance is not considered, as making the same *self*. But the same continued consciousness, in which several Substances may have been united, and again separated from it, which, whilst they continued in a vital union with that, wherein this consciousness then resided, made a part of that same *self*.[86]

Locke needed to find a criterion for moral accountability that was not only based on a non-substantialist account of personhood, given his agnosticism on

---

[82] Ibid., II.xxvii.10, pp. 335–336.   [83] Ibid., II.xxvii.16, p. 340.
[84] Ibid., II.xxvii.17, p. 341.   [85] Ibid., II.xxvii.18, p. 341.
[86] Ibid., II.xxvii.25, pp. 345–346.

substance, but also different from spatio-temporally continuous, "ungapped" life, given his views on death and the resurrection of the dead. As I have said above, Locke explained in *Essay* II.xxvii.6 that the identity of a "man" consists in "a participation of the same continued Life, by constantly fleeting Particles of Matter, in succession vitally united to the same organized Body."[87] However, the hypothesis of "the same Man being presumed to be the same Person," which Locke considered and rejected in the above-quoted *Essay* II. xxvii.20,[88] would be impractical on Judgment Day, given Locke's stance on the resurrection of the dead – not of their bodies. Locke admitted that life is "ungapped" and, thus, living creatures – including human beings or, as he put it, "man" – are *spatio-temporal* continuous things *in this life*. But, given Locke's views on soul-death and the resurrection of the dead (and not of their bodies), there is a gap and, consequently, no *spatio-temporal* continuity in human beings between death and resurrection on Judgment Day. Nevertheless, there ought to be, and to Locke there is indeed, some sort of continuity between one's self in their earthly life and in the afterlife upon resurrection, since resurrection is not a new *beginning* but a *continuation* of this self. Considering resurrection as a *beginning* would actually be inconsistent with a corollary of Locke's notion of the *principium individuationis*, namely, that all things only have a single beginning in time and place. For all these reasons, Locke's criterion for moral accountability ought to be, and indeed was, unrelated not only to the (unknown) substance or substances underlying a person's thinking and a person's life, but also to the unity of spatio-temporally continuous *life*. Locke's criterion for moral accountability was, simply, personal identity, which consciousness alone makes.

Locke described a "person" as a subject of accountability in two sections of *Essay* II.xxvii.[89] When distinguishing between "man" and "person" in *Essay* II.xxvii.9, he maintained that a person "is a thinking intelligent Being, that has reason and reflection, and can consider it self as it self, the same thinking thing in different times and places."[90] Every element of this definition is relevant to the moral implications of Locke's theory of personal identity. Reason, if utilized properly, is what allows a thinking, intelligent being to discern between what is moral and what is immoral. Reflection is necessary to realizing that one has freedom, which, as Locke put it in *Essay* II.xxi.56, "consists in a Power to do, or not to do; to do, or forbear doing as we *will*."[91] Reflection is

---

[87] Ibid., II.xxvii.6, pp. 331–332.   [88] Ibid., II.xxvii.20, pp. 342–343.

[89] On "person" as a subject of accountability in Locke, see Ruth Boeker, "The Moral Dimension in Locke's Account of Persons and Personal Identity," *History of Philosophy Quarterly*, 31:3 (2014): pp. 229–247 (239–241).

[90] Locke, *Essay*, II.xxvii.9, p. 335.

[91] Ibid., II.xxi.56, p. 270. As I have explained in Chapter 1, Locke included a revised, extended version of *Essay* II.xxi, "Of Power," in the second edition of 1694. Since here and below

indeed necessary to recognizing that one has the power to suspend the carrying out of some action until investigation has concluded whether this action is compatible, or not, with one's true happiness. Locke regarded true happiness as consistent with morality, since he equated the pursuit of true happiness to "the highest perfection of intellectual nature."[92] Moreover, he insisted on the necessity of keeping in mind "the true intrinsick good or ill, that is in things" in order to act in accordance with "the eternal Law and Nature of things [which] must not be alter'd," thus complying with "the Will and Power of the Law-maker" – i.e., God – who has the prerogative to reward and punish.[93] As to considering "it self as it self, the same thinking thing in different times and places," without this ability a thinking, intelligent being could not act morally or recognize the justness of punishment or reward. In fact, one is punished or rewarded for what one has done at some other time and (in most cases) in some other place. Therefore, one needs to consider oneself the same thinking thing at different times and places to make the connection between crime and punishment. Locke elaborated on his notion of person as a subject of account-ability in *Essay* II.xxvii.26, in which he called attention to the moral and legal connotations of the term "person":

[Person] is a Forensick Term appropriating Actions and their Merit; and so belongs only to intelligent Agents capable of a Law, and Happiness and Misery. This personality extends it *self* beyond present Existence to what is past, only by consciousness, whereby it becomes concerned and accountable, owns and imputes to it *self* past Actions, just upon the same ground, and for the same reason, as it does the present.[94]

Locke's characterization and use of "person" as a forensic term denote one more point in common with the Socinian tradition, despite the Socinians' substantialist account of personhood. Concerning the equivalence of "person" and "substance," Socinus's and his followers' understanding of person was inspired by the Boethian view of personhood. However, in regard to the moral and legal aspects of personhood, the Socinians' views were indebted to Roman law, in which the word "*persona*" is a forensic term. Since Roman law deals with persons, things, and actions, a major implication of the Socinians' borrowing from Roman law is that *personality* – not essence or substance – is the key characteristic of an active entity.[95] Briefly, both the Socinians and Locke paid great attention to person as a thinking, intelligent *moral* agent. Locke's attention to persons as moral agents has led some interpreters, such as

---

I concentrate particularly on another chapter (i.e., II.xxvii) added to the second edition of the *Essay*, I abstain from comparing the first and second editions when referring to *Essay* II.xxi.
[92] Ibid., II.xxi.51, p. 266.   [93] Ibid., II.xxi.53, p. 268, II.xxi.56, p. 271, II.xxviii.5, p. 351.
[94] Ibid., II.xxvii.26, p. 346.
[95] Sarah Mortimer, *Reason and Religion in the English Revolution: The Challenge of Socinianism* (Cambridge: Cambridge University Press, 2010), p. 35.

J. L. Mackie and Gideon Yaffe, to overemphasize the moral and legal aspects of his theory of personal identity. Mackie has even stated that Locke's theory is "hardly a theory of personal identity at all, but might be better described as a theory of action appropriation."[96] Moreover, Yaffe has argued that, in Locke's theory, it is the suitability of rewards and punishments to function as a criterion of personal identity and that, therefore, Locke "is reversing the assumed order of priority of the metaphysical and the moral."[97] I am convinced, however, by David Anderson's and Udo Thiel's interpretations, which, responding to Yaffe in particular, reaffirm that Locke's theory is actually a theory of personal identity.[98] In Thiel's words:

For Locke, personal identity is the *foundation* for "all the Right and Justice of Reward and Punishment" (*Essay*, II.xxvii.18). Identity, for Locke, is presupposed by appropriate rewards and punishments. Thus, the latter cannot function as criteria of the former. *Pace* Yaffe, for Locke personal identity cannot "consist in any thing but consciousness" (*Essay*, II.xxvii.21).[99]

In other words, to Locke personal identity, which consciousness alone makes, is ontologically prior to moral accountability. Yet, his theory of personal identity certainly complements, and is indeed conditioned by, his moral and theological commitments to a system of otherworldly rewards and punishments.[100] In fact, Locke's theory of personal identity combines well with his stance on the resurrection of the dead and the Last Judgment. Although Locke expounded his views on this matter in comprehensive terms only in the late 1690s, the second edition of the *Essay* and the *Reasonableness*, both published in the mid-1690s, already denoted his position on this subject. In fact, following the publication of these two works, Locke's views on the resurrection of the dead – not of their "frail Mortal Bodies"[101] – were largely perceived as heterodox and were connected to his theory of personal identity. Stillingfleet, in particular, called attention to this issue during his dispute with

---

[96] J. L. Mackie, *Problems with Locke* (Oxford: Clarendon Press, 1976), p. 183. Other studies describe Locke's account of personal identity in terms of appropriation. See, for instance, Antonia LoLordo, *Locke's Moral Man* (Oxford: Oxford University Press, 2012). Whereas a detailed discussion of this issue is irrelevant to my point in this chapter, I refer the reader to: Ruth Boeker, "The Role of Appropriation in Locke's Account of Persons and Personal Identity," *Locke Studies*, 16 (2016): pp. 3–39.

[97] Gideon Yaffe, "Locke on Ideas of Identity and Diversity," in Lex Newman (ed.), *The Cambridge Companion to Locke's "Essay concerning Human Understanding"* (Cambridge: Cambridge University Press, 2007), pp. 192–230 (227).

[98] David J. Anderson, "Susceptibility to Punishment: A Response to Yaffe," *Locke Studies*, 8 (2008): pp. 101–106; Thiel, *Early Modern Subject*, pp. 214–215.

[99] Ibid., p. 215.

[100] Marshall, "Locke, Socinianism," p. 160; Shelley Weinberg, "Locke on Personal Identity," *Philosophy Compass*, 6:6 (2011): pp. 398–407 (398); Boeker, "Moral Dimension," p. 242.

[101] Locke, *Reasonableness*, p. 115.

Locke in 1697–1699, which saw the publication of three writings each by these two philosophers. He argued that Locke's understanding of the resurrection of the dead, which he considered grounded in Locke's consciousness-based theory of personal identity, was incompatible with the Christian religion.[102] To Stillingfleet, the identity of the body at resurrection was an article of the Christian faith. He defended the view that each individual *human* person consists of a particular union of soul and body and, consequently, the identity of a human person as a specific union of soul and body must be the same in this life and at resurrection.[103] Locke's three replies to Stillingfleet provided further textual evidence from the Bible, as well as rational arguments to defend his theory of personal identity.[104] Responding to Stillingfleet, Locke reaffirmed the difference between "body" and "man" and argued that neither sameness of the body, nor sameness of the man is needed at resurrection. What matters, when it comes to the resurrection of the dead, is personal identity, which is made by consciousness alone. To make his argument stronger, Locke wrote in his third and last response to Stillingfleet:

The resurrection of the dead, I acknowledge to be an article of the Christian faith: but that the resurrection of the same body ... is an article of the Christian faith, is what, I confess, I do not yet know. ... I do not remember in any place of the New Testament (where the general resurrection at the last day is spoken of) any such expression as the resurrection of the body, much less of the same body.[105]

Locke added an interesting reflection on the fact that our bodies change in time: one's body at the age of five was not the same body it is at fifteen or fifty, and so will the body be different at resurrection.[106] But, despite Locke's clarification of his position on this subject, the debate on his views on personal identity and the resurrection of the dead continued for several decades after his death and involved various famous theologians of different persuasions, such as the Congregationalist ministers Isaac Watts and Philip Doddridge and the

---

[102] On this aspect of the Locke-Stillingfleet controversy, see Alan P. F. Sell, *John Locke and the Eighteenth-Century Divines* (Cardiff: University of Wales Press, 1997), pp. 250–262; Dan Kaufman, "The Resurrection of the Same Body and the Ontological Status of Organisms: What Locke Should Have (and Could Have) Told Stillingfleet," in David Owen, Paul Hoffman, Gideon Yaffe (eds.), *Contemporary Perspectives on Early Modern Philosophy* (Peterborough: Broadview Press, 2008), pp. 191–214; Thiel, *Early Modern Subject*, pp. 134–139.

[103] Stillingfleet, *Discourse in Vindication*, p. 261; Stillingfleet, *Answer to Locke's Second Letter*, pp. 33–44, 175.

[104] See especially Locke, "Reply to the ... Answer to His Second Letter," pp. 303–332; Jolley, *Locke's Touchy Subjects*, pp. 50–66.

[105] Locke, "Reply to the ... Answer to His Second Letter," pp. 303–304. Here, Locke disregarded the fact that John 2:19–22 was usually referred to in support of belief in the resurrection of the same body, because it relates Jesus speaking of raising "the temple of his body" in three days.

[106] Ibid., p. 308.

Church of England clergyman Joseph Butler.[107] Anyhow, starting with the controversy between Locke and Stillingfleet, this debate concentrated mainly on the metaphysical (and not the moral) aspects of Locke's theory of personal identity.

Consciousness, Repentance, and Salvation

The moral implications of Locke's theory of personal identity inform his considerations on the Last Judgment. As Udo Thiel has noted, in Locke "moral responsibility is founded in personal identity and personal identity in consciousness."[108] This conviction contradicts original sin, which Locke expressly denied in various public as well as private writings, as I have explained in Chapter 3. *Essay* II.xxvii, too, presents several passages incompatible with the doctrine of original sin and highlighting, instead, individual responsibility in matters of salvation. In this chapter of the *Essay*, Locke stated that only one's own actions will be considered on Judgment Day, when "the Sentence shall be justified by the consciousness all Persons shall have, that they *themselves* in what Bodies soever they appear, or what Substances soever that consciousness adheres to, are the *same*, that committed those Actions, and deserve that Punishment for them."[109] Locke took into account the possibility that a person's memory is transferred to another person – a possibility entailing that one might be rewarded or punished for another's actions. However, he trusted "the Goodness of God, who as far as the Happiness or Misery of any of his sensible Creatures is concerned in it, will not by a fatal Error of theirs transfer from one to another, that consciousness, which draws Reward or Punishment with it."[110] In the same chapter, Locke maintained that "in the great Day, wherein the Secrets of all Hearts shall be laid open, it may be reasonable to think, no one shall be made to answer for what he knows nothing of; but shall receive his Doom, his Conscience accusing or excusing him."[111] All these passages confirm Locke's denial of original sin and his firm belief in individual responsibility.

Concerning punishment on Judgment Day, however, Thiel has argued that there is a dichotomy between Locke's consciousness-based theory of personal identity and his notion of repentance, which *The Reasonableness of Christianity* describes as necessary to salvation. Calling attention to *Essay* II.xxvii.22, Thiel has maintained the following:

---

[107] On this debate, see Sell, *John Locke*, pp. 239–267.
[108] Thiel, *Early Modern Subject*, p. 131.   [109] Locke, *Essay*, II.xxvii.26, p. 347.
[110] Ibid., II.xxvii.13, p. 338.
[111] Ibid., II.xxvii.22, p. 344. As I have noted in Chapter 3, and as I repeat below in this chapter, Locke drew on 1 Cor. 14:25 in this section of the *Essay*.

If I am still conscious of my "past misdeeds," Locke would have to say that despite my genuine repentance I would nevertheless be subject to punishment for them, because "punishment [is] annexed to personality, and personality to consciousness." Thus it seems that repentance, even of the kind that Locke envisages, is not consistent with his account of personal identity in terms of consciousness. His distinction between thinking substance, man, and person does not help here. The inconsistency concerns his notion of repentance and his claim that just rewards and punishments depend only on consciousness.[112]

Briefly, in Thiel's opinion, a person's consciousness of their past misdeeds still makes this person subject to punishment and, consequently, this will result in punishment on the Last Judgment, regardless of their repentance. However, nowhere does Locke claim (as Thiel has argued) that "just rewards and punishments depend only on consciousness." Moreover, Thiel has neglected two other, interconnected elements of Locke's soteriology as explained in the *Reasonableness* – namely, that repentance is *necessary but not sufficient* to salvation, and that the fact that a sin deserves punishment does not mean that God will necessarily punish the sinner.[113] Finally, and incidentally, Thiel has not considered the case of misdeeds one commits against their will, although to Locke another condition for moral accountability, and hence for punishment, is freedom. If one is forced to perform a criminal act, this person can be conscious of it. But it would be unjust to punish this person for this act, because this person lacked freedom to do otherwise.

Galen Strawson, too, has discussed the apparently problematic relationship between Locke's theory of personal identity and his notion of repentance. Commenting on *Essay* II.xxvii, Strawson has written that "guilt (apart from being a painful emotion) is surely a form of Concernment, and entails Consciousness; and Consciousness entails same Personhood; and same Personhood entails present accountability and punishability."[114] Strawson has stressed the inseparableness of consciousness and concernment regarding a person's past misdeeds, given that repentance might not cancel one's consciousness of, and concernment with, their past misdeeds. Accordingly, he has observed that, given Locke's account of personal identity and punishment, the latter seems unavoidable on Judgment Day:

Tying punishment and reward to actual Consciousness and Concernment isn't going to allow anyone to get away with anything they shouldn't get away with, for what one is Conscious of – what one still feels Concerned or involved in – is, again, not something one can do anything about, on Locke's view.[115]

---

[112] Thiel, *Early Modern Subject*, p. 143. This passage includes a quote from Locke, *Essay*, II. xxvii.22, p. 344.
[113] See Chapter 3.   [114] Strawson, *Locke on Personal Identity*, p. 140.   [115] Ibid., p. 143.

In an attempt to accommodate repentance, Strawson has hypothesized that repentance might lead one to lose consciousness of their past misdeeds:

If Consciousness is genuinely lost ... then Locke's theory gives the right result. The person one is now can't be rightly punished for the action of which Consciousness has been lost. This core idea lifts easily out of its eschatological context, and seems better expressed in an entirely nonreligious and nonepistemological way. It's simply the idea that there is at any time a fact of the matter about a person's overall moral nature, shape, constitution, or being, whether or not it is ever revealed or made the basis of action. This is an idea that has considerable resonance and plausibility for many people. One's moral identity is not simply a matter of an accumulated bag of actions. It's something that can change (e.g. improve) over time, and not just by a change in the proportion of good and bad actions in the bag. And this improvement can be not only correlative with, but also partly constitutive of, one's losing touch with some of one's past actions in such a way that one is no longer appropriately punished for them.[116]

Nevertheless, as Strawson himself has recognized, this solution rests on "one terminological choice among others, made to suit a case that Locke didn't consider in print."[117] It is instead likely that, as Strawson himself has noted, to Locke "our capacities for recall will be exceptionally vivid on the Day of Judgment."[118] Drawing on 1 Cor. 14:25 ("And thus are the secrets of his heart made manifest ..."), Locke actually declared in the above-quoted *Essay* II.xxvii.22 that "in the great Day ... the Secrets of all Hearts shall be laid open."[119] It is thus likely that, according to Locke, on Judgment Day we will be able to remember our past actions accurately – that is, in Locke's words, we will be able to "repeat the *Idea* of any past Action with the same consciousness [we] had of it at first, and with the same consciousness [we have] of any present Action."[120] In fact, when talking of Judgment Day in an above-quoted passage from *Essay* II.xxvii.26, Locke mentioned "the consciousness all Persons shall have, that they *themselves* ... are the *same*, that committed those Actions."[121] However, while implicitly dismissing the aforesaid, ill-grounded solution, Strawson has taken into account another option:

Alternatively, the gap can be closed by appeal to God's mercy. On this view one is indeed still punish*able* for absolutely everything one is Conscious of, and one is still Conscious of absolutely everything one experiences as one's own, even if one now experiences it as one's own only in a wholly affectively neutral, wholly morally disengaged way. Nevertheless, God won't actually punish one for any of the things from which one has disengaged.[122]

---

[116] Ibid., pp. 148–149.   [117] Ibid., p. 147.   [118] Ibid., p. 148.

[119] Locke, *Essay*, II.xxvii.22, p. 344.   [120] Ibid., II.xxvii.10, p. 336.

[121] Ibid., II.xxvii.26, p. 347. Whereas Locke believed that on Judgment Day everyone will have accurate memories of their deeds, including their sins, and will understand that they deserve punishment for their sins, he never considered the possibility and effectiveness of *post-mortem* repentance.

[122] Strawson, *Locke on Personal Identity*, p. 147.

Whereas this hypothesis is more plausible than Strawson's other option, he has not endorsed it expressly, perhaps because he has not supported it with a thorough analysis of Locke's views on salvation. Moreover, the scarce attention that Strawson has paid to Locke's soteriology has led him to suppose, incorrectly, that one's "appeal to God's mercy" enables one to experience their past misdeeds "in a wholly affectively neutral, wholly morally disengaged way." However, Locke's account of repentance in *The Reasonableness of Christianity* does not involve affective neutrality or moral disengagement from one's past sins. To Locke, repentance actually brings about a moral renovation in the repentant faithful, thanks to the latter's acknowledgment of, and sorrow for, their sins; and this sorrow must be accompanied by a genuine endeavor to obey the divinely given moral law.[123] This attitude, I think, is far from entailing affective neutrality or moral disengagement.

It is true that one's repentance for their misdeeds, along with a sincere and constant effort to lead a righteous life, does not cancel these misdeeds and, hence, does not make them less deserving of punishment. This is the case in human affairs, in which repentance for one's crime, accompanied by one's commitment to live a just life, actually does not exempt the culprit from punishment. As regards human justice, according to Locke, even one's (momentary) unconsciousness (with one's subsequent lack of memory) of their own misdeeds is not an excuse strong enough to exempt the offender from punishment. Locke's position on this matter emerges from the famous passage about the drunk and sober man in *Essay* II.xxvii.22 (which is the same section Thiel refers to, and quotes in part, when claiming that Locke's theory of personal identity contradicts his notion of repentance):

For though punishment be annexed to personality, and personality to consciousness, and the Drunkard perhaps be not conscious of what he did; yet Humane Judicatures justly punish him; because the Fact is proved against him, but want of consciousness cannot be proved for him.[124]

Nevertheless, when it comes to eternal salvation, things are more complex. In *Essay* II.xxvii.22, Locke maintains that, on Judgment Day, everyone "shall receive his Doom, his Conscience accusing or excusing him."[125] Harold Noonan has suggested that, in this passage, Locke uses the term "conscience" as a synonym for "consciousness."[126] This interpretation supports the view that, to Locke, all that counts when it comes to divine judgment is one's awareness of their deeds, including their sins. I disagree with Noonan. I believe

---

[123] See Chapters 2 and 3.   [124] Locke, *Essay*, II.xxvii.22, p. 344.   [125] Ibid.
[126] Harold W. Noonan, "Locke on Personal Identity," in Gary Fuller, Robert Stecker, John P. Wright (eds.), *John Locke, An Essay concerning Human Understanding in Focus* (London: Routledge, 2000), pp. 210–235 (232).

that in this passage (which is the only place in *Essay* II.xxvii where Locke uses the term "conscience") by "conscience" Locke means the same thing he does in *Essay* I.iii.7–9, where he defines conscience as "our own Opinion or Judgment of the Moral Rectitude or Pravity of our own Actions."[127] In other words, to Locke conscience is one's own moral evaluation of one's acts (including thoughts), whereas consciousness is non-evaluative awareness. Locke's discussion of this subject in *Essay* I.iii.7–9 indeed shows that what he means by "opinion or judgment" is not mere consciousness (i.e., non-evaluative awareness) of our actions. What Locke means by "opinion or judgment" is actually an assessment of our actions that, if matched by a proper consideration of the eternal moral law, is accompanied by a sound judgment of their righteousness or wrongness and, hence, by feelings of confidence and serenity in the case of good works, or by remorse in the case of misdeeds.[128] Therefore, I believe that when Locke states, in *Essay* II.xxvii.22, that on Judgment Day everyone "shall receive his Doom, his Conscience accusing or excusing him,"[129] he is talking not only of one's awareness of their sins, but also of whether one, during their earthly life, has understood, or not, the evilness of these sins and has felt remorse, or not, for these sins. In other words, *pace* Noonan (and Thiel, too), the adequacy (or inadequacy) of one's moral evaluation of their sins and, hence, one's repentance (or lack thereof) for these sins during their life – and not simply one's (non-evaluative) awareness thereof – will be taken into consideration on the Last Judgment. And repentance must be accompanied by a sincere commitment to abide by the divine moral law.[130]

In *The Reasonableness of Christianity*, however, Locke argued that one's salvation depends not only on their repentance for their sins and on the consequent resolution to obey the divine moral law, but also on one's faith in Jesus the Messiah and one's commitment to understanding God's Revealed Word. To Locke, Christ assured humanity of otherworldly rewards and sanctions and emphasized God's mercy, which makes salvation possible despite human weakness and imperfection. According to Locke, God has the power to abstain from punishing the repentant faithful for their sins, even if these sins are deserving of punishment. Thus, the repentant faithful will receive "the Pardon and Forgiveness of Sins and Salvation" thanks to their faith.[131] And, when talking of "sins," Locke meant both the sins committed before accepting the Law of Faith and those committed after conversion to Christianity. To Locke, in fact, the weakness and imperfection of human nature make sin inevitable, even when one sincerely endeavors to obey the moral law. Therefore, the Last Judgment will not be based simply on a consideration of one's

---

[127] Locke, *Essay*, I.iii.8, p. 70.   [128] Ibid., I.iii.7–9, pp. 69–72.
[129] Ibid., II.xxvii.22, p. 344.   [130] See Chapter 3.   [131] Locke, *Reasonableness*, 133.

mere consciousness of their sins. God will show his mercy to the faithful and will not punish them – despite their consciousness of their sins and despite these sins being deserving of punishment – on condition that, in their life, they have repented for their sins and have wholeheartedly committed themselves to observing the divine law and living a Christian life.

5   The Trinity and Christ

According to Locke, adherence to the fundamentals of Christianity – namely, faith in Jesus the Messiah, repentance for sin, and obedience to the divine moral law – along with the diligent study of Scripture is what the Law of Faith prescribes as essential to achieving eternal life. All other beliefs and practices are non-fundamental and, hence, irrelevant to salvation. For this reason, Locke did not take into consideration non-fundamentals in *The Reasonableness of Christianity*. One of the beliefs omitted from Locke's elucidation of the Christian religion in the *Reasonableness* is belief in the Trinity. The omission of the Trinitarian dogma from the fundamental tenets of Christianity was controversial because it implicitly made belief in the Trinity unnecessary to salvation. This omission attracted much criticism to Locke and led various critics to accuse him of Socinianism. Locke never gave a public explanation of his position on the Trinitarian doctrine, even when some of his opponents, particularly John Edwards and Edward Stillingfleet, pressured him to do so. His public silence on the Trinity was surprising to many because the *Reasonableness* appeared in the middle of a Trinitarian controversy that caused significant turmoil in the English theological arena. This controversy saw the opposition of Unitarian authors, who were mainly, but not exclusively, inspired by Socinian ideas, and Trinitarian divines, who gave different explanations of the Trinity and consequently clashed with one another. A proper appreciation of this controversy and its context facilitates a better understanding of the significance of Locke's public silence on the Trinity, of the heterodoxy of his reflections on Christological and Trinitarian issues, and of the reasons behind his obstinate public silence on the Trinitarian doctrine. Locke actually expressed, unsystematically and at times ambiguously, his views on Christ's nature and mission in his public writings on religion and in various manuscript notes. Moreover, he focused on Trinitarian issues in *Adversaria Theologica* and other manuscripts. When examined meticulously, his Christological reflections and his consideration of Trinitarian issues denote a non-Trinitarian conception of the Godhead, presenting both Socinian and Arian elements, although he never expressly denied the Trinity. Both irenic and prudential reasons contributed to his choice to avoid public discussion of the

134

Trinitarian doctrine. Locke indeed deemed it inappropriate and immoral to fuel pointless and divisive debates about non-fundamentals. Furthermore, he considered it unwise to cause himself unnecessary troubles with the ecclesiastical and political authorities, in a time when it was inadvisable to discuss the Trinitarian doctrine.

The Trinitarian Controversy

Socinian ideas spread in England during the Civil War and Interregnum, provoking the harsh reaction of Puritan writers and the persecution of anti-Trinitarians such as Paul Best and John Biddle.[1] After the Restoration of the Stuart monarchy, various Socinian writings, mostly printed in the Netherlands, such as the multi-volume *Bibliotheca Fratrum Polonorum*, circulated clandestinely in England. Starting in 1687, with *A Brief History of the Unitarians, called also Socinians*, by the Church of England clergyman Stephen Nye, many anti-Trinitarian books, including five collections of Unitarian tracts (1691–1703), were written and published in England, mainly thanks to funds provided by the wealthy merchant and philanthropist Thomas Firmin. The English anti-Trinitarians, most of whom by that time were calling themselves Unitarians,[2] were encouraged to make their views public by the Declaration of Indulgence of 1687, in which the Catholic King James II extended religious liberty in a failed attempt to draw support from the Nonconformists. The Trinitarian controversy was also triggered by problems inherent to the Protestant doctrine of *sola Scriptura*. Protestants rejected the Catholic dogma of transubstantiation as unscriptural and illogical. In England, John Tillotson's *Discourse against Transubstantiation*, which received seven editions between 1684 and 1687, revived the debate on this subject. But the Continental Socinians argued that belief in the Trinity, too, could not be derived from clear and intelligible passages in the Bible. This enabled English Catholic polemicists to attack *sola Scriptura* and insist on the necessity to ground biblical exegesis in ecclesiastical tradition – the Catholic rule of faith – in order to salvage the Trinity.[3] The idea that the Trinitarian doctrine could be inferred from Scripture alone was further challenged by Richard Simon's *Critical History of the Text of the New Testament*, published, and promptly

---

[1] See Chapter 2.

[2] The English word "Unitarian" first appeared in a book by a former student of Biddle: Henry Hedworth, *Controversy Ended* (London, 1673), p. 53. The Latin term "*Unitarius*" was widely used in reference to the Socinians in the second half of the seventeenth century and appeared in the title of the *Bibliotheca Fratrum Polonorum quos Unitarios vocant*, 9 vols. (Irenopoli – Eleutheropoli [Amsterdam], "post annum Domini 1656" [1665–1692]).

[3] [Abraham Woodhead?], *The Protestants Plea for a Socinian* (London, 1686); Anonymous, *A Dialogue between a New Catholic Convert and a Protestant* (London, 1686).

translated into English, in 1689. Simon questioned the existence of indisputable manuscript support for Trinitarian proof texts, including the Johannine Comma, and reaffirmed the necessity of ecclesiastical tradition to define Christian doctrine.[4] In that situation, English Protestant theologians had three choices: to maintain their commitment to Scripture as the rule of faith and prove the Socinians wrong about the Trinity; to maintain their commitment to Scripture as the rule of faith and concur with the Socinians' denial of the Trinity; or to renounce *sola Scriptura* and admit that only the Catholic rule of faith, namely ecclesiastical tradition, could secure the Trinity.[5] English Protestant theologians inevitably chose the first of these three options, although they employed different historical or philosophical methods to defend the Trinity. Conversely, Nye and other Unitarians rejected both the Trinitarian dogma and ecclesiastical tradition, and they described themselves as the truly "orthodox" Christians adhering to *sola Scriptura* completely and unquestionably.

While the turbulent political context of James II's reign enabled the Unitarians to propagate their views, the events following the Glorious Revolution of 1688–1689 did not discourage them from maintaining their cause. In May 1689, the Toleration Act of 1688 received royal assent. This Act expressly excluded non-Trinitarian Christians from toleration while relieving Trinitarian Nonconformists from various civil disabilities.[6] This did not deter English anti-Trinitarian writers from publishing their works, although most of them preferred to remain anonymous. The few Unitarian authors who did not remain anonymous paid a high price for expressing their ideas. Nye remained the rector of the parish of Little Hormead, a small hamlet in Hertfordshire, for all his life. He did not advance in his ecclesiastical career despite his vast theological learning. Moreover, Arthur Bury saw his *Naked Gospel* (1690) – a work of creedal minimalism describing belief in the Trinity as unnecessary to salvation – promptly condemned by a convocation of the University of Oxford as "impious and heretical" and, consequently, seized and burnt. Following these events, the Bishop of Exeter, Jonathan Trelawney, deprived Bury of his rectorship of Exeter College at Oxford in July 1690. Four years later, William Freke was forced to recant the Arian views he had expressed in *A Dialogue by way of Question and Answer, concerning the Deity* (1693). Shortly afterwards, the clockmaker and self-taught writer John Smith, author of *A Designed End to the Socinian Controversy* (1695), was required to renounce his irenic ideas. Finally, in 1703, the Presbyterian divine Thomas Emlyn was sentenced for

---

[4] See Chapter 2.

[5] Jason E. Vickers, *Invocation and Assent: The Making and Remaking of Trinitarian Theology* (Grand Rapids: Eerdmans, 2008), p. 70.

[6] The long title of the Toleration Act is "An Act for Exempting Their Majestyes Protestant Subjects Dissenting from the Church of England from the Penalties of certaine Lawes."

blasphemy in Dublin for having written a controversial anti-Trinitarian treatise, *An Humble Inquiry into the Scripture Account of Jesus Christ* (1702). It is therefore understandable that most of the anti-Trinitarians who took part in the controversy opted to remain anonymous.[7]

Despite the authorities' attempts at repressing Unitarianism, the Church of England and the political institutions were unable to contain the spread of anti-Trinitarian ideas after the Glorious Revolution, which had brought about an atmosphere of uncertainty within the Anglican establishment and had contributed to an increase in the hostility between latitudinarian clergymen and High Church divines. This situation, which prevented the ecclesiastical and political authorities from organizing a concerted strategy to suppress Unitarianism, even fueled the Trinitarian controversy. The Unitarians, with their focus on individual will and reason, led an attack (later continued and intensified by deists and freethinkers) on the politically demarcated boundaries of faith in order to relocate the source of belief from public authority to the epistemological criteria of individual reason, conscience, and scholarship.[8] Their revolt combined with the serious crisis that, at that time, was taking place within ecclesiastical authority. As Brent Sirota has noted, "the Trinitarian controversy repeatedly exposed the absence of any Anglican consensus on the methods and instruments of enforcing orthodoxy, whether through the universities, Parliament, or convocation."[9] Moreover, the Commons' refusal to renew the 1662 Licensing Act in 1695 made things relatively easier for the Unitarians, while at the same time encouraging the ecclesiastical and political authorities to undertake new measures to put an end to that controversy.

At first, the controversy revolved around the question of whether the Church of England doctrine of the Trinity could be historically justified – or, in other words, whether this doctrine could be traced back to the earliest period of Christianity.[10] The Unitarians aimed to demonstrate that the Trinitarian dogma was illogical and unscriptural. They argued that this dogma had originated in

---

[7] On the persecutions of Unitarians during the Trinitarian controversy, see Earl M. Wilbur, *A History of Unitarianism*, 2 vols. (Cambridge, MA: Harvard University Press, 1945–1952), vol. 2, pp. 231, 244–247; H. John McLachlan, *Socinianism in Seventeenth-Century England* (Oxford: Oxford University Press, 1951), pp. 333–334; Philip Dixon, *Nice and Hot Disputes: The Doctrine of the Trinity in the Seventeenth Century* (London: T&T Clark, 2003), pp. 108–109, 131–132; Christopher J. Walker, *Reason and Religion in Late Seventeenth-Century England: The Politics and Theology of Radical Dissent* (London: I. B. Tauris, 2013), pp. 170–175, 185–193, 218–219, 240.

[8] Justin Champion, *The Pillars of Priestcraft Shaken: The Church of England and Its Enemies 1660–1730* (Cambridge, Cambridge University Press, 1992), pp. 99–132.

[9] Brent Sirota, "The Trinitarian Crisis in Church and State: Religious Controversy and the Making of the Post-Revolutionary Church of England, 1687–1702," *Journal of British Studies*, 52:1 (2013): pp. 26–54 (31).

[10] Kristine L. Haugen, "Transformations of the Trinity Doctrine in English Scholarship: From the History of Beliefs to the History of Texts," *Archiv für Religionsgeschichte*, 3 (2001): pp. 149–168 (150).

the corruption of Christian theology by pagan, especially Platonic, philoso-phies in the early centuries of Christianity.[11] Nye and other Unitarians main-tained that neither Scripture, nor Patristic sources testifying to the beliefs of the first Christians, also called "Nazarens," substantiate belief in the Trinity.[12] Therefore, they thought that the Trinitarian dogma should not be among the tenets of the Church of England or, at least, should not be forced on all members of this church.

Despite the Unitarians' aversion to the Trinitarian dogma, their front was not homogeneous in its theological positions. Those who, in late seventeenth-century England, opposed the Trinitarian doctrine had different views on the fundamentals of Christianity, the nature of the Godhead, and ecclesiological matters. Although their enemies generally labeled all of them "Socinians," some of them, such as the Arian William Freke and the deist Matthew Tindal, held theological views different from Socinus's and his disciples' ideas.[13] Even those who agreed with Socinian theology, soteriology, and ethics further elaborated on the history of early Christianity and the origins of the Trinitarian dogma. Nye himself borrowed not only from Socinian authors like John Biddle and the German physician Daniel Zwicker, but also from the Arian Christoph Sand, Arminians like Grotius, Courcelles, and Episcopius, and the Jesuit Denis Petau. Briefly, late seventeenth-century English Unitarianism was a new phase in the development of early modern anti-Trinitarianism. In late seventeenth-century England, many Unitarians actually did not describe them-selves as representatives of a specific theological current endorsing a particular system of divinity. They rather emphasized their commitment to Scripture and the early Christian teachings. At the same time, they downplayed the doctrinal differences within their party.[14] Some of those who joined the Unitarian cause, such as Arthur Bury and John Smith, were indeed creedal minimalists, and a

[11] On the seventeenth-century English debate about early Christianity and its corruption, see Dmitri Levitin, *Ancient Wisdom in the Age of the New Science: Histories of Philosophy in England, c. 1640–1700* (Cambridge: Cambridge University Press, 2015), pp. 447–541; Diego Lucci, "Ante-Nicene Authority and the Trinity in Seventeenth-Century England," *Intellectual History Review*, 28:1 (2018): pp. 101–124.

[12] See, for instance, Stephen Nye, *A Brief History of the Unitarians, Called Also Socinians* (London, 1687), pp. 24–33; Stephen Nye, *A Letter of Resolution* (London, 1691), pp. 11–17. The rediscovery of the Nazarenes' non-Trinitarian Christianity, inaugurated by the German Socinian Daniel Zwicker's *Irenicum Irenicorum* (1658), also informed Henry Stubbe's and John Toland's considerations on primitive Christianity. See Justin Champion, "Introduction" to John Toland, *Nazarenus*, ed. Justin Champion (Oxford: Voltaire Foundation, 1999), pp. 1–106; Nabil Matar (ed.), *Henry Stubbe and the Beginnings of Islam: The Originall & Progress of Mahometanism* (New York: Columbia University Press, 2014); Levitin, *Ancient Wisdom*, pp. 484, 506–507, 524–531; Lucci, "Ante-Nicene Authority," pp. 106, 112–113.

[13] Diego Lucci, "From Unitarianism to Deism: Matthew Tindal, John Toland, and the Trinitarian Controversy," *Études Epistémè*, 35 (2019), https://journals.openedition.org/episteme/4223.

[14] John Marshall, "Locke, Socinianism, 'Socinianism,' and Unitarianism," in M. A. Stewart (ed.), *English Philosophy in the Age of Locke* (Oxford: Clarendon Press, 2000), pp. 111–182 (113).

conciliatory and irenic attitude characterized the works of most Unitarian writers, who valued conciliation, toleration, morality, and the right to freely interpret Scripture more than their own particular theological positions.

While the anti-Trinitarians tried to overcome their divergences and find some common ground, the Trinitarian party became increasingly fragmented. During the work of an Ecclesiastical Commission appointed in 1689 to alter the liturgy and canons of the Church of England, several latitudinarian clergymen, including Gilbert Burnet and Edward Stillingfleet, took into serious consideration the opportunity to declare the markedly Trinitarian Athanasian Creed to be only an inessential, optional element of the Anglican faith.[15] This attempt at a compromise solution was part of the latitudinarians' efforts to achieve a higher degree of "comprehension" within the established Church. However, no comprehension scheme reached the table of Convocation because of the conservatives' inflexibility. Those latitudinarian clergymen's proposal concerning the Athanasian Creed inspired two books that disparaged Athanasius and his followers – the aforementioned *Naked Gospel* by Arthur Bury and the anonymous *Brief Notes on the Creed of St. Athanasius* (1690), commonly attributed to Stephen Nye, given its stylistic and thematic affinities with other writings by this author.[16] These two books, along with the second edition of Nye's *Brief History* (1691), contributed to the hardening of the debate. Despite their common opposition to integrating the Unitarians within the Church of England, the Anglican apologists who defended the Trinitarian dogma soon found themselves entangled in the difficulties of refuting the anti-Trinitarians' attacks. After some initial attempts, in the late 1680s, by Anglican divines such as William Sherlock, Edward Stillingfleet, and Thomas Tenison to defend the Trinitarian doctrine through historical-critical methods, Trinitarian polemicists realized that historical arguments in favor of the Trinity were hard to prove and easy to ridicule.[17] Therefore, in the 1690s, several Anglican theologians endeavored to elucidate the doctrine of the Trinity in philosophical terms. They employed Platonic, Aristotelian, or Cartesian concepts and formulated divergent views of the Godhead. But, once the Trinitarians accepted to consider the Trinity no more as a mystery, they had to face difficulties and contradictions that led them to disagree and clash with one another, thus further exposing the weaknesses of the Trinitarian doctrine. The most controversial book in the Trinitarian camp was Sherlock's *Vindication of the Trinity* (1690), written in response to Nye's *Brief History* and *Brief Notes*. Drawing on Cartesian metaphysics, Sherlock described the three divine persons as three

---

[15] Sirota, "Trinitarian Crisis," pp. 36–41.
[16] Arthur Bury, *The Naked Gospel* (London, 1690), pp. 29–31, 37–43, 57–58; Stephen Nye, *Brief Notes on the Creed of St. Athanasius* (London, 1690).
[17] Haugen, "Transformations," p. 154.

distinct "minds," self-conscious and reciprocally conscious of one another.[18] Nye promptly responded to Sherlock in *The Acts of the Great Athanasius* (1690), which depicted the Trinitarian doctrine as an invention devised by the immoral, crafty, and seditious Athanasius – an invention that corrupted the true Christian religion and contributed to the emergence of popery.[19] To Sherlock's disappointment, other Trinitarian apologists concentrated their fire not on Nye's and other Unitarians' works, but on his *Vindication of the Trinity*. *Contra* Sherlock's theory, which was widely perceived as tritheistic (that is, as implying that the three persons of the Trinity are three distinct deities), the Oxford mathematician John Wallis and the Calvinistic theologian Robert South argued that the Father, the Son, and the Holy Spirit were three manifestations, aspects, or modes of existence of the same divine substance.[20] However, Wallis and South were not exempt from criticism, because their views on the Trinity were open to the charge of modalism (i.e., the belief that the three persons of the Trinity are merely three modes or aspects of God). In fact, the Calvinistic divine, and Locke's archenemy, John Edwards leveled the charge of modalism at these two authors and reaffirmed the idea that the three persons of the Trinity are "three distinct subsistences."[21] In the end, "there appeared to be as many Trinities as there were writers."[22] The clash among Church of England divines about Trinitarian issues caused deep embarrassment to the ecclesiastical and political authorities. Therefore, in 1696, the Archbishop of Canterbury, Thomas Tenison, persuaded King William III to issue a Royal Injunction that forbade discussion of the Trinity in terms different from those contained in the Scriptures, the Apostolic, Nicene, and Athanasian creeds, and the Thirty-Nine Articles of the Church of England. One year later, the Parliament passed a Blasphemy Act that declared the denial of the Trinity by Christians, like other forms of "blasphemy," to be a crime. These measures did not put an abrupt end to the Trinitarian controversy, which waned only

---

[18] William Sherlock, *A Vindication of the Doctrine of the Holy and Ever Blessed Trinity* (London, 1690), pp. 48–50, 55–57, 66–68.

[19] Stephen Nye, *The Acts of the Great Athanasius* (London, 1690), pp. 4–10.

[20] Wallis criticized Sherlock in eight "letters" written between 1690 and 1692 and collected in: John Wallis, *Theological Discourses* (London, 1692). For the polemic between South and Sherlock, see Robert South, *Animadversions upon Dr. Sherlock's Book* (London, 1693); William Sherlock, *A Defence of Dr. Sherlock's Notion of a Trinity in Unity* (London, 1694); Robert South, *Tritheism Charged upon Dr. Sherlock's New Notion of the Trinity* (London, 1695). On Sherlock's Trinitarianism and the debate it elicited, see Udo Thiel, "The Trinity and Human Personal Identity," in Stewart (ed.), *English Philosophy*, pp. 217–243 (220–236); Dixon, *Nice and Hot Disputes*, pp. 109–125; Vickers, *Invocation and Assent*, pp. 79–133; Stephen Hampton, *Anti-Arminians: The Anglican Reformed Tradition from Charles II to George I* (Oxford, Oxford University Press, 2008), pp. 136–159; Walker, *Reason and Religion*, pp. 164–179, 195–201.

[21] John Edwards, *Theologia Reformata*, 2 vols. (London, 1713), vol. 1, pp. 282–290.

[22] Dixon, *Nice and Hot Disputes*, p. 125.

gradually in the late 1690s to early 1700s, when Nye and other Unitarians assumed a mollifying attitude while Trinitarian divines abstained from engaging in other internal disputes on this subject.[23]

In that situation of theological conflict involving various practicing members and clergymen of the Church of England, Locke, who was himself a conforming member of this church, showed great interest in Simon's work on the New Testament, Nye's writings, and Bury's book and the turmoil it caused. In June 1688, he informed Limborch about the then upcoming publication of Simon's *Critical History of the Text of the New Testament*.[24] Moreover, he corresponded with Limborch, Le Clerc, and others about various Unitarian works, mainly Nye's *Brief History* and Bury's *Naked Gospel*, and he took care of sending copies of these two books to Le Clerc, who promptly wrote a defense of Bury's treatise.[25] Furthermore, Locke extensively cited Nye, Biddle, and other anti-Trinitarian authors, including several Continental Socinians, in some of his manuscripts, as I explain below. But he decided to stay out of the Trinitarian controversy, he disregarded the Trinitarian doctrine in *The Reasonableness of Christianity*, and then he obstinately abstained from clarifying his position on this subject. Nevertheless, an accurate analysis of Locke's Christological views, which he expressed, albeit unsystematically, in his public as well as private writings, and a reassessment of his consideration of Trinitarian issues in several manuscripts demonstrate that he actually held a non-Trinitarian Christology comprising both Socinian and Arian elements.

Locke's Messianic and Non-Trinitarian Christology

Locke's theological manuscripts and his public writings on religion present several points in common with Socinianism, although he did not subscribe to all tenets of Socinian theology. He had good knowledge of anti-Trinitarian, particularly Socinian, literature, for he owned (and often cited in his manuscripts) many anti-Trinitarian, Socinian, and Unitarian books and was friends with various intellectuals who held heterodox views on the Trinity.[26] Locke

---

[23] See, for instance, Stephen Nye, *The Agreement of the Unitarians with the Catholick Church* (London, 1697); Stephen Nye, *The Doctrine of the Holy Trinity* (London, 1701).

[24] Locke to Philipp van Limborch, June 12/22, 1688, in John Locke, *The Correspondence of John Locke*, ed. E. S. de Beer, 8 vols. (Oxford: Oxford University Press, 1979–1989), vol. 3, no. 1058.

[25] Jean Le Clerc, *An Historical Vindication of the Naked Gospel* (London, 1691). For Locke's correspondence concerning Unitarian works, see Locke to Philipp van Limborch, March 12, 1689, in Locke, *Correspondence*, vol. 3, no. 1120; James Tyrrell to Locke, February 18, 1690, in Locke, *Correspondence*, vol. 4, no. 1248; Benjamin Furly to Locke, October 16/26, 1690, in Locke, *Correspondence*, vol. 4, no. 1325; Jean Le Clerc to Locke, October 22/November 1, 1690, in Locke, *Correspondence*, vol. 4, no. 1329.

[26] See Chapter 2.

himself was unorthodox when considering Christological and Trinitarian issues in some of his manuscripts and, in less explicit terms, in his theological writings intended for publication. His Christology deviated significantly from the Trinitarian norm and had much more in common with the *Messianic* Christology of anti-Trinitarians like the Socinians than with the *incarnational* Christology that is at the basis of Trinitarian Christianity. These are the two main types of Christology and are conceptually distinct, as Victor Nuovo has explained:

Although both make Christ the centre of salvation, a Messianic Christ achieves this goal through deeds, and, he being a king, the benefits of his saving activity are distributed to those who become his subjects after a judicial process; an incarnational Christ, although not inactive, accomplishes salvation through the communication of his divine being, which he makes available to his beneficiaries by becoming human.[27]

Along with these two types of Christology, the latter of which has largely prevailed in the history of Greek as well as Latin Christianity, there are two other Christological models: "One represents Christ as a mediator between God and man, the *Logos*, the other as a heavenly man, the founder of a new race, the second Adam."[28] Locke's views on the atonement and the Law of Faith show that these two models, along with the notion of a "Messianic Christ," play a role in his version of Christianity. In fact, various theological systems adopt and combine different Christological models. In Locke's case, his Christology is predominantly Messianic, while also describing Christ as a mediator and the second Adam, but is non-incarnational and, hence, non-Trinitarian.

The manuscript *Adversaria Theologica*, which Locke composed for the most part in 1694–1695, presents eight entries concerning Trinitarian questions – that is, "Trinitas" and "Non Trinitas," "Christus Deus Supremus" and "Christus non Deus Supremus," "Christus merus homo" and "Christus non merus homo," and, finally, "Spiritus Sanctus Deus" and "Spiritus Sanctus non Deus."[29] In these entries, Locke recorded a total of only eight arguments supporting the Trinitarian dogma, while he related thirty-six arguments against a Trinitarian view of the Godhead. This imbalance is partly due to the fact that Locke's main sources, in this case, were two works by the anti-Trinitarian John Biddle – *Twelve Arguments Drawn out of the Scripture* (1647) and *A Confession of Faith Touching the Holy Trinity* (1648). The anti-Trinitarian

---

[27] Victor Nuovo, *Christianity, Antiquity, and Enlightenment: Interpretations of Locke* (Dordrecht: Springer, 2011), p. 76.

[28] Ibid.

[29] John Locke, "Adversaria Theologica 94," in John Locke, *Writings on Religion*, ed. Victor Nuovo (Oxford: Oxford University Press, 2002), pp. 19–33 (23–28). For more details of this manuscript, see Chapter 3.

arguments in *Adversaria Theologica* support the view that Jesus had only a human nature. This view is in line with Socinian Christology. But, despite the numerical prevalence of anti-Trinitarian arguments consonant with Socinian Christology in *Adversaria*, Locke's position on the Trinity and on Christ's nature in this manuscript is still subject to interpretation. In *Adversaria*, both Trinitarian and anti-Trinitarian arguments are actually substantiated with references to Scripture. Moreover, Locke endorsed with his initials only one argument in the eight entries on Trinitarian issues, precisely in the note under "Christus non merus homo." Based on 1 Peter 1:11 ("Searching what, or what manner of time the Spirit of Christ which was in them [i.e., the prophets] did signify, when it testified beforehand the sufferings of Christ, and the glory that should follow"), this argument states that "his [i.e., Christ's] spirit was in the ancient prophets."[30] This statement indicates the pre-existence of Christ's *spirit* to his conception and birth. What does Locke's endorsement of this argument mean? Did he infer from 1 Peter 1:11 that Christ had not only a human nature, given that the spirits of those who have only a human nature do not pre-exist their conception and birth? If taken literally, this argument is compatible with a later suggestion on Christ's pre-existence in *A Paraphrase and Notes on the Epistles of St Paul*, which I examine below in this chapter. But even if we suppose that Locke, in *Adversaria Theologica*, endorsed the idea that Christ had pre-existed his conception and birth, his acceptance of Christ's pre-existence does not mean that he believed in Christ's *eternal* pre-existence and, consequently, does not make him a Trinitarian. Locke's endorsement might indeed denote an Arian notion of Christ as *pre-existent but created*, namely, begotten by God the Father at a point in time. At any rate, there is no evidence to maintain that Locke pursued a specifically Arian agenda in *Adversaria* or in other, later theological writings. Moreover, if we consider the context of his reference to the pre-existence of Christ's *spirit* in *Adversaria Theologica*, we may actually reach a different conclusion. Perhaps, in writing his note on 1 Peter 1:11, Locke meant to draw attention to Biddle's disregard of this biblical verse and thus criticize, although indirectly, Biddle's view of the Holy Spirit.[31] Unlike Continental Socinians, who considered the Holy Spirit as God's power, Biddle, in his early writings, upheld an uncommon notion of the Holy Spirit, which he portrayed as the "principal Minister of God and Christ ... singled out of the number of the other heavenly Ministers or Angels."[32] But 1 Peter 1:11 contradicts this view, in that it describes the spirit

---

[30] Locke, "Adversaria Theologica," p. 27.

[31] John Marshall and Victor Nuovo consider this hypothesis plausible: Marshall, "Locke, Socinianism," pp. 121–122; Nuovo, *Christianity*, p. 29.

[32] John Biddle, *A Confession of Faith Touching the Holy Trinity* (London, 1648), p. 44. This view echoes Arius's notion of the Holy Spirit as an angel.

of the prophets as the spirit of Christ – not as a heavenly minister or angel. It is therefore possible that, when commenting on 1 Peter 1:11 in *Adversaria*, Locke was talking of the Holy Spirit, which had inspired first the ancient prophets and then Christ. Given his divine inspiration, Christ was not a common man, for he was the Messiah. But acknowledging merely Christ's divine inspiration and Messiahship is still compatible with a view of the Son as *created as a man* (although not a common man) – and not as an *uncreated divine person* or as a *creature pre-existing his conception and birth*. Briefly, this interpretation does not dismiss the hypothesis that Locke, when writing *Adversaria* (and the *Reasonableness* as well) in the mid-1690s, might have endorsed a view of Christ essentially in line with Socinian Christology, whereas later, in the *Paraphrase*, he developed a different understanding of Christ's nature, consonant with Arian Christology in at least one respect – namely, concerning Christ's pre-existence, as we will see below. Moreover, this interpretation is consistent with the unorthodox, non-Trinitarian ideas on Christ's nature and divine inspiration that Locke expressed in various manuscript notes, written in the same period as *Adversaria Theologica*, about the unscriptural, pagan, Platonic roots of the Trinitarian dogma.

In 1695, Locke took some notes on Trinitarian issues in the notebook *Lemmata Ethica*. In one of these notes, under the heading "Trinity," he observed that "the papists deny that the doctrine of the Trinity can be proved by the Scripture."[33] Furthermore, in the entry on "Unitarians" in this notebook – an entry concerning the unscriptural origins of the Trinitarian dogma – Locke referred to anti-Trinitarian authors like Johann Crell, Johann Ludwig von Wolzogen, and Stephen Nye when stating that in the Bible there is "scarce one text alledgd by the Trinitarians which is not otherwise expounded by their own writers."[34] He further noted that the Scriptures present "a multitude of texts that deny those things of Christ which can not be denied of god; & that affirme such things of him that cannot agree to him if he were a person of god. In like manner of the holy ghost."[35] *Lemmata Ethica* is important to us for yet another reason. The entry on the Trinity in this manuscript presents clear signs of Locke's interest in the corruption of early Christianity, particularly by Platonic concepts – an interest that also emerges from other manuscript notes of the period, such as some notes in Locke's interleaved copies of the polyglot New Testament and of *Censura celebriorum authorum* (1690) by Sir Thomas Pope Blount.[36] Locke's curiosity in this subject dated back to at least the late

---

[33] MS Locke d. 10, "Lemmata Ethica, Argumenta et Authores," p. 167.   [34] Ibid., p. 177.

[35] Ibid. Concerning the denial of the divinity of the Holy Ghost, Locke referred, in particular, to Wolzogen's *Praeparatio ad utilem S. S. Litterarum lectionem* (in *Bibliotheca Fratrum Polonorum*, vol. 8, pp. 238–356) and Crell's *De uno Deo Patre libri duo* (Racoviae, 1631).

[36] LL 2864, BOD Locke 9.103–9.107, *Le Nouveau Testament* (Mons, 1673), interleaved and bound in 5 vols.; LL 358, BOD Locke 15.38, Thomas Pope Blount, *Censura celebriorum authorum* (London, 1690), interleaved. On Locke's views on Platonism, see Marshall, "Locke,

1670s, as is demonstrated by a journal note of December 20, 1678. In this note, Locke described several manuscripts of the New Testament that he had seen when visiting the Abbey of Saint-Germain-des-Prés in Paris with his friend, the clergyman and natural philosopher John Covel, later vice-chancellor of the University of Cambridge:

In the library of the Abbé of St. Germains, M. Covell and I saw two very old manuscripts of the New Testament, the newest of which was, as appeared by the date of it, at least 800 years old, in each of which 1 John c. v. v. 7. was quite wanting, and the end of the eighth verse ran thus, "tres unum sunt"; in an other old copy the seventh verse was, but with interlining; in another much more modern copy, v. 7. was also, but differently from the old copy; and in two other old manuscripts, also, v. 7. was quite out, but as I remember in all of them the end of the eighth verse was "tres unum sunt."[37]

In this journal note, Locke was referring to the Johannine Comma, namely, 1 John 5:7–8 ("For there are three that bear record in heaven, the Father, the Word, and the Holy Ghost: and these three are one. And there are three that bear witness in earth, the Spirit, and the water, and the blood: and these three agree in one"). This passage was at the center of a long controversy in the early modern era, since Erasmus excluded it from the first two editions of his Greek New Testament.[38] The rejection of the Comma as inauthentic was crucial to the development of anti-Trinitarian biblical criticism in the early modern period, not only among Socinians and other overt anti-Trinitarians, but also among scholars who were hesitant to express their doubts on, or even their hostility to, the Trinitarian doctrine. This was the case of Isaac Newton, who, in 1690, asked Locke to help him to publish *An Historical Account of Two Notable Corruptions of Scripture*.[39] The two "corruptions" of the title were the

---

Socinianism," pp. 120–131; G. A. J. Rogers, "Locke, Plato, and Platonism," in Douglas Hedley, Sarah Hutton (eds.), *Platonism at the Origins of Modernity: Studies on Platonism and Early Modern Philosophy* (Dordrecht: Springer, 2008), pp. 193–205; Nuovo, *Christianity*, pp. 163–179. On *Censura* by Thomas Pope Blount, who was the elder brother of the deist Charles Blount, and on Locke's interest in this book, see Kelsey Jackson Williams, "Canon before Canon, Literature before Literature: Thomas Pope Blount and the Scope of Early Modern Learning," *Huntington Library Quarterly*, 77:2 (2014): pp. 177–199.

[37] MS Locke f. 3, p. 386, quoted in Peter King, *The Life of John Locke* (London: Colburn, 1829), p. 78.

[38] See Chapter 2.

[39] Isaac Newton, "An Historical Account of Two Notable Corruptions of Scripture," in Isaac Newton, *The Correspondence of Isaac Newton*, 7 vols. (Cambridge: Cambridge University Press, 1959–1977), vol. 3 (1961), ed. H. W. Turnbull, pp. 83–146. On this treatise and on Newton's and Locke's aborted attempt at publishing it, see Stephen D. Snobelen, "'To Us There Is But One God, the Father': Anti-Trinitarian Textual Criticism in Seventeenth- and Early Eighteenth-Century England," in Ariel Hessayon, Nicholas Keene (eds.), *Scripture and Scholarship in Early Modern England* (Aldershot: Ashgate, 2006), pp. 116–136 (128–131); Rob Iliffe, "Friendly Criticism: Richard Simon, John Locke, Isaac Newton and the *Johannine Comma*," in Hessayon, Keene (eds.), *Scripture and Scholarship*, pp. 137–157; Rob Iliffe, *Priest of Nature: The Religious Worlds of Isaac Newton* (Oxford: Oxford University Press, 2017),

Johannine Comma and another passage frequently alleged to support the Trinitarian dogma, 1 Tim. 3:16 ("And without controversy great is the mystery of godliness: God was manifest in the flesh, justified in the Spirit, seen of angels, preached unto the Gentiles, believed on in the world, received up into glory"). These two verses were expressly rejected as inauthentic by Stephen Nye in his *Brief History*. Nye called attention to the absence of the Johannine Comma from the most ancient Greek manuscripts; Coptic, Arabic, Syriac, and Ethiopic Bibles; the most ancient Latin versions of Scripture; and the works of the Fathers.[40] As to 1 Tim. 3:16, Nye argued that the word "God" in this verse was an interpolation, because it appeared neither in the most ancient texts of the Bible nor in the Fathers' citations of this verse.[41] Newton's, and Locke's, interest in these passages was probably triggered by Nye's remarks, since *An Historical Account* advances arguments similar to Nye's points, although in a more thorough manner.[42] The debate raised by Bury's *Naked Gospel*, too, probably furthered Newton's and Locke's interest in the Johannine Comma, given also that, in a defense of the Trinitarian doctrine from Bury's creedal minimalism, the clergyman William Nicholls asserted the authenticity of the Comma based on Cyprian's authority.[43] Newton drew on Greek, Syriac, Ethiopic, and other ancient versions of Scripture republished in modern times, on Patristic sources that disregarded the Johannine Comma, and on modern scholars, such as Sand and Erasmus, to argue that the Comma was an interpolation introduced by later copyists who were part of "the great Athanasian conspiracy."[44] Newton sent *An Historical Account* to Locke with a letter, dated November 14, 1690, in which he wrote that he wanted this treatise to be first translated into French and then published – obviously in order to conceal his authorship of this text, although he considered the opportunity to subsequently publish it in English.[45] Probably, Locke had raised the possibility that Le Clerc could translate and publish *An Historical Account*. In late December 1690, he indeed sent Newton's treatise to Le Clerc, who, a few months later, accepted to translate and publish it in a volume with other tracts, although he criticized its

pp. 354–389. On Newton's anti-Trinitarianism, see Stephen D. Snobelen, "Isaac Newton, Socinianism and 'the One Supreme God,'" in Martin Mulsow, Jan Rohls (eds.), *Socinianism and Arminianism: Antitrinitarians, Calvinists and Cultural Exchange in Seventeenth-Century Europe* (Leiden: Brill, 2005), pp. 241–298; Iliffe, *Priest of Nature*, pp. 132–138. On the friendship and mutual interests, including theological interests, of Newton and Locke, see Peter Anstey, "Newton and Locke," in Eric Schliesser, Chris Smeenk (eds.), *The Oxford Handbook of Newton* (Oxford: Oxford University Press, 2017), pp. 1–23.

[40] Nye, *Brief History*, pp. 151–153.   [41] Ibid., pp. 137–139.

[42] Iliffe, *Priest of Nature*, pp. 365–369.

[43] William Nicholls, *An Answer to an Heretical Book Called the Naked Gospel* (London, 1691), p. 63.

[44] Iliffe, *Priest of Nature*, p. 383.

[45] Isaac Newton to Locke, November 14, 1690, in Locke, *Correspondence*, vol. 4, no. 1338.

author for disregarding Simon's position on the difficulty, or even the impossibility, to substantiate the Trinitarian doctrine through Scripture alone.[46] Nevertheless, Newton changed his mind more than one year after sending this treatise to Locke. He was probably troubled by the prospect of publishing his heterodox views on such a controversial issue, which were likely to be understood by only a few and to cause him problems with the ecclesiastical and political authorities.[47] Therefore, after providing Locke with some additions concerning Richard Simon's and Gilbert Burnet's observations on the Johannine Comma, and after further corresponding with Locke on this matter, in February 1692 he eventually decided to stop the publication of *An Historical Account*, thus upsetting Le Clerc who, in the meantime, had completed its French translation.[48] Almost two decades later, in 1709, Newton tried, once again, to publish this treatise; but, this time too, the publication was held back, and *An Historical Account* was eventually printed for the first time, posthumously and imperfectly, in 1754.[49] While these events tell much about Newton's problematic personality, they are also revealing of Locke's receptiveness to heterodox, and particularly anti-Trinitarian, readings of biblical passages commonly alleged to endorse the Trinitarian dogma. In fact, Locke, like Newton, abhorred the corruption of early Christianity by scheming priests – a corruption furthered by the influence of pagan, Platonic views among the early Christians.

In *Lemmata Ethica* and in his interleaved copy of Blount's *Censura*, Locke made reference to various works by Nye, including the aforesaid *Brief History*, when exposing the Platonic distortion of early Christianity. In the entry on the Trinity in *Lemmata Ethica*, he called attention to the "parallelism betwixt the Ancient or Genuine Platonick, and the Christian Trinity"[50] – a parallelism that the Cambridge Platonist Ralph Cudworth had tried to explain in *The True Intellectual System of the Universe* (1678). In an attempt to justify the similarities between Platonism and Christian Trinitarianism, Cudworth claimed that the doctrine of the Trinity had found "such Admittance and Entertainment in the Pagan World, and [was] received by the wisest of all their Philosophers, before the times of Christianity; thereby to prepare a more easie way for the Reception of Christianity amongst the Learned Pagans."[51] Despite Cudworth's

---

[46] Jean Le Clerc to Locke, April 1/11, 1691, in Locke, *Correspondence*, vol. 4, no. 1381; Jean Le Clerc to Locke, July 21/31, 1691, in Locke, *Correspondence*, vol. 4, no. 1410.

[47] Stephen D. Snobelen, "Isaac Newton, Heresy Laws and the Persecution of Religious Dissent," *Enlightenment and Dissent*, 25 (2009): pp. 204–259.

[48] Isaac Newton to Locke, February 16, 1692, in Locke, *Correspondence*, vol. 4, no. 1465; Jean Le Clerc to Locke, April 1/11, 1692, in Locke, *Correspondence*, vol. 4, no. 1486.

[49] Iliffe, *Priest of Nature*, p. 370.   [50] MS Locke d. 10, pp. 167–168.

[51] Ralph Cudworth, *The True Intellectual System of the Universe* (London, 1678), p. 625. On Cudworth's views on the Trinity and their reception in late seventeenth-century England, see Dixon, *Nice and Hot Disputes*, pp. 88–90, 110–111, 127; Sarah Hutton, "The Neoplatonic

pious intentions, his book provided the Unitarian cause with additional arguments to denounce the Platonic corruption of Christianity and the pagan origins of Trinitarianism. When considering the Platonic roots of the Trinitarian doctrine in *Lemmata Ethica*, Locke expressly made reference to Cudworth's thesis, which one of his sources, Nye's *Letter of Resolution* (1691), largely utilized to debunk the Trinitarian dogma.[52] Besides various tracts by Stephen Nye, other writings such as Sand's *Nucleus Historiae Ecclesiasticae* (1669), Fontenelle's *Histoire des Oracles* (1687), and the works of the heterodox Huguenot refugee Jacques Souverain proved useful to Locke's criticism of the "Platonizing" of Christianity. From Sand and Nye, Locke borrowed the thesis that "the fathers of the three first Centuries ... speake rather like Arians than Orthodox" and "all antiquity was Arian," as he noted in his copy of Blount's *Censura*.[53] He made the same claim in *Lemmata Ethica*, maintaining that "the fathers before the Council of Nice speak rather like Arians than Orthodox."[54] However, as Locke read in Fontenelle's *Histoire des Oracles*, and as he noted in his copy of Blount's book, Plato soon became a "philosopher in fashion among the learned Christians of the first ages," who regarded him as a "kind of prophet, who had found out several important matters of Christianity, especially the Trinity."[55] As regards the ante-Nicene Fathers' views on the Godhead, it is possible that, in the mid-1690s, Locke conversed with his friend, the anti-Trinitarian Alexander Beresford, about the difficulty to infer Trinitarian views from the works of the early Christian writers. In a letter sent to Locke on March 24, 1695, Beresford wrote of his desire to "peruse" Eusebius and Epiphanius and to tell Locke "whether or not they are as much misrepresented as Irenaeus," whom Beresford considered to be "more against than for" Trinitarianism. In this letter, Beresford also gave Locke his "own thoughts of the Trinity-texts of Scripture," refuting Trinitarian readings of several biblical verses and openly declaring that the Bible was "against this Doctrine" (i.e., the Trinitarian doctrine). Beresford openly rejected the theory that Christ had pre-existed his conception and birth. He described Jesus as a man, although he, like Locke, believed that Jesus was *literally* the Son of

---

Roots of Arianism: Ralph Cudworth and Theophilus Gale," in Lech Szczucki (ed.), *Socinianism and Its Role in the Culture of the XVIth to XVIIIth Centuries* (Warsaw – Lodz: Polish Academy of Sciences, 1983), pp. 139–145; Leslie Armour, "Trinity, Community and Love: Cudworth's Platonism and the Idea of God," in Hedley, Hutton (eds.), *Platonism*, pp. 113–129; Levitin, *Ancient Wisdom*, pp. 509–514; Lucci, "Ante-Nicene Authority," pp. 109–111, 114.

[52] MS Locke d. 10, pp. 167–168; Nye, *Letter of Resolution*, pp. 11–18. See, also, Stephen Nye, *Considerations on the Explications of the Doctrine of the Trinity by Dr. Wallis, Dr. Sherlock, Dr. S-th, Dr. Cudworth, and Mr. Hooker* (London, 1693), pp. 13–19. As I have said in Chapter 3, Locke referred to Nye's *Considerations* when relating Socinian arguments against the satisfaction doctrine in "Adversaria Theologica," p. 32.

[53] LL 358, BOD Locke 15.38, interleaved pp. 620–621.   [54] MS Locke d. 10, p. 177.

[55] LL 358, BOD Locke 15.38, interleaved p. 119.

God.[56] Although no letter from Locke to Beresford on Trinitarian and Christological issues survives, Beresford and Locke remained good friends and correspondents, and Locke even recommended Beresford to others. Therefore, the fact that Beresford felt comfortable enough to express overtly anti-Trinitarian ideas to Locke indicates that Locke was receptive to these ideas.[57]

As regards Jacques Souverain, Locke was so interested in his views that, at some point in the 1690s, he had one of Souverain's manuscripts copied by his amanuensis Sylvester Brownover. This manuscript, entitled *Some General Reflections upon the Beginning of St. John's Gospel* and now part of MS Locke e. 17, presents ideas that Souverain also expounded in his book *Le Platonisme dévoilé*, published in 1700 and translated into English the same year, shortly after his death in 1699.[58] Locke also owned a copy of *Le Platonisme dévoilé*, and he knew of Souverain since at least 1691, for Souverain was an acquaintance of Locke's Unitarian friend William Popple and, in the 1690s, Locke followed the persecution of various Huguenots (including Souverain) suspected of Socinianism by their orthodox coreligionists. Souverain's views actually had much in common with the English Unitarians' ideas, especially with Nye's anti-Platonism. Locke was interested in Souverain's thought because this author denounced the Platonic corruption of Christianity and saw faith in Jesus the Messiah as the core tenet of Christianity. In *Le Platonisme dévoilé*, Souverain declared faith in Jesus the Messiah to be sufficient for baptism into the Church. In *Some General Reflections*, he advanced a clearly anti-Trinitarian interpretation of John's Gospel. He argued that John had described Jesus not as part of the Godhead, but simply as the Messiah – namely, as a prophet inspired by God the Father, through the Holy Spirit, in a more constant and excellent way than any other prophet before him. According to Souverain, Christ had a divine office, and Christ's words were of divine authority because they were divinely inspired. A manuscript note that Locke wrote most probably at some point in the first half of the 1690s, and that is now part of MS Locke f. 30, contains some comments on Jesus' divine inspiration remarkably similar to Souverain's views on this subject. This note on John 3:34 ("For he whom God hath sent speaketh the words of God: for God giveth not the Spirit by measure unto him"), which also includes an

---

[56] Alexander Beresford to Locke, March 24, 1695, in Locke, *Correspondence*, vol. 5, no. 1865.

[57] Marshall, "Locke, Socinianism," p. 135.

[58] MS Locke e. 17, pp. 175–223, "Some General Reflections upon the Beginning of St. John's Gospel"; Jacques Souverain, *Le Platonisme dévoilé* (Cologne [Amsterdam], 1700); Jacques Souverain, *Platonism Unveil'd* (London, 1700). On Souverain, see Paul C. H. Lim, *Mystery Unveiled: The Crisis of the Trinity in Early Modern England* (Oxford: Oxford University Press, 2012), pp. 311–317; Paul C. H. Lim, "The Platonic Captivity of Primitive Christianity and the Enlightening of Augustine," in William J. Bulman, Robert G. Ingram (eds.), *God in the Enlightenment* (Oxford: Oxford University Press, 2016), pp. 136–156.

interpretation of Col. 2:9 ("For in him dwelleth all the fulness of the Godhead bodily"), reads as follows:

The last & highest degree of Revelation was that given to our Saviour expressed here by the *Spirit given not by measure*. there was noe stint of it, noe intervals where in our Saviour had not the presence & assistance of this Spirit whereby every thing he said was of divine authority every thing he did was according to the will of god. And by this I think we may understand that expression of St Pauls Col. II. 9 *for in him dwelleth all the fulnesse of the Godhead bodily* viz. that the Spirit of god without stint or measure was as certainly & constantly in him to be the sourse of all his words & actions, as our souls are annexed & fixd to our bodys as the principle of action in us. The context will lead us to this sense, for the Apostle there is perswading the Colossians to rest satisfied in the truth & wisdom of the Gospel revealed by Jesus Christ. JL[59]

The content of this note on Jesus' divine inspiration supports my interpretation of what Locke probably meant when, in *Adversaria Theologica*, he made reference to Christ's spirit as present in the ancient prophets. In *Adversaria Theologica*, Locke most likely meant that what he called "the Spirit of god" in the note on John 3:34 (i.e., the Holy Spirit) had also inspired other prophets before Christ. In fact, this note refers to "the fulnesse of the Godhead bodily" dwelling in Christ as denoting not a divine nature, but only the presence of the "Spirit of god" in the Savior. Therefore, I agree with John Marshall that this note seems "to indicate disbelief in the Trinity," as does the fact that the *Reasonableness* was "silent about baptism in the name of the Holy Ghost, Jesus Christ, and God the Father, which many trinitarians adduced in support of the Trinity."[60] In the *Reasonableness*, Locke affirmed the miraculous conception and birth of Christ, "conceived in the Womb of a Virgin (that had not known Man) by the immediate Power of God."[61] However, he used the term "Son of God" as a synonym for "Messiah" and mainly to parallel Jesus' sonship with that of Adam. Locke never subscribed to the eternal generation of Christ and, in the *Reasonableness*, he did not even mention John 1:1 ("In the beginning was the Word, and the Word was with God, and the Word was God"). To Locke, the Gospel of John, far from substantiating the Trinitarian dogma, had the central purpose to teach that Jesus was the Messiah.

Whereas Locke firmly believed in Christ's Messiahship, he recognized Jesus' "Messianic secrecy," namely, Jesus' reticence about his being the Messiah, and he tried to understand the reasons behind this secrecy, as he explained in the *Reasonableness*:

---

[59] MS Locke f. 30, f. 43r, "Note on John 3:34," quoted in Nuovo, *Christianity*, p. 66. On this note, see also Marshall, "Locke, Socinianism," p. 131; Victor Nuovo, *John Locke: The Philosopher As Christian Virtuoso* (Oxford: Oxford University Press, 2017), p. 233.

[60] Marshall, "Locke, Socinianism," pp. 131, 164.

[61] John Locke, *The Reasonableness of Christianity, As Delivered in the Scriptures*, ed. John C. Higgins-Biddle (Oxford: Clarendon Press, 1999), p. 113.

This concealment of himself will seem strange, in one who was come to bring light into the world, and was to suffer death for the testimony of the truth. This reservedness will be thought to look, as if he had a mind to conceal himself, and not to be known to the world for the Messiah, nor to be believed on as such. But we shall be of another mind, and conclude this proceeding of his according to divine wisdom, and suited to a fuller manifestation and evidence of his being the Messiah; when we consider that he was to fill out the time foretold of his ministry; and after a life illustrious in miracles and good works, attended with humility, meekness, patience, and suffering, and every way conformable to the prophesies of him; should be led as a sheep to the slaughter, and with all quiet and submission be brought to the cross, though there were no guilt, nor fault in him.[62]

Over one-third of the *Reasonableness* is devoted to the question of Jesus' secrecy about his Messiahship. Locke argued that Jesus' behavior was part of a strategy of gradual self-disclosure. Locke explained this strategy by referring to the history of Jesus' Messianic actions (i.e., his miraculous birth, his miracles, and his resurrection) in the four Gospels and the Acts of the Apostles, which, according to Locke, relate the fulfillment of Old Testament Messianic prophecies. Locke's narrative of Jesus' Messianic activity denotes his involvement in one of the main projects of early modern biblical scholarship – the reconstruction of biblical harmony, especially of the harmony of the gospel narrative. As Victor Nuovo has noted:

The aim of this project, overall, was to rearrange all the parts of the Bible into a single chronological order, relocating whole books, transposing parts of them, and reconciling different accounts of the same events, fitting all the parts into a single continuous history. The general purpose of this undertaking was to facilitate the retrieval of the meaning of the several parts of the Bible by placing them in their proper context.[63]

Locke knew several harmonies, including those written by John Lightfoot, Jean Le Clerc, and William Whiston, which, toward the end of his life, he also recommended to the young clergyman Richard King.[64] Moreover, in 1679 his friend, the French philologist Nicolas Toinard had given him a draft of what was later published posthumously as *Evangeliorum Harmonia Graeco-Latina* (1707).[65] Locke considered these works helpful to read the Scriptures, particularly the Gospels, in "harmony." His reconstruction of Jesus' Messianic

---

[62] Ibid., pp. 40–41.   [63] Nuovo, *Christianity*, pp. 114–115.

[64] Locke to Richard King, September 27, 1703, in Locke, *Correspondence*, vol. 8, no. 3339; Justin Champion, "'An Intent and Careful Reading': How John Locke Read His Bible," in Luisa Simonutti (ed.), *Locke and Biblical Hermeneutics: Conscience and Scripture* (Cham: Springer, 2019), pp. 143–160 (151–152). Locke also recommended to King the works of biblical critics like Henry Hammond, Daniel Whitby, Joseph Mede, and Matthew Poole, but merely as tools to facilitate the understanding of Scripture – the only infallible source of religious truth.

[65] Nuovo, *Christianity*, pp. 37, 114–115; Giuliana Di Biase, *John Locke e Nicolas Thoynard. Un'amicizia ciceroniana* (Pisa: ETS, 2018), pp. 42–45, 154–165, 200–206, 233–239.

activity presents striking similarities with that of Toinard and focuses on the role, and the intentions, of all the figures involved in the fulfillment of the Messianic prophecies. Among these figures were not only Jesus and his disciples, but also the Jewish priests who opposed Jesus' teaching, the Roman officials and soldiers who condemned and executed him, and even ordinary Jewish people who were awaiting the Messiah but conceived of him as "a Mighty Temporal Prince, that should raise their Nation into an higher degree of Power, Dominion, and Prosperity than ever it had enjoyed. They were filled with the expectation of a Glorious Earthly Kingdom."[66] It is mainly for this reason that Jesus revealed himself only gradually:

It was not fit to open himself too plainly or forwardly, to the heady Jews, that he himself was the *Messiah*; That was to be left to the Observation of those who would attend to the Purity of his Life, and the Testimony of his Miracles, and the Conformity of all with the Predictions concerning him. By these marks those he lived amongst were to find it out without an express promulgation that he was the *Messiah*, till after his Death. His Kingdom was to be opened to them by degrees, as well to prepare them to receive it, as to enable him to be long enough amongst them; to perform what was the work of the *Messiah* to be done; and fulfil all those several parts of what was foretold of him in the Old Testament, and we see applyed to him in the New.[67]

Even Jesus' Apostles, who were simple persons, were often perplexed by his words, and they could fully understand his message only after his resurrection. In this regard, Locke speculated "whether St. *Paul* was not for this reason, by his Learning, Parts, and warmer Temper, better fitted for an Apostle after, than during our Saviour's Ministry: And therefore, though a chosen Vessel, was not by the Divine Wisdom called till after Christ's Resurrection."[68] It is therefore no accident that Locke devoted a significant part of his later years to studying Paul's epistles. According to Locke, Jesus' actions were part of a providential plan that placed him in circumstances suited to his mission. Jesus' mission unfolded in a time when the Jews were subject to a foreign, oppressive power (i.e., the Roman Empire) and lived in a period of decadence, during which their monotheism needed to be revived and perfected by the Messiah promulgating God's universal dominion. It is in this situation that the Law of Moses gave way to the Law of Faith, before the Jewish theocracy that God had established eventually came to an end with the destruction of the Second Temple in the year 70 CE. Locke saw this event as a divine act of (deserved) vengeance putting an end to the Jews' "Church, Worship, and Commonwealth," which were superseded by the Christian Church.[69] According to Locke, Jesus' miraculous birth, miracles, and resurrection were not only the means through which the Savior gradually revealed his Messianic nature and mission, but also

[66] Locke, *Reasonableness*, p. 89.   [67] Ibid., pp. 88–89.   [68] Ibid., p. 91.
[69] Ibid., p. 95. On Locke's supersessionist views, see Chapter 6.

three crucial steps in a biblical chronology that did not end with Jesus' death and resurrection, but looked ahead to the future – namely, to the establishment of the Kingdom of God.[70] In this regard, the *Reasonableness* makes no mention of the millennium – that is, the one-thousand-year reign of Christ on earth – even when dealing with the Jews' notion of the Messiah as a temporal prince who will establish a glorious earthly kingdom. This omission can be taken as denoting adherence to amillennialism – that is, the standard position among Eastern Orthodox, Catholic, Lutheran, Reformed, and Anglican denominations, according to which there will be no literal, thousand-year-long, physical reign of Jesus on earth, and the "thousand years" mentioned in Revelation 20:3 are just a symbolic number (interpreted variously, but not literally). However, in the years preceding the composition of the *Reasonableness*, Locke was at least interested in millenarian speculations. Three of his manuscripts, all titled "Chronologia Sacra" and written between 1692 and 1695, testify to his eschatological expectations.[71] The longest of these manuscripts presents an annotated biblical chronology based on *Seder Olam* (1693) by the Flemish alchemist and kabbalist Franciscus Mercurius van Helmont, who was a guest at Oates in 1693–1694. Nevertheless, nowhere did Locke expressly share the millenarian expectations of van Helmont and others – for example, his friend Newton, or the early seventeenth-century biblical scholar Joseph Mede, whose work he admired. When examining Rom. 11 in the *Paraphrase*, Locke wrote that "the Jews shall be a flourishing nation again, professing Christianity, in the land of promise, for that is to be reinstated again, in the promise made to Abraham, Isaac, and Jacob."[72] He maintained that the Jews will convert to Christianity and "be reestablished the people of God" when "the whole Gentile world shall enter into the Church, and make profession of Christianity."[73] These words denote Locke's belief in the Restoration of the Jews in Palestine.[74] But Locke did not clarify whether this Restoration will take place upon Christ's Second Coming and mark the beginning of his one-thousand-year reign on earth. He just explained that, in these verses, Paul speaks "not [of] eternal happiness in heaven," but of "the profession of the true religion, here on earth."[75] Moreover, in the manuscript *Resurrectio et quae sequuntur* (c.1699) and when examining 1 Cor. 15 in the *Paraphrase*, he maintained that Christ's Second Coming will be followed by

[70] Locke, *Reasonableness*, pp. 93–108.   [71] MS Locke c. 27, ff. 90, 91, 258–263.

[72] John Locke, *A Paraphrase and Notes on the Epistles of St Paul to the Galatians, 1 and 2 Corinthians, Romans, Ephesians*, ed. Arthur W. Wainwright, 2 vols. (Oxford: Clarendon Press, 1987), Rom. 11:23, vol. 2, p. 578.

[73] Ibid., Rom. 11:24–26, vol. 2, p. 577.

[74] Nabil Matar, "John Locke and the Jews," *Journal of Ecclesiastical History*, 44:1 (1993): pp. 45–62 (57–61).

[75] Locke, *Paraphrase*, Rom. 11:26, vol. 2, p. 578.

the resurrection of the "Beleivers," the resurrection of the wicked, the Last Judgment, and Christ's delivering his "Kingdome to God his father." At this point "cometh the end ... after which there shall be noe death noe change."[76] He did not speculate about the intervals of time between these events. On this issue, he just wrote:

How long after this [i.e., the resurrection of the saved] the wicked shall rise shall be enquired hereafter I shall only at present take notice only I think it is plain it shall be before our Saviour delivers up the Kingdom to his father, for then is the end.[77]

These words might be taken as being consistent with premillennialism, namely, the belief (upheld by Mede and Newton, among others) that Christ's Second Coming will inaugurate the millennium, which will come to an end on Judgment Day. However, in his third and last letter to Stillingfleet in 1699, Locke mentioned "the New Testament (where the general resurrection at the last day is spoken of)."[78] And these words indicate belief that both the resurrection of the saved and the resurrection of the unsaved will take place on Judgment Day, although separated by an undefined interval of time. Given also that Locke never talked of the millennium taking place between Christ's Second Coming and the general resurrection of the dead, it is likely that he thought that Christ's Second Coming, too, will occur on Judgment Day, shortly before the resurrection of the dead.

Anyhow, while none of Locke's theological writings denotes belief in the millennium, the *Reasonableness* emphasizes the office of the Messiah as a divinely appointed king much more than his offices as prophet and priest. According to Locke, Jesus never expressly claimed the title of priest for himself, and he spoke of himself as a prophet only seldom and incidentally. Locke's stress on the Messiah's kingly role diverges from the Socinians' emphasis on Christ's prophetic role. However, the Socinians also emphasized the exaltation and reinstatement of Christ as head of the Church and lord in the Kingdom of God.[79] Moreover, other writings by Locke show that he also believed in Christ's priestly office. In an addition, composed probably in the mid-1670s, to the 1667 manuscript *Essay concerning Toleration*, Locke indeed described Jesus as "the Great high preist" and "the last preist" in whom "all preisthood terminated."[80] A quarter of a century later, Locke highlighted

---

[76] John Locke, "Resurrectio et quae sequuntur," in Locke, *Writings on Religion*, pp. 232–237 (237). See, also, Locke, *Paraphrase*, 1 Cor. 15, vol. 1, pp. 246–256. See Chapter 4.

[77] Locke, "Resurrectio," p. 234.

[78] John Locke, "Reply to the Right Reverend the Lord Bishop of Worcester's Answer to His Second Letter," in John Locke, *Works*, 9 vols., 12th ed. (London, 1824), vol. 3, pp. 191–499 (304).

[79] Marshall, "Locke, Socinianism," pp. 175–176.

[80] John Locke, *An Essay concerning Toleration and Other Writings on Law and Politics, 1667–1683*, ed. J. R. Milton and Philip Milton (Oxford: Clarendon Press, 2006), p. 313. Four

Christ's priestly office once again, in a short manuscript analysis of the Epistle to the Hebrews that he composed around the year 1700 – perhaps in preparation of a paraphrase, since Locke (mistakenly) believed that Paul was most probably the author of Hebrews.[81] Several passages in Hebrews describe Jesus as "a priest for ever after the order of Melchisedec," who was "priest of the most high God."[82] Based on a belief already widespread among Jews before the time of Christ, Hebrews associates the Messiah with Melchisedec and his priestly office: ". . . after the similitude of Melchisedec there ariseth another priest, Who is made, not after the law of a carnal commandment, but after the power of an endless life."[83] According to Locke, Hebrews stresses Christ's priestly office and attempts to demonstrate that "under the gospel the covenant is much better than that under the law."[84] The main objective of the author of Hebrews was indeed to confirm the Jewish converts to Christianity in their belief that Jesus was the Messiah and, thus, dissuade them from apostatizing back to Judaism.[85]

While describing Jesus as the Messiah and considering his offices as king (above all), prophet, and priest, Locke never portrayed Christ as a person of the Trinity and never referred to the Son or the Holy Spirit as "God." The *Reasonableness* completely disregarded the Trinitarian doctrine in the midst of the Trinitarian controversy of the late seventeenth century. Likewise, the word "Trinity" does not appear even once in the *Paraphrase*, in which Locke interpreted in non-Trinitarian terms several passages often referred to in support of the Trinitarian dogma (e.g., Rom. 1:3–4, Rom. 9:5, 1 Cor. 1:2, and Eph. 3:9). Locke considered and used the term "Son of God" as an equivalent for "Messiah" not only in the *Reasonableness*, but also in the *Paraphrase*. Moreover, when paraphrasing and commenting on Rom. 1:3–4 ("Concerning his Son Jesus Christ our Lord, which was made of the seed of

---

manuscript versions of *An Essay concerning Toleration* exist: MS HM 584 (Huntington Library, San Marino, CA), the earliest version; MS Locke c. 28, ff. 21–32 (Bodleian Library); "Adversaria 1661," pp. 106–125 (see Chapter 1 for more details of this manuscript); PRO 30/24/47/1 (British National Archives). The original of the addition cited here is in "Adversaria 1661," pp. 125, 270–271. On this *Essay* and its composition, see Carlo Augusto Viano, "L'abbozzo originario e gli stadi di composizione di 'An Essay concerning Toleration' e la nascita delle teorie politico-religiose di Locke," *Rivista di filosofia*, 52:3 (1961): pp. 285–311; John Dunn, *The Political Thought of John Locke: An Historical Account of the Argument of the "Two Treatises of Government"* (Cambridge: Cambridge University Press, 1969), pp. 27–40; J. R. Milton, "Locke's *Essay on Toleration*: Text and Context," *British Journal for the History of Philosophy*, 1:2 (1993): pp. 45–63; J. R. Milton, Philip Milton, "General Introduction" to Locke, *Essay concerning Toleration*, pp. 1–161; J. R. Milton, Philip Milton, "Textual Introduction" to Locke, *Essay concerning Toleration*, pp. 162–263.

[81] John Locke, "On the Priesthood of Christ: Analysis of Hebrews," in Locke, *Writings on Religion*, pp. 238–241. For more details of this manuscript note, see Chapter 3.

[82] Heb. 5:6, 7:1. See, also, Heb. 5:10, 6:20, 7:10, 7:11, 7:15, 7:16, 7:17, 7:21.

[83] Heb. 7:15–16.   [84] Locke, "Priesthood," p. 240.   [85] Ibid.

David according to the flesh; And declared to be the Son of God with power, according to the spirit of holiness, by the resurrection from the dead") a few months before his death, he deviated from the traditional view that this passage attests the "union of the two natures" in Christ. While not expressly denying Christ's divine nature, which he did not mention at all when examining this Pauline passage, he considered the "flesh" to be simply Christ's body (not his human nature) and "the spirit of holiness" to be merely Christ's "more pure and spiritual part" (not a divine nature).[86] Briefly, although Locke never committed himself to an unequivocally anti-Trinitarian stance, his consider- ations on Christ in his theological writings, particularly in the *Paraphrase*, imply a denial of the Trinity.

Yet, the Christology that emerges from the *Paraphrase* is not completely in line with a Socinian notion of Jesus' nature, as is shown by Locke's paraphrase and note on Eph. 1:10 ("That in the dispensation of the fulness of times he might gather together in one all things in Christ, both which are in heaven, and which are on earth; even in him"). Locke paraphrased this verse as: "Until the Coming of the due time of that dispensation wherein he had predetermined to reduce all things again, both in Heaven and Earth under one Head in Christ."[87] He further explained in a note on this verse: "'Tis plain in Sacred Scripture, that Christ at first had the Rule and Supremacy over all, and was Head over all."[88] Satan's rebellion disrupted Christ's unitary rule and supremacy over all, but "Christ recovered this Kingdom, and was re-instated in the Supremacy and Headship, in the fullness of time … at his death and resurrection."[89] There is now wide consensus among historians that Locke's paraphrase and note on Eph. 1:10 denote belief in Christ's pre-existence, although not in Christ's divinity, and thus reveal an incipient Arianism.[90] This was not the first time that the theme of Christ's pre-existence emerged from Locke's theological reflection. He had already reflected upon this subject some time before 1679, when drafting a set of comments on twelve biblical texts in his interleaved Bentley Bible.[91] In these comments, Locke made reference to the heterodox

---

[86] Arthur W. Wainwright, "Introduction" to Locke, *Paraphrase*, vol. 1, pp. 1–88 (35–39); Marshall, "Locke, Socinianism," pp. 173–176. Locke benefited from Newton's feedback when revising his paraphrase and notes on Rom. 1:3–4: see Kim Ian Parker, "Newton, Locke and the Trinity: Sir Isaac's Comments on Locke's *A Paraphrase and Notes on the Epistle of St Paul to the Romans*," *Scottish Journal of Theology*, 62:1 (2009): pp. 40–52.

[87] Locke, *Paraphrase*, Eph. 1:10, vol. 2, p. 616. This paraphrase might indicate a view of Christ's kingdom as a merely terrestrial one – a hypothesis that, however, Locke neither endorsed nor rejected, as I explain below, when considering, also, his use of Col. 1:15–17 as a gloss on Eph. 1:10.

[88] Ibid.   [89] Ibid.

[90] Wainwright, "Introduction," p. 38; Marshall, "Locke, Socinianism," pp. 173–176; Nuovo, *Christianity*, pp. 36–37, 41–43.

[91] Ibid., p. 36. Nuovo has published this set of comments from Locke's interleaved Bentley Bible (i.e., LL 309, BOD Locke 16.25) in ibid., pp. 100–101.

views on the Trinity expressed by a certain "G," whom Victor Nuovo has identified with the seventeenth-century Anglican clergyman Nicholas Gibbon, the Younger. Locke probably drew on a still unidentified manuscript by this author, according to which the Godhead consists of three subsistences – the Father and Creator, the Word, and the Spirit. According to this manuscript, immediately after the Fall, the Father created the intellectual nature or soul of the Messiah, which was united with the Word and remained with it in the bosom of the Father until incarnation. This view was certainly heterodox and tended to a sort of Origenism, although the third-century theologian Origen thought that Jesus' (human) soul had become fused with the *Logos* only at incarnation. However, Locke did not express any support for this view. Conversely, Locke's paraphrase of Eph. 1:10 – especially the words "to reduce all things again, both in Heaven and Earth under one Head in Christ" – and his note stating that "Christ at first had the Rule and Supremacy over all, and was Head over all" clearly avow Christ's pre-existence. This position is incompatible with Socinianism – even with the views of a second-generation Socinian like Jonas Schlichting, who argued that "Christ's pre-existence" simply meant that Christ's Coming had been *foreseen*.[92] It would indeed be incorrect to interpret Locke's comments on Eph. 1:10 as consistent with Schlichting's Christology, because Christ could not lose his power if he had possessed it only as foreseen.[93] That Locke held neither a Trinitarian nor a properly Socinian Christology is confirmed by his citation of Col. 1:15–17 as a gloss on Eph. 1:10, given that in Col. 1:15–17 the Son is described as "the firstborn of every creature" and as being "before all things"[94] (although these terms do not necessarily denote primacy *in time*). Locke's paraphrase and note on Eph. 1:10, with his reference to Col. 1:15–17, rather indicate a Christology echoing Arianism. Nevertheless, Locke's considerations on Christ and the Godhead, taken as a whole, do not allow for the conclusion that he was an "Arian" proper. Even his note on Eph. 1:10 indicating belief in Christ's

---

[92] Jonas Schlichting, *Confessio fidei Christianae* (n.p., 1642), pp. 5–11.

[93] Marshall, "Locke, Socinianism," p. 174.

[94] Locke, *Paraphrase*, Eph. 1:10, vol. 2, pp. 616–617. Col. 1:15–17 reads: "[The Son] Who is the image of the invisible God, the firstborn of every creature: For by him were all things created, that are in heaven, and that are in earth, visible and invisible, whether they be thrones, or dominions, or principalities, or powers: all things were created by him, and for him: And he is before all things, and by him all things consist." Concerning this gloss, Locke suggested in the same note on Eph. 1:10 that "things in heaven" and "things on earth" might signify, respectively, Jews and Gentiles. Victor Nuovo has observed that, if this is what Paul actually meant in Eph. 1:10, then "Christ's kingdom might be a merely terrestrial one" (Nuovo, *Christianity*, p. 42). At any rate, Locke neither endorsed nor rejected this interpretation, as he stated the following: "However, this interpretation I am not positive in; but offer it as a matter of inquiry" (Locke, *Paraphrase*, Eph. 1:10, vol. 2, p. 616).

pre-existence denotes a purpose typical of Socinianism, as John Marshall has convincingly argued:

The note itself includes emphasis on Christ's death and resurrection as reinstating him in his power, and leading to his position as head of the Church as what was significant for humans to know. Focus on that exaltation and on Christ's lordship following the resurrection – his headship of the Church and position as lord in the kingdom of God – was thus what this note itself made most important, and the issue of his pre-existence only came up in this one note and nowhere else in the text. Such focus was more distinctive of Socinian emphases than of Arian or trinitarian emphases.[95]

In this regard, Victor Nuovo has correctly observed that, in Locke's note on Eph. 1:10, "Christ is a far more exalted and sublime figure than the one represented in the Gospels and in the *Reasonableness*."[96] Christ's resurrection and exaltation actually play a prominent role in the *Paraphrase*, as is shown by other passages in this work, including a note on the aforesaid Rom. 1:4 in which Locke judged "Christs resurrection from the dead and his entring into immortalitie to be the most eminent and characteristical marke whereby Christ is certainly known and as it were determined to be the Son of god."[97] Locke's emphasis, in the *Paraphrase*, on Christ's resurrection as the distinguishing mark of his being the son of God denotes a subtle theological shift from the *Reasonableness*.[98] In the *Reasonableness*, Locke described Jesus' sonship as being *"The First-born from the dead"* – a phrase he borrowed from Col. 1:18.[99] However, in the *Reasonableness*, Locke also stressed Jesus' virgin birth as an indicator of his literal sonship of God entailing his immortality since birth, which distinguished him from the mortal descendants of Adam, who had forfeited the state of immortality when committing his sin in Paradise:

God nevertheless, out of his Infinite Mercy, willing to bestow Eternal Life on Mortal Men, sends Jesus Christ into the World; Who being conceived in the Womb of a Virgin (that had not known Man) by the immediate Power of God, was properly the Son of God. ... So that being the Son of God, he was, like his Father, *Immortal*.[100]

In the *Reasonableness*, Locke argued that Jesus, being immortal since birth, did not have to suffer death, but chose to die in order to fulfill his Messianic office because, without his death, his resurrection would not be possible. Locke also stated that "the great Evidence that Jesus was the *Son of God*, was his Resurrection. Then the Image of his Father appeared in him, when he

---

[95] Marshall, "Locke, Socinianism," p. 175.   [96] Nuovo, *John Locke*, p. 245.
[97] Locke, *Paraphrase*, Rom. 1:4, vol. 2, p. 487.
[98] Parker, "Newton, Locke," p. 49. As Parker has noted, Locke's interpretation benefited from Newton's suggestions concerning this subject, too.
[99] Locke, *Reasonableness*, p. 114.
[100] Ibid., p. 113. On Jesus as literally the Son of God in the *Reasonableness*, see Chapter 3 in the present book.

visibly entered into the state of Immortality."[101] Yet, according to the *Reason-ableness*, Jesus' immortality since birth has a primary role in his salvific mission, because, by the "*Spirit of Adoption*" mentioned in Rom. 8:15, the faithful become Christ's brethren (and hence "adoptive" sons of God) and are eventually admitted to eternal life: "And we by Adoption, being for his sake made his Brethren, and the Sons of God, come to share in that Inheritance, which was his Natural Right; he being by Birth the Son of God: Which Inheritance is Eternal Life."[102] But in the *Paraphrase* it is essentially Christ's resurrection that distinguishes him as the Son of God. Thus, the *Paraphrase* echoes the Socinian stress on Christ's resurrection and exaltation, rather than his virgin birth (although the Socinians described Christ as created mortal and then made immortal by divine miracle upon his death, while Locke never wavered from what he wrote in the *Reasonableness* about Christ's immortality since birth).[103] One more argument supports the thesis that what really counts, in the Christology of the *Paraphrase*, is Christ's resurrection and exaltation, not his pre-existence or his birth: while the aforesaid note on Eph. 1:10 may denote an Arian notion of Christ, it does not clarify whether Locke conceived of Christ's pre-existence as pre-cosmic.[104] Along with the fact that this note is the only place in Locke's production that clearly denotes belief in Christ's pre-existence, the absence of further specifications might indicate that this subject does not play a major role in Locke's Christology, which, instead, strongly emphasizes Christ's exaltation and lordship following his resurrection.

Briefly, Locke's views on the Trinity, Christ's nature, and Christ's relation to God the Father present several similarities with Socinian thought, and the *Paraphrase* also presents an important point in common with Arian concep-tions of Christ. Locke's reflections on these themes actually benefited from his knowledge of various theological – especially anti-Trinitarian – currents and authors. However, his Christological views largely resulted from his effort to comprehend relevant biblical passages on his own.

The Debate on Locke and the Trinity

In the 1690s and 1700s, Locke's religious views elicited a number of unfavor-able responses. Many of these responses concentrated on the Socinian elem-ents and the anti-Trinitarian implications of Locke's theology and philosophy, although he was also accused of being a creedal minimalist, a deist, a skeptic, and even a Spinozist, a Hobbist, and a covert atheist. Whereas the debate revolved mainly around Locke's statements in, and omissions from, the *Reasonableness*, some of his critics focused their attention on other works,

---

[101] Locke, *Reasonableness*, p. 115.   [102] Ibid., pp. 114–115.   [103] See Chapter 3.
[104] Marshall, "Locke, Socinianism," p. 175.

particularly *An Essay concerning Human Understanding*. Locke replied to his critics in only a few cases, and he became involved in heated disputes with two of his detractors – the Calvinistic divine John Edwards and the latitudinarian Bishop of Worcester, Edward Stillingfleet, both of whom associated him with anti-Trinitarian positions. In four books published between 1695 and 1697,[105] Edwards described the author of the *Reasonableness* as "all over Socinianized"[106] and labeled him "a well-Willer to the *Racovian* way."[107] Edwards's attacks led Locke to write two vindications of the *Reasonableness*, published respectively in 1695 and 1697. Stillingfleet criticized Locke's way of ideas, and particularly his concepts of substance and person, in *A Discourse in Vindication of the Doctrine of the Trinity* (1697).[108] Although Stillingfleet did not judge Locke to be an anti-Trinitarian proper, he blamed *An Essay concerning Human Understanding* for having provided the anti-Trinitarians – especially "the author of *Christianity Not Mysterious*," namely, John Toland – with a powerful weapon to question the Trinitarian dogma. Stillingfleet's attack on Locke in 1697 was only the beginning of a harsh dispute, during which Stillingfleet composed two more writings against Locke, and Locke responded to Stillingfleet in three replies. This heated exchange of opinions came to an end only with Stillingfleet's death in 1699. Edwards's and Stillingfleet's critiques of Locke's theological and philosophical views encouraged other theologians, particularly the nonjuror John Milner, to find elements of Socinianism in Locke's religious thought.[109]

---

[105] John Edwards, *Some Thoughts concerning the Several Causes and Occasions of Atheism* (London, 1695); John Edwards, *Socinianism Unmask'd* (London, 1696); John Edwards, *The Socinian Creed* (London, 1697); John Edwards, *A Brief Vindication of the Fundamental Articles of the Christian Faith* (London, 1697). Edwards attacked Locke for his allegedly reduced creed, once again, in 1708, four years after Locke's death: see John Edwards, *The Doctrine of Faith and Justification Set in a True Light* (London, 1708), pp. 63, 139–140.

[106] Edwards, *Some Thoughts*, p. 113.   [107] Edwards, *Socinian Creed*, p. 120.

[108] Edward Stillingfleet, *A Discourse in Vindication of the Doctrine of the Trinity* (London, 1697). On the controversy between Stillingfleet and Locke, see Robert Todd Carroll, *The Common-Sense Philosophy of Religion of Bishop Edward Stillingfleet (1635–1699)* (The Hague: Nijhoff, 1975), pp. 86–100; G. A. J. Rogers, "Stillingfleet, Locke, and the Trinity," in Allison P. Coudert, Sarah Hutton, Richard H. Popkin, Gordon M. Weiner (eds.), *Judaeo-Christian Culture in the Seventeenth Century: A Celebration of the Library of Narcissus Marsh (1638–1713)* (Dordrecht: Springer, 1999), pp. 207–224; M. A. Stewart, "Stillingfleet and the Way of Ideas," in Stewart (ed.), *English Philosophy*, pp. 245–280; Dixon, *Nice and Hot Disputes*, pp. 143–162; E. D. Kort, "Stillingfleet and Locke on Substance, Essence, and Articles of Faith," *Locke Studies*, 5 (2005): pp. 149–178; Chiara Giuntini, *Presenti a se stessi. La centralità della coscienza in Locke* (Florence: Le Lettere, 2015), pp. 299–331; Matthew Stuart, "The Correspondence with Stillingfleet," in Matthew Stuart (ed.), *A Companion to Locke* (Chichester: Wiley-Blackwell, 2016), pp. 354–369; Jonathan S. Marko, *Measuring the Distance between Locke and Toland: Reason, Revelation, and Rejection during the Locke-Stillingfleet Debate* (Eugene: Pickwick, 2017), pp. 13–59.

[109] Alan P. F. Sell, *John Locke and the Eighteenth-Century Divines* (Cardiff: University of Wales Press, 1997), pp. 189–197, 212–229; John C. Higgins-Biddle, "Introduction" to Locke,

When Edwards first attacked the *Reasonableness* in 1695, Locke was only suspected to be the author of this book, which had been published anonymously. Therefore, Edwards did not mention Locke as the author of this book in *Some Thoughts concerning the Several Causes and Occasions of Atheism* (1695). In this tract, Edwards described Socinianism as promoting atheism. In his opinion, Socinian thinkers like Socinus himself and Johann Crell excessively trusted the capacities of human reason in all fields of inquiry, including biblical interpretation, and refused to believe anything incomprehensible to natural reason. According to Edwards, such an excessive confidence in the powers of reason undermined not simply the Christian religion, but also even theism and morality altogether, given the limits and imperfections of reason.[110] He claimed (on the basis of weak evidence, namely, some isolated and decontextualized passages from Socinus's and Crell's works) that the Socinians denied several essential attributes of God, such as immensity, omnipresence, immateriality, and prescience.[111] Depicting *The Reasonableness of Christianity* as contributing to Socinianism and hence atheism, Edwards argued that the interpretation and use of the term "Son of God" as a mere synonym for "Messiah" in this book clearly denoted its Socinian nature.[112] Moreover, he observed that the "creedal minimalism" of the *Reasonableness* was well-matched by its silence on the Trinity and on beliefs and practices supporting the Trinitarian dogma – for example, baptism in the name of the Father, the Son, and the Holy Spirit; Christ's divine nature; the Son's consubstantiality, coequality, and coeternity with God the Father; the incarnation; and the satisfaction theory of atonement. According to Edwards, the silence on these themes in the *Reasonableness* implied a rejection of these beliefs and practices.[113] He reiterated his charges against the *Reasonableness* in three more writings in the second half of the 1690s. In *Socinianism Unmask'd* (1696), he disapproved of the distinction between fundamental and non-fundamental doctrines made in the *Reasonableness* – a distinction that, in his opinion, endorsed creedal minimalism – but he still abstained from naming Locke as the author of this book. He referred to Locke as the author of *The Reasonableness of Christianity* for the first time in *The Socinian Creed* (1697), a tract dedicated to Bishop Stillingfleet, whose first attack on Locke's way of ideas was published shortly before Edwards's third book against Socinianism and the *Reasonableness*. In *The Socinian Creed*, Edwards followed Stillingfleet's example in portraying Locke's philosophy as

---

Reasonableness, pp. xv–cxv (xlii–lxxiv); Stephen D. Snobelen, "Socinianism, Heresy and John Locke's *Reasonableness of Christianity*," *Enlightenment and Dissent*, 20 (2001): pp. 88–125.

[110] Edwards, *Some Thoughts*, p. 66.   [111] Ibid.   [112] Ibid., pp. 112–113.

[113] Ibid., pp. 105–111. See, also, Chapter 2 in the present study.

buttressing the anti-Trinitarians' views. Finally, in *A Brief Vindication of the Fundamental Articles of the Christian Faith* (1697), Edwards ridiculed not only Locke's work, but also his character, deliberately treating his philosophical and religious views "with Satyr rather than Argument."[114]

Edwards's *Brief Vindication* angered Locke so much that he sought satisfaction through Archbishop Tenison, since four members of the University of Cambridge – including Locke's friend John Covel, who apologized to him – had given the imprimatur to this book.[115] Locke's annoyance at Edwards's attacks emerges from his two vindications of the *Reasonableness*, in which he replied to Edwards's charges point by point. Besides clarifying his position, or in some cases the reasons for his silence, about some of the controversial issues that Edwards had addressed in his critiques, Locke observed that his hermeneutical and soteriological views were similar to the ideas of various theologians affiliated with the Church of England, including William Chillingworth, Archbishop John Tillotson, and Bishop Simon Patrick.[116] Locke denied that he had adopted theories typical of Socinianism regarding, for instance, the use of the title "Son of God" as a synonym for "Messiah" and reliance, above all, on the Gospels and the Acts of the Apostles. He was not alone in defending the *Reasonableness* from Edwards's charges. A defense that particularly pleased Locke, as he himself declared in the *Second Vindication*, came from Samuel Bold, rector of the parish of Steeple in Dorset and author of a sermon and a commentary on the *Reasonableness*, both contained in a volume published in 1697.[117] Bold reaffirmed Locke's theory that belief in Jesus the Messiah is required to *become* a Christian, while those who have already accepted the Christian faith also have the duty to diligently study Scripture. Moreover, Bold pointed out that, to Locke, faith relies not merely on *intellectual* assent to the proposition that Jesus is the Messiah. Nonetheless, Bold's notion of faith differed from that of Locke, since Bold considered faith as a gift of grace, regardless of one's natural capacities and works. Conversely, Locke argued that true faith ought to be complemented by repentance and obedience to the divine moral law, as he restated in the *Second Vindication*.[118] Furthermore, Bold listed in his sermon several doctrines that all true Christians ought to accept, based on their study of Scripture; and his list included doctrines that

---

[114] Edwards, *Brief Vindication*, sig. A4r.   [115] Higgins-Biddle, "Introduction," pp. xlvii–xlviii.

[116] John Locke, "A Second Vindication of the Reasonableness of Christianity," in John Locke, *Vindications of the Reasonableness of Christianity*, ed. Victor Nuovo (Oxford: Clarendon Press, 2012), pp. 27–233 (110–111, 131, 181).

[117] Ibid., pp. 33–37; Samuel Bold, *A Short Discourse of the True Knowledge of Christ Jesus. To Which Are Added, Some Passages in the Reasonableness of Christianity, & c., and Its Vindication* (London, 1697); Sell, *John Locke*, pp. 197–199, 252–254; Higgins-Biddle, "Introduction," pp. liv–lvi.

[118] Locke, "Second Vindication," pp. 39–46.

Locke had not considered in the *Reasonableness*, such as Christ's divinity, incarnation, and sacrificial death, and even the Trinitarian dogma. Others, besides Bold, defended the *Reasonableness*. However, with a few remarkable exceptions, the other writings favorable to Locke, instead of supporting his cause, offered new arguments to Edwards and encouraged other critics to further attack him.[119] Among the most provocative defenses of the *Reasonableness* was an anonymous letter, published in September 1695 in the London periodical *Miscellaneous Letters* and attributed to Toland, which slandered Edwards while praising Locke as a herald of reason.[120] The anonymous pamphlet *The Exceptions of Mr. Edwards, in His Causes of Atheism, against The Reasonableness of Christianity* (1695) was even more controversial, in that it drew on the *Reasonableness* in expressly refuting the Trinitarian dogma. Another defense not in line with Locke's intentions was *An Account of the Growth of Deism in England* (1696) by the Whig clergyman William Stephens, who argued, among other things, that deism had emerged as a reaction to priestcraft and abstruse doctrines (e.g., the Trinity). Finally, an anonymous *Letter to the Deists* (1696) commended the *Reasonableness* for emphasizing the inherent *rationality* of Jesus' teachings. Some of these writings tended to anti-Trinitarianism or deism, to such an extent that Locke felt compelled to disassociate himself, in his *Second Vindication*, from the use that some defenses of the *Reasonableness*, as well as Toland's *Christianity Not Mysterious*, had made of his philosophical and religious ideas.

In the *Second Vindication*, Locke also disassociated himself from the Socinians.[121] However, we know that he had several anti-Trinitarian friends, with some of whom he corresponded and talked about Christological and Trinitarian questions. He owned a large number of Socinian books, which he started reading extensively at least in the late 1670s and which he frequently referred to in his private writings.[122] His familiarity with Socinian themes emerges from his public writings, as not only Edwards but also the nonjuror John Milner observed. In *An Account of Mr. Lock's Religion*, published in 1700, Milner gave a comprehensive list of parallels between Locke's religious thought and Socinian theology. Milner's analysis was based on various Socinian works and some of Locke's books – that is, *An Essay concerning Human Understanding, Some Thoughts concerning Education* (1693), the *Reasonableness* with its two vindications, and Locke's three replies to Stillingfleet. Milner's list of parallels between Locke's religion and Socinianism includes

---

[119] Higgins-Biddle, "Introduction," pp. l–lviii.

[120] The Huguenot intellectual Pierre Desmaizeaux republished this letter, as "Toland to the Reverend Mr. ***, London, 12 Sept. 1695," in John Toland, *A Collection of Several Pieces*, 2 vols. (London, 1726), vol. 1, pp. 314–317.

[121] Locke, "Second Vindication," p. 126.   [122] See Chapter 2.

the use of the term "Son of God" as a synonym for "Messiah," an emphasis on faith in Jesus the Messiah as the core article of Christianity, the denial of original sin, the rejection of innate ideas, and various aspects and implications of some Socinian authors' and Locke's mortalist ideas, such as the opinions that the wicked will be annihilated and that the bodies of the dead do not literally resurrect.[123] Milner's accurate list demonstrates that Locke's opponents aimed at associating his religious views not so much with English Unitarianism as with Continental Socinianism – a theological tradition that Milner and other critics of Locke, including Edwards, knew well. Both Locke and his critics wrote during or shortly after the Trinitarian controversy of the late seventeenth century. Moreover, Locke was well acquainted with various English Unitarians, such as Thomas Firmin, William Popple, and Alexander Beresford, and he possessed several texts published during the controversy, including various writings by Stephen Nye and the first three collections of Unitarian tracts. However, the Continental Socinians' works, especially but not exclusively those collected in *Bibliotheca Fratrum Polonorum*, were available not only to Locke and other heterodox intellectuals, but also to a number of Anglican clergymen. Some of these clergymen had an impressive theological erudition and an excellent command of Latin, which enabled them to identify the numerous similarities between Locke's religious thought and the Socinian theological tradition. Thus, Edwards, Milner, and other critics correctly noted that Locke's views on scriptural authority, justification, and the afterlife overlapped, in many respects, with the ideas of Socinus, or second-generation Socinians like Crell and Schlichting, or the editors of the final version of the *Racovian Catechism*.[124]

Nevertheless, Locke always denied any association with Socinianism, and he always maintained that his religious ideas were based exclusively on his reading of Scripture. In fact, he was not a Socinian or Unitarian proper, because his theological ideas diverged from Socinian thought in many significant respects – for instance, concerning the relationship between the natural and revealed law, the atonement, and Christ's pre-existence. Moreover, whereas he often agreed with Socinian authors, he always made sure that his religious views were consistent with, and indeed grounded in, Scripture. He actually considered one's being a Christian as more important than belonging to a specific denomination or tradition and, when taking distance from the Socinians, he blamed them for their sectarianism and "Zeal for their Orthodoxy."[125] Briefly, Locke's disassociation from Socinianism reflected the actual differences between his religious thought and Socinian systems of theology, although he had good knowledge of Socinian and Unitarian sources and he

---

[123] John Milner, *An Account of Mr. Lock's Religion* (London, 1700), pp. 180–188.
[124] Snobelen, "Socinianism, Heresy," p. 102.   [125] Locke, "Second Vindication," p. 126.

certainly approved of some Socinian and Unitarian theories – but only because he found these theories compatible with Scripture.

When responding to Edwards and disassociating himself from Socinianism, Locke protested to have never denied the Trinitarian doctrine, but he never took the trouble to affirm belief in the Trinity. He abstained from clarifying his position on the Trinity also during his controversy with Stillingfleet. In *A Discourse in Vindication of the Doctrine of the Trinity*, written in the later stages of the Trinitarian controversy, Stillingfleet pursued a threefold purpose: he contested the Unitarians' allegations of disunity within the Trinitarian party, he offered an "answer to the late Socinian objections"[126] to the Trinitarian dogma, and he provided a complex, although conservative in tone and contents, defense of the Trinity. While not mentioning by name any of the writers involved in the Trinitarian controversy, and while refraining from detailing their specific views on the Trinity, Stillingfleet rejected the distinction (made by Nye and Tindal)[127] between Trinitarians like Wallis and South, whom the anti-Trinitarians depicted as modalists, and those who, like Sherlock, were accused of tritheism. In the first four chapters of his book, Stillingfleet described Unitarianism as a recent current, unknown among the early Christians and employing a narrow view of knowledge as necessitating clear and distinct ideas.[128] He blamed the Unitarians for employing in Godtalk concepts of substance, nature, and person that are pertinent exclusively to created, finite, *human* persons. The core of his argument was in a clarification of scholastic notions of substance (or essence), nature, and person, and in the use of these notions in Godtalk. He maintained that "one common Nature subsists in several Individuals" and that "Personality ... doth not consist in a meer Intelligent Being, but in that peculiar manner of Subsistence in that Being which can be in no other."[129] He added that "we never conceive a Person without the Essence in Conjunction with it."[130] Individuals of the same kind, including human persons, are separate and different "because of their different Accidents and separate Existence. . . .. But where there can be no Accidents nor Division, there must be perfect Unity."[131] Thus, he described the "divine essence" as indivisible:

Because there can be no difference of Accidents, or Place, or Qualities in the divine Nature; and there can be no separate Existence, because the Essence and Existence are the same in God; and if necessary Existence be an inseparable Attribute of the divine

---

[126] Stillingfleet, *Discourse in Vindication*, p. 1.
[127] Nye, *Considerations*; Matthew Tindal, *A Letter . . . concerning the Trinity and the Athanasian Creed* (London, 1694).
[128] Stillingfleet, *Discourse in Vindication*, pp. 1–54.   [129] Ibid., pp. 72–74.   [130] Ibid., p. 73.
[131] Ibid.

Essence, it is impossible there should be any separate Existence; for what always was and must be, can have no other Existence than what is implied in the very Essence.[132]

Stillingfleet was aware that his views on the "divine essence" could be accused of leading to modalism. Therefore, he clarified that the term "person," when used in Godtalk, "signifies the Essence with a particular manner of Subsistence, which the Greek Fathers called an Hypostasis."[133] According to Stillingfleet, both the Scriptures and the Fathers insisted on the indivisible unity of the Godhead, thus excluding any "division of the substance" or "division in nature."[134] Consequently, he condemned the Unitarians' narrow understanding of the term "person" in Godtalk – a term they took as signifying a *separate* intelligent being. Briefly, Stillingfleet attempted to speak of the Trinity in traditional, scholastic terms, which were obviously at odds with Locke's way of ideas. Stillingfleet indeed criticized the Lockean theory that certainty ought to be based on "clear and distinct ideas" – a theory that had enabled the author of *Christianity Not Mysterious*, namely, John Toland, to reduce faith to rational assent to what is intelligible and thus to question, although indirectly, the Trinitarian doctrine.[135] During their dispute, neither Stillingfleet nor Locke ever called Toland by his name. They referred to him as, simply, "the author of *Christianity Not Mysterious*" – a book that Stillingfleet regarded as a Lockean-influenced contribution to the Unitarian cause.

In *Christianity Not Mysterious*, Toland drew on *An Essay concerning Human Understanding*, but he modified Locke's way of ideas for his own purposes. *Christianity Not Mysterious* was actually indebted, above all, to Spinoza's biblical hermeneutics thematically, methodologically, and in terms of operative principle – not to Locke's way of ideas and biblical theology.[136] Toland concurred with Locke that "it still belongs to *Reason*, to judge of the Truth of [a proposition's] being a Revelation, and of the signification of the Words, wherein it is delivered."[137] Like Locke, Toland acknowledged that "in Matters of common Practice [we] must of necessity sometimes admit *Probability* to supply the Defect of *Demonstration*."[138] But, while Locke, in the *Essay*, described faith as assent to merely *probable* matters of fact, Toland did not admit probability in matters of fact wherein faith was the intended consequence. Toland's insistence on demonstrable certainty – not merely probability – as the ground of assent, when it comes to revelations contained in the

---

[132] Ibid., p. 74.   [133] Ibid., p. 75.   [134] Ibid., pp. 75–100.   [135] Ibid., pp. 230–292.

[136] Ian Leask, "The Undivulged Event in Toland's *Christianity Not Mysterious*," in Wayne Hudson, Diego Lucci, Jeffrey R. Wigelsworth (eds.), *Atheism and Deism Revalued: Heterodox Religious Identities in Britain, 1650–1800* (Farnham: Ashgate, 2014), pp. 63–80; Lucci, "From Unitarianism to Deism."

[137] John Locke, *An Essay concerning Human Understanding*, ed. Peter H. Nidditch (Oxford: Clarendon Press, 1975), IV.xviii.8, p. 694.

[138] John Toland, *Christianity Not Mysterious* (London, 1696), p. 21.

Bible, was a significant point of divergence from Locke, as James Lancaster has noted:

Toland differed from Locke in one fundamental respect, and this was his belief that the matters of faith revealed in the Bible could be known as matters of fact with demonstrable certainty. Where Locke argued that assent could properly be called "faith" because it was assent to probable matters of fact, Toland argued that assent should only be given to matters of fact that attained the level of the intuitive, not those which were merely probable.[139]

As Toland explained in *Christianity Not Mysterious*:

When all these Rules concur in any Matter of Fact, I take it then for *Demonstration*, which is nothing else but *Irresistible Evidence from proper Proofs*: But where any of these Conditions are wanting, the thing is *uncertain*, or, at best, but *probable*, which, with me, are not very different.[140]

While Locke classified propositions into three categories – according to reason, above reason, and contrary to reason[141] – Toland stated that "there is nothing in the Gospel Contrary to Reason, Nor Above it," and that "an implicite Assent to any thing above Reason ... contradicts the Ends of Religion, the Nature of Man, and the Goodness and Wisdom of God."[142] Consequently, to Toland the "Subject of Faith" must be intelligible to all and must be built upon "very strict Reasoning from Experience."[143]

According to Stillingfleet, Toland's dismissal of mysteries entailed a denial of the Trinitarian dogma, because this dogma was not based on a "clear and distinct idea."[144] But, *contra* both Toland and Locke, Stillingfleet argued that certainty "is not placed upon any clear and distinct Ideas, but upon the force of Reason distinct from it."[145] Stillingfleet's attack on Locke's way of ideas rested on his reaffirmation of a scholastic notion of substance, based on a view of certain knowledge as "*adaequatio rei et intellectus*," against Locke's agnosticism on substance. He openly rejected Locke's characterization of substance as an unknown substratum or support of qualities.[146] To Stilling-fleet, our perception of the "qualities we find existing" in a certain being leads us to conceive of this being's substance as not simply the "support of those qualities," but as this being's very essence; and by "essence" Stillingfleet meant not merely a notion in the mind (as could follow, in his opinion, from Locke's way of ideas), but something existing in reality.[147] Stillingfleet

---

[139] James A. T. Lancaster, "From Matters of Faith to Matters of Fact: The Problem of Priestcraft in Early Modern England," *Intellectual History Review*, 28:1 (2018): pp. 145–165 (158).
[140] Toland, *Christianity*, pp. 17–18.   [141] Locke, *Essay*, IV.xvii.23, p. 687.
[142] Toland, *Christianity*, pp. 77, 139.   [143] Ibid., p. 137.
[144] Stillingfleet, *Discourse in Vindication*, p. 252.   [145] Ibid.
[146] Locke, *Essay*, II.xxiii.1–6, pp. 295–299.
[147] Stillingfleet, *Discourse in Vindication*, pp. 236–238.

employed an anti-nominalist, "realist" approach in covering "the Distinction between Nature and Person, and of this," he continued, "we can have no clear and distinct Idea from Sensation or Reflection. And yet all our Notions of the Doctrine of the Trinity, depend upon the right understanding of it."[148] He dismissed the option (which, in his opinion, could follow from Locke's philosophy) that "nature" is only an abstraction devised by our discriminating and categorizing understanding. Consequently, he denied that the essence of a being is merely a "nominal essence." He maintained, instead, that "there must be a Real Essence in every individual of the same kind" and that "the general Idea is not made from the simple Ideas by the meer Act of the Mind abstracting from Circumstances, but from Reason and Consideration of the true Nature of Things."[149] Finally, he reasserted and further clarified his concept of "personality," maintaining that "a Person is a compleat Intelligent Substance, with a peculiar manner of Subsistence."[150] In other words, according to Stillingfleet, what makes an individual person, and distinguishes this individual person from all other persons, is the "peculiar manner of subsistence" adopted by the common nature in that specific case. Stillingfleet's definition of "person" as "a compleat Intelligent Substance" – a definition in line with the Boethian understanding of personhood – could be taken as denying a Trinity consisting of three *consubstantial* persons. He was aware of this possibility. Therefore, in order to avoid misunderstandings, he restated his distinction (already employed against the Unitarians' identification of "person" with "substance" in Godtalk) between *human* and *divine* persons:

When we speak of Finite Substances and Persons, we are certain that distinct Persons do imply distinct Substances, because they have a distinct and separate Existence; but this will not hold in an infinite Substance, where necessary Existence doth belong to the Idea of it. ... For necessary Existence doth imply a Co-existence of the Divine Persons; and the Unity of the Divine Essence, that there cannot be such a difference of individual Substances, as there is among mankind.[151]

During the intense exchange of ideas between Locke and Stillingfleet, neither of the two disputants conceded anything to the other. Replying to Stillingfleet's attacks, Locke repeatedly claimed that his opponent had misinterpreted the *Essay* and was trying to push him to talk of a subject – the Trinitarian doctrine – that he had not intended to cover in his works.[152] He protested that he had written the *Essay* "without any thought of the controversy between the trinitarians and the unitarians" and that, consequently, this book did not

---

[148] Ibid., p. 252.   [149] Ibid., pp. 258–259.   [150] Ibid., p. 261.   [151] Ibid., pp. 261–262.

[152] John Locke, "A Letter to the Right Reverend the Lord Bishop of Worcester," in Locke, *Works*, vol. 3, pp. 1–96 (30, 68–69); Locke, "Reply to the ... Answer to His Second Letter," pp. 407–408.

contain anything concerning the Trinity.[153] Locke frequently noted that he, unlike the author of *Christianity Not Mysterious*, admitted mysteries in religion, since his faith was based on Scripture.[154] He added that, if others had made ill use of his theories, Stillingfleet should blame them, instead of making a case against him that rested merely on guilt by association.[155] As Locke wrote in his last reply to Stillingfleet:

[The author of *Christianity Not Mysterious*] says something which has a conformity with some of the notions in my book. But it is to be observed he speaks them as his own thoughts, and not upon my authority, nor with taking any notice of me.[156]

Locke maintained that he had not attempted to "discard substance out of the reasonable part of the world."[157] In fact, he had simply refused to assert that he knew anything about substance, which he nonetheless considered as part of the reasonable world since human reason supposes substance as a substratum. In defending his way of ideas, Locke even pressed Stillingfleet to show how we can have an understanding of a thing's substance beyond the idea we have of it.[158] He also argued that Stillingfleet had claimed that we need clear and distinct ideas of "nature" and "person" to maintain the doctrine of the Trinity; but Stillingfleet had failed to provide such ideas, thus harming the Trinitarian dogma even more than Locke's philosophy had supposedly done.[159] Furthermore, in his third and last reply (characterized by a more abusive and offensive tone than the previous two), Locke openly accused Stillingfleet of having completely misread the *Essay*, or of having "got some strange copy of it, whereof I know nothing,"[160] and he ridiculed the bishop's Trinitarianism with the following words:

My lord, my Bible is faulty again; for I do not remember that I ever read in it either of these propositions, in these precise words, "there are three persons in one nature, or, there are two natures and one person".... I deny that these very propositions are in express words in my Bible.[161]

Stillingfleet's tone was equally rough in his two answers to Locke. He insisted that Locke had provided the anti-Trinitarians' theoretical arsenal with powerful

---

[153] Locke, "Letter to the Right Reverend," p. 68; John Locke, "Reply to the Right Reverend the Lord Bishop of Worcester's Answer to His Letter," in Locke, *Works*, vol. 3, pp. 97–185 (150).

[154] Locke, "Letter to the Right Reverend," pp. 30, 95–96; Locke, "Reply to the ... Answer to His Letter," pp. 110, 119, 127–130; Locke, "Reply to the ... Answer to His Second Letter," pp. 201–209, 259–270.

[155] Locke, "Reply to the ... Answer to His Letter," p. 126.

[156] Locke, "Reply to the ... Answer to His Second Letter," pp. 204–205.

[157] Locke, "Letter to the Right Reverend," p. 5; Locke, "Reply to the ... Answer to His Second Letter," p. 454.

[158] Locke, "Letter to the Right Reverend," pp. 27–28.

[159] Locke, "Reply to the ... Answer to His Letter," pp. 155–164.

[160] Locke, "Reply to the ... Answer to His Second Letter," p. 408.   [161] Ibid., p. 343.

weapons. As *Christianity Not Mysterious* demonstrated, the Unitarians' rejection of the Trinity drew on the Lockean theory that certainty necessitates clear and distinct ideas and on the opinion, which they inferred from Locke's way of ideas, that there can be no clear and distinct ideas of substance and person. If the terms "substance" and "person" denoted only notions in the mind instead of real things, as Locke's philosophy indicated according to Stillingfleet, then the doctrine of the Trinity would become indefensible.[162] Given Locke's agnosticism on substance, Stillingfleet maintained that Locke's philosophy "leads to Scepticism, or at least, that I could find no way to attain to Certainty in it upon your own grounds."[163] He stated that Locke's "own Grounds of Certainty, tend to Scepticism," that his way of ideas "must lay the Foundation of Scepticism," and that his "Notion of Ideas tends to Scepticism."[164] Stillingfleet also noted that Locke's new philosophical terminology had been used "by ill men to promote Scepticism and Infidelity, and to overthrow the Mysteries of our Faith"[165] – a clear allusion to those who, like Nye, Tindal, and Toland, denied mysteries in Christianity. Against the skeptical implications of Locke's empiricism, Stillingfleet claimed to have demonstrated that we can know the real essence of things by means of reasoning, as the scholastic tradition teaches.

Stillingfleet was not the only one to see Locke's way of ideas as leading to skepticism. In *Solid Philosophy Asserted* (1697), the Roman Catholic priest John Sergeant argued that Locke's concept of substance laid "Grounds for Scepticism, to the utter Subversion of all Science."[166] A few years later, the Church of England clergyman Henry Lee wrote a corrosive critique of Locke's *Essay* entitled *Anti-Scepticism* (1702). Lee, like Stillingfleet, argued that Locke's view of certain knowledge as grounded on the perception of the agreement or disagreement of ideas not only threatened the Christian religion, but also ruled out any knowledge of real things. Moreover, both Lee in *Anti-Scepticism* and Leibniz in *Nouveaux essais sur l'entendement humain* wondered about what a "substance" would be, if stripped of all its qualities and properties. And Leibniz shared Stillingfleet's opinion that Locke's treatment of substance was inconsistent with the doctrine of the Trinity.[167] However,

[162] Edward Stillingfleet, *An Answer to Mr. Locke's Letter* (London, 1697), pp. 14, 103; Edward Stillingfleet, *An Answer to Mr. Locke's Second Letter* (London, 1698), pp. 49–60.
[163] Stillingfleet, *Answer to Mr. Locke's Letter*, p. 125.
[164] Stillingfleet, *Answer to Mr. Locke's Second Letter*, pp. 20, 107, 177.
[165] Stillingfleet, *Answer to Mr. Locke's Letter*, p. 23.
[166] John Sergeant, *Solid Philosophy Asserted, against the Fancies of the Ideists* (London, 1697), p. 238.
[167] On the charge of skepticism leveled at Locke by contemporaries, see Sell, *John Locke*, pp. 30–42; Edwin McCann, "Locke's Theory of Substance under Attack!," *Philosophical Studies*, 106:1–2 (2001): pp. 87–105; Dmitri Levitin, "Reconsidering John Sergeant's Attacks on Locke's *Essay*," *Intellectual History Review*, 20:4 (2010): pp. 457–477; H. T. Adriaenssen,

Stillingfleet's arguments failed to persuade not only Locke, but also the Unitarians, given the complexity of his scholastic terminology. The Unitarian leader Stephen Nye even complained that reading Stillingfleet's attacks on Locke had given him a jaw ache.[168] Nye's criticism of Stillingfleet's attempt at salvaging the Trinitarian dogma was particularly harsh, because Stillingfleet had deliberately avoided unconventional terminologies in his defense of the Trinity. He had intentionally employed a language typical of scholastic metaphysics, which he considered crucial to his point, for he believed that doctrine and language were inextricably linked. He was afraid that abandoning the language of the doctrine would lead to discarding the doctrine itself. He was afraid, therefore, that some Unitarian writers' adoption of Locke's language, along with various Trinitarian divines' use of different metaphysical terminologies, could deal a death blow to the Trinitarian doctrine.[169] This, of course, did not happen. But the fact that some Trinitarian divines, such as Francis Gastrell in the 1690s and Daniel Waterland in the first half of the eighteenth century,[170] approved and even utilized Locke's language, methods, and concepts shows that, by that time, the scholastic terminological and conceptual categories employed by Stillingfleet were already outdated. A new way of conceiving human understanding – a way indebted to Lockean epistemology – was rapidly developing and spreading in philosophical and theological investigation.

What remains to be answered is why Locke never elucidated his views on the Trinity in clear and unequivocal terms. He abstained from commenting on the Trinitarian doctrine in the *Reasonableness*. Moreover, when he touched upon Christological and Trinitarian issues in other public as well as private writings, he was always careful to avoid clarifying his stance on the Trinitarian dogma. Finally, yet importantly, he always refrained from publicly explaining his position on the Trinity when his critics, especially Edwards and Stillingfleet, pressured him to do so. In my opinion, his circumspection on this issue indicates his disbelief in the Trinity. If he believed in the Trinity, he could easily follow the example of other Trinitarian Protestant irenicists committed to the way of fundamentals, such as his friend Limborch. While describing belief in the Trinity as inessential to salvation, and while advocating toleration of anti-Trinitarian Christians, Limborch indeed declared himself a Trinitarian and defended the Trinitarian doctrine against the Socinians' objections.[171] Locke, conversely, never adopted such an approach. However, he never

"An Early Critic of Locke: The Anti-Scepticism of Henry Lee," *Locke Studies*, 11 (2011): pp. 17–47.
[168] Nye, *Agreement*, p. 50.   [169] Dixon, *Nice and Hot Disputes*, pp. 159–160.
[170] Francis Gastrell, *Some Considerations concerning the Trinity* (London, 1696); Daniel Waterland, *Works*, 10 vols. (Oxford, 1823).
[171] See Chapter 2.

expressly denied the Trinity. I believe that the irenicism resulting from his biblical theology and moralist soteriology played a role in his decision to avoid public discussion, and denial, of the Trinitarian doctrine. Locke's biblical theology was informed by his attempt to promote the practice of morality and the development of moral character through a Scripture-based theological ethics. In his public writings on religion, he largely disregarded issues concerning the metaphysical constitution of the Godhead. He explored, instead, the moral, soteriological, and eschatological meaning of Scripture. Thus, he focused on the fundamentals of Christianity, which he regarded as plainly revealed in Scripture and, hence, essential to salvation and acceptable to all Christians. The doctrine of the Trinity was not deducible from Scripture in an indisputable way. This is why the Trinitarian dogma was a matter of controversy among Christians, and this is why Locke gave it no role in justification. Taking a clear stance about the Trinity would only add new fuel to the Trinitarian controversy. But Locke abhorred theological disputes about non-fundamentals, which he considered pointless and even harmful because these disputes revolved around issues unnecessary to salvation and were likely to cause enmity among Christians and even to disturb the civil peace. Locke indeed deemed it inappropriate and even immoral and intolerable to disseminate *opinions* (which are different from *matters of knowledge*) "which are in their naturall tendency absolutely destructive to humane society," and he argued that one should not feel entitled to "broach & propagate any opinion he beleives himself" when such opinions could lead to socially destructive consequences.[172]

Furthermore, Locke was generally keen to avoid debate, controversy, and polemic. Negative reactions to his writings aroused irritation and even anger in him, as his responses to Edwards and Stillingfleet show. Questioning the Trinitarian doctrine publicly, in late seventeenth-century England, would certainly elicit a backlash of opposition (which Locke would definitely dislike) and prove not only troublesome, but also dangerous, as several Unitarians experienced firsthand. In those circumstances, Locke's silence on the Trinity in the *Reasonableness* and in other public writings was also inspired by his intention to avoid making statements that could be perceived as heretical, at a time when the debate over the Licensing Act was ongoing and when heresy laws were quite a sensitive issue.[173] Even after the Commons refused to renew the Licensing Act in 1695, new legal measures, such as the aforesaid Royal

---

[172] Locke, *Essay concerning Toleration*, pp. 288–289. See G. A. J. Rogers, "John Locke: Conservative Radical," in Roger D. Lund (ed.), *The Margins of Orthodoxy: Heterodox Writing and Cultural Response, 1660–1750* (Cambridge: Cambridge University Press, 1995), pp. 97–116 (110).

[173] Marshall, "Locke, Socinianism," pp. 176–182; Snobelen, "Isaac Newton, Heresy Laws."

Injunction of 1696 and Blasphemy Act of 1697, still made it advisable to abstain from expressing ideas on the Trinity that could be charged with heterodoxy. Moreover, in December 1696 a twenty-year-old student of the University of Edinburgh, Thomas Aikenhead, was sentenced to death for blasphemy. Denial of the Trinity was among the charges made against Aikenhead. Although carried out in Scotland, his execution by hanging on January 8, 1697 shocked many Christian irenicists in England, including Locke.[174] Briefly, it was also – or rather mainly – for reasons of caution that Locke refrained from specifying his position on the Trinity during his disputes with Edwards and Stillingfleet.

In conclusion, there were several motivations to keep Locke from elucidating his views on the Trinity. His intention to concentrate only on elements of Christianity essential to salvation, and unquestionably deducible from Scripture, conditioned his decision to leave the Trinity out of his account of the Christian religion in the *Reasonableness*. Moreover, his irenicism led him to eschew theological disputes concerning non-fundamentals, which he considered pointless, contrary to charity among Christians, and even harmful to civil peace. Therefore, he resolved to offer no contribution to the particularly divisive Trinitarian controversy of the late seventeenth century. Finally, his intent to avoid unnecessary troubles with his critics and, above all, with the ecclesiastical and political authorities certainly played a major role in his choice to avoid clarifying his position on the Trinity, in a time when denying or questioning the Trinitarian dogma could lead to undesirable consequences.[175]

---

[174] Michael Hunter, "'Aikenhead the Atheist': The Context and Consequences of Articulate Irreligion in the Late Seventeenth Century," in Michael Hunter, David Wootton (eds.), *Atheism from the Reformation to the Enlightenment* (Oxford: Clarendon Press, 1992), pp. 221–254; Michael F. Graham, *The Blasphemies of Thomas Aikenhead: Boundaries of Belief on the Eve of the Enlightenment* (Edinburgh: Edinburgh University Press, 2008), pp. 117–118, 137–138, 158, on Locke's interest in this affair.

[175] On Locke's notion and practice of prudence, see Giuliana Di Biase, *La morale di Locke. Fra prudenza e mediocritas* (Rome: Carocci, 2012); Giuliana Di Biase, "The Development of the Concept of *Prudentia* in Locke's Classification of Knowledge," *Society and Politics*, 7:2 (2013): pp. 85–125.

6   Religious Toleration and Christian Irenicism

One of the reasons behind Locke's public silence on the Trinitarian doctrine was that he abhorred unnecessary and divisive controversies among Christians. While being inspired mainly by moral and soteriological concerns, Locke's doctrine of the fundamentals indeed has important irenic implications. His omission of "disputed doctrines" from his account of the Christian religion in *The Reasonableness of Christianity* implies toleration of all those accepting the Law of Faith, regardless of their views on non-fundamentals. Thus, the *Reasonableness* and, generally, Locke's later writings on religion denote a more advanced position on toleration than merely the affirmation of the distinction between the state and religious societies. Locke advocated the principle of the state-church separation in *A Letter concerning Toleration*, written in 1685 and published in 1689,[1] and in three more letters on toleration, written in 1690, 1692, and 1704, during a dispute with the High Church clergyman Jonas Proast, who rejected separation.[2] But in the *Reasonableness* and other theological writings, while portraying adherence to the Law of Faith as crucial to achieving eternal life, Locke did not describe affiliation to a church as critical to salvation. This position implicitly made denominationally uncommitted Christians tolerable. However, in the *Reasonableness*, Locke also suggested that accepting the Christian Law of Faith was the best way to

---

[1] *A Letter concerning Toleration* was first published, anonymously and in Latin, as *Epistola de Tolerantia* in Gouda in 1689. An English translation by the Unitarian merchant William Popple appeared in London in the same year. In this chapter, I refer to the following edition: John Locke, "A Letter concerning Toleration," in John Locke, *A Letter concerning Toleration and Other Writings*, ed. Mark Goldie (Indianapolis: Liberty Fund, 2010), pp. 1–62.

[2] On the Locke-Proast controversy, see Mark Goldie, "John Locke, Jonas Proast, and Religious Toleration, 1688–1692," in John Walsh, Colin Haydon, Stephen Taylor (eds.), *The Church of England, c.1689–c.1833: From Toleration to Tractarianism* (Cambridge: Cambridge University Press, 1993), pp. 143–171; Richard Vernon, *The Career of Toleration: John Locke, Jonas Proast, and After* (Montreal-Kingston: McGill-Queen's University Press, 1997); Adam Wolfson, "Toleration and Relativism: The Locke-Proast Exchange," *The Review of Politics*, 59:2 (1997): pp. 213–232; Adam Wolfson, *Persecution or Toleration: An Explication of the Locke-Proast Quarrel, 1689–1704* (Lanham: Lexington, 2010); John William Tate, *Liberty, Toleration and Equality: John Locke, Jonas Proast and the Letters concerning Toleration* (New York: Routledge, 2016).

pursue the chief business of humankind, namely, morality. This position is problematic, given also that Locke, in the *Letter* of 1689 and during his dispute with Proast, avoided extending the principle of toleration from competing conceptions of salvation to competing conceptions of the moral good.[3] Nevertheless, Locke's Christian irenicism in his writings on religion, far from putting new and narrower limits to toleration, complemented and expanded the tolerationism of the *Letter*. In this regard, I argue that, to Locke, all those believing in a divine creator and legislator can acknowledge and respect the divinely given Law of Nature in its basic tenets (which Locke described when explaining natural rights and duties in the *Second Treatise of Civil Government*), even though they reject the Law of Faith. Thus, they can meet at least minimally decent moral standards and are hence tolerable. This is, I think, the main reason why he did not exclude non-Christian believers from toleration, while he was always intolerant of atheists and he censured the immorality of some ideas held by Roman Catholics. Briefly, the inclusive model of toleration inherent to the irenicism of the *Reasonableness* represents the culmination of Locke's developing tolerationism, which was pervaded by a markedly religious conception of life and morality since at least the drafting of *An Essay concerning Toleration* in 1667.

The Theoretical Framework of *A Letter concerning Toleration*

The question of religious toleration attracted Locke's attention since at least the early 1660s.[4] His first writings on toleration, the manuscript *Two Tracts on Government*, were occasioned by the publication of Edward Bagshaw's *The Great Question concerning Things Indifferent in Religious Worship* (1660). Bagshaw argued, mainly on scriptural grounds, that individuals should be allowed to observe or disregard religious ceremonies (which he considered "indifferent") according to their conscience. Refuting Bagshaw's theory point by point, Locke's *Two Tracts* endorsed religious uniformity, thus expressing a position different from his views in his later writings on this subject, starting with the 1667 manuscript *Essay concerning Toleration*. Locke composed this essay amidst an outpouring of works about the issue of "indulgence" or "comprehension" of Nonconformity, in a period when the political authorities needed the Dissenters' support after the Dutch raid on the Medway and the

---

[3] Wolfson, "Toleration and Relativism," p. 230.

[4] Richard Ashcraft, *Revolutionary Politics and Locke's Two Treatises of Government* (Princeton: Princeton University Press, 1986), pp. 75–127; John W. Gough, "The Development of Locke's Belief in Toleration," in John P. Horton, Susan Mendus (eds.), *John Locke: "A Letter concerning Toleration" in Focus* (London: Routledge, 1991), pp. 57–77.

subsequent English defeat in the Second Anglo-Dutch War.[5] At that time, the Act of Uniformity (1662), the Conventicle Act (1664), and the Five Mile Act (1665) severely limited Nonconformists' religious freedom, making it extremely difficult for them to meet and worship. Therefore, persecutions conducted under these acts alienated Nonconformists. When advocating toleration, mainly but not exclusively of Nonconformists, in *An Essay concerning Toleration*, Locke advanced many of the arguments that he later refined in the *Letter*. He stigmatized the dangers of state-imposed religious uniformity, while highlighting the benefits of toleration of different religious societies, in various other manuscripts written before the *Letter*, such as his *Critical Notes* (c.1681) on Edward Stillingfleet's *The Mischief of Separation* (1680) and *The Unreasonableness of Separation* (1681). In these *Critical Notes*, Locke advocated the separation of the state and religious societies by employing some of the arguments he later used in the *Letter* and arguing that "a national Church [that] tends to the support of a national Religion" is unable to promote true religion, preserve the civil peace, and prevent dangerous errors.[6] Locke was eventually prompted to write *A Letter concerning Toleration* by Louis XIV's revocation of the Edict of Nantes (1598) in October 1685. This event led many French Huguenots to flee to surrounding Protestant countries – especially to the Netherlands, where Locke was living at that time. Moreover, the Catholic James II's accession to the English throne in early 1685 increased Locke's and other Whig or radical intellectuals' concerns over the new monarch's political and religious policies – an issue that raised an international controversy.[7]

Locke attributed the causes of intolerant policies to competition among churches aiming to gain power from the state. In his opinion, the main cause of state-supported intolerance toward some religious groups was the rivalry among power-seeking churches themselves. He thought that this persecuting attitude on the part of some Christian churches contradicted the precepts of the Gospel, which, he observed, "frequently declares that the true Disciples of Christ must suffer Persecution; but that the Church of Christ should persecute

---

[5] Between August 1667 and May 1668, over twenty pamphlets on this subject appeared. See J. R. Milton, Philip Milton, "General Introduction" to John Locke, *An Essay concerning Toleration and Other Writings on Law and Politics, 1667–1683*, eds. J. R. Milton and Philip Milton (Oxford: Clarendon Press, 2006), pp. 1–161 (152–157). On the extant manuscripts of *An Essay concerning Toleration*, see Chapter 5.

[6] John Locke, "Critical Notes upon Edward Stillingfleet's *Mischief* and *Unreasonableness of Separation* – Extracts," in John Locke, *Writings on Religion*, ed. Victor Nuovo (Oxford: Oxford University Press, 2002), pp. 73–79 (77–78). The 170-page manuscript of the *Critical Notes*, still unpublished in its entirety, is MS Locke c. 34, "Critical Notes on Stillingfleet." Timothy Stanton is currently preparing a critical edition of this manuscript for Clarendon Press. Other manuscripts on toleration, written by Locke between the *Essay* of 1667 and the *Letter*, are in: John Locke, *Political Essays*, ed. Mark Goldie (Cambridge: Cambridge University Press, 1997).

[7] Ashcraft, *Revolutionary Politics*, pp. 467–520.

others, and force others by Fire and Sword, to embrace her Faith and Doctrine, I could never yet find in any of the Books of the New Testament."[8] Locke also disapproved of the imprudence of civil magistrates whose willingness to favor a sect over another reflected a grievous failure to properly comprehend the grounds, purpose, and limits of political authority. This is why the *Letter* begins with a plea for "mutual toleration of Christians"[9] and gives arguments against undesirable alliances between the civil magistrate and one or more religious societies. Accordingly, the *Letter* argues for the separation between the state and religious organizations and expressly advocates toleration of all those subscribing to organized religion, be they Christians, Jews, Muslims, or pagans.

The *Letter* presents three arguments delineating the purview and aims of the commonwealth, which Locke defined as "a Society of Men constituted only for the procuring, preserving, and advancing of their own *Civil Interests*."[10] By civil interests, Locke meant "Life, Liberty, Health, and Indolency of Body; and the Possession of outward things, such as Money, Lands, Houses, Furniture, and the like."[11] It follows that the civil magistrate's power does not extend to "the Care of Souls," as Locke maintained in the first of his arguments – the argument from the mandate of the state:

The Care of Souls is not committed to the Civil Magistrate any more than to other Men. It is not committed unto him, I say, by God; because it appears not that God has ever given any such Authority to one Man over another, as to compell any one to his Religion. Nor can any such Power be vested in the Magistrate by the *Consent of the People;* because no man can so far abandon the care of his own Salvation, as blindly to leave it to the choice of any other, whether Prince or Subject, to prescribe to him what Faith or Worship he shall embrace.[12]

Consequently, "there is absolutely no such thing, under the Gospel, as a Christian Commonwealth."[13] To Locke, there can only be a *civil* common-wealth. Moreover, the political authorities cannot impose religious uniformity because of the nature of the power they exercise, as Locke explained in his second argument – the argument from belief:

The care of Souls cannot belong to the Civil Magistrate, because his Power consists only in outward force: But true and saving Religion consists in the inward perswasion of the Mind; without which nothing can be acceptable to God. And such is the nature of the Understanding, that it cannot be compell'd to the belief of any thing by outward Force.[14]

Finally, Locke's third argument – the argument from error – states that, even "though the rigour of Laws and the force of Penalties were capable to convince

---

[8] Locke, "Letter," p. 18.   [9] Ibid., p. 7.   [10] Ibid., p. 12.   [11] Ibid.   [12] Ibid., p. 13.
[13] Ibid., p. 42.   [14] Ibid., p. 13.

and change Mens minds, yet would not that help at all to the Salvation of their Souls."[15] According to Locke, there is only one true religion and many false ones. Therefore, in most cases, imposing the "Religion of the Court" on the subjects would put them "under an Obligation of following their Princes in the ways that lead to Destruction."[16]

These arguments are far from being *positive* arguments in support of religious toleration. In the *Letter*, Locke supplied only a *negative* justification of a limited toleration on the part of the state, as he rejected several arguments for the civil magistrate's *complete* control of religious affairs. Locke's denial of the magistrate's complete control of religious affairs led him to denounce coercion in matters of faith as irrational and ineffective to establish belief of any sort. In rejecting separation during his dispute with Locke, Jonas Proast focused especially on Locke's views on the irrationality and ineffectiveness of coercion, which he considered to be at the core of Locke's advocacy of toleration. *Contra* Locke, Proast argued that the civil magistrate had a duty to concern themselves with religious affairs, because religious matters had an impact on communal life. Therefore, even though belief could not be coerced, the magistrate could still make use of coercion in order to place an individual in a situation apt to inspire true belief. Thus, according to Proast, coercion was still reasonable and justifiable.[17] Proast's objection has even contributed to Jeremy Waldron's conclusion that Locke's argument against coercion in matters of belief is flawed. According to Waldron, Locke's argument does not prevent religious persecution for ends different from conversion (e.g., to preserve the civil peace) and, as Proast maintained, coercion might still be indirectly effective in changing people's beliefs.[18] In this regard, I disagree with Waldron, as I argue that Locke's (negative) justification of toleration in the *Letter* is based on a broader set of considerations rooted in a sort of political skepticism.[19] Although Proast (mistakenly) portrayed the tolerationism of the

[15] Ibid., p. 14.

[16] Ibid., p. 15. See, also, John Locke, "A Third Letter for Toleration," in John Locke, *Locke on Toleration*, ed. Richard Vernon (Cambridge: Cambridge University Press, 2010), pp. 123–163 (123–124).

[17] For Proast's two writings of 1690 and 1691 against Locke, and Locke's three replies to Proast, see Locke, *Locke on Toleration*.

[18] Jeremy Waldron, "Locke: Toleration and the Rationality of Persecution," in Susan Mendus (ed.), *Justifying Toleration: Conceptual and Historical Perspectives* (Cambridge: Cambridge University Press, 1988), pp. 61–86.

[19] Several scholars have highlighted the significance of Locke's political skepticism, regarding mainly his views on toleration. See, for instance, Vernon, *Career of Toleration*, pp. 35–51, 124–144; Sam Black, "Toleration and the Skeptical Inquirer in Locke," *Canadian Journal of Philosophy*, 28:4 (1998): pp. 473–504; Alex Tuckness, "Rethinking the Intolerant Locke," *American Journal of Political Science*, 46:2 (2002): pp. 288–298; Diego Lucci, "Political Scepticism, Moral Scepticism, and the Scope and Limits of Toleration in John Locke," *Yearbook of the Maimonides Centre for Advanced Studies*, 3 (2018): pp. 109–143.

Letter as promoting religious skepticism, Locke's *political* skepticism actually did not entail *religious* skepticism, in that it was not about true religion in itself.[20] Locke never questioned the existence of true religion. He was confident that the existence of a divine creator and lawgiver, laying down positive commands to humanity, could actually be proven through rational arguments. Concerning God's positive commands, Locke deemed the divine moral law not only rationally demonstrable (at least in principle), but also revealed in Scripture, which he judged infallible. Thus, he identified true religion with "the truth of the Gospel," containing all things "necessary to salvation."[21] According to Locke, "all charitable Admonitions, and affectionate Endeavours to reduce Men from Errors ... are indeed the greatest Duty of a Christian."[22] But he argued that "all Force and Compulsion are to be forborn" when "one Man does not violate the Right of another, by his Erroneous Opinions, and undue manner of Worship, nor is his Perdition any prejudice to another Mans Affairs," because "the care of each Mans Salvation belongs only to himself."[23] Locke's rejection of "force and compulsion" in religious matters not affecting others' civil interests is rooted in his skepticism about the human ability to perfectly comprehend and effectively communicate religious truth. Locke recognized that, although there can be but one true religion, differences in human understanding and the difficulties of communication had produced a plethora of divergent dogmas and ceremonies. As a result, "every one is Orthodox to himself"[24] and believes that all others are heretics. This happens because most religious doctrines are simply a matter of opinion, not a matter of certain knowledge.[25] However, divergences in religious opinions ought not to hinder civil coexistence, as Locke argued in *An Essay concerning Human Understanding*:

Since therefore it is unavoidable to the greatest part of Men, if not all, to have several *Opinions*, without certain and indubitable Proofs of their Truths; and it carries too great an imputation of ignorance, lightness, or folly, for Men to quit and renounce their former Tenets, presently upon the offer of an Argument, which they cannot immediately answer, and shew the insufficiency of: It would, methinks, become all Men to maintain *Peace*, and the common Offices of Humanity, *and Friendship, in the diversity of Opinions*, since we cannot reasonably expect, that any one should readily and obsequiously quit his own Opinion, and embrace ours, with a blind resignation to an Authority, which the Understanding of Man acknowledges not. For however it may often mistake, it can own no other Guide but Reason, nor blindly submit to the Will and

---

[20] Nicholas Jolley, *Toleration and Understanding in Locke* (Oxford: Oxford University Press, 2016), pp. 37–42.

[21] Locke, "Letter," p. 66; John Locke, "A Second Letter concerning Toleration," in Locke, *Locke on Toleration*, pp. 67–107 (79).

[22] Locke, "Letter," p. 46.   [23] Ibid., pp. 45–46.   [24] Ibid., p. 7.

[25] Jolley, *Toleration and Understanding*, pp. 37–90.

Dictates of another. .... We should do well to commiserate our mutual Ignorance, and endeavour to remove it in all the gentle and fair ways of Information; and not instantly treat others ill, as obstinate and perverse, because they will not renounce their own, and receive our Opinions, or at least those we would force upon them, when 'tis more than probable, that we are no less obstinate in not embracing some of theirs.[26]

As Locke maintained in the *Letter*, in order to facilitate peaceful coexistence between people holding different religious opinions, "indifferent" beliefs and practices unharmful to the civil interests ought to be tolerated. Nevertheless, Locke was aware that making a case for toleration based on the concept of "things indifferent," also called "*adiaphora*," had two drawbacks. First, it was difficult to reach consensus about the boundary between "things necessary" and "things indifferent." Second, the very notion of "things indifferent" could lead to an argument for intolerance. Since some doctrines and rituals are "indifferent," one might wish to impose them by authority – for instance, for the sake of decency and good order. This was the position of several latitudinarians who, as Mark Goldie has remarked, "were in fact intolerant, for their intention was to embrace moderate nonconformists, by softening the rigidities of the church's 'good order,' before penalizing the recalcitrant minority who refused to accept such revised terms."[27] Locke too, in his *Two Tracts* of the early 1660s, used the distinction between *fundamenta* and *adiaphora* to affirm, *contra* Bagshaw, the civil magistrate's complete authority over religious matters. By 1667 – the year when he wrote *An Essay concerning Toleration* – he had already made a 180-degree turn on this subject. This change in perspective indicates Locke's shift to a greater optimism regarding human nature in the *Essay* of 1667 and in his later political writings. This change in perspective indeed led Locke to endorse, in *An Essay concerning Human Understanding* and *Two Treatises of Government*, probabilistic judgment as a new standard of public judgment – *contra* the absolutist views that he had embraced earlier in *Two Tracts* and that denoted a more extreme (and indeed pessimistic) skeptical approach to political issues.[28] In *A Letter concerning Toleration*, Locke's political skepticism – originating in his recognition of the burden of incommunicability and, thus, of the limits of civil communication and the limited scope of public reason – led him to conclude that "indifferent" beliefs and practices ought to be tolerated, even when the magistrate or other citizens consider these beliefs and practices erroneous and ineffective or detrimental to salvation.[29] In the *Letter* and in the

---

[26] John Locke, *An Essay concerning Human Understanding*, ed. Peter H. Nidditch (Oxford: Clarendon Press, 1975), IV.xvi.4, pp. 659–660.

[27] Mark Goldie, "Introduction" to Locke, *Letter*, pp. ix–xxiii (xvii–xviii).

[28] Douglas J. Casson, *Liberating Judgment: Fanatics, Skeptics, and John Locke's Politics of Probability* (Princeton: Princeton University Press, 2011), pp. 75–91, 126–158. For more details of *Two Tracts* and their original manuscripts, see Chapter 1.

[29] Vernon, *Career of Toleration*, pp. 35–51, 124–144.

Second Treatise of Civil Government, the difficulties of communication restrict the purview of political power to what can be publicly conveyed and largely agreed upon. To Locke, what can be largely agreed upon depends on practical reasoning, which leads human beings to take steps for preserving themselves and the rest of humankind while avoiding principles destructive of human interests and society.[30] Adopting principles detrimental to life, property, and freedom would be inconsistent with the principles of natural reason – specifically with practical reasoning, which is at the basis of public reason. The proper use of practical reasoning leads to consensus about the necessity to procure, preserve, and advance the civil interests of the members of the commonwealth. Therefore, political power can be rightfully exercised for this purpose. Conversely, it is impossible to reach consensus on religious beliefs and practices that do not harm anyone's life, property, or freedom and are irrelevant to worldly interests. Such beliefs and practices are and ought to be left open to human choice.[31] Thus, Locke concluded (convincingly in my opinion, *pace* Waldron) that human beings cannot "stipulate" about "their spiritual and eternal Interest," they cannot "submit this Interest to the Power of the Society, or any Soveraign they should set over them," and no one can undertake to provide salvation to another through authoritarian, paternalistic means.[32] In fact, truth does not need to be imposed, and true religion can only benefit from toleration. True religion, according to Locke, "is not taught by Laws, nor has she any need of Force to procure her entrance into the minds of men. ... If Truth makes not her way into the Understanding by her own Light, she will be but the weaker for any borrowed force Violence can add to her."[33] And by "truth" Locke meant the *Christian* truth, which, in his opinion, better spread without "force and compulsion" and, at the same time, without finding impediments:

The Christian religion ... grew, and spread, and prevailed, without any aid from force or the assistance of the powers in being; and if it be a mark of the true religion that it will prevail by its own light and strength, but that false religions will not, but have need of force and foreign helps to support them, nothing certainly can be more for the advantage of true religion, than to take away compulsion everywhere.[34]

---

[30] John Locke, *Two Treatises of Government*, rev. ed., ed. Peter Laslett (Cambridge: Cambridge University Press, 1988), pp. 285–302. Several scholars have correctly observed that Locke's line of reasoning in the *Letter* is illuminated by the wider political arguments he advanced in *Two Treatises of Government*. See, for instance, Ian Harris, *The Mind of John Locke: A Study of Political Theory in Its Intellectual Setting* (Cambridge: Cambridge University Press, 1994), pp. 191–192; Selina Chen, "Locke's Political Arguments for Toleration," *History of Political Thought*, 19:2 (1998): pp. 167–185; Timothy Stanton, "Locke and the Politics and Theology of Toleration," *Political Studies*, 54:3 (2006): pp. 84–102; Jolley, *Toleration and Understanding*, pp. 107–125.

[31] Wolfson, *Persecution or Toleration*, pp. 21–38; Tate, *Liberty*, pp. 31–37.

[32] Locke, "Letter," p. 75.   [33] Ibid., p. 45.   [34] Locke, "Second Letter," p. 69.

Briefly, the *Letter* of 1689 and the letters Locke wrote against Proast suggest that every individual, left to their own devices and suitably encouraged (but not pressured) by friendly others, has the ability, the right, and, under natural law, the duty to seek religious truth for themselves. Therefore, neither the civil magistrate nor anyone else can impede the search for truth, which, if left free, might lead the searcher to the true religion. Besides being useless and even detrimental to salvation, the imposition of religious conformity by the political authorities proves destructive to human society because it is likely to spread discontent and harm the civil peace. Thus, practical reasoning disposes human beings to shun the imposition of religious uniformity as a principle and practice destructive of their own interests, both spiritual and civil, and of the public good. Concerning Locke's notion of the public good, Alex Tuckness has correctly observed:

The public good and the fundamental law of nature which commands that as much as possible mankind is to be preserved are, for Locke, more or less interchangeable. When God issues such a commission, he takes into account the fact that fallible persons will have to interpret and carry out the commission. God, as a rational legislator, will not define the public good broadly if a narrower conception that would be misapplied less often would better promote the good.[35]

However, Tuckness's analysis of human fallibility in Locke's thought focuses not on the perspective of citizens disputing about true religion, but on the perspective of a civil legislator putting forward a principle aimed at guiding the disputants.[36] *Pace* Tuckness, I believe that Locke's notion of the civil magistrate or legislator in the *Letter* needs to be considered in the wider context of his political thought. In the *Second Treatise*, it is indeed a prerogative of the community to delegate the legislative function – "the supreme power of the common-wealth" – to magistrates representing the people and accountable to the people. Thus, the civil magistrate's powers flow from the citizens' consent, natural law, and the tasks of government.[37] Moreover, when advocating toleration of different opinions in the above-quoted passage from *An Essay concerning Human Understanding*, Locke considered relationships between individual citizens or persons in general, not between citizens and the magistrate.[38] Briefly, Locke stressed not simply the magistrate's fallibility, but something more basic – that is, *human* fallibility in general.

The tolerationist implications of Locke's political skepticism denote several similarities with the Socinians' discourse on religious freedom, especially with

[35] Tuckness, "Rethinking the Intolerant Locke," p. 291. See, also, Alex Tuckness, *Locke and the Legislative Point of View: Toleration, Contested Principles, and the Law* (Princeton: Princeton University Press, 2002), pp. 57–84.
[36] Tuckness, "Rethinking the Intolerant Locke," p. 291.
[37] Locke, *Two Treatises*, pp. 355–363.   [38] Locke, *Essay*, IV.xvi.4, pp. 659–660.

Johann Crell's *Vindiciae pro religionis libertate*. Crell wrote this treatise in 1632, when the Polish-based Socinians were afraid that the new King of Poland and Grand Duke of Lithuania, Wladyslaw IV Vasa, might disregard the terms of the Warsaw Confederation of 1573 – an act granting religious freedom in the Polish-Lithuanian Commonwealth. However, *Vindiciae* was published posthumously, in Amsterdam, only in 1637, four years after its author's death and a few months before the Polish parliament – the Sejm – ordered the closure of the Polish Brethren's academy and press in Rakow in April 1638, under pressure by Catholic clergymen and politicians. This event triggered the Socinian diaspora, which intensified after the expulsion of anti-Trinitarians from Poland in 1658, when the Netherlands became the new center of Socinianism. In his plea for religious freedom, which was translated into English in 1646,[39] Crell reaffirmed Socinus's emphasis on the importance of free will and morality to both salvation and communal life. Crell argued that human beings voluntarily join in civil societies and establish political institutions for the sake of security and peace and for the preservation of rights sanctioned by the Law of Nature. According to Crell, political authority does not extend to matters pertaining to eternal salvation, the pursuit of which depends exclusively on one's free choice – a choice made possible by natural liberty, albeit necessitating knowledge of Scripture in order to lead to saving belief. Therefore, the magistrate cannot forbid religious doctrines and practices that do not affect the civil interests or communal life. The magistrate has a duty to protect all citizens in their religious observances and beliefs, which are an essential part of their liberty. The magistrate's duty to preserve the citizens' religious freedom must be ratified in civil covenants, which both the magistrate and the subjects are bound to respect. Briefly, around half a century before Locke's *Letter concerning Toleration*, Crell's *Vindiciae pro religionis libertate* affirmed the magistrate's duty to preserve the civil interests of all citizens, including their religious freedom, regardless of their theological ideas and confessional affiliation. Therefore, Crell's *Vindiciae* envisaged a separation between the state and religious societies. There is, nevertheless, a significant point of divergence between Socinian tolerationism and Locke's toleration in the *Letter*. Socinus, Crell, and other Socinians considered human beings primarily as individuals. To the Socinians, salvation depends on the individual's free choice to accept the assistance of divine grace and, consequently, to have faith and live by the divine revealed law.[40] They claimed that every

---

[39] Johann Crell, *A Learned and Exceeding Well-Compiled Vindication of Liberty of Religion*, trans. N. Y. (London, 1646). As I have noted in Chapter 3, this translation is commonly attributed to the irenicist Scottish Calvinist minister John Dury, but I have found no evidence for this attribution.

[40] On the differences between natural and revealed law according to the Socinians, see Chapter 3.

believer had the right to study Scripture and choose their way to salvation. Although the Socinians acknowledged the individual's right to create and join religious organizations, they did not consider affiliation to a religious society as crucial to salvation or to toleration. Socinus himself never officially joined the Minor Reformed Church of Poland, to which most of his disciples belonged. Conversely, in the *Letter*, Locke talked of believers as essentially members of religious societies. Concentrating on *organized* religion, he made a distinction between the civil commonwealth, which he envisioned as a *general* entity consisting of all citizens, and religious organizations, which he described as *particular* societies, each composed of people who had freely joined it for a precise purpose, which Locke clarified as follows:

The end of a Religious Society . . . is the Publick Worship of God, and by means thereof the acquisition of Eternal Life. All Discipline ought therefore to tend to that End, and all Ecclesiastical Laws to be thereunto confined. Nothing ought, nor can be transacted in this Society, relating to the Possession of Civil and Worldly Goods.[41]

In this passage, Locke not only delineated the ends of religious societies as distinct from the state's aims, but also suggested that "the Publick Worship of God" within the bosom of a religious society was critical to "the acquisition of Eternal Life." In fact, the *Letter* nowhere considers the possibility to grant toleration to believers belonging to no religious society. Nowhere in the *Letter* does Locke affirm the right of denominationally uncommitted believers to toleration or clarify their status. And this is a significant omission, which reduces Locke's theory of toleration in the *Letter* to essentially a theory of the separation between state and churches. Yet, according to Locke, religious societies ought to be free and voluntary. Thus, he argued that "excommunication neither does, nor can deprive the excommunicated Person of any of those Civil Goods that he formerly possessed. All those things belong to the Civil Government, and are under the Magistrate's Protection."[42] He explained in which relation religious organizations must stand to each other and to private persons as well:

No private Person has any Right, in any manner, to prejudice another Person in his Civil Enjoyments, because he is of another Church or Religion. . ... What I say concerning the mutual Toleration of private Persons differing from one another in Religion, I understand also of particular Churches; which stand as it were in the same relation to each other as private Persons among themselves; nor has any one of them any manner of Jurisdiction over any other, no not even when the Civil Magistrate (as it sometimes happens) comes to be of this or the other Communion.[43]

---

[41] Locke, "Letter," p. 18.   [42] Ibid., p. 19.   [43] Ibid., p. 20.

Briefly, to Locke, differences in denominational affiliation ought to have no impact on civil life. Accordingly, he limited the authority of ecclesiastical ministers to the boundaries of their churches and denied that such authority could "be extended to Civil Affairs."[44] All these conditions applied to both Christian and non-Christian organizations, for he expressly advocated toleration of Jews, Muslims, and pagans:

Neither *Pagan,* nor *Mahumetan,* nor *Jew,* ought to be excluded from the Civil Rights of the Commonwealth, because of his Religion. The Gospel commands no such thing. The Church, which *judges not those that are without,* 1 Corinthians 5:12–13, wants it not. And the Commonwealth, which embraces indifferently all men that are honest, peaceable, and industrious, requires it not.[45]

Locke repeated his advocacy of toleration of non-Christian believers in his dispute with Proast. During this dispute, Locke called attention to the aforesaid benefits that Christianity could gain from reciprocal toleration, which would permit the Christian religion to be practiced, and propagated, in Muslim and "pagan" countries.[46] In fact, many Muslim and pagan states already granted toleration to Christians, as Locke observed in his writings on toleration.[47] Locke obviously hoped that toleration (and, in the case of Jews, even naturalization, which he openly endorsed in his *Third Letter for Toleration* of 1692) could facilitate the conversion to Christianity of non-Christian believers living under English rule, such as Jews residing in England and in its colonies and pagans inhabiting the English colonies in America. However, according to Locke, the preservation of non-Christian believers' civil rights had priority over attempts at conversion, which should be made by means of "charitable Admonitions, and affectionate Endeavours to reduce Men from Errors" – not through "Force and Compulsion."[48] This "charitable" and non-coercive attitude toward non-Christian believers had already emerged in the *Fundamental Constitutions of Carolina* of 1669, to whose drafting Locke and his patron Anthony Ashley Cooper, 1st Earl of Shaftesbury, significantly contributed.[49] Article 97 of this legal document indeed states:

That Jews, heathens, and other dissenters from the purity of Christian religion may not be scared and kept at a distance from it, but, by having an opportunity of acquainting themselves with the truth and reasonableness of its doctrines, and the peaceableness and inoffensiveness of its professors, may, by good usage and persuasion, and all those

---

[44] Ibid., p. 24.   [45] Ibid., pp. 58–59.   [46] Locke, "Second Letter," pp. 69–70.

[47] See, for instance, Locke, "Letter," pp. 21, 41.   [48] Ibid., pp. 45–46.

[49] On Locke's and Shaftesbury's involvement with this legal document, see David Armitage, "John Locke, Carolina, and the *Two Treatises of Government*," *Political Theory,* 32:5 (2004): pp. 602–627. At that time, Locke was working as a physician and secretary for Shaftesbury, who was one of the eight Lord Proprietors of Carolina.

convining methods of gentleness and meekness, suitable to the rules and design of the gospel, be won over to embrace and unfeignedly receive the truth.[50]

Whereas some Jews and "heathens" lived under English rule, Muslims represented a different, and more complex, case.[51] There were no Muslim subjects to the English crown in the seventeenth century. Moreover, Locke lived in a time when Europe was under the "Ottoman threat" – a threat that became concrete with the Ottoman attack on Vienna in 1683 – and when Muslims were often conflated with "Turks" in European imagination. Locke himself was afraid of the Ottoman threat, as is proven by a letter he sent in March 1684 to his friend Edward Clarke, to whom he expressed the hope that Christian Europe would unite against the Ottoman enemy.[52] However, as Nabil Matar has noted, Locke's fear of the Ottoman threat did not prevent him from advocating toleration and even endenization of Muslims:

Locke feared the Ottomans but he categorically separated between the military danger which the "turbanned nations" posed against Europe and members of those Muslim nations who might become subjects to the English crown. Furthermore, Locke did not allow the Turkish military threat to undermine the possible endenization of law-abiding Muslims in London nor to cause irreverence for their religion and habit.[53]

The only condition that Locke posed to Muslims willing to become citizens of a civil commonwealth was to renounce their "blind obedience to the *Mufti* of *Constantinople;* who himself is intirely obedient to the *Ottoman* Emperor, and frames the feigned Oracles of that Religion according to his pleasure."[54] This inaccurate understanding of the mufti's authority, which was partly compared to that of the pope and hence (incorrectly) considered as politically destabilizing, was common in seventeenth-century England, particularly among intellectuals who, like Paul Rycaut, Robert Withers, and John Greaves, wrote about Ottoman history, politics, and society.[55] Locke too, although manifesting a sincere interest in Islamic culture, was misled into adopting this misconception, which, nevertheless, did not prevent him from endorsing endenization of Muslims willing to reject the mufti's (supposed) political authority in favor of that of the civil commonwealth.[56] Locke's hypothesis, however, remained

---

[50] *The Fundamental Constitutions of Carolina* (London, 1670), art. 97.

[51] Nabil Matar, "John Locke and the 'Turbanned Nations,'" *Journal of Islamic Studies*, 2:1 (1991): pp. 67–77 (73–76); Nabil Matar, "England and Religious Plurality: Henry Stubbe, John Locke and Islam," in Charlotte Methuen, Andrew Spicer, John Wolffe (eds.), *Christianity and Religious Plurality* (Woodbridge: Boydell Press, 2015), pp. 181–203 (191–196).

[52] Locke to Edward Clarke, March 7/17, 1684, in John Locke, *The Correspondence of John Locke*, ed. E. S. de Beer, 8 vols. (Oxford: Oxford University Press, 1979–1989), vol. 2, no. 776.

[53] Matar, "John Locke," pp. 74–75.   [54] Locke, "Letter," p. 52.

[55] Matar, "John Locke," pp. 75–76; Matar, "England and Religious Plurality," pp. 200–203.

[56] On Locke's interest in Islamic culture, see Matar, "John Locke," p. 70; Matar, "England and Religious Plurality," p. 191.

only theoretical, given that no endenizations of Muslims in England are recorded from the seventeenth century.[57]

The model of religious toleration advocated by Locke in the *Letter* was far ahead of his time. Even after the Glorious Revolution, the new policy sanctioned by the Toleration Act of 1688, which received royal assent in May 1689 and carried the long title of "An Act for Exempting their Majestyes Protestant Subjects dissenting from the Church of England from the Penalties of certaine Lawes," presented several limits. Significantly, this Act did not grant toleration to "any Papist or Popish recusant whatsoever or any person that shall deny in his Preaching or Writeing the Doctrine of the Blessed Trinity." Furthermore, this Act ignored the situation of non-Christian believers. Locke was aware of the limits of the Toleration Act. In a letter sent to Limborch in June 1689, he observed that the toleration established by this Act was "not perhaps so wide in scope as might be wished for by you and those like you who are true Christians and free from ambition or envy."[58] As a Remonstrant, Limborch was in favor of wide toleration in the form of "comprehension," regardless of disagreements concerning non-fundamental issues like the Trinitarian doctrine. But Locke opposed this model of toleration, which in England was advocated by latitudinarian clergymen and which still entailed intolerance of those Dissenters who would still refuse to join a less doctrinally rigid national church. Locke did not "feel any hopes that ecclesiastical peace will be established in that way," as he wrote in another letter to Limborch in September 1689.[59] In this letter, he maintained that "men will always differ on religious questions and rival parties will continue to quarrel and wage war on each other unless the establishment of equal liberty for all provides a bond of mutual charity by which all may be brought together into one body."[60] Nevertheless, Locke's theory in *A Letter concerning Toleration* was itself not devoid of limits, given his express advocacy of "equal liberty" for religious "parties" alone.

Locke's Omissions and Exceptions to Toleration in the *Letter* and Other Writings

While extending toleration to Christian as well as non-Christian religious societies, *A Letter concerning Toleration* did not consider the situation of those belonging to no religious society. When talking of "private persons" in

---

[57] Matar, "John Locke," p. 75; Matar, "England and Religious Plurality," p. 202.
[58] Locke to Philipp van Limborch, June 6, 1689, in Locke, *Correspondence*, vol. 3, no. 1147.
[59] Locke to Philipp van Limborch, September 10, 1689, in Locke, *Correspondence*, vol. 3, no. 1182.
[60] Ibid.

the *Letter*, Locke meant, in essence, *members of religious societies*. In fact, he argued that no one's civil rights could be limited "because he is of another Church or Religion"[61] – not because one held heterodox ideas, for instance, ideas that could not be attributed to any church or religion. What counted, for Locke, was whether one belonged to one or another religious society. As Jonathan Israel has noted, in Locke's *Letter* "those who subscribe to no organized religion, be they agnostics, Deists or *indifferenti*, in confessional matters while not explicitly excluded are left in a vague limbo without any clear status or guaranteed freedom."[62] In his other writings advocating religious toleration – from the *Essay* of 1667 and the *Critical Notes* on Stillingfleet to his letters against Proast – Locke concentrated mainly on justifying the right of Dissenting Protestants and, also, of some other believers to have their own religious societies. In the *Letter* and his other tolerationist writings, one of Locke's main objectives was indeed to prevent any church from gaining power from the political rulers and oppressing other churches. Therefore, far from endorsing complete freedom of conscience, he simply delineated the criteria regulating the relationships between political authorities and religious societies, as well as between different religious societies.

Moreover, Locke expressly denied toleration to Roman Catholics and atheists, and he did so for moral reasons. Although Locke called attention to the narrow scope of knowledge in religious and moral matters, his toleration did not extend beyond the boundaries of moral standards that he considered beneficial, or at least harmless, to the civil commonwealth and its members' civil interests. To Locke, surrendering to moral relativism would be as dangerous as its opposite – namely, allowing religious fanaticism, enthusiasm, and dogmatism to influence civil life.[63] As Locke wrote in the *Letter*, "No Opinions contrary to human Society, or to those moral Rules which are necessary to the preservation of Civil Society, are to be tolerated by the Magistrate."[64] For this reason, the *Letter* explicitly denies toleration to atheists, whom Locke considered devoid of morality, and to Roman Catholics, who, in Locke's opinion, held some morally unacceptable principles.

Locke's best-known argument against Catholics is of a prudential nature. He maintained that the magistrate could not trust, and hence tolerate, subjects who owed their primary allegiance to a foreign prince, such as the pope. Roman

[61] Locke, "Letter," p. 20.
[62] Jonathan I. Israel, "Spinoza, Locke and the Enlightenment Battle for Toleration," in Ole P. Grell, Roy Porter (eds.), *Toleration in Enlightenment Europe* (Cambridge: Cambridge University Press, 1999), pp. 102–113 (103).
[63] J. B. Schneewind, "Locke's Moral Philosophy," in Vere Chappell (ed.), *The Cambridge Companion to Locke* (Cambridge: Cambridge University Press, 1994), pp. 199–225 (208); Wolfson, "Toleration and Relativism," p. 230; Wolfson, *Persecution or Toleration*, pp. 88–99.
[64] Locke, "Letter," pp. 49–50.

Catholics' allegiance to a foreign power made them dangerous to the commonwealth, because their religion bound them to obey the pope's dictates in political matters.[65] Furthermore, Catholic morals, according to Locke, promoted evil behaviors and were hence harmful to human and civil society. Locke mentioned in the *Letter* several opinions that Protestants, especially in England, commonly ascribed to Catholics – that is, "*that Faith is not to be kept with Hereticks,*" "that Kings excommunicated *forfeit their Crowns and Kingdoms,*" and "*that Dominion is founded in Grace.*"[66] Moreover, Catholics were widely blamed for their intolerance, which Locke too had deplored already in *An Essay concerning Toleration*, arguing that Catholics did not deserve toleration because they denied toleration to others in the countries where they had power.[67] Finally, Locke obviously had the pope in mind when he criticized, in the *Letter*, "the absolute Authority of the same Person; who has not only power to perswade the Members of his Church to whatsoever he lists, (either as purely Religious, or as in order thereunto) but can also enjoyn it them on pain of Eternal Fire."[68] This is a point Locke frequently made in his writings on toleration, starting at least in 1659, with his response to Henry Stubbe's *Essay in Defence of the Good Old Cause* (1659). Commenting on Stubbe's proposal to tolerate Roman Catholics in England, on condition that they swore allegiance to the English political authorities, Locke wrote:

Since I cannot see how they can at the same time obey two different authoritys carrying on contrary intrest espetially where that which is destructive to ours ith backd with an opinion of infalibility and holinesse supposd by them to be immediatly derivd from god.[69]

Two years later, Locke further condemned Catholics' belief in papal infallibility in a Latin manuscript on this subject, in which he wrote that Catholic priests aimed to "establish a complete dominion over the conduct and

---

[65] Ibid., pp. 51–52.   [66] Ibid., pp. 50–51.

[67] Locke, *Essay concerning Toleration*, pp. 290–293. On Catholic intolerance and its representations in England from the 1670s to the 1690s, see John Marshall, *John Locke, Toleration and Early Enlightenment Culture* (Cambridge: Cambridge University Press, 2006), pp. 17–93.

[68] Locke, "Letter," p. 52. Concerning Locke's view of Catholics as dominated by the papacy in political as well as moral matters, see Jeffrey R. Collins, *In the Shadow of Leviathan: John Locke and the Politics of Conscience* (Cambridge: Cambridge University Press, 2020), pp. 271–314.

[69] Locke to S. H. [Henry Stubbe], [mid-September? 1659], in Locke, *Correspondence*, vol. 1, no. 75. For Stubbe's position, see Henry Stubbe, *An Essay in Defence of the Good Old Cause* (London, 1659), pp. 133–140. Significantly, Stubbe thought that Jesuits would not accept to declare their loyalty to the English authorities and should, therefore, be "executed ... for *Traytors*" (ibid., p. 139).

consciences of men, a dominion to which they zealously lay claim."[70] To this purpose, they "usurped" the power to make and interpret laws:

> They force upon the church traditions of their own that spring forth spontaneously as the occasion requires, and they argue that these traditions have the force of law and are binding on human consciences. They set up the Roman Pontiff as the sole infallible interpreter of Holy scripture.[71]

Affirming that the words of God's "messengers" (i.e., "Prophets, Apostles, even his own son") in Scripture were comprehensible and sufficient, Locke concluded that "it is not necessary to grant that there be an Infallible Interpreter of holy Scripture in the Church."[72] According to Locke, belief in papal infallibility was not only unnecessary to salvation, but also harmful to society, given Catholic churchmen's cunning attitude and their habit to assert, endorse, and spread unethical principles whenever they deemed it convenient to themselves. Later on in his life, Locke always disapproved of the concept of papal infallibility and its unfortunate consequences concerning Catholics' morals and conduct, as the *Letter* demonstrates. Given Locke's disapproval of Catholic "immorality" in the *Letter* and other writings on toleration, I agree with Mark Goldie about the main reason why Locke excluded Catholics from toleration. According to Goldie, Locke intended to preclude not Catholicism as such, but Catholic "antinomianism" – namely, the opinion that a sort of divinely given "superiority" takes priority over ordinary moral rules and can thus inform the faithful's conduct.[73] Locke denied toleration to Catholics not because of "indifferent" beliefs or practices that Protestants considered absurd but had no moral implications – for instance, belief in transubstantiation, about which he wrote in the *Letter*: "If a *Roman Catholick* believe that to be really the Body of Christ, which another man calls Bread, he does no injury thereby to his Neighbour."[74] To Locke, what was perceived as the "absurdity" of another's religious belief or practice was not, in itself, a ground for intolerance and coercion. Therefore, in the *Letter*, he did not dismiss the theoretical possibility of tolerating Catholics, on condition that they discarded practical principles harmful to human and civil society – principles largely deriving from their blind obedience to their allegedly infallible leader, the pope. If they renounced practical principles destructive to society, they would be cleared of the accusation of immorality and hence become tolerable, even though they still held speculative opinions that others considered absurd. This hypothesis is, however, only implied in the *Letter*, which appears to describe Roman Catholics'

---

[70] John Locke, "Infallibility," in Locke, *Writings on Religion*, pp. 69–72 (69), in English translation. For the details of this manuscript, see Chapter 2.
[71] Locke, "Infallibility," p. 69.   [72] Ibid., p. 70.   [73] Goldie, "Introduction," pp. xix–xx.
[74] Locke, "Letter," p. 44.

allegiance to the pope in all matters – not only theological, but also moral and political – as an "*ipso facto*" element of Catholicism *as an organized religion*:

That Church can have no right to be tolerated by the Magistrate, which is constituted upon such a bottom, that all those who enter into it, do thereby, *ipso facto*, deliver themselves up to the Protection and Service of another Prince.[75]

Locke's early writings on toleration were more explicit on this matter. In a recently discovered manuscript entitled *Reasons for Tolerateing Papists Equally with Others* and composed, most probably, shortly before *An Essay concerning Toleration*, Locke first built a case for tolerating Catholics, but then, in his conclusion, he excluded Catholics from toleration.[76] In doing so, he clarified that the reason for not tolerating Catholics was their absolute loyalty to the pope, which entailed practical principles destructive to society:

I doubt whether upon Protestant principles we can justifie punishing of Papists for their speculative opinions as Purgatory transubstantiation &c if they stopd there. But possibly noe reason nor religion obleiges us to tolerate those whose practicall principles necessarily lead them to the eager persecution of all opinions, & the utter destruction of all societys but their owne. soe that it is not the difference of their opinion in religion, or of their ceremonys in worship; but their dangerous & factious tenents in reference to the state. *which are blended with & make a part of their religion* that excludes them from the benefit of toleration.[77]

In *An Essay concerning Toleration*, Locke expressly took into account the possibility of separating Catholics' "dangerous opinions" from their "religious worship," although he considered this distinction a "very hard" thing to do:

Roman Catholicks … therefor blending such opinions with their religion, reverencing them as fundamentall truths, & submitting to them as articles of their faith, ought not to be tolerated by the magistrate in the exercise of their religion unlesse he can be securd, that he can allow one part, without the spreading of the other, & that the propagation of these dangerous opinions may be separated from their religious worship, which I suppose is very hard to be donne.[78]

Later, in the mid-1670s, Locke endorsed with the words "Papists Test" a manuscript draft of a test of allegiance for Catholic priests in the hand of the Irish Franciscan Peter Walsh, which expunged "dangerous opinions" from the tenets of Catholicism.[79] Briefly, the idea that practical principles harmful to

---

[75] Ibid., p. 52.

[76] J. C. Walmsley, Felix Waldmann, "John Locke and the Toleration of Catholics: A New Manuscript," *The Historical Journal*, 62:4 (2019): pp. 1093–1115. Locke's manuscript "Reasons for Tolerateing Papists Equally with Others" (BR1610.L8232, Greenfield Library, St. John's College, Annapolis) is copied in the appendix to this article at pp. 1111–1115.

[77] Ibid., p. 1115.   [78] Locke, *Essay concerning Toleration*, pp. 284–285.

[79] "The Particular Test for Priests," in Locke, *Political Essays*, pp. 222–224. The original of this manuscript is MS Locke c. 27, ff. 30a–b. See Anthony J. Brown, "Anglo-Irish Gallicanism,

human and civil society (and not speculative opinions) made Roman Catholics intolerable was a constant in Locke's thought, although he expressed this idea with different nuances in various writings concerning toleration.

Locke's objections to Catholic "antinomianism," in the *Letter* and other writings, could also apply to others who claimed to be divinely inspired to rule or exempt from ordinary moral norms. This was the case of several radical Nonconformist groups in seventeenth-century England. In this regard, I agree with Goldie that Locke conceived of religious fanatics of various stripes as *potentially* intolerable.[80] Goldie's thesis is confirmed by the parallel that Locke made, in *An Essay concerning Human Understanding*, between enthusiasts' persuasion of their divine inspiration and Roman Catholics' belief in papal infallibility:

> Take an intelligent *Romanist*, that ... hath had this Principle constantly inculcated, *viz.* That he must believe as the Church (*i.e.* those of his Communion) believes, or that the Pope is Infallible. ... Let an *Enthusiast* be principled, that he or his Teacher is inspired, and acted by an immediate Communication of the Divine Spirit, and you in vain bring the Evidence of clear Reasons against his Doctrines.[81]

Locke's hostility to the antinomian attitude of enthusiasts emerges clearly in *Essay* IV.xix, "Of Enthusiasm," which Locke added to the fourth edition of the *Essay* in 1700, but which bears many resemblances with Locke's previous writings on the subject, as I have explained in Chapter 1. In *Essay* IV.xix.5, Locke indeed observed that enthusiasts' persuasion of being "under the peculiar guidance of Heaven" could lead them to hold opinions and commit actions divergent from common knowledge and morality.[82] Given Locke's stance against the antinomian implications of enthusiasm, his stigmatization of Catholic "antinomianism" was, in fact, also a warning against the *potentially* dangerous outcomes of others' antinomian attitudes. And, here, I want to highlight my use of the adverb "*potentially*," which is crucial to my thesis, explained further in this chapter, concerning why Locke did not call for intolerance of Protestant antinomians while he excluded Roman Catholics from toleration.

As to atheists, Locke lived in a time when the term "atheism" was utilized to define several sorts of religious heterodoxy, including, among others, Socinianism, Arianism, and deism.[83] Locke's works – not only the *Essay*, his works on toleration, and his theological writings, but also his treatises on education and the conduct of the understanding – take into account different

---

c.1635–c.1685," PhD dissertation, University of Cambridge, 2004, pp. 266–267; Milton, Milton, "General Introduction," pp. 147–148.

[80] Goldie, "Introduction," p. xix.   [81] Locke, *Essay*, IV.xx.10, p. 713.

[82] Ibid., IV.xix.5, pp. 698–699.   [83] Marshall, *John Locke, Toleration*, pp. 256–263.

forms of atheism.[84] Locke's approach to atheism was quite original if we consider that, in seventeenth-century England, most theologians – including, also, those who did not use the term "atheism" in a broad sense – regarded the idea of God as innate to all human beings. They deemed it impossible to genuinely deny God's existence and, thus, to be a "speculative atheist."[85] For instance, Edward Stillingfleet wrote in *Origines Sacrae* (1662) that "God hath imprinted an universal character of himself on the minds of men" and that "the existence of a Deity [is] a thing so consonant to our natural reason, that as long as there are men in the world it will continue."[86] Moreover, in a Boyle Lecture delivered in 1692, Richard Bentley pointed out (and challenged) "the commonly received notion of an Innate Idea of God, imprinted upon every Soul of Man at their Creation, in Characters that can never be defaced."[87] Furthermore, Robert Boyle and Ralph Cudworth judged speculative atheism self-contradictory, irrational, and conceptually impossible.[88] These and other theologians of the time only admitted the existence of "practical atheists," whom Bentley described as people who, although "believing [in God's] Existence, do yet seclude him from directing the Affairs of the World, from observing and judging the Actions of Men."[89] Conversely, Locke's rejection of innate ideas made it possible to conceive of what J. K. Numao has termed "the 'ignorant atheist,' an atheist who has simply not yet developed the notion of a God."[90] Moreover, Locke's empiricist, anti-innatist epistemology contributed to raise the conceptual problem of the "speculative atheist … one who 'rationally' reached the wrong conclusion that God does not exist, and obstinately held fast to this view."[91] To Locke, the speculative atheist was the "true" atheist and, hence, the truly intolerable one. Like other seventeenth-century theist intellectuals, Locke considered speculative atheism irrational. But, unlike most of his contemporaries, he denied that the idea of God is an innate idea, since he

---

[84] John Locke, *Some Thoughts concerning Education* (London, 1693); John Locke, "Of the Conduct of the Understanding," in John Locke, *Posthumous Works* (London, 1706), pp. 1–137; J. K. Numao, "Locke on Atheism," *History of Political Thought*, 34:2 (2013): pp. 252–272.

[85] David Berman, *A History of Atheism in Britain: From Hobbes to Russell*, 2nd ed. (London: Routledge, 2013), pp. 1–47; Gianluca Mori, *L'ateismo dei moderni. Filosofia e negazione di Dio da Spinoza a d'Holbach* (Rome: Carocci, 2016), pp. 11–34.

[86] Edward Stillingfleet, *Origines Sacrae* (London, 1662), pp. 384–385.

[87] Richard Bentley, "The Folly of Atheism, and (What Is Now Called) Deism," in Richard Bentley, *Eight Sermons Preach'd at the Honourable Robert Boyle's Lecture* (Cambridge, 1724), pp. 1–44 (5).

[88] Robert Boyle, *Some Considerations Touching the Usefulnesse of Experimental Naturall Philosophy* (Oxford, 1663), p. 101; Ralph Cudworth, *The True Intellectual System of the Universe* (London, 1678), pp. 183–208. On Cudworth's notion of atheism, see Mori, *L'ateismo dei moderni*, pp. 71–78.

[89] Bentley, "Folly of Atheism," pp. 4–5.   [90] Numao, "Locke on Atheism," p. 260.

[91] Ibid., p. 267.

denied any innate idea. Locke judged natural reason able to demonstrate God's existence based on the observation of Creation and one's own existence. This is why he employed the argument from design and the anthropological argument to prove God's existence in the *Essays on the Law of Nature* and *An Essay concerning Human Understanding*.[92] To Locke, since atheists fail to infer God's existence from a proper consideration of the order of nature, it means that atheists deny a "discovery" that "carries such a weight of thought and communication with it."[93] Atheists are also unable to appreciate the implications of their own being, since they fail to deduce God's existence from their own existence and constitution. Briefly, Locke judged atheism to be irrational; but he considered the irrationality of atheism dissimilar to the irrationality of some "indifferent" beliefs that, although absurd, had no moral implications and consequently ought to be tolerated – as was the case, for instance, with belief in transubstantiation. To Locke, failure to recognize God's existence entails the incapability of engaging in at least minimally decent moral conduct. He expressed this point already in *An Essay concerning Toleration*:

> The beleif of a deitie is not to be recond amongst purely speculative opinions for it being the foundation of all morality & that which influences the whole life & actions of men without which a man is to be counted noe other then one of the most dangerous sorts of wild beasts & so uncapeable of all societie.[94]

In the first of his two arguments against atheists in *A Letter concerning Toleration*, Locke further stressed the main reason why atheists are so dangerous to society:

> Those are not at all to be tolerated who *deny the Being of a God.* Promises, Covenants, and Oaths, which are the Bonds of Humane Society, can have no hold upon an Atheist. The taking away of God, though but even in thought, dissolves all.[95]

Locke's definition of atheists as "those ... who *deny the Being of a God*" confirms that he, unlike most theologians of the time, admitted that some people actually fail to acknowledge God's existence. Therefore, when Locke talked of "atheists" in the *Letter*, he essentially meant speculative atheists – that is, people who do not employ experience-based reasoning properly and who, consequently, fail to infer God's existence from the observation of Creation and their own existence. To Locke, atheists, being unable to recognize the existence of a divine creator and lawgiver, are unable to understand

---

[92] See Chapter 1.   [93] Numao, "Locke on Atheism," p. 267.

[94] Locke, *Essay concerning Toleration*, p. 308. This passage is part of an addition that Locke made to this *Essay* in MS Locke c. 28 and does not appear in the other three manuscripts of this work.

[95] Locke, "Letter," pp. 52–53.

their duties toward their creator (whose workmanship, servants, and property all human beings are) and to acknowledge, and obey, the God-given moral law (which humans are bearers of). Thus, they are intrinsically devoid of morality and, consequently, cannot be trustworthy members of society. Additionally, atheists do not believe in an afterlife with reward and punishment, which Locke, in *The Reasonableness of Christianity*, described as a powerful incentive to behave morally – a conclusion already hinted at in some of his previous writings, including *An Essay concerning Human Understanding*.[96] Briefly, as Locke stated in *A Vindication of the Reasonableness of Christianity* (1695), "Atheism [is] a Crime, which for its Madness as well as Guilt, ought to shut a Man out of all Sober and Civil Society."[97] To Locke, religious belief, with its moral implications, was always an essential prerequisite to enjoy toleration in a civil society. In his other argument against tolerating atheists in the *Letter*, he maintained that "those that by their Atheism undermine and destroy all Religion, can have no pretence of Religion whereupon to challenge the Privilege of a Toleration."[98] The *Letter* actually advocates toleration of those who have religion – namely, those who believe in God, pursue eternal salvation, and have voluntarily joined a church "in order to the publick worshipping of God, in such a manner as they judge acceptable to him, and effectual to the Salvation of their Souls."[99] But atheists deny belief in God, do not pursue eternal salvation, and do not belong to any religious society.

Locke's model of toleration in the *Letter* is much less inclusive than other seventeenth-century theories of toleration, such as Spinoza's philosophical advocacy of freedom of thought and Bayle's skeptical justification of wide toleration.[100] While Spinoza grounded religious liberty in the freedom to philosophize, and while Bayle endorsed religious toleration by separating morality from theological belief, Locke's approach to toleration was always informed by his religious conception of life and morality. Moreover, Locke's exceptions to toleration and his focus on the separation between the state and religious societies, which entails a disregard of the status of denominationally uncommitted believers, are significant shortcomings in the theory of toleration

---

[96] See Chapter 1.

[97] John Locke, "A Vindication of the Reasonableness of Christianity," in John Locke, *Vindications of the Reasonableness of Christianity*, ed. Victor Nuovo (Oxford: Clarendon Press, 2012), pp. 3–26 (8). For Locke's rejection of atheism, see, also, John Locke, "Atheism," in Locke, *Political Essays*, pp. 245–246 (a journal note dated July 29, 1676 and contained in MS Locke f. 1, pp. 367–370, "Essay [de] morall, A deity, God, Atheisme"); John Locke, "Law," in Locke, *Political Essays*, pp. 328–329 (a handwritten note taken circa 1693, in MS Locke c. 28, ff. 141–142, "Ethica B").

[98] Locke, "Letter," p. 53.   [99] Ibid., p. 15.

[100] Benedict de Spinoza, *Theological-Political Treatise*, trans. Michael Silverthorne and Jonathan I. Israel, ed. Jonathan I. Israel (Cambridge: Cambridge University Press, 2007), pp. 238–259; Pierre Bayle, *Commentaire philosophique*, 4 vols. (Cantorbery [Amsterdam?], 1686–1688).

expounded in the *Letter*. However, Locke's religious writings, especially *The Reasonableness of Christianity*, overcome the limitations of the *Letter* regarding, at least, toleration of unaffiliated believers.

Salvation and Toleration in Locke's Theological Writings

In *The Reasonableness of Christianity*, Locke argued that faith in Jesus the Messiah, repentance for sin, and obedience to the divinely given moral law, along with the diligent study of Scripture, are all that is required for salvation. He admitted that different non-fundamental beliefs might arise from divergent interpretations of biblical texts not dealing with the fundamentals of Christianity. To Locke, non-fundamentals are irrelevant to morality and salvation and, consequently, must not hinder peace among Christians. All those committed to pursuing salvation by observing the Law of Faith should tolerate each other, instead of showing hostility to one another because of divergences about non-fundamentals and differences in denominational affiliation. Locke's moralist soteriology even implies toleration of denominationally uncommitted Christians, although Locke lived and died a conforming member of the Church of England and never aimed at dissolving churches as formal associations with their specific doctrines, norms, institutions, and ceremonies. He always granted churches the right to be uniformitarian. To Locke, there can be no forced church membership, but voluntary membership entails submission to the discipline of the religious society to which one has chosen to belong with the purpose of performing the public worship of God. In the *Reasonableness*, Locke addressed public acts of worship, performed within religious societies, in the section concerning Jesus' attempt to reform the public worship among the Jews of his time. To Locke, Christ intended to deprive "the outward forms of *Worshipping the Deity*" of "Stately Buildings, costly Ornaments, peculiar and uncouth Habits, And a numerous huddle of pompous, phantastical, cumbersome Ceremonies," formerly, and mistakenly, "thought the principal part, if not the whole of Religion."[101] According to Locke, Jesus revealed the following:

To be Worshipped in Spirit and in Truth; With application of Mind and sincerity of Heart, was what God henceforth only required. . ... Decency, Order, Edification, were to regulate all their publick Acts of Worship. . ... Praises and Prayer, humbly offered up to the Deity, were the Worship he now demanded; And in these every one was to look after his own Heart, And know that it was that alone which God had regard to, and accepted.[102]

---

[101] John Locke, *The Reasonableness of Christianity, As Delivered in the Scriptures*, ed. John C. Higgins-Biddle (Oxford: Clarendon Press, 1999), p. 159.
[102] Ibid., p. 160.

To me, it seems that, while endorsing the renovation of public acts of worship advocated by Jesus in the name of "Decency, Order, Edification," this section of the *Reasonableness* does not describe *public* worship, and hence affiliation to a church, as essential to salvation. Here, Locke stresses that God requires only "application of Mind, and sincerity of Heart" from those who "humbly" offer up "Praises and Prayer ... to the Deity" – a form of worship demanded by God and certainly practicable, publicly and collectively, by the members of a church, but not necessarily connected to public worship. Thus, in my opinion, the *Reasonableness* does not preclude the possibility of salvation to those who accept the Law of Faith but consider themselves as "mere Christians" – as was, for instance, Locke's friend, the Rotterdam-based English merchant, writer, and bibliophile Benjamin Furly, after renouncing Quakerism in the early 1690s. Whether Locke, in his theological works, conceived of unaffiliated Christians as simply "traveling" in search of a church with doctrines and rites they could approve, or as believers who could remain denominationally uncommitted throughout their lives, is not crucial to my argument. It is true that Locke suggests nowhere in the *Reasonableness*, or in his other theological writings, that an individual Christian might remain unaffiliated throughout their life. However, nowhere in the *Reasonableness*, or in Locke's other writings on religion composed between the mid-1690s and his death in 1704, is denominational affiliation described, or even only hinted at, as indispensable to moral conduct or to the achievement of salvation.[103] As John Marshall has accurately noted, Locke's later writings on religion actually show that he "was opposed to dividing and denominating Christians on the basis of non-fundamentals, stressing the express words of Scripture and his status as a Christian, not the member of any sect."[104] The *Reasonableness* and Locke's other theological writings indeed extend the possibility of salvation to all those accepting the Law of Faith, regardless of non-fundamentals and confessional affiliation. This position allows for toleration of denominationally uncommitted Christians who adhere to the Law of Faith and the ethics it entails. Locke's later theological writings express the conviction that only the Law of Faith – disclosing the God-given moral law plainly and completely, and complementing it with the promise of otherworldly rewards and sanctions and an emphasis

---

[103] I believe that Locke's manuscript *Sacerdos* (1698) does not require confessional affiliation as essential to salvation. In this manuscript, Locke stated that Christ, reuniting religion and morality, had reformed "outward ceremonie" to fit with what "decency & order requird in actions of publique assemblys." Concerning religious ministers' right to regulate and perform public worship and "to teach Men their dutys of Morality," Locke was obviously talking of a right limited to the boundaries of their churches, which he always considered as voluntary societies. See John Locke, "Sacerdos," in Locke, *Writings on Religion*, pp. 17–18. See Chapter 1 for more details of this manuscript.

[104] John Marshall, "Locke, Socinianism, 'Socinianism,' and Unitarianism," in M. A. Stewart (ed.), *English Philosophy in the Age of Locke* (Oxford: Clarendon Press, 2000), pp. 111–182 (171).

on God's mercy – effectively facilitates moral conduct and enables the pursuit of salvation. Locke unambiguously highlighted the ethical value of the Christian message when commenting on Eph. 2:15 in *A Paraphrase and Notes on the Epistles of St Paul*:

> The Subjects of [God's] Kingdom whereof this is now the Law, can be at no doubt or less about their Duty, if they will but read and consider the Rules of Morality, which our Saviour and his Apostles have deliver'd in very plain words in the holy Scriptures of the New Testament.[105]

In this regard, Victor Nuovo has observed that Locke's views on morality and salvation in his theological works imply that, "if morality is the chief business of mankind, then the best way of pursuing it is to become a Christian"[106] – or, more precisely, to accept and observe the Law of Faith and thus become a Christian holding a moralist soteriology. This issue was already raised by John Dunn in his important book of 1969 on Locke's political thought, in which he wrote that Locke's theological ethics "restricts reasonableness, effective access to knowledge of the obligatory force of *recta ratio*, to those privileged to receive the Christian revelation."[107] While Dunn considered this "restriction" as one of the factors that determined what he saw as the intrinsic incoherence of Locke's thought, Nuovo has argued that Locke's Christian, moralist soteriology is compatible with his views on religious toleration – particularly on toleration of non-Christian believers. I concur with Nuovo's conclusion and, below in this chapter, I add new arguments in support of his thesis. But, before focusing on this issue, it is necessary to examine the implications of Locke's soteriology regarding those who do not subscribe to the Law of Faith. Locke's soteriology indeed implies a denial of the possibility of salvation to those refusing the Law of Faith – not only antinomians and deists, but also heathens, Muslims, and Jews.

Concerning "pagans," Locke manifested an ambivalent position on "uncivilized" peoples, particularly those discovered in the Americas. In *Essay* I.iii.9, drawing on various European travel reports, he talked of peoples in the Caribbean Islands, Peru, and Brazil who made "No Acknowledgment of any God, no Religion, no Worship," and who habitually engaged in cannibalism.[108] He mentioned these habits along with "Robberies, Murders, Rapes,"

---

[105] John Locke, *A Paraphrase and Notes on the Epistles of St Paul to the Galatians, 1 and 2 Corinthians, Romans, Ephesians*, ed. Arthur W. Wainwright, 2 vols. (Oxford: Clarendon Press, 1987), Eph. 2:15, vol. 2, p. 635.

[106] Victor Nuovo, *John Locke: The Philosopher As Christian Virtuoso* (Oxford: Oxford University Press, 2017), p. 245.

[107] John Dunn, *The Political Thought of John Locke: An Historical Account of the Argument of the "Two Treatises of Government"* (Cambridge: Cambridge University Press, 1969), p. 189.

[108] Locke, *Essay*, I.iii.9, p. 71.

and "Murders in Duels" to support his skeptical anthropology in contrast to theories of innate moral ideas.[109] He indeed considered cannibalism and atheism as extreme cases showing that different human societies hold, and live by, different practical principles and that, consequently, moral innatism is untenable.[110] At any rate, despite his skeptical anthropology, Locke did not condone atheism, cannibalism, and disregard of practical principles "that are absolutely necessary to hold Society together, which commonly too are neglected betwixt distinct Societies."[111] Besides being detrimental to salvation, these sorts of misconduct are indeed harmful to the civil interests, destructive of society, and hence intolerable in a civil commonwealth. As regards heathens' speculative opinions, Locke disliked polytheism, which, in the *Reasonableness*, he associated with idolatry, superstition, and "wrong Opinions of the Deity."[112] He called attention to polytheists' false notions of the deity in one of his arguments against innatism in *Essay* I.iv.15:

What true or tolerable Notion of a *Deity*, could they have, who acknowledged, and worshipped hundreds? Every Deity, that they owned above one, was an infallible evidence of their ignorance of Him, and a proof, that they had no true Notion of God, where Unity, Infinity, and Eternity, were excluded. To which if we add their gross Conceptions of Corporeity, expressed in their Images, and Representations of their Deities; the Amours, Marriages, Copulations, Lusts, Quarrels, and other mean Qualities, attributed by them to their gods; we shall have little reason to think, that the heathen World, *i.e.* the greatest part of mankind, had such *Ideas* of God in their minds, as he himself, out of care, that they should not be mistaken about him, was Author of.[113]

However, although Locke deplored polytheists' incorrect notions of the deity, he could not deny that polytheists still acknowledged divine power and authority and still had a religion, although one he considered wrong. This means that some "pagans," although practicing polytheism, were still able to behave morally, as Locke's descriptions of some Native Americans demonstrate. In fact, Locke portrayed some American peoples, particularly those living in North America, as intelligent, honest, just, truthful, virtuous, and courageous in various letters, in his colonial memoranda, and in the chapter-length "discourse" on Carolina that he wrote for John Ogilby's atlas *America* (1671).[114] Briefly, despite Locke's denunciation of atheism, cannibalism, and

---

[109] Ibid., I.iii.9, pp. 70–72.

[110] Ibid. On Locke's skeptical anthropology and references to American "savages" to strengthen his point, see Daniel Carey, *Locke, Shaftesbury, and Hutcheson: Contesting Diversity in the Enlightenment and Beyond* (Cambridge: Cambridge University Press, 2005), pp. 34–97; James Farr, "Locke, 'Some Americans,' and the Discourse on 'Carolina,'" *Locke Studies*, 9 (2005): pp. 19–94.

[111] Locke, *Essay*, I.iii.10, p. 72.   [112] Locke, *Reasonableness*, pp. 144–145.

[113] Locke, *Essay*, I.iv.15, p. 93.

[114] John Ogilby, *America* (London, 1671), pp. 205–212, now in Farr, "Locke, 'Some Americans,'" pp. 80–94. On the attribution of the discourse on Carolina to Locke, see ibid.,

other despicable customs and absurd beliefs among some "uncivilized" heathens in the Americas, his description of other Native Americans largely matched the Enlightenment idea of the noble savage.

Things are complicated by Locke's reference to (supposedly) atheistic *but civilized* societies in *Essay* I.iv, particularly in his refutation of the argument that belief in God is innate. In this chapter of the *Essay*, he took into consideration some Asian societies, which he knew mainly from the writings of seventeenth-century Catholic missionaries, such as Domingo Fernandez Navarrete, Jacques de Bourges, and François Timoleon de Choisy.[115] He described the "Siamites" – that is, the Siamese, who were Buddhist – as either polytheists or atheists.[116] Concerning Confucians, he wrote that "the Missionaries of *China*, even the Jesuits themselves, the Encomiasts of the *Chinese*, do all to a Man agree and will convince us that the Sect of the *Litterati*, or *Learned*, keeping to the old Religion of *China*, and the ruling Party there, are all of them *Atheist*."[117] But several years later, in a set of manuscript notes on China composed in 1702 or later and now contained in MS Locke c. 27, he recorded Confucians' belief in a material heaven and a material God, besides their morals and their ancestor cult, which particularly impressed him.[118] He wrote that Confucians, or at least some of them, believed in "an intelligent & active principle or nature that creates and governs all things."[119] Although he noted that Buddhist and Confucian beliefs could be considered essentially atheistic, as European travel reports suggested, he described both the Siamese's religion and "the old Religion of China" as institutional religions with specific moral principles and norms, ceremonies, and institutions. Furthermore, he portrayed those (possibly) atheistic Asians as virtuous and their societies as civilized. It is perhaps for these reasons that he never equated them to the atheists he condemned in *A Letter concerning Toleration* and other writings. Concerning both "noble savages" and *civilized* heathens, but obviously not atheistic cannibals, in the *Reasonableness* Locke even extended the possibility of salvation to those who had "never heard of the Promise or News of a Saviour."[120] He could not accept that God, in his goodness and mercy, would damn those people for not accepting a revelation they had never heard of. Therefore, he argued that God, "by the Light of Reason," had enabled them to grasp and respect the essential tenets of the Law of Nature and "to find also

---

pp. 60–73. On Locke's references to Native Americans in his letters and colonial memoranda, see ibid., pp. 20–29, 33–36, 51–58, 70–75.

[115] Ann Talbot, *"The Great Ocean of Knowledge": The Influence of Travel Literature on the Work of John Locke* (Leiden: Brill, 2010), pp. 179–199.

[116] Locke, *Essay*, I.iv.15, p. 93.   [117] Ibid., I.iv.8, p. 88.

[118] MS Locke c. 27, ff. 179–211 (179–200). See Talbot, *Great Ocean*, pp. 190–194.

[119] MS Locke c. 27, f. 181.   [120] Locke, *Reasonableness*, p. 139.

the way to Reconciliation and Forgiveness" when they transgressed this divine rational law:[121]

The Author of this Law, and God of Patience and Consolation, who is rich in Mercy, would forgive his frail Off-spring; if they acknowledged their Faults, disapproved the Iniquity of their Transgressions, beg'd his Pardon, and resolved in earnest for the future to conform their Actions to this Rule, which they owned to be Just and Right.[122]

Nevertheless, in the *Reasonableness* Locke did not extend the possibility of salvation to those who, although reached by the Christian message, still preferred to profess another religion. Later, in the *Paraphrase*, he refrained from making any concession to the heathen world – even to those who had "never heard of the Promise or News of a Saviour."[123] This omission was probably due to his notion of faith in the *Paraphrase*, which represented a development of his concept of faith expressed in the *Essay*. In the *Paraphrase*, Locke indeed presented saving faith as entailing an element of trust in and allegiance to Christ. In other words, in the *Paraphrase* saving faith entails trustful reliance on, and commitment to, Christ's message – not merely rational assent, although Christ's salvific message never contradicts natural reason, for it actually "enlarges" natural reason and is acceptable to it.[124]

As regards Muslims, Locke mentioned "the *Mahometan* Religion" only once in the *Reasonableness*, when he observed that this religion had "derived and borrowed" its monotheism from Christianity.[125] In the *Second Vindication*, he referred to Islam only in responding to John Edwards's charge of holding a non-Trinitarian, "Socinian," "Mahometan" view of Jesus as merely a prophet.[126] In his theological writings, however, Locke neither affirmed nor implied the possibility of salvation for Muslims, whom, I believe, he deemed excluded from salvation, despite the sincerity of their faith, because of their refusal of what he considered the true religion. In his writings on toleration, Locke depicted Muslims as sincere believers. In his *Third Letter*, he declared that "there are many Turks who sincerely seek truth."[127] This passage denotes Locke's willingness to regard Muslims as honest truth-seekers, exactly as he considered Christians; but this does not mean that Locke equated quranic and biblical revelations, for he always favored the latter. In fact, Locke portrayed Muslims as sincere truth-seekers, and hence as error-prone, when stressing, in

---

[121] Ibid., pp. 139–140.   [122] Ibid., p. 140.

[123] On this omission, see Arthur W. Wainwright, "Introduction" to Locke, *Paraphrase*, vol. 1, pp. 1–88 (41–43); John Marshall, *John Locke: Resistance, Religion and Responsibility* (Cambridge: Cambridge University Press, 1994), pp. 447–451.

[124] See Chapter 3.   [125] Locke, *Reasonableness*, p. 145.

[126] John Locke, "A Second Vindication of the Reasonableness of Christianity," in Locke, *Vindications*, pp. 27–233 (33, 116, 179, 180–181).

[127] Locke, "Third Letter," p. 154.

the *Third Letter*, the difficulty to "convince them of the truth of the Christian religion."[128] A few lines below in the same text, he drew a line between *belief* and *believers* in order to reject persecution of believers, including those who persevered in their theological error, and thus to advocate their toleration by the civil authorities.[129] When calling for toleration of those holding theological errors, Locke argued that judgment on their errors lies with God – not with the civil magistrate or other human beings.[130] Nonetheless, while being aimed at protecting the civil rights of "mistaken" believers, Locke's argument entails that God's judgment will eventually come for those obstinate in their error and unwilling to embrace the true religion. This was obviously the case with, among others, Muslims, whom Locke indeed mentioned, in the *Third Letter*, in the context of his distinguishing between human and divine judgment.

Concerning Jews who lived before Jesus, in the *Reasonableness* Locke drew on Rom. 4:18–22 to emphasize "the strength and firmness of *Abraham's* Faith," which "was *accounted to him for Righteousness*."[131] From this, Locke inferred that "the *Faith* of those before *Christ*; (believing that God would send the *Messiah*, to be a Prince, and a Saviour to his People, as he had promised) ... shall be accounted to them for Righteousness."[132] But, when rejecting antinomian ideas and salvaging the importance of good works for salvation in the *Reasonableness*, Locke expressed views typical of supersessionism – that is, the Christian doctrine, also called "replacement theology," according to which the New Covenant through Christ has superseded the Old Covenant and, hence, the Christian Church has succeeded and replaced the Jewish people as the definitive people of God. Moreover, in the *Paraphrase*, he openly disparaged the Jewish religion. In his religious writings, Locke countered antinomian readings of Paul's epistles and, thus, he aimed at demonstrating that Paul's concept of justification cohered with his own moralist soteriology. To this purpose, he distinguished between the Christian concept of "works" and the Mosaic notion of "works of the law." In the *Reasonableness*, Locke argued that Paul had not opposed good works. To Locke, when Paul spoke against "works," he meant the "works of the law," namely, the ceremonial part of the Law of Moses, which had only temporary validity. Conversely, the moral part of the Law of Moses, being identical to the Law of Nature, is eternally valid:

Some of God's Positive Commands being for peculiar Ends, and suited to particular Circumstances of Times, Places, and Persons, have a limited and only temporary Obligation by vertue of God's positive Injunction; such as was that part of *Moses*'s Law which concerned the outward Worship, or Political Constitution of the Jews, and is called the Ceremonial and Judaical law, in contradistinction to the Moral part of it;

---

[128] Ibid.   [129] Ibid., p. 155.   [130] Ibid.   [131] Locke, *Reasonableness*, pp. 136–137.
[132] Ibid., p. 139.

Which being conformable to the Eternal Law of Right, is of Eternal Obligation, and therefore remains in force still under the Gospel; nor is abrogated by the *Law of Faith*.[133]

Locke's view of the Mosaic Law is emblematic of the "theory of condescension," according to which, as Eldon Eisenach has put it, "the Old Testament law is consigned to the dustbin of history."[134] Several seventeenth-century latitudinarian theologians, including John Tillotson and Edward Stillingfleet, upheld this theory. In the early eighteenth century, the Newtonian scholar and clergyman Samuel Clarke unambiguously formulated the core tenets of this theory in a sermon entitled *The End and Design of the Jewish Law*: "The Jewish Law was an Institution of Religion adapted by God in great condescension to the weak apprehension of that people."[135] Locke's remarks on Judaism in the *Paraphrase* are even more demeaning than Clarke's words and indicate why Locke's theological works do not contemplate the possibility of salvation for post-biblical Jews. In several places in the *Paraphrase*, Locke distinguished between two concepts of justification – the "Jewish" concept, which revolves around obedience to the Law of Moses, and the "Christian" concept, according to which salvation depends on conformity to the Law of Faith. This distinction led him to argue that, when Paul used the terms "we" and "us," he meant "the Gentile converts" to Christianity, who accepted the Christian concept of justification, as opposed to Jews – even to Jewish converts to Christianity who still upheld the misleading "Jewish" notion of justification.[136] Accordingly, in his paraphrase of Gal. 1:4 – a verse stating that Christ came to "deliver us from this present evil world" – Locke maintained that by "evil world" Paul meant "the Jewish nation under the Mosaical constitution."[137] On this point, when commenting on Gal. 3:19–25, Locke argued that Christ's

---

[133] Ibid., p. 19.

[134] Eldon J. Eisenach, "Religion and Locke's Two Treatises of Government," in Edward J. Harpham (ed.), *John Locke's Two Treatises of Government: New Interpretations* (Lawrence: University Press of Kansas, 1992), pp. 50–81 (73). See, also, Nabil Matar, "John Locke and the Jews," *Journal of Ecclesiastical History*, 44:1 (1993): pp. 45–62; Raffaele Russo, *Ragione e ascolto. L'ermeneutica di John Locke* (Naples: Guida, 2001), pp. 205–246; Raffaele Russo, "Locke and the Jews: From Toleration to the Destruction of the Temple," *Locke Studies*, 2 (2002): pp. 199–223; Raffaele Russo, "The Thread of Discourse: Primary and Secondary Paraphrase in Locke's Hermeneutics," in Luisa Simonutti (ed.), *Locke and Biblical Hermeneutics: Conscience and Scripture* (Cham: Springer, 2019), pp. 121–141; Diego Lucci, "The Law of Nature, Mosaic Judaism, and Primitive Christianity in John Locke and the English Deists," *Entangled Religions: Interdisciplinary Journal for the Study of Religious Contact and Transfer*, 8 (2019), https://er.ceres.rub.de/index.php/ER/article/view/8354/7703.

[135] Samuel Clarke, "The End and Design of the Jewish Law," in Samuel Clarke, *Works*, 4 vols. (London, 1738), vol. 2, pp. 307–316 (313).

[136] Jean-Michel Vienne, "Hermeneutics and the Reasonableness of Belief," in Simonutti (ed.), *Locke and Biblical Hermeneutics*, pp. 105–119 (114–118).

[137] Locke, *Paraphrase*, Gal. 1:4, vol. 1, pp. 121–122.

ministry on earth had marked the end of the Mosaic Law.[138] In other words, the Law of Faith had superseded the Law of Moses. According to Locke, 2 Cor. 3:6 ("the letter killeth, but the spirit giveth life") indicates that "the New Testament or covenant was also, though obscurely, held forth in the law [of Moses]."[139] But the bulk of the Jewish people were unable to discard their literalist, legalistic reading of the Scriptures, and thus to accept Jesus as the Messiah, because a sort of hermeneutic "veil" conditioned their biblical exegesis. Locke expressed this opinion in his paraphrase of 2 Cor. 3:15 ("But even unto this day, when Moses is read, the vail is upon their heart"): in Locke's words, "even until now when the writings of Moses are read, the veil remains upon their hearts, they see not the spiritual and evangelical truths contained in them."[140] To Locke, even the Jews who converted to Christianity shortly after Christ's Coming were unwilling to abandon the "works of the law." Thus, they caused tensions and divisions among the early Christians. When talking of these Jewish converts to Christianity, Locke wrote in a note to 1 Cor. 2:6 ("Howbeit we speak wisdom amongst them that are perfect: yet not the wisdom of this world, nor of the princes of this world, that come to nought"):

St. Paul here tells the Corinthians that the wisdom and learning of the Jewish nation led them not into the knowledge of the wisdom of God, i.e. the Gospel revealed in the Old Testament, evident in this, that it was their rulers and rabbies, who, stiffly adhering to the notions and prejudices of their nation, had crucified Jesus, the Lord of glory, and were now themselves, with their state and religion, upon the point to be swept away and abolished.[141]

In this passage, Locke claimed that Paul had foreseen the then imminent destruction of the Jewish nation, state, and religion as a deserved punishment for having "crucified Jesus." Locke even justified this "destruction" in a note to Rom. 3:8, in which Paul maintained that the "damnation" of "some" who had slandered him was "just." Locke thought that, by "some," Paul meant the Jews:

"Some." It is past doubt that these were the Jews. But St. Paul, always tender towards his own nation, forbears to name them, when he pronounces this sentence, that their casting-off and destruction now at hand, for this scandal and their opposition to the Christian religion, was just.[142]

Briefly, Locke's later writings on religion depict the Jews as bound to their superseded law and hence incapable of pursuing salvation, like all those refusing the Christian Law of Faith, although he believed, based on Rom. 11, that both Gentiles and Jews will eventually all convert to the true religion.[143] When focusing his attention on heathens and Jews in his

---

[138] Ibid., Gal. 3:19–25, vol. 1, p. 138.   [139] Ibid., 2 Cor. 3:6, vol. 1, p. 278.
[140] Ibid., 2 Cor. 3:15, vol. 1, p. 280.   [141] Ibid., 1 Cor. 2:6, vol. 1, p. 174.
[142] Ibid., Rom. 3:8, vol. 2, p. 506.   [143] See Chapter 5.

theological works, Locke obviously had the issue of salvation in mind. Explicit political considerations, concerning whether the religious and moral ideas of heathens and Jews make them tolerable or intolerable in a civil commonwealth, are absent from Locke's theological writings. Yet, his moralist soteriology has powerful political implications, as Eisenach has noted:

> Only when the truth of morality is seen as part of a system of divine rewards and punishments will it attain both psychological force and historical reality. Only under these conditions will morality provide the basis for a civil law with teeth in it.[144]

Concerning the moral and political implications of Locke's biblical theology, Victor Nuovo has observed that "Locke's theology is a political theology at least in this respect, that the sovereign legislator of the moral law is God, or his viceregent Christ."[145] Locke's political theology is grounded in Messianism, since he thought that Christ had restated the moral law, affirming it completely and plainly, besides complementing it with new, revealed truths. To Locke, Christ was indeed the restorer of the divine moral law, a king, and the supreme archetype or model for humankind.[146] However, as Nuovo has correctly noted, Locke did "not propose a Christian commonwealth as the proper way to do the business of morality."[147] Locke actually labored to ensure that the *Second Treatise of Civil Government*, with its advocacy of a *civil* commonwealth, would become part of his intellectual legacy. Moreover, he always opposed the institutionalization of Christianity as a national religion, which in practice had done as much to disturb as to reinforce civil society and moral conduct. According to Nuovo, Locke never endorsed a *Christian* commonwealth for two main reasons – namely, his Christian view of history, which emerges from the *Reasonableness* and other theological writings, and his concept of the Law of Nature as expressed in the *Second Treatise*. On this issue, Nuovo has explained:

> According to the Scriptures, it was not God's intention to establish his kingdom or the kingdom of Christ – they are the same thing – until the history of redemption had run its course, until the resurrection and the last judgment. In the meantime, whether in a state of nature or in a civil state, the law of nature is the only proper rule to govern human behavior and civil institutions to safeguard human life and property.[148]

In the *Second Treatise*, Locke described human beings as bound to the God-given Law of Nature, which they are bearers of, in that they are God's

---

[144] Eldon J. Eisenach, *Two Worlds of Liberalism: Religion and Politics in Hobbes, Locke, and Mill* (Chicago: The University of Chicago Press, 1981), p. 85.
[145] Nuovo, *John Locke*, p. 246.
[146] Victor Nuovo, *Christianity, Antiquity, and Enlightenment: Interpretations of Locke* (Dordrecht: Springer, 2011), pp. 75–101. See, also, Chapters 3 and 5 in the present study.
[147] Nuovo, *John Locke*, p. 246.   [148] Ibid.

workmanship, servants, and property.[149] Nevertheless, Locke's position on the Law of Nature in the *Reasonableness* makes things problematic because, in this book, Locke maintained that unassisted reason had never "made out an entire body of the *Law of Nature*."[150] According to Locke, even when the Law of Nature became easily accessible through the Old Testament (since the moral part of the Law of Moses, i.e., the Law of Works, was identical to the Law of Nature), the Law of Moses was still ineffective to promote moral conduct. Locke concluded that only the *Christian* Law of Faith effectively facilitates the chief business of humankind, namely, morality, and makes salvation possible, because Christ complemented the Law of Nature with the assurance of otherworldly reward and punishment and the promise of God's forgiveness of the sins of the repentant faithful who, during their life, endeavor to obey the divine moral law. However, in the *Reasonableness* and his other theological writings, Locke did not invoke the civil power against pagans, Muslims, and Jews. He also ruled out any such use of the civil power in the *Two Treatises of Government*, in his letters on toleration, and in several of his mature manuscripts. Conversely, in *A Letter concerning Toleration* and other writings on this subject, he expressly excluded atheists and Roman Catholics from toleration, and he did so mainly for moral reasons. So, why did he not deny toleration to heathens, Jews, and Muslims too for moral reasons? We can answer this question if we consider Locke's views on the different moralities of atheists, Roman Catholics, and non-Christian believers. Locke judged atheists intrinsically immoral, and hence socially dangerous, because of their failure to acknowledge the existence of a divine creator and legislator and their consequent inability to appreciate, and observe, the God-given moral law. Concerning Roman Catholics, Locke considered them intolerable because of some of their practical principles, which he judged harmful to society. He did not exclude the theoretical possibility of tolerating Catholics, on condition that the latter renounced their antisocial principles. As to pagans, Jews, and Muslims, things are different, because they, believing in divine power and authority, are able to recognize and respect the divinely given moral law, at least in its core tenets (i.e., the natural rights and duties that Locke explained in the *Second Treatise*). Therefore, they are not intrinsically immoral and are not comparable to atheists. Heathens of different stripes can comprehend, "by the Light of Reason," the essential principles of the Law of Nature, which, as Locke declared in the *Reasonableness*, God has enabled them to grasp and follow.[151] Jews can also know the Law of Nature in the form of the Law of Works accessible through their Scriptures. In fact, Locke did not attribute any socially dangerous principle, contradicting the ordinary rules of morality and

---

[149] Locke, *Two Treatises*, p. 271. See Chapter 1 in the present study.
[150] Locke, *Reasonableness*, pp. 148–150.   [151] Ibid., pp. 139–140.

sociability, to pagans, Jews, and Muslims as well. And this distinguished them from Roman Catholics. Briefly, according to Locke, the religious and moral views of non-Christian believers, although defective and imperfect, still enable them to meet at least minimally decent moral standards. This conclusion is supported by a letter that Locke wrote in August 1690 to his friend, the Whig political thinker James Tyrrell, who had misread his considerations on morality in the *Essay*. In this letter, Locke clarified that, in the *Essay*, he had examined "whence man had moral ideas," not which ideas were moral. He explained that human beings may achieve a notion of morality by "comparing their actions to a rule" stemming from "divine law." Accordingly, he described non-Christian believers like Jews and Muslims as people who conceive of "a divine moral law" and who, consequently, have "notions of morality or Moral Ideas."[152] In other words, Locke thought that non-Christians who believe in a divine creator and lawmaker are able to behave morally. Their refusal of the Law of Faith certainly prevents them from achieving eternal salvation. However, as Locke argued in *A Letter concerning Toleration*, "the Care of Souls" falls outside of the purview of political authority, as long as a religious opinion or practice is not destructive of the civil interests or communal life. Therefore, Locke's more or less explicit denial of the possibility of salvation to non-Christian believers in his theological writings does not invalidate what the *Letter* states in this regard, namely, that "neither *Pagan*, nor *Mahumetan*, nor *Jew*, ought to be excluded from the Civil Rights of the Commonwealth, because of his Religion."[153]

It is, finally, worth considering the cases of deists and antinomians – Locke's main polemical targets in his later works on religion. Locke opposed deism, with its reliance on natural reason alone, as incapable of establishing morality and ineffective to salvation. However, he did not call for intolerance of deists, whom he described as significantly different from atheists. According to Locke, deists maintained belief in a divine creator and lawgiver and, hence, acknowledged the existence of the divinely given moral law, although they believed only in natural religion. By the light of natural reason, deists, like heathens, could comprehend and respect at least the essential principles of the Law of Nature. Whereas Locke questioned the human capacity to *actually* and *adequately* grasp the content of the Law of Nature *in its entirety* through the operation of natural reason, deists' commitment to live by this moral law could be sufficient to make them tolerable in a civil commonwealth. It is true that, according to Locke, reliance on natural reason alone was ineffective to eternal salvation. Accordingly, Locke thought that the deists' rejection of the Law of Faith prevented them from achieving the

---

[152] Locke to James Tyrrell, August 4, 1690, in Locke, *Correspondence*, vol. 4, no. 1309.
[153] Locke, "Letter," pp. 58–59.

salvation of their souls. But, to Locke, the civil magistrate's power does not extend to "the Care of Souls." A possible objection might be that deists did not belong to any "deistic church" and thus, given Locke's focus on *organized* religion in the *Letter*, they could not be tolerated as people having "religion." However, I believe that the scarce importance that Locke gave to church membership in the *Reasonableness*, along with his emphasis, in his political works, on the Law of Nature as the only proper rule to govern human conduct and civil institutions in order to preserve the civil interests, allows for toleration of deists and, by extension, of denominationally unaffiliated non-Christian believers in general.

As regards antinomianism, Locke's exclusion of Roman Catholics from toleration because of their "antinomian" practical principles implies that other, if not all, forms of antinomianism are intolerable, at least in principle. But, whereas Locke criticized Calvinistic antinomianism and, generally, belief in predestination as injurious to salvation, he did not declare Protestant antinomians "intolerable" in any of his writings. I believe that Locke judged Protestant antinomianism to be not as socially dangerous as some of the practical principles held by Roman Catholics. In the *Letter*, he indeed condemned some specific antisocial ideas, which Protestant polemicists commonly attributed to Roman Catholics, and he connected these ideas with the obedience that Catholics owed to their indisputable religious leader, who was also a foreign prince. Concerning Calvinistic antinomians, Locke was probably aware of their *potential* intolerability, in that their claims of divine inspiration could *possibly* lead them to act regardless of ordinary moral norms and, thus, to harm human and civil society. Nonetheless, this *theoretical* possibility (unlike some specific immoral principles held by Roman Catholics and *actually* informing their conduct, at least according to Locke and other Protestant writers of the time) was not enough to make Protestant antinomians *actually* intolerable, as long as they did not really engage in illegal actions. Therefore, Locke never called for intolerance of Protestant antinomians and, by extension, of other Christians who, maintaining doctrines like predestination or justification by faith alone (which Locke considered detrimental to salvation), rejected the moralist soteriology inherent to the Law of Faith while not necessarily engaging in immoral conduct. Nevertheless, Locke never went so far as to advocate complete freedom of conscience, because his religious conception of life and morality always conditioned his tolerationism.

Conclusion

In this book, I have attempted to elucidate Locke's religion, which, although expounded unsystematically in his public as well as private writings, is an original and internally coherent version of Protestant Christianity, essentially grounded in his painstaking analysis of Scripture. Locke's endeavor as a theologian was typical of a *biblical* theologian who, rather than concentrating on God's nature and attributes, paid particular attention to the moral, soteriological, and eschatological meaning of Scripture. He always considered the moral law as God-given and, hence, discoverable by natural reason (at least in principle) or through divine revelation. He regarded obedience to the divine moral law as a *duty* toward God as a creator and legislator, whose workmanship, servants, and property human beings are. However, he did not provide a rational demonstration of morality. Although he believed in the rationality and demonstrability of morality in itself, he was skeptical about the human capacity to *actually* establish morality on scientific or theoretical grounds, while he considered Scripture infallible and, hence, trumping rational doubt. Therefore, in his later years, he resolutely turned to biblical theology in an attempt to promote the practice of morality and the development of moral character whereas a *scientia* of morality, although possible in principle, was actually nowhere in view. Locke's acknowledgment of the failure of natural reason to provide epistemological foundations for morality up until his time led him to endorse what he took to be a convincing theological ethics based on Scripture, especially on the New Testament. He criticized the deists' belief in the sufficiency of a natural religion based on the Law of Nature alone, which, in Locke's opinion, they mistakenly viewed as actually and perfectly known by natural reason alone. According to Locke, only the Christian Law of Faith, besides reaffirming the Law of Nature in its entirety, provides an effective incentive to moral conduct, in the form of otherworldly rewards and sanctions, and enables the believer to pursue salvation despite their sins, thanks to the promise of God's forgiveness of the repentant faithful. This is why Locke judged faith in Jesus the Messiah, and hence in his salvific message, to be the central article of Christianity. He emphasized repentance for sin and obedience to the divine moral law as the other two fundamentals of Christianity emerging unequivocally from Scripture, the diligent study of which he deemed required of all Christians. Consequently, he opposed antinomianism and, generally, any form of predestinarianism, to such an extent that he denied original sin and excluded the satisfaction theory of atonement from his account of the Christian religion. It is in this sense that, to Locke, Christianity has a predominantly moral meaning. He thought that the justifying faith includes good works. Thus, far from reducing Christianity to morality, he utilized Christianity to elevate morality to a status above nature.[1]

While Locke's moralist soteriology is at the core of his theological reflection, other elements of his religious thought converge to create an internally coherent form of Protestant Christianity. His proof of scriptural authority (which revolved around the excellence of Christ's moral precepts, the fulfillment of Old Testament Messianic prophecies in the New Testament, and Christ's miracles confirming his Messianic mission) was intended to support his effort to provide a Scripture-based account of the Christian religion (and, thus, to endorse a Scripture-based theological ethics). Likewise, his historical method of biblical interpretation, according to which the scriptural texts ought to be studied in relation to both their historical context and the wider framework of the biblical discourse, stressed the internal consistency of the Bible. Whereas Locke was committed to the Protestant doctrine of *sola Scriptura*, he approached Scripture as a divinely given source of moral and religious truth complementing God-given natural reason. He regarded natural reason as the ultimate judge "of the Truth of [a proposition's] being a revelation, and of the signification of the Words, wherein it is delivered."[2] This approach enabled him to avoid a literalist reading of the Bible while leading him to reject, or at least exclude from his account of Christianity, doctrines grounded in "tradition" but unwarranted by Scripture. This was the case not only with original sin and satisfaction, but also with the doctrine of the Trinity, which he omitted from his elucidation of the Christian religion and which he definitely did not uphold, as some of his manuscripts and his Christological considerations in his public writings indicate. Locke's reliance on Scripture led him to formulate some theological ideas extremely similar, or even corresponding, to several tenets of Socinianism and Arminianism – two Protestant currents that, like Locke, adhered to *sola Scriptura* and pursued the way of fundamentals. But, whereas "on the theological map of his day" Locke's religion can be

---

[1] Victor Nuovo, *John Locke: The Philosopher As Christian Virtuoso* (Oxford: Oxford University Press, 2017), p. 250.

[2] John Locke, *An Essay concerning Human Understanding*, ed. Peter H. Nidditch (Oxford: Clarendon Press, 1975), IV.xviii.8, p. 694.

located "somewhere between Socinianism and Arminianism,"[3] his points of disagreement with the Socinian and Arminian theological traditions demonstrate that his version of Christianity cannot be subsumed under any denomination in particular. Given its specificity and uniqueness, Locke's religion resists any attempt at categorization and can only be described as "Locke's Christianity."

The main focus of this book has been on Locke's writings on religion – particularly *The Reasonableness of Christianity* and its two vindications, his three replies to Stillingfleet in the late 1690s, the unfinished *A Paraphrase and Notes on the Epistles of St Paul*, and several letters and theological manuscripts he wrote in his later years. My analysis of Locke's religion has also benefited from a consideration of *An Essay concerning Human Understanding*, *Two Treatises of Government*, *A Letter concerning Toleration*, and other writings by Locke, many of which he left in manuscript form. My examination of these works has enabled me to reassess the religious dimension pervading virtually all areas of Locke's production. While abstaining from providing a comprehensive analysis of Locke's thought as the thought of a Christian thinker – namely, of a thinker whose writings in several fields were conditioned by his Christian conception of life – I have highlighted the religious character of his reflections on some epistemological, moral, and political issues closely connected to his theological inquiry. In the *Essay*, for instance, Locke provided rational arguments for the existence of God as a creator and a legislator, he maintained the necessity of divine revelation as "enlarging" natural reason, and he affirmed the need to believe in things *above reason* revealed in Scripture. Therefore, although the *Essay* is a philosophical work, it definitely tends toward theological investigation, and it does so primarily for reasons relevant to morality and salvation. Locke indeed affirmed in several works – including, among others, the *Essay*, the *Second Treatise*, and the *Reasonableness* – his conviction that belief in a divine creator and legislator, whose existence can be proven by natural reason and is confirmed by Scripture, is indispensable to moral conduct. Moreover, in the *Essay*, the *Reasonableness*, and other writings, he talked of an afterlife with reward and punishment, the existence of which is revealed by Scripture, as a powerful incentive to act morally. Concerning Locke's views on the afterlife, I have argued that his consciousness-based theory of personal identity in *Essay* II.xxvii is consistent with his mortalist ideas, besides being conditioned by his agnosticism on substance and his moral and theological commitments to a system of other-worldly rewards and punishments. When formulating his theory of personal

---

[3] Arthur W. Wainwright, "Introduction" to John Locke, *A Paraphrase and Notes on the Epistles of St Paul to the Galatians, 1 and 2 Corinthians, Romans, Ephesians*, ed. Arthur W. Wainwright, 2 vols. (Oxford: Clarendon Press, 1987), vol. 1, pp. 1–88 (58).

identity, he paid special attention to the role of consciousness on Judgment Day – a role that, as I have explained, is compatible with his soteriology. To Locke, in fact, salvation is not only a matter of one's consciousness of their sins. In Locke's soteriology, repentance for sin, the endeavor to obey the divine law, faith in Jesus the Messiah (which involves hope in God's mercy), and the diligent study of Scripture all play a part in the pursuit of eternal life.

Locke's rethinking of personal identity in non-substantialist terms led Stillingfleet and others to accuse his way of ideas of promoting skepticism. Locke indeed stressed the limitations of human knowledge in ontological matters and believed that the amount of knowledge available in several domains, above all in religion and ethics, was very narrow, although he regarded most theological knowledge as falling within the scope of probability while he considered morality demonstrable. Locke's doubts about the prospects for increasing human knowledge of religion and ethics led him, on the one hand, to adopt a sort of "mitigated skepticism" in advocating religious toleration and, on the other, to rely on Scripture in moral matters. While Locke's reliance on Scripture in moral matters is obvious in the *Reasonableness*, his political writings, too, present numerous references to the Bible, especially when discussing moral and legal issues. The *Second Treatise* provides mixed arguments, based on both natural reason and biblical revelation, to found natural rights and duties. While Locke considered the Law of Nature as knowable by natural reason (at least in principle) or through divine revelation, he regarded scriptural revelation as sufficient to establish natural rights and duties, for he judged Scripture to be infallible. Accordingly, he never questioned true religion in itself, which he identified with the truth revealed by Scripture. However, he acknowledged the imperfection and weakness of human nature and he admitted that human beings utilize their understanding (and consequently interpret the Bible) in different, and often flawed, ways. According to Locke, these factors make human knowledge of religion limited and fallible, especially concerning non-fundamental issues that cannot be inferred unequivocally from Scripture, and thus contribute to the creation of disparate theological dogmas, doctrines, and ceremonies. Being skeptical about humans' ability to perfectly comprehend and effectively communicate religious truth, Locke called for toleration of any religious beliefs and practices unharmful to the commonwealth and its members – regardless of what the civil magistrate or others might think of the soundness, or lack thereof, of such beliefs and practices, and even regardless of their saving power or lack thereof. This form of political skepticism, rooted in Locke's reflections on human fallibility in the *Essay* and the *Second Treatise*, plays, I have argued, a crucial role in his case for the separation of the state and religious societies in *A Letter concerning Toleration*. I have also maintained that Locke's irenicism in the *Reasonableness* and other writings on religion complements and expands the tolerationism of the *Letter*. In his theological writings, Locke extended the possibility of salvation and, implicitly, toleration to all those accepting the Christian Law of Faith, regardless of their being affiliated or not with a church. However, he never denied toleration to Protestant antinomians and non-Christian believers, such as deists, Jews, Muslims, and heathens, who, although refusing the Law of Faith (and its advantages concerning the practice of morality and the pursuit of salvation), still believed in a divine creator and lawgiver and could hence acknowledge, and observe at least in its essential tenets, the God-given moral law. Locke did not dismiss even the theoretical possibility of tolerating Roman Catholics, whom he excluded from toleration not because of their theological doctrines, but because, in his opinion, they held some moral ideas harmful to human and civil society. Conversely, he always considered atheists as inherently intolerable, given his oft-repeated connection between belief in God and morally decent, socially harmless conduct. Locke's exclusion of atheists from toleration is further proof of the role of his religious worldview in his moral and political thought.

As regards the legacy of Locke as a theologian, his religious views had an impact on various Protestant authors and currents, despite the controversies that his theological ideas raised among contemporaries and despite the mixed reception that his thought met with among English divines in the eighteenth century.[4] Whereas the authorities of the University of Oxford proscribed the reading of *An Essay concerning Human Understanding* in 1703, at Cambridge Locke's writings, along with the works of Isaac Newton and Samuel Clarke, became for a number of years standard books for students and scholars.[5] Among Dissenters, too, Locke's ideas received a mixed reception, but his works were widely studied at dissenting academies and attracted the attention (and sometimes the criticism) of many prominent Nonconformist theologians, including, among others, Philip Doddridge and Joseph Priestley. In the eighteenth century, several thinkers with anti-Trinitarian leanings, such as Whiston and Priestley, spoke favorably of Locke's biblical hermeneutics, particularly of the *Paraphrase*.[6] Moreover, in the 1720s and 1730s, Dissenting ministers James Peirce, Joseph Hallett, and George Benson continued Locke's work and took his *Paraphrase* as a model in paraphrasing and explaining the New

---

[4] Ibid., pp. 59–73; Philip Dixon, *Nice and Hot Disputes: The Doctrine of the Trinity in the Seventeenth Century* (London: T&T Clark, 2003), pp. 160–162; Alan P. F. Sell, *John Locke and the Eighteenth-Century Divines* (Cardiff: University of Wales Press, 1997), pp. 16–108, 185–267; Stephen D. Snobelen, "Socinianism, Heresy and John Locke's *Reasonableness of Christianity*," *Enlightenment and Dissent*, 20 (2001): pp. 88–125 (95–97).

[5] Sell, *John Locke*, p. 5.

[6] William Whiston, "Advice for the Study of Divinity," in William Whiston, *Sermons and Essays upon Several Subjects* (London, 1709), pp. 235–326 (254–255); Joseph Priestley, "On the Reasoning of the Apostle Paul," in Joseph Priestley, *Theological and Miscellaneous Works*, ed. John Towill Rutt, 25 vols. (London, 1817–1832), vol. 7, pp. 365–415 (377, 411).

Testament epistles he had not had the chance to elucidate.[7] Here, it is worth noting that in 1719, in the context of the eighteenth-century controversies within English Nonconformity, Peirce and Hallett's father (whose name was also Joseph) refused to subscribe to the statement that the Son was one God with the Father, while Hallett himself became notorious for his unorthodox Christology, and Benson clashed with his fellow Presbyterians because of his "Arminian" views about predestination.[8] Thus, exercising an influence on several divines holding heterodox Christological and soteriological ideas, Locke's hermeneutics also influenced, more or less directly, the development of Unitarianism. Conversely, the Congregationalist ministers Isaac Watts (who was himself accused of Socinianism) and Ezra Stiles, president of Yale from 1778 to 1795, criticized Locke's new method of paraphrasing the biblical text, which they considered neither orthodox nor rigorous.[9] Nevertheless, Locke's adherence to *sola Scriptura*, along with his rejection of human authorities in exegetical and soteriological matters, contributed, in most cases indirectly, to the growth of Protestant movements such as Methodism, several Baptist churches, and various evangelical groups in the eighteenth and nineteenth centuries. Briefly, despite the use that deists and freethinkers like John Toland and Anthony Collins made of Locke's way of ideas in their attacks on mystery and priestcraft, Locke's theological legacy extended to various Protestant currents and theologians. In this regard, I concur with Stephen Snobelen that, "considering Locke's status as an icon and herald of the Enlightenment, this particular legacy of Locke is more than a little ironic."[10]

An accurate examination of Locke's oeuvre belies depicting him as a "secular" philosopher and shows that his conception of life was distinctly religious. Although Locke's way of ideas and political theory played a significant role in the development of modern epistemology and the liberal tradition respectively, he was definitely a *Christian* thinker. Throughout his life, he combined the use of natural reason with recourse to scriptural revelation in his epistemological inquiry, he employed both natural and biblical theology in his political thought, and he always maintained a markedly religious conception of

---

[7] James Peirce, *A Paraphrase and Notes on the Epistles of St. Paul to the Colossians, Philippians, and Hebrews* (London, 1727); Joseph Hallett, *A Paraphrase, and Notes on the Three Last Chapters of the Epistle to Hebrews* (London, 1733); George Benson, *A Paraphrase and Notes on St. Paul's Epistles*, 6 vols. (London, 1731–1734). See Sell, *John Locke*, pp. 105–106; Arthur W. Wainwright, "Locke's Influence on the Exegesis of Peirce, Hallett, and Benson," in Luisa Simonutti (ed.), *Locke and Biblical Hermeneutics: Conscience and Scripture* (Cham: Springer, 2019), pp. 189–205.

[8] Ibid., pp. 189–190, 195–196.

[9] Isaac Watts, "Horae Lyricae," in Isaac Watts, *Works*, 9 vols. (London, 1813), vol. 9, pp. 231–309 (262); Ezra Stiles, *The Literary Diary*, ed. Franklin Bowditch Dexter, 3 vols. (New York: Scribners, 1901), vol. 1, pp. 556–558.

[10] Snobelen, "Socinianism, Heresy," p. 97.

morality, even before decisively turning to biblical theology in his moral and soteriological investigations in the *Reasonableness*. It is therefore no accident that his intellectual struggle culminated in the religious writings he composed in his later years. For these reasons, Locke's thought can be considered as an expression of what David Sorkin and other scholars have called "the religious Enlightenment."[11] Locke was indeed the archetype of a "religious Enlightener" – namely, of a philosopher endorsing *reasonable belief* as "the coordination of reason and revelation [which] did not contradict because by definition, as the two God-given 'lights,' they could not."[12] His emphasis on the interplay of natural reason and biblical revelation in philosophical, political, moral, and theological matters is emblematic of what J. G. A. Pocock has defined "the Protestant Enlightenment,"[13] which in England, developing gradually in the second half of the seventeenth century, spread particularly after the Glorious Revolution. In that context, the emergence of forms of socio-political relations and intellectual debate less hegemonic than before 1689 facilitated the discussion and dissemination of new, heterodox (albeit still theological in nature) methods and concepts. Locke's philosophical, political, and religious writings provide an emblematic example of an original, heterodox way of thinking that is definitely theological in nature. Therefore, the religious dimension of Locke's thought calls into question the enduring stereotype of the Age of Enlightenment as a completely secular, or even irreligious, "Age of Reason." As Charles Taylor has put it in *A Secular Age* (2007), according to the "modern subtraction story of the Enlightenment," in that period of western history "people started to use Reason and Science, instead of Religion and Superstition, and ... the conclusions they then came to simply reflect this salutary shift in method."[14] And by "reason" Taylor means "disengaged reason," which enables human beings to "acquire knowledge by exploring impersonal orders" and to form "societies under the normative provisions of the Modern Moral Order" – namely, of an order defined by merely contractarian, atheological notions of mutual benefit.[15] This may be true if we consider the long-term effects of intellectual and sociocultural dynamics activated in seventeenth- and eighteenth-century Europe, when the source of belief was gradually relocated from public authority, both political and ecclesiastical, to the epistemological criteria of individual reason, conscience, and scholarship. Nevertheless, individual reason, conscience, and scholarship were not

---

[11] David Sorkin, *The Religious Enlightenment: Protestants, Jews, and Catholics from London to Vienna* (Princeton: Princeton University Press, 2008).

[12] Ibid., p. 12.

[13] J. G. A. Pocock, "Enthusiasm: The Antiself of Enlightenment," *Huntington Library Quarterly*, 60:1–2 (1997): pp. 7–28 (26).

[14] Charles Taylor, *A Secular Age* (Cambridge, MA: Harvard University Press, 2007), p. 273.

[15] Ibid., p. 294.

necessarily disconnected from religious concerns, interests, and ideas in Enlightenment authors whose works triggered, in some cases inadvertently, secularization processes in western culture, society, and politics. Thus, I concur with Sorkin's conclusion that "the Enlightenment origins of modern culture were neither secular nor religious but a complex amalgam."[16]

Locke was one of the authors involved in this "complex amalgam." His attention to scriptural revelation, to the supernatural, and to eternal salvation played a major role in the definition of his philosophical, moral, and political ideas, which, in many respects, ultimately converged in his theological reflection. Therefore, a proper appreciation of the role that natural and biblical theology played in Locke's thought is crucial to recognizing the religious origins of the Enlightenment and, hence, to comprehending in which regards the "Age of Reason" was rooted in attempts at a "reasonable Christianity" – attempts based on both a rational understanding of Creation and a critical reassessment of the meaning of Scripture.[17] However, Locke's work, or rather, *the selective reception of Locke's work* between the eighteenth and twentieth centuries contributed to the making of modern secular societies. His intellectual legacy was largely molded to suit a narrative of the Enlightenment as a quintessentially secular phenomenon. First the English deists and then the French *philosophes* dismissed Locke's acceptance of things above reason as a secondary, and negligible, element of his way of ideas. They reinterpreted Locke's way of ideas, and transmitted it to the following generations, as a radically empiricist theory, describing human knowledge and thought as based exclusively on experience and natural reason. As Brian Young has correctly observed, Lockean epistemology was eventually fused with Newtonianism, and Locke's and Newton's ideas were portrayed as paving the way to a "high Enlightenment."[18] Moreover, Locke's *political-theological* arguments, concerning issues such as natural rights and duties and religious toleration, were gradually removed from the discourse of liberalism and were largely ignored, misunderstood, or underestimated even by Locke experts until the 1960s. His inclusion in the canon of early modern philosophy has entailed, or perhaps even required, the neglect of his Scripture-based theological ethics and of his biblical theology as a whole. Thus, his thought has been accommodated to the grand narrative of the development of two great philosophical traditions – rationalism and empiricism – eventually converging in Kant's final synthesis. In the end, teleological views of the Age of Enlightenment have led to the

---

[16] Sorkin, *Religious Enlightenment*, p. 21.

[17] Justin Champion, "'An Intent and Careful Reading': How John Locke Read His Bible," in Simonutti (ed.), *Locke and Biblical Hermeneutics*, pp. 143–160 (159–160).

[18] B. W. Young, *Religion and Enlightenment in Eighteenth-Century England: Theological Debate from Locke to Burke* (Oxford: Clarendon Press, 1998), pp. 113–119.

making of a distorted image of Locke's mind and work. But the intellectual historian, in their struggle to clarify an author's questions, methods, ideas, and context, has to shun teleology, eschew the influence of a posteriori evaluations, avoid acontextual, ahistorical, anachronistic considerations, and leave aside their personal opinions, beliefs, and aspirations. Briefly, the intellectual historian needs to exercise intellectual honesty in considering the historical value of the subjects they examine. The intellectual historian of the Enlightenment, in particular, should promote a better understanding of this complex phenomenon by reconstructing the conceptual and terminological categories of the period, by identifying the different concerns, questions, and interests of Enlightenment thinkers in various fields, and by comprehending and highlighting the significance of these thinkers' views on the subjects they examined.

Locke's case is important because of several reasons. In developing his way of ideas, he referred not only to natural reason, but also to scriptural revelation, for he saw God-given natural reason and divine revelation as mutually sustaining and complementary. His reliance on Scripture led him to affirm belief in things above reason, including an afterlife with reward and punishment. Moreover, his political theory is substantiated by both natural and biblical theological arguments, especially regarding natural law, natural rights, and toleration. This demonstrates that the seventeenth- and early eighteenth-century roots of liberalism, including Locke's contributions to this political tradition, are indebted to points made on religious grounds. Only later, following the emergence of atheological notions of natural reason in the eighteenth and nineteenth centuries, were the core principles of the liberal tradition widely considered objectively valid regardless of the existence (or inexistence) of a divine creator and legislator. Finally, Locke's biblical theology was not an accidental appendage to his intellectual path. In fact, his thought reached its climax in his later writings on religion, in which he examined, and gave his final answers to, what he considered the ultimate questions of life – namely, questions regarding moral conduct and the pursuit of salvation. It is no accident that, shortly before Locke's death, his friend Anthony Collins called him the "Great Lay Priest" of the age.[19] What I have said of Locke in this book, particularly in this conclusion, can be said (with all differences considered) of other intellectuals often referred to as "fathers of modernity" – from Galileo to Newton, and from Descartes to Kant, to name a few. Therefore, I hope that my analysis and interpretation of Locke's Christianity and, to a lesser extent, of the impact of his theological ideas on other areas of his thought will contribute to further reassessing the complexity of the Enlightenment origins of modern western culture.

---

[19] Anthony Collins to Locke, May 27, 1704, in John Locke, *The Correspondence of John Locke*, ed. E. S. de Beer, 8 vols. (Oxford: Oxford University Press, 1979–1989), vol. 8, no. 3546.

Bibliography

Locke's Unpublished Manuscripts

Bodleian Library

LL 309, BOD Locke 16.25, Bentley Bible, interleaved.
LL 358, BOD Locke 15.38, Thomas Pope Blount, *Censura celebriorum authorum* (London, 1690), interleaved.
LL 2864, BOD Locke 9.103–9.107, *Le Nouveau Testament* (Mons, 1673), interleaved and bound in 5 vols.
MS Locke b. 1, f. 185.
MS Locke c. 27, ff. 90, 91, 258–263, "Chronologia sacra."
MS Locke c. 27, ff. 179–211.
MS Locke c. 34, "Critical Notes on Stillingfleet" (published in part).
MS Locke d. 10, "Lemmata Ethica, Argumenta et Authores" (published in part).
MS Locke e. 17, pp. 23–71.
MS Locke e. 17, pp. 175–223, "Some General Reflections upon the Beginning of St. John's Gospel."
MS Locke f. 14.

Locke's Published Writings

The Correspondence of John Locke, ed. E. S. de Beer, 8 vols. (Oxford: Oxford University Press, 1979–1989).
Drafts for the Essay concerning Human Understanding and Other Philosophical Writings, eds. Peter H. Nidditch and G. A. J. Rogers (Oxford: Clarendon Press, 1990).
An Early Draft of Locke's Essay: Together with Excerpts from His Journals, eds. Richard I. Aaron and Jocelyn Gibb (Oxford: Clarendon Press, 1936).
An Essay concerning Human Understanding (London, 1690).
An Essay concerning Human Understanding, ed. Peter H. Nidditch (Oxford: Clarendon Press, 1975).
An Essay concerning Toleration and Other Writings on Law and Politics, 1667–1683, eds. J. R. Milton and Philip Milton (Oxford: Clarendon Press, 2006).
Essays on the Law of Nature, ed. Wolfgang von Leyden (Oxford: Clarendon Press, 1954).

A Letter concerning Toleration and Other Writings, ed. Mark Goldie (Indianapolis: Liberty Fund, 2010).

Locke on Toleration, ed. Richard Vernon (Cambridge: Cambridge University Press, 2010).

A Paraphrase and Notes on the Epistles of St. Paul to the Galatians, 1 and 2 Corinthians, Romans, Ephesians, ed. Arthur W. Wainwright, 2 vols. (Oxford: Clarendon Press, 1987).

Political Essays, ed. Mark Goldie (Cambridge: Cambridge University Press, 1997).

Posthumous Works (London, 1706).

The Reasonableness of Christianity, As Delivered in the Scriptures, ed. John C. Higgins-Biddle (Oxford: Clarendon Press, 1999).

Some Thoughts concerning Education (London, 1693).

Two Tracts on Government, ed. Philip Abrams (Cambridge: Cambridge University Press, 1967).

Two Treatises of Government, rev. ed., ed. Peter Laslett (Cambridge: Cambridge University Press, 1988).

Vindications of the Reasonableness of Christianity, ed. Victor Nuovo (Oxford: Clarendon Press, 2012).

Works, 9 vols., 12th ed. (London, 1824).

Writings on Religion, ed. Victor Nuovo (Oxford: Oxford University Press, 2002).

Other Primary Sources

[Allestree, Richard?], *The Practice of Christian Graces: Or, the Whole Duty of Man* (London, 1658).

Anonymous, *A Dialogue between a New Catholic Convert and a Protestant* (London, 1686).

   The Exceptions of Mr. Edwards, in His Causes of Atheism, against The Reasonableness of Christianity (London, 1695).

   A Letter to the Deists (London, 1696).

Arminius, Jacobus, *Arminius and His Declaration of Sentiments*, trans. and ed. W. Stephen Gunter (Waco: Baylor University Press, 2012).

   Works, trans. and ed. James Nichols and W. R. Bagnall, 3 vols. (Auburn – Buffalo: Derby, Miller, Orton and Mulligan, 1853).

Bagshaw, Edward, *The Great Question concerning Things Indifferent in Religious Worship* (London, 1660).

Barclay, Robert, *The Possibility and Necessity of the Inward and Immediate Revelation of the Spirit of God* (London, 1686).

Barlow, Thomas, *De Studio Theologiae* (Oxford, 1699).

Barrow, Isaac, *Theological Works*, ed. Alexander Napier, 9 vols. (Cambridge: Cambridge University Press, 1859).

Baxter, Richard, *More Reasons for the Christian Religion, and No Reason against It* (London, 1672).

Bayle, Pierre, *Commentaire philosophique*, 4 vols. (Cantorbery [Amsterdam?], 1686–1688).

Benson, George, *A Paraphrase and Notes on St. Paul's Epistles*, 6 vols. (London, 1731–1734).

Bentley, Richard, *Eight Sermons Preach'd at the Honourable Robert Boyle's Lecture* (Cambridge, 1724).

Observations upon a Sermon Intituled, A Confutation of Atheism from the Faculties of the Soul (London, 1692).

Best, Paul, *Mysteries Discovered* (London, 1647).

Bibliotheca Fratrum Polonorum quos Unitarios vocant, 9 vols. (Irenopoli – Eleutheropoli [Amsterdam], "post annum Domini 1656" [1665–1692]).

Biddle, John, *The Apostolical and True Opinion concerning the Holy Trinity Revived and Reasserted* (London, 1653).

A Confession of Faith Touching the Holy Trinity (London, 1648).

Twelve Arguments Drawn out of the Scripture (London, 1647).

A Twofold Catechism (London, 1654).

Blount, Charles, *Great Is Diana of the Ephesians* (London, 1680).

Miscellaneous Works, 2 vols. (London, 1695).

Blount, Thomas Pope, *Censura celebriorum authorum* (London, 1690).

Bold, Samuel, *A Short Discourse of the True Knowledge of Christ Jesus. To Which Are Added, Some Passages in the Reasonableness of Christianity, & c., and Its Vindication* (London, 1697).

Boyle, Robert, *A Discourse of Things above Reason* (London, 1681).

Some Considerations about the Reconcileableness of Reason and Religion (London, 1675).

Some Considerations Touching the Usefulnesse of Experimental Naturall Philosophy (Oxford, 1663).

Bradley, Thomas, *Nosce te ipsum, in a Comparison between the First, and the Second Adam* (York, 1668).

The Second Adam (York, 1668).

Burnet, Thomas, *Remarks on John Locke, with Locke's Replies*, ed. George Watson (Doncaster: Brynmill, 1989).

Bury, Arthur, *The Naked Gospel* (London, 1690).

Butler, Joseph, *The Analogy of Religion, Natural and Revealed, to the Constitution and the Course of Nature* (London, 1736).

Calvin, John, *Expositio impietatis Valentini Gentilis* (Geneva, 1561).

Institutio Christianae Religionis (Geneva, 1559).

Carroll, William, *A Dissertation upon the Tenth Chapter of the Fourth Book of Mr Locke's Essay concerning Humane Understanding* (London, 1706).

Chillingworth, William, *The Religion of Protestants a Safe Way to Salvation* (Oxford, 1638).

Clarke, Samuel, *A Discourse concerning the Unchangeable Obligations of Natural Religion, and the Truth and Certainty of the Christian Revelation* (London, 1706).

Works, 4 vols. (London, 1738).

Collins, Anthony, *An Essay concerning the Use of Reason in Propositions* (London, 1707).

Courcelles, Etienne de, *Opera Theologica* (Amsterdam, 1675).

Crell, Johann, *Ad librum Hugonis Grotii ... de satisfactione Christi* (Racoviae, 1623).

De uno Deo Patre libri duo (Racoviae, 1631).

A Learned and Exceeding Well-Compiled Vindication of Liberty of Religion, trans. N. Y. (London, 1646).

Prima ethices elementa (Racoviae, 1635).

Vindiciae pro religionis libertate (Eleutheropoli [Amsterdam], 1637).

Crisp, Tobias, *Christ Alone Exalted* (London, 1643).

Croft, Herbert, *The Naked Truth* (London, 1675).

Cudworth, Ralph, *The True Intellectual System of the Universe* (London, 1678).

da Costa, Uriel, *Examination of Pharisaic Traditions*, trans. and ed. H. P. Salomon and I. S. D. Sassoon (Leiden: Brill, 1993).

Dryden, John, *Absalom and Achitophel* (London, 1681).

Edwards, John, *A Brief Vindication of the Fundamental Articles of the Christian Faith* (London, 1697).

The Doctrine of Faith and Justification Set in a True Light (London, 1708).

The Socinian Creed (London, 1697).

Socinianism Unmask'd (London, 1696).

Some Thoughts concerning the several Causes and Occasions of Atheism (London, 1695).

Theologia Reformata, 2 vols. (London, 1713).

Edwards, Jonathan, *A Preservative against Socinianism*, 3rd ed. (Oxford, 1698).

Emlyn, Thomas, *An Humble Inquiry into the Scripture Account of Jesus Christ* (Dublin?, 1702).

Episcopius, Simon, *Opera theologica*, 2 vols. (Amsterdam, 1650).

Filmer, Robert, *Patriarcha, or the Natural Power of Kings* (London, 1680).

Fontenelle, Bernard de, *Histoire des Oracles* (Paris, 1687).

Freke, William, *A Dialogue by way of Question and Answer, concerning the Deity* (London, 1693).

The Fundamental Constitutions of Carolina (London, 1670).

Gastrell, Francis, *Some Considerations concerning the Trinity* (London, 1696).

Gother, John, *A Papist Misrepresented and Represented* (London, 1665).

Grotius, Hugo, *Defensio fidei Catholicae de satisfactione Christi adversus Faustum Socinum* (Leiden, 1617).

The Rights of War and Peace, ed. Richard Tuck, 3 vols. (Indianapolis: Liberty Fund, 2005).

Sensus librorum sex, quos pro veritate religionis Christianae ... (Paris, 1627).

Hallett, Joseph, *A Paraphrase, and Notes on the Three Last Chapters of the Epistle to Hebrews* (London, 1733).

Harris, Robert, *A Brief Discourse of Man's Estate in the First and Second Adam* (London, 1654).

Hedworth, Henry, *Controversy Ended* (London, 1673).

Herbert of Cherbury, Edward, *De veritate* (Paris, 1624).

Pagan Religion, trans. and ed. John A. Butler (Ottawa: Dovehouse, 1996).

Hobbes, Thomas, *Leviathan*, ed. C. B. Macpherson (London: Penguin, 1985).

Hooker, Richard, *Of the Laws of Ecclesiastical Polity*, ed. W. Speed Hill, 2 vols. (Binghamton: Folger Library, 1993).

Howard, Robert, *The History of Religion* (London, 1694).

Law, William, *The Case of Reason* (London, 1731).

Le Clerc, Jean, *An Historical Vindication of the Naked Gospel* (London, 1691).

Sentimens de quelques theologiens de Hollande (Amsterdam, 1685).

Lee, Henry, *Anti-Scepticism* (London, 1702).

Leibniz, Gottfried Wilhelm, *New Essays on Human Understanding*, trans. and ed. Peter Remnant and Jonathan Bennett (Cambridge: Cambridge University Press, 1982).

Leland, John, *A View of the Principal Deistical Writers*, 2 vols. (London, 1757).

Limborch, Philipp van, *De Veritate Religionis Christianae amica collatio cum Erudito Judaeo* (Gouda, 1687).

   Theologia Christiana (Amsterdam, 1686).

Lobb, Stephen, *The Growth of Error* (London, 1697).

Melanchthon, Philipp, *On Christian Doctrine: Loci Communes 1555*, trans. and ed. Clyde L. Manschrek (Oxford: Oxford University Press, 1965).

Milner, John, *An Account of Mr. Lock's Religion* (London, 1700).

Newton, Isaac, *The Correspondence of Isaac Newton*, 7 vols. (Cambridge: Cambridge University Press, 1959–1977).

   An Historical Account of Two Notable Corruptions of Scripture (London, 1754).

Nicholls, William, *An Answer to an Heretical Book Called the Naked Gospel* (London, 1691).

Norris, John, *An Account of Reason and Faith, in Relation to the Mysteries of Christianity* (London, 1697).

Nye, Stephen, *The Acts of the Great Athanasius* (London, 1690).

   The Agreement of the Unitarians with the Catholick Church (London, 1697).

   A Brief History of the Unitarians, Called Also Socinians (London, 1687).

   Brief Notes on the Creed of St. Athanasius (London, 1690).

   Considerations on the Explications of the Doctrine of the Trinity by Dr. Wallis, Dr. Sherlock, Dr. S-th, Dr. Cudworth, and Mr. Hooker (London, 1693).

   The Doctrine of the Holy Trinity (London, 1701).

   A Letter of Resolution (London, 1691).

Ogilby, John, *America* (London, 1671).

Overton, Richard, *Mans Mortalitie* (Amsterdam [London], 1644).

Payne, William, *The Mystery of the Christian Faith and of the Blessed Trinity Vindicated* (London, 1697).

Peirce, James, *A Paraphrase and Notes on the Epistles of St. Paul to the Colossians, Philippians, and Hebrews* (London, 1727).

Priestley, Joseph, *Theological and Miscellaneous Works*, ed. John Towill Rutt, 25 vols. (London, 1817–1832).

Przypkowski, Samuel, *Dissertatio de pace et concordia ecclesiae* (Eleutheropoli [Amsterdam], 1628).

   Dissertatio de pace, &c. Or, A Discourse Touching the Peace and Concord of the Church (London, 1653).

Pufendorf, Samuel, *Of the Law of Nature and Nations*, trans. Basil Kennett (London, 1729).

The Racovian Catechism, trans. and ed. Thomas Rees (London, 1818).

Sand, Christoph, *Nucleus historiae ecclesiasticae* (Cosmopoli [Amsterdam], 1669).

Schlichting, Jonas, *Confessio fidei Christianae* (n.p., 1642).

Sergeant, John, *Solid Philosophy Asserted, against the Fancies of the Ideists* (London, 1697).

Sherlock, William, *A Defence of Dr. Sherlock's Notion of a Trinity in Unity* (London, 1694).

   A Vindication of the Doctrine of the Holy and Ever Blessed Trinity (London, 1690).

Simon, Richard, *A Critical History of the Old Testament* (London, 1682).
  A Critical History of the Text of the New Testament (London, 1689).
Skelton, Philip, *Deism Revealed*, 2 vols., 2nd rev. ed. (London, 1751).
Smith, John, *A Designed End to the Socinian Controversy* (London, 1695).
Socinus, Faustus, *An Argument for the Authority of Holy Scripture*, trans. Edward
  Combe (London, 1731).
South, Robert, *Animadversions upon Dr. Sherlock's Book* (London, 1693).
  Tritheism Charged upon Dr. Sherlock's New Notion of the Trinity (London, 1695).
Souverain, Jacques, *Le Platonisme dévoilé* (Cologne [Amsterdam], 1700).
  Platonism Unveil'd (London, 1700).
Spinoza, Benedict de, *Theological-Political Treatise*, trans. Michael Silverthorne and
  Jonathan I. Israel, ed. Jonathan I. Israel (Cambridge: Cambridge University Press,
  2007).
Stephens, William, *An Account of the Growth of Deism in England* (London, 1696).
Stiles, Ezra, *The Literary Diary*, ed. Franklin Bowditch Dexter, 3 vols. (New York:
  Scribners, 1901).
Stillingfleet, Edward, *An Answer to Mr. Locke's Letter* (London, 1697).
  An Answer to Mr. Locke's Second Letter (London, 1698).
  A Discourse in Vindication of the Doctrine of the Trinity (London, 1697).
  The Doctrines and Practices of the Church of Rome Truly Represented (London, 1687).
  A Letter to a Deist (London, 1677).
  The Mischief of Separation (London, 1680).
  Origines Sacrae (London, 1662).
  The Unreasonableness of Separation (London, 1681).
Stubbe, Henry, *An Essay in Defence of the Good Old Cause* (London, 1659).
Taylor, Jeremy, *Treatises* (London, 1648).
  Unum necessarium, 4th ed. (London, 1705).
Tillotson, John, *A Discourse against Transubstantiation* (London, 1684).
  Sermons, concerning the Divinity and Incarnation of Our Blessed Saviour (London,
  1693).
  Works, ed. Thomas Birch, 3 vols. (London, 1752).
Tindal, Matthew, *A Letter ... concerning the Trinity and the Athanasian Creed*
  (London, 1694).
Toinard, Nicolas, *Evangeliorum Harmonia Graeco-Latina* (Paris, 1707).
Toland, John, *Christianity Not Mysterious* (London, 1696).
  A Collection of Several Pieces, 2 vols. (London, 1726).
  Letters to Serena (London, 1704).
Trotter Cockburn, Catharine, *Philosophical Writings*, ed. Patricia Sheridan
  (Peterborough: Broadview Press, 2006).
van Helmont, Franciscus Mercurius, *Seder Olam sive Ordo Seculorum, historica
  enarratio doctrinae* (n.p., 1693).
Völkel, Johannes, *De vera religione libri quinque* (Amsterdam, 1642).
Wallis, John, *Theological Discourses* (London, 1692).
Waterland, Daniel, *Works*, 10 vols. (Oxford, 1823).
Watts, Isaac, *Works*, 9 vols. (London, 1813).
West, Richard, *Animadversions on a Late Book Entituled The Reasonableness of
  Christianity* (Oxford, 1698).

Whiston, William, *Sermons and Essays upon Several Subjects* (London, 1709).
Whitby, Daniel, *A Paraphrase and Commentary on All the Epistles of the New Testament* (London, 1700).
Williams, Daniel, *Gospel Truth, Stated and Vindicated* (London, 1692).
Willis, Richard, *The Occasional Paper*, 10 vols. (London, 1697–1698).
[Woodhead, Abraham?], *The Protestants Plea for a Socinian* (London, 1686).
Zwicker, Daniel, *Irenicum Irenicorum* (Amsterdam, 1658).

Secondary Sources

Adriaenssen, H. T., "An Early Critic of Locke: The Anti-Scepticism of Henry Lee," *Locke Studies*, 11 (2011): pp. 17–47.
Almond, Philip C., *Heaven and Hell in Enlightenment England* (Cambridge: Cambridge University Press, 1994).
Anderson, David J., "Susceptibility to Punishment: A Response to Yaffe," *Locke Studies*, 8 (2008): pp. 101–106.
Anstey, Peter, *John Locke and Natural Philosophy* (Oxford: Oxford University Press, 2011).
    "Locke and Natural Philosophy," in Matthew Stuart (ed.), *A Companion to Locke* (Chichester: Wiley-Blackwell, 2016), pp. 64–81.
    "Locke, the Quakers and Enthusiasm," *Intellectual History Review*, 29:2 (2019): pp. 199–217.
    "Newton and Locke," in Eric Schliesser, Chris Smeenk (eds.), *The Oxford Handbook of Newton* (Oxford: Oxford University Press, 2017), pp. 1–23.
Armitage, David, "John Locke, Carolina, and the *Two Treatises of Government*," *Political Theory*, 32:5 (2004): pp. 602–627.
Armour, Leslie, "Trinity, Community and Love: Cudworth's Platonism and the Idea of God," in Douglas Hedley, Sarah Hutton (eds.), *Platonism at the Origins of Modernity: Studies on Platonism and Early Modern Philosophy* (Dordrecht: Springer, 2008), pp. 113–129.
Artis, Aderemi, "Locke on Original Sin," *Locke Studies*, 12 (2012): pp. 201–219.
Ashcraft, Richard, "Faith and Knowledge in Locke's Philosophy," in John W. Yolton (ed.), *John Locke: Problems and Perspectives* (Cambridge: Cambridge University Press, 1969), pp. 194–223.
    "John Locke's Library: Portrait of an Intellectual," *Transactions of the Cambridge Bibliographical Society*, 5:1 (1969), pp. 47–60.
    "Locke's State of Nature: Historical Fact or Moral Fiction?," *American Political Science Review*, 62:3 (1968): pp. 898–915.
    "Religion and Lockean Natural Rights," in Irene Bloom, J. Paul Martin, Wayne L. Proudfoot (eds.), *Religious Diversity and Human Rights* (New York: Columbia University Press, 1996), pp. 195–212.
    Revolutionary Politics and Locke's Two Treatises of Government (Princeton: Princeton University Press, 1986).
Babcock, William S., "A Changing of the Christian God," *Interpretation*, 45:2 (1991): pp. 133–146.
Ball, Bryan W., *The Soul Sleepers: Christian Mortalism from Wycliffe to Priestley* (Cambridge: James Clarke, 2008).

Bangs, Carl, *Arminius: A Study in the Dutch Reformation* (Nashville: Abingdon Press, 1971).

Berman, David, *A History of Atheism in Britain: From Hobbes to Russell*, 2nd ed. (London: Routledge, 2013).

Bernier, Jean, "Le Problème de la tradition chez Richard Simon et Jean Le Clerc," *Revue des Sciences Religieuses*, 82:2 (2008): pp. 199–223.

Biddle, John C., "John Locke's Essay on Infallibility: Introduction, Text, and Translation," *Journal of Church and State*, 19:2 (1977): pp. 301–327.

"Locke's Critique of Innate Principles and Toland's Deism," *Journal of the History of Ideas*, 37:3 (1976): pp. 411–422.

Black, Sam, "Toleration and the Skeptical Inquirer in Locke," *Canadian Journal of Philosophy*, 28:4 (1998): pp. 473–504.

Boeker, Ruth, "Locke on Personal Identity: A Response to the Problems of His Predecessors," *Journal of the History of Philosophy*, 55:3 (2017): pp. 407–434.

"The Moral Dimension in Locke's Account of Persons and Personal Identity," *History of Philosophy Quarterly*, 31:3 (2014): pp. 229–247.

"The Role of Appropriation in Locke's Account of Persons and Personal Identity," *Locke Studies*, 16 (2016): pp. 3–39.

Brown, Anthony J., "Anglo-Irish Gallicanism, c.1635–c.1685," PhD dissertation, University of Cambridge, 2004.

Brown, Stuart, "'Theological Politics' and the Reception of Spinoza in the Early English Enlightenment," *Studia Spinozana*, 9 (1993): pp. 181–200.

Burns, Norman T., *Christian Mortalism from Tyndale to Milton* (Cambridge, MA: Harvard University Press, 1972).

Carey, Daniel, *Locke, Shaftesbury, and Hutcheson: Contesting Diversity in the Enlightenment and Beyond* (Cambridge: Cambridge University Press, 2005).

Carroll, Robert Todd, *The Common-Sense Philosophy of Religion of Bishop Edward Stillingfleet (1635–1699)* (The Hague: Nijhoff, 1975).

Casson, Douglas J., *Liberating Judgment: Fanatics, Skeptics, and John Locke's Politics of Probability* (Princeton: Princeton University Press, 2011).

Champion, Justin, "'An Intent and Careful Reading': How John Locke Read His Bible," in Luisa Simonutti (ed.), *Locke and Biblical Hermeneutics: Conscience and Scripture* (Cham: Springer, 2019), pp. 143–160.

"Introduction" to John Toland, *Nazarenus*, ed. Justin Champion (Oxford: Voltaire Foundation, 1999), pp. 1–106.

"Père Richard Simon and English Biblical Criticism, 1680–1700," in James E. Force, David S. Katz (eds.), *Everything Connects: In Conference with Richard H. Popkin. Essays in His Honor* (Leiden: Brill, 1999), pp. 37–61.

The Pillars of Priestcraft Shaken: The Church of England and Its Enemies 1660–1730 (Cambridge: Cambridge University Press, 1992).

Chen, Selina, "Locke's Political Arguments for Toleration," *History of Political Thought*, 19:2 (1998): pp. 167–185.

Colie, Rosalie L., "Spinoza and the Early English Deists," *Journal of the History of Ideas*, 20:1 (1959): pp. 23–46.

"Spinoza in England, 1665–1730," *Proceedings of the American Philosophical Society*, 107:3 (1963): pp. 183–219.

Collins, Jeffrey R., *In the Shadow of Leviathan: John Locke and the Politics of Conscience* (Cambridge: Cambridge University Press, 2020).

Colman, John, *John Locke's Moral Philosophy* (Edinburgh: Edinburgh University Press, 1983).

Connolly, Patrick J., "Locke's Theory of Demonstration and Demonstrative Morality," *Philosophy and Phenomenological Research*, 98:2 (2019): pp. 435–451.

Corneanu, Sorana, *Regimens of the Mind: Boyle, Locke, and the Early Modern Cultura Animi Tradition* (Chicago: The University of Chicago Press, 2011).

De Tommaso, Emilio Maria, "'Some Reflections upon the True Grounds of Morality': Catharine Trotter in Defence of John Locke," *Philosophy Study*, 7:6 (2017): pp. 326–339.

Dempsey, Liam P., "'A Compound Wholly Mortal': Locke and Newton on the Metaphysics of (Personal) Immortality," *British Journal for the History of Philosophy*, 19:2 (2011): pp. 241–264.

"John Locke, 'Hobbist': Of Sleeping Souls and Thinking Matter," *Canadian Journal of Philosphy*, 47:4 (2017): pp. 454–476.

Di Biase, Giuliana, "The Development of the Concept of *Prudentia* in Locke's Classification of Knowledge," *Society and Politics*, 7:2 (2013): pp. 85–125.

John Locke e Nicolas Thoynard. Un'amicizia ciceroniana (Pisa: ETS, 2018).

La morale di Locke. Fra prudenza e mediocritas (Rome: Carocci, 2012).

Dixon, Philip, *Nice and Hot Disputes: The Doctrine of the Trinity in the Seventeenth Century* (London: T&T Clark, 2003).

Dumsday, Travis, "Locke on Competing Miracles," *Faith and Philosophy*, 25:4 (2008): pp. 416–424.

Dunn, John, "The Contemporary Political Significance of John Locke's Conception of Civil Society," *Iyyun: The Jerusalem Philosophical Quarterly*, 45 (1996): pp. 103–124.

The Political Thought of John Locke: An Historical Account of the Argument of the "Two Treatises of Government" (Cambridge: Cambridge University Press, 1969).

Eisenach, Eldon J., "Religion and Locke's Two Treatises of Government," in Edward J. Harpham (ed.), *John Locke's Two Treatises of Government: New Interpretations* (Lawrence: University Press of Kansas, 1992), pp. 50–81.

Two Worlds of Liberalism: Religion and Politics in Hobbes, Locke, and Mill (Chicago: The University of Chicago Press, 1981).

Ellis, Brannon, *Calvin, Classical Trinitarianism, and the Aseity of the Son* (Oxford: Oxford University Press, 2012).

Farr, James, "Locke, 'Some Americans,' and the Discourse on 'Carolina,'" *Locke Studies*, 9 (2005): pp. 19–94.

Foisneau, Luc, "Personal Identity and Human Mortality: Hobbes, Locke, Leibniz," in Sarah Hutton, Paul Schuurman (eds.), *Studies on Locke: Sources, Contemporaries, and Legacy* (Dordrecht: Springer, 2008), pp. 88–105.

Forstrom, K. Joanna S., *John Locke and Personal Identity: Immortality and Bodily Resurrection in 17th-Century Philosophy* (London: Continuum, 2010).

Giuntini, Chiara, *Presenti a se stessi. La centralità della coscienza in Locke* (Florence: Le Lettere, 2015).

Goldie, Mark, "Introduction" to John Locke, *A Letter concerning Toleration and Other Writings*, ed. Mark Goldie (Indianapolis: Liberty Fund, 2010), pp. ix–xxiii.

"John Locke, Jonas Proast, and Religious Toleration, 1688–1692," in John Walsh, Colin Haydon, Stephen Taylor (eds.), *The Church of England, c.1689–c.1833: From Toleration to Tractarianism* (Cambridge: Cambridge University Press, 1993), pp. 143–171.

"John Locke, the Early Lockeans, and Priestcraft," *Intellectual History Review*, 28:1 (2018): pp. 125–144.

Gordon-Roth, Jessica, "Catharine Trotter Cockburn's Defence of Locke," *The Monist*, 98:1 (2015): pp. 64–76.

"Locke on Personal Identity," *Stanford Encyclopedia of Philosophy* (2019), https:// plato.stanford.edu/entries/locke-personal-identity/.

Gough, John W., "The Development of Locke's Belief in Toleration," in John P. Horton, Susan Mendus (eds.), *John Locke: "A Letter concerning Toleration" in Focus* (London: Routledge, 1991), pp. 57–77.

Graham, Michael F., *The Blasphemies of Thomas Aikenhead: Boundaries of Belief on the Eve of the Enlightenment* (Edinburgh: Edinburgh University Press, 2008).

Griffin, Martin I. J., Jr., *Latitudinarianism in the Seventeenth-Century Church of England* (Leiden: Brill, 1992).

Hampton, Stephen, *Anti-Arminians: The Anglican Reformed Tradition from Charles II to George I* (Oxford: Oxford University Press, 2008).

Harris, Ian, *The Mind of John Locke: A Study of Political Theory in Its Intellectual Setting* (Cambridge: Cambridge University Press, 1994).

Harrison, John R., Peter Laslett, *The Library of John Locke* (Oxford: Oxford University Press, 1965).

Haugen, Kristine L., "Transformations of the Trinity Doctrine in English Scholarship: From the History of Beliefs to the History of Texts," *Archiv für Religionsgeschichte*, 3 (2001): pp. 149–168.

Hicks, John Mark, "The Theology of Grace in the Thought of Jacobus Arminius and Philip van Limborch," PhD dissertation, Westminster Theological Seminary, 1985.

Higgins-Biddle, John C., "Introduction" to John Locke, *The Reasonableness of Christianity, As Delivered in the Scriptures*, ed. John C. Higgins-Biddle (Oxford: Clarendon Press, 1999), pp. xv–cxv.

Hindess, Barry, "Locke's State of Nature," *History of the Human Sciences*, 20:3 (2007): pp. 1–20.

Holden, Thomas, "Robert Boyle on Things above Reason," *British Journal for the History of Philosophy*, 15:2 (2007): pp. 283–312.

Hudson, Wayne, *The English Deists: Studies in Early Enlightenment* (London: Pickering & Chatto, 2009).

Enlightenment and Modernity: The English Deists and Reform (London: Pickering & Chatto, 2009).

Hunt, Bruce A., Jr., "Locke on Equality," *Political Research Quarterly*, 69:3 (2016): pp. 546–556.

Hunter, Michael, "'Aikenhead the Atheist': The Context and Consequences of Articulate Irreligion in the Late Seventeenth Century," in Michael Hunter, David Wootton (eds.), *Atheism from the Reformation to the Enlightenment* (Oxford: Clarendon Press, 1992), pp. 221–254.

Hutton, Sarah, "The Neoplatonic Roots of Arianism: Ralph Cudworth and Theophilus Gale," in Lech Szczucki (ed.), *Socinianism and Its Role in the Culture of the XVIth to XVIIIth Centuries* (Warsaw – Lodz: Polish Academy of Sciences, 1983), pp. 139–145.

Iliffe, Rob, "Friendly Criticism: Richard Simon, John Locke, Isaac Newton and the *Johannine Comma*," in Ariel Hessayon, Nicholas Keene (eds.), *Scripture and Scholarship in Early Modern England* (Aldershot: Ashgate, 2006), pp. 137–157.

Priest of Nature: The Religious Worlds of Isaac Newton (Oxford: Oxford University Press, 2017).

Israel, Jonathan I., *Radical Enlightenment: Philosophy and the Making of Modernity 1650–1750* (Oxford: Oxford University Press, 2001).

"Spinoza, Locke and the Enlightenment Battle for Toleration," in Ole P. Grell, Roy Porter (eds.), *Toleration in Enlightenment Europe* (Cambridge: Cambridge University Press, 1999), pp. 102–113.

Jolley, Nicholas, *Leibniz and Locke: A Study of the New Essays concerning Human Understanding* (Oxford: Oxford University Press, 1984).

"Locke on Faith and Reason," in Lex Newman (ed.), *The Cambridge Companion to Locke's "Essay concerning Human Understanding"* (Cambridge: Cambridge University Press, 2007), pp. 436–455.

Locke's Touchy Subjects: Materialism and Immortality (Oxford: Oxford University Press, 2015).

"Reason's Dim Candle: Locke's Critique of Enthusiasm," in Peter Anstey (ed.), *The Philosophy of John Locke: New Perspectives* (London: Routledge, 2003), pp. 179–191.

Toleration and Understanding in Locke (Oxford: Oxford University Press, 2016).

Kaufman, Dan, "The Resurrection of the Same Body and the Ontological Status of Organisms: What Locke Should Have (and Could Have) Told Stillingfleet," in David Owen, Paul Hoffman, Gideon Yaffe (eds.), *Contemporary Perspectives on Early Modern Philosophy* (Peterborough: Broadview Press, 2008), pp. 191–214.

King, Peter, *The Life of John Locke* (London: Colburn, 1829).

Kort, E .D., "Stillingfleet and Locke on Substance, Essence, and Articles of Faith," *Locke Studies*, 5 (2005): pp. 149–178.

Lancaster, James A. T., "From Matters of Faith to Matters of Fact: The Problem of Priestcraft in Early Modern England," *Intellectual History Review*, 28:1 (2018): pp. 145–165.

Lascano, Marcy, "Locke's Philosophy of Religion," in Matthew Stuart (ed.), *A Companion to Locke* (Chichester: Wiley-Blackwell, 2016), pp. 469–485.

Laslett, Peter, "Introduction" to John Locke, *Two Treatises of Government*, rev. ed., ed. Peter Laslett (Cambridge: Cambridge University Press, 1988), pp. 3–126.

Leask, Ian, "The Undivulged Event in Toland's *Christianity Not Mysterious*," in Wayne Hudson, Diego Lucci, Jeffrey R. Wigelsworth (eds.), *Atheism and Deism Revalued: Heterodox Religious Identities in Britain, 1650–1800* (Farnham: Ashgate, 2014), pp. 63–80.

Leiter, Yechiel J. M., *John Locke's Political Philosophy and the Hebrew Bible* (Cambridge: Cambridge University Press, 2018).

Levitin, Dmitri, *Ancient Wisdom in the Age of the New Science: Histories of Philosophy in England, c. 1640–1700* (Cambridge: Cambridge University Press, 2015).

"Reconsidering John Sergeant's Attacks on Locke's *Essay*," *Intellectual History Review*, 20:4 (2010): pp. 457–477.

Lim, Paul C. H., *Mystery Unveiled: The Crisis of the Trinity in Early Modern England* (Oxford: Oxford University Press, 2012).

"The Platonic Captivity of Primitive Christianity and the Enlightening of Augustine," in William J. Bulman, Robert G. Ingram (eds.), *God in the Enlightenment* (Oxford: Oxford University Press, 2016), pp. 136–156.

LoLordo, Antonia, *Locke's Moral Man* (Oxford: Oxford University Press, 2012).

Lucci, Diego, "Ante-Nicene Authority and the Trinity in Seventeenth-Century England," *Intellectual History Review*, 28:1 (2018): pp. 101–124.

"From Unitarianism to Deism: Matthew Tindal, John Toland, and the Trinitarian Controversy," *Études Epistémè*, 35 (2019), https://journals.openedition.org/episteme/4223.

"John Locke on Atheism, Catholicism, Antinomianism, and Deism," *Ethics & Politics*, 20:3 (2018): pp. 201–246.

"The Law of Nature, Mosaic Judaism, and Primitive Christianity in John Locke and the English Deists," *Entangled Religions: Interdisciplinary Journal for the Study of Religious Contact and Transfer*, 8 (2019), https://er.ceres.rub.de/index.php/ER/article/view/8354/7703.

"Political Scepticism, Moral Scepticism, and the Scope and Limits of Toleration in John Locke," *Yearbook of the Maimonides Centre for Advanced Studies*, 3 (2018): pp. 109–143.

"Reconciling Locke's Consciousness-Based Theory of Personal Identity and His Soteriology," *Locke Studies*, 20 (2020), https://ojs.lib.uwo.ca/index.php/locke/article/view/7321.

Scripture and Deism: The Biblical Criticism of the Eighteenth-Century British Deists (Bern: Lang, 2008).

Lupoli, Agostino, "Boyle's Influence on Locke's 'Study of the Way to Salvation'," in Luisa Simonutti (ed.), *Locke and Biblical Hermeneutics: Conscience and Scripture* (Cham: Springer, 2019), pp. 21–54.

MacIntosh, J. J., "Locke and Boyle on Miracles and God's Existence," in Michael Hunter (ed.), *Robert Boyle Reconsidered* (Cambridge: Cambridge University Press, 1994), pp. 193–214.

Mackie, J. L., *Problems with Locke* (Oxford: Clarendon Press, 1976).

Marko, Jonathan S., *Measuring the Distance between Locke and Toland: Reason, Revelation, and Rejection during the Locke-Stillingfleet Debate* (Eugene: Pickwick, 2017).

Marshall, John, "John Locke and Latitudinarianism," in Richard W. F. Kroll, Richard Ashcraft, Perez Zagorin (eds.), *Philosophy, Science, and Religion in England 1640–1700* (Cambridge: Cambridge University Press, 1992), pp. 253–282.

John Locke: Resistance, Religion and Responsibility (Cambridge: Cambridge University Press, 1994).

John Locke, Toleration and Early Enlightenment Culture (Cambridge: Cambridge University Press, 2006).

"Locke, Socinianism, 'Socinianism,' and Unitarianism," in M. A. Stewart (ed.), *English Philosophy in the Age of Locke* (Oxford: Clarendon Press, 2000), pp. 111–182.

Matar, Nabil, "England and Religious Plurality: Henry Stubbe, John Locke and Islam," in Charlotte Methuen, Andrew Spicer, John Wolffe (eds.), *Christianity and Religious Plurality* (Woodbridge: Boydell Press, 2015), pp. 181–203.

(ed.), *Henry Stubbe and the Beginnings of Islam: The Originall & Progress of Mahometanism* (New York: Columbia University Press, 2014).

"John Locke and the Jews," *Journal of Ecclesiastical History*, 44:1 (1993): pp. 45–62.

"John Locke and the 'Turbanned Nations'," *Journal of Islamic Studies*, 2:1 (1991): pp. 67–77.

McCann, Edwin, "Locke's Theory of Substance under Attack!," *Philosophical Studies*, 106:1–2 (2001): pp. 87–105.

McClure, Kirstie M., *Judging Rights: Lockean Politics and the Limits of Consent* (Ithaca: Cornell University Press, 1996).

McDonald, Grantley, *Biblical Criticism in Early Modern Europe: Erasmus, the Johannine Comma and Trinitarian Debate* (Cambridge: Cambridge University Press, 2016).

McLachlan, H. John, *The Religious Opinions of Milton, Locke, and Newton* (Manchester: Manchester University Press, 1941).

Socinianism in Seventeenth-Century England (Oxford: Oxford University Press, 1951).

Milton, J. R., "Locke's *Essay on Toleration*: Text and Context," *British Journal for the History of Philosophy*, 1:2 (1993): pp. 45–63.

Milton, J. R., Philip Milton, "General Introduction" to John Locke, *An Essay concerning Toleration and Other Writings on Law and Politics, 1667–1683*, eds. J. R. Milton and Philip Milton (Oxford: Clarendon Press, 2006), pp. 1–161.

"Textual Introduction" to John Locke, *An Essay concerning Toleration and Other Writings on Law and Politics, 1667–1683*, eds. J. R. Milton and Philip Milton (Oxford: Clarendon Press, 2006), pp. 162–263.

Mooney, T. Brian, Anthony Imbrosciano, "The Curious Case of Mr. Locke's Miracles," *International Journal for Philosophy of Religion*, 57:3 (2005): pp. 147–168.

Mori, Gianluca, *L'ateismo dei moderni. Filosofia e negazione di Dio da Spinoza a d'Holbach* (Rome: Carocci, 2016).

Mortimer, Sarah, "Freedom, Virtue and Socinian Heterodoxy," in Quentin Skinner, Martin van Gelderen (eds.), *Freedom and the Construction of Europe*, 2 vols. (Cambridge: Cambridge University Press, 2013), vol. 1, pp. 77–93.

"Human and Divine Justice in the Works of Grotius and the Socinians," in Sarah Mortimer, John Robertson (eds.), *The Intellectual Consequences of Religious Heterodoxy, 1600–1750* (Leiden: Brill, 2012), pp. 75–94.

"Human Liberty and Human Nature in the Works of Faustus Socinus and His Readers," *Journal of the History of Ideas*, 70:2 (2009): pp. 191–211.

Reason and Religion in the English Revolution: The Challenge of Socinianism (Cambridge: Cambridge University Press, 2010).

Noonan, Harold W., "Locke on Personal Identity," in Gary Fuller, Robert Stecker, John P. Wright (eds.), *John Locke, An Essay concerning Human Understanding in Focus* (London: Routledge, 2000), pp. 210–235.

Numao, J. K., "Locke on Atheism," *History of Political Thought*, 34:2 (2013): pp. 252–272.

Nuovo, Victor, *Christianity, Antiquity, and Enlightenment: Interpretations of Locke* (Dordrecht: Springer, 2011).

"Enthusiasm," in S.-J. Savonius-Wroth, Paul Schuurman, Jonathan Walmsley (eds.), *The Continuum Companion to Locke* (London: Continuum, 2010), pp. 141–143.

"Introduction" to John Locke, *Writings on Religion*, ed. Victor Nuovo (Oxford: Oxford University Press, 2002), pp. xv–lvii.

(ed.), *John Locke and Christianity: Contemporary Responses to The Reasonableness of Christianity* (Bristol: Thoemmes, 1997).

John Locke: The Philosopher As Christian Virtuoso (Oxford: Oxford University Press, 2017).

"Locke's Hermeneutics of Existence and His Representation of Christianity," in Luisa Simonutti (ed.), *Locke and Biblical Hermeneutics: Conscience and Scripture* (Cham: Springer, 2019), pp. 77–103.

Olson, Roger E., *Arminian Theology: Myths and Realities* (Downers Grove: Intervarsity Press, 2000).

Parker, Kim Ian, *The Biblical Politics of John Locke* (Waterloo: Wilfried Laurier University Press, 2004).

"Newton, Locke and the Trinity: Sir Isaac's Comments on Locke's *A Paraphrase and Notes on the Epistle of St Paul to the Romans*," *Scottish Journal of Theology*, 62:1 (2009): pp. 40–52.

"Spinoza, Locke, and Biblical Interpretation," in Luisa Simonutti (ed.), *Locke and Biblical Hermeneutics: Conscience and Scripture* (Cham: Springer, 2019), pp. 163–188.

Pitassi, Maria-Cristina, *Le philosophe et l'écriture: John Locke exégète de Saint Paul* (Geneva: Cahiers de la Revue de Théologie et de Philosophie, 1990).

"Locke's Pauline Hermeneutics: A Critical Review," in Luisa Simonutti (ed.), *Locke and Biblical Hermeneutics: Conscience and Scripture* (Cham: Springer, 2019), pp. 243–256.

Placher, William C., *The Domestication of Transcendence: How Modern Thinking about God Went Wrong* (Louisville: Westminster John Knox Press, 1996).

Pocock, J. G. A., "Enthusiasm: The Antiself of Enlightenment," *Huntington Library Quarterly*, 60:1–2 (1997): pp. 7–28.

Quabeck, Franziska, *John Locke's Concept of Natural Law from the Essays on the Law of Nature to the Second Treatise of Government* (Zurich-Berlin: Lit Verlag, 2013).

Rabieh, Michael S., "The Reasonableness of Locke, or the Questionableness of Christianity," *The Journal of Politics*, 53:4 (1991): pp. 933–957.

Rockwood, Nathan, "Lockean Essentialism and the Possibility of Miracles," *The Southern Journal of Philosophy*, 56:2 (2018): pp. 293–310.

Rogers, G. A. J., "John Locke and the Sceptics," in Gianni Paganini (ed.), *The Return of Scepticism: From Hobbes and Descartes to Bayle* (Dordrecht: Kluwer, 2003), pp. 37–53.

"John Locke: Conservative Radical," in Roger D. Lund (ed.), *The Margins of Orthodoxy: Heterodox Writing and Cultural Response, 1660–1750* (Cambridge: Cambridge University Press, 1995), pp. 97–116.

"Locke and the Latitude-Men: Ignorance As a Ground of Toleration," in Richard W. F. Kroll, Richard Ashcraft, Perez Zagorin (eds.), *Philosophy, Science, and*

Religion in England 1640–1700 (Cambridge: Cambridge University Press, 1992), pp. 230-252.

"Locke, Plato, and Platonism," in Douglas Hedley, Sarah Hutton (eds.), *Platonism at the Origins of Modernity: Studies on Platonism and Early Modern Philosophy* (Dordrecht: Springer, 2008), pp. 193–205.

"Stillingfleet, Locke, and the Trinity," in Allison P. Coudert, Sarah Hutton, Richard H. Popkin, Gordon M. Weiner (eds.), *Judaeo-Christian Culture in the Seventeenth Century: A Celebration of the Library of Narcissus Marsh (1638–1713)* (Dordrecht: Springer, 1999), pp. 207–224.

Russo, Raffaele, "Locke and the Jews: From Toleration to the Destruction of the Temple," *Locke Studies*, 2 (2002): pp. 199–223.

Ragione e ascolto. L'ermeneutica di John Locke (Naples: Guida, 2001).

"The Thread of Discourse: Primary and Secondary Paraphrase in Locke's Hermeneutics," in Luisa Simonutti (ed.), *Locke and Biblical Hermeneutics: Conscience and Scripture* (Cham: Springer, 2019), pp. 121–141.

Schaff, Philip, *The Creeds of Christendom, with a History and Critical Notes*, 3 vols. (New York: Harper, 1877).

Schneewind, J. B., "Locke's Moral Philosophy," in Vere Chappell (ed.), *The Cambridge Companion to Locke* (Cambridge: Cambridge University Press, 1994), pp. 199–225.

Seidler, Michael J., "The Politics of Self-Preservation: Toleration and Identity in Pufendorf and Locke," in T. J. Hochstrasser, Peter Schröder (eds.), *Early Modern Natural Law Theories: Contexts and Strategies in the Early Enlightenment* (Dordrecht: Kluwer, 2003), pp. 227–255.

Seliger, Martin, "Locke's Natural Law and the Foundation of Politics," *Journal of the History of Ideas*, 24:3 (1963): pp. 337–354.

Sell, Alan P. F., *John Locke and the Eighteenth-Century Divines* (Cardiff: University of Wales Press, 1997).

Shagan, Ethan H., *The Birth of Modern Belief: Faith and Judgment from the Middle Ages to the Enlightenment* (Princeton: Princeton University Press, 2018).

Sidgwick, Henry, *Outlines of the History of Ethics for English Readers* (London: Macmillan, 1886).

Simmons, A. John, *The Lockean Theory of Rights* (Princeton: Princeton University Press, 1992).

Simonutti, Luisa, "John Locke e il socinianesimo," in Mariangela Priarolo, Maria Emanuela Scribano (eds.), *Fausto Sozzini e la filosofia in Europa* (Siena: Accademia Senese degli Intronati, 2005), pp. 211–249.

"Locke's Biblical Hermeneutics on Bodily Resurrection," in Luisa Simonutti (ed.), *Locke and Biblical Hermeneutics: Conscience and Scripture* (Cham: Springer, 2019), pp. 55–74.

"Premières réactions anglaises au *Traité théologique-politique*," in Paolo Cristofolini (ed.), *The Spinozistic Heresy: The Debate on the "Tractatus Theologico-Politicus," 1670–77* (Amsterdam: APA – Holland University Press, 1995), pp. 123–137.

"Religion, Philosophy, and Science: John Locke and Limborch's Circle in Amsterdam," in James E. Force, David S. Katz (eds.), *Everything Connects: In*

Conference with Richard H. Popkin. Essays in His Honor (Leiden: Brill, 1999), pp. 295–324.

"Spinoza and the English Thinkers: Criticism on Prophecies and Miracles: Blount, Gildon, Earbery," in Wiep van Bunge, Wim Klever (eds.), *Disguised and Overt Spinozism around 1700* (Leiden: Brill, 1996), pp. 191–211.

Sina, Mario, "Testi teologico-filosofici lockiani dal MS. Locke c.27 della Lovelace Collection," *Rivista di filosofia neo-scolastica*, 64:1 (1972): pp 54–75, and 64:3 (1972): pp. 400–427.

Sirota, Brent, "The Trinitarian Crisis in Church and State: Religious Controversy and the Making of the Post-Revolutionary Church of England, 1687–1702," *Journal of British Studies*, 52:1 (2013): pp. 26–54.

Skinner, Quentin, *Liberty before Liberalism* (Cambridge: Cambridge University Press, 1998).

Snobelen, Stephen D., "Isaac Newton, Heresy Laws and the Persecution of Religious Dissent," *Enlightenment and Dissent*, 25 (2009): pp. 204–259.

"Isaac Newton, Socinianism and 'the One Supreme God'," in Martin Mulsow, Jan Rohls (eds.), *Socinianism and Arminianism: Antitrinitarians, Calvinists and Cultural Exchange in Seventeenth-Century Europe* (Leiden: Brill, 2005), pp. 241–298.

"Socinianism, Heresy and John Locke's *Reasonableness of Christianity*," *Enlightenment and Dissent*, 20 (2001): pp. 88–125.

"'To Us There Is But One God, the Father': Anti-Trinitarian Textual Criticism in Seventeenth- and Early Eighteenth-Century England," in Ariel Hessayon, Nicholas Keene (eds.), *Scripture and Scholarship in Early Modern England* (Aldershot: Ashgate, 2006), pp. 116–136.

Sorkin, David, *The Religious Enlightenment: Protestants, Jews, and Catholics from London to Vienna* (Princeton: Princeton University Press, 2008).

Spellman, William M., *John Locke and the Problem of Depravity* (Oxford: Clarendon Press, 1988).

The Latitudinarians and the Church of England, 1660–1700 (Athens: University of Georgia Press, 1993).

Spitz, Jean-Fabien, "Le concept d'état de nature chez Locke et chez Pufendorf: Remarques sur le rapport entre épistémologie et philosophie morale au XVIIe siècle," *Archives de Philosophie*, 49:3 (1986): 437–452.

Spurr, John, "'Latitudinarianism' and the Restoration Church," *The Historical Journal*, 31:1 (1988): pp. 61–82.

Stanton, Timothy, "Locke and the Politics and Theology of Toleration," *Political Studies*, 54:3 (2006): pp. 84–102.

Stewart, M. A., "Stillingfleet and the Way of Ideas," in M. A. Stewart (ed.), *English Philosophy in the Age of Locke* (Oxford: Clarendon Press, 2000), pp. 245–280.

Strauss, Leo, "Locke's Doctrine of Natural Law," *American Political Science Review*, 52:2 (1958): pp. 490–501.

Natural Rights and History (Chicago: The University of Chicago Press, 1953).

Strawson, Galen, *Locke on Personal Identity: Consciousness and Concernment*, 2nd rev. ed. (Princeton: Princeton University Press, 2014).

Stuart, Matthew, "The Correspondence with Stillingfleet," in Matthew Stuart (ed.), *A Companion to Locke* (Chichester: Wiley-Blackwell, 2016), pp. 354–369.

Sugg, Richard, *The Smoke of the Soul: Medicine, Physiology and Religion in Early Modern England* (Basingstoke: Palgrave Macmillan, 2013).

Tabb, Kathryn, "Locke on Enthusiasm and the Association of Ideas," *Oxford Studies in Early Modern Philosophy*, 9 (2019): pp. 75–104.

Talbot, Ann, *"The Great Ocean of Knowledge": The Influence of Travel Literature on the Work of John Locke* (Leiden: Brill, 2010).

Tate, John William, *Liberty, Toleration and Equality: John Locke, Jonas Proast and the Letters Concerning Toleration* (New York: Routledge, 2016).

Taylor, Charles, *A Secular Age* (Cambridge, MA: Harvard University Press, 2007).

Thiel, Udo, *The Early Modern Subject: Self-Consciousness and Personal Identity from Descartes to Hume* (Oxford: Oxford University Press, 2011).

"The Trinity and Human Personal Identity," in M. A. Stewart (ed.), *English Philosophy in the Age of Locke* (Oxford: Clarendon Press, 2000), pp. 217–243.

Thompson, Jon William, "Personal and Bodily Identity: The Metaphysics of Resurrection in 17th Century Philosophy," PhD dissertation, King's College London, 2019.

Tuck, Richard, *Natural Rights Theories: Their Origin and Development* (Cambridge: Cambridge University Press, 1979).

Tuckness, Alex, "The Coherence of a Mind: John Locke and the Law of Nature," *Journal of the History of Philosophy*, 37:1 (1999): pp. 73–90.

Locke and the Legislative Point of View: Toleration, Contested Principles, and the Law (Princeton: Princeton University Press, 2002).

"Locke's Political Philosophy," *Stanford Encyclopedia of Philosophy* (2016), https://plato.stanford.edu/entries/locke-political/.

"Rethinking the Intolerant Locke," *American Journal of Political Science*, 46:2 (2002): pp. 288–298.

Vernon, Richard, *The Career of Toleration: John Locke, Jonas Proast, and After* (Montreal-Kingston: McGill-Queen's University Press, 1997).

Viano, Carlo Augusto, "L'abbozzo originario e gli stadi di composizione di 'An Essay concerning Toleration' e la nascita delle teorie politico-religiose di Locke," *Rivista di filosofia*, 52:3 (1961): pp. 285–311.

Vickers, Jason E., *Invocation and Assent: The Making and Remaking of Trinitarian Theology* (Grand Rapids: Eerdmans, 2008).

Vienne, Jean-Michel, "Hermeneutics and the Reasonableness of Belief," in Luisa Simonutti (ed.), *Locke and Biblical Hermeneutics: Conscience and Scripture* (Cham: Springer, 2019), pp. 105–119.

von Leyden, Wolfgang, "Introduction" to John Locke, *Essays on the Law of Nature*, ed. Wolfgang von Leyden (Oxford: Clarendon Press, 1954), pp. 1–92.

Wainwright, Arthur W., "Introduction" to John Locke, *A Paraphrase and Notes on the Epistles of St Paul to the Galatians, 1 and 2 Corinthians, Romans, Ephesians*, ed. Arthur W. Wainwright, 2 vols. (Oxford: Clarendon Press, 1987), vol. 1, pp. 1–88.

"Locke's Influence on the Exegesis of Peirce, Hallett, and Benson," in Luisa Simonutti (ed.), *Locke and Biblical Hermeneutics: Conscience and Scripture* (Cham: Springer, 2019), pp. 189–205.

Waldron, Jeremy, *God, Locke, and Equality: Christian Foundations in Locke's Political Thought* (Cambridge: Cambridge University Press, 2002).

"Locke: Toleration and the Rationality of Persecution," in Susan Mendus (ed.), *Justifying Toleration: Conceptual and Historical Perspectives* (Cambridge: Cambridge University Press, 1988), pp. 61–86.

Walker, Christopher J., *Reason and Religion in Late Seventeenth-Century England: The Politics and Theology of Radical Dissent* (London: I. B. Tauris, 2013).

Wallace, Dewey D., "Socinianism, Justification by Faith, and the Sources of John Locke's *The Reasonableness of Christianity*," *Journal of the History of Ideas*, 45:1 (1984): pp. 49–66.

Wallace, Robert, *Antitrinitarian Biography*, 3 vols. (London: Whitfield, 1850).

Walmsley, J. C., Felix Waldmann, "John Locke and the Toleration of Catholics: A New Manuscript," *The Historical Journal*, 62:4 (2019): pp. 1093–1115.

Walmsley, J. C., Hugh Craig, John Burrows, "The Authorship of the *Remarks upon An Essay concerning Human Understanding*," *Eighteenth-Century Thought*, 6 (2016): pp. 205–243.

Weinberg, Shelley, *Consciousness in Locke* (Oxford: Oxford University Press, 2016). "Locke on Personal Identity," *Philosophy Compass*, 6:6 (2011): pp. 398–407.

White, Morton, *The Philosophy of the American Revolution* (Oxford: Oxford University Press, 1978).

Wigelsworth, Jeffrey R., *Deism in Enlightenment England: Theology, Politics, and Newtonian Public Science* (Manchester: Manchester University Press, 2009).

Wilbur, Earl M., *A History of Unitarianism*, 2 vols. (Cambridge, MA: Harvard University Press, 1945–1952).

Wiles, Maurice, *Archetypal Heresy: Arianism through the Centuries* (Oxford: Oxford University Press, 2001).

Williams, George H. (ed.), *The Polish Brethren: Documentation of the History and Thought of Unitarianism in the Polish-Lithuanian Commonwealth and in the Diaspora 1601–1685*, 2 vols. (Missoula: Scholars Press, 1980).

Williams, Kelsey Jackson, "Canon before Canon, Literature before Literature: Thomas Pope Blount and the Scope of Early Modern Learning," *Huntington Library Quarterly*, 77:2 (2014): pp. 177–199.

Wojcik, Jan W., *Robert Boyle and the Limits of Reason* (Cambridge: Cambridge University Press, 1997). "The Theological Context of Boyle's Things above Reason," in Michael Hunter (ed.), *Robert Boyle Reconsidered* (Cambridge: Cambridge University Press, 1994), pp. 139–156.

Wolfson, Adam, *Persecution or Toleration: An Explication of the Locke-Proast Quarrel, 1689–1704* (Lanham: Lexington, 2010). "Toleration and Relativism: The Locke-Proast Exchange," *The Review of Politics*, 59:2 (1997): pp. 213–232.

Wolterstorff, Nicholas, *John Locke and the Ethics of Belief* (Cambridge: Cambridge University Press, 1996). "Locke's Philosophy of Religion," in Vere Chappell (ed.), *The Cambridge Companion to Locke* (Cambridge: Cambridge University Press, 1994), pp. 172–198.

Woolhouse, Roger, *Locke: A Biography* (Cambridge: Cambridge University Press, 2007).

Wootton, David, "John Locke: Socinian or Natural Law Theorist?," in James E. Crimmins (ed.), *Religion, Secularization and Political Thought: Thomas Hobbes to J. S. Mill* (London: Routledge, 1989), pp. 39–67.

Yaffe, Gideon, "Locke on Ideas of Identity and Diversity," in Lex Newman (ed.), *The Cambridge Companion to Locke's "Essay concerning Human Understanding"* (Cambridge: Cambridge University Press, 2007), pp. 192–230.

Yeo, Richard, "John Locke and Polite Philosophy," in Conal Condren, Stephen Gaukroger, Ian Hunter (eds.), *The Philosopher in Early Modern Europe: The Nature of a Contested Identity* (Cambridge: Cambridge University Press, 2006), pp. 254–275.

"John Locke's 'Of Study' (1677): Interpreting an Unpublished Essay," *Locke Studies*, 3 (2003): pp. 147–165.

Yolton, John W., *John Locke and the Way of Ideas* (Oxford: Clarendon Press, 1956).

The Two Intellectual Worlds of John Locke: Man, Person, and Spirits in the "Essay" (Ithaca: Cornell University Press, 2004).

Young, B. W., *Religion and Enlightenment in Eighteenth-Century England: Theological Debate from Locke to Burke* (Oxford: Clarendon Press, 1998).

Index